Major League Baseball
Players of 1884

ALSO BY PAUL BATESEL
AND FROM MCFARLAND

*Major League Baseball Players of 1916:
A Biographical Dictionary* (2007)

Major League Baseball Players of 1884

A Biographical Dictionary

Paul Batesel

McFarland & Company, Inc., Publishers
Jefferson, North Carolina, and London

LIBRARY OF CONGRESS CATALOGUING-IN-PUBLICATION DATA

Batesel, Paul, 1938 –
Major league baseball players of 1884 :
a biographical dictionary / Paul Batesel.
    p.   cm.
Includes bibliographical references and index.

ISBN 978-0-7864-5905-6
softcover : 50# alkaline paper ∞

1. Baseball players — United States — Biography — Dictionaries.
2. Baseball players — United States — Statistics. I. Title.
GV865.A1B3857 2011   796.3570922 — dc22 [B]   2010043879

British Library cataloguing data are available

© 2011 Paul Batesel. All rights reserved

*No part of this book may be reproduced or transmitted in any form
or by any means, electronic or mechanical, including photocopying
or recording, or by any information storage and retrieval system,
without permission in writing from the publisher.*

On the cover (left to right): (top row) Cap Anson, Pete Browning;
(middle row) Charles Comiskey, Buck Ewing *(T. Scott Brandon),*
Pretzels Getzein, King Kelly; *(bottom row)* John Morrell, Charley Radbourn,
Danny Richardson *(both from Mark Fimoff),* Fleet Walker *(public domain)*
(All photographs from the Library of Congress except where noted)

Manufactured in the United States of America

McFarland & Company, Inc., Publishers
Box 611, Jefferson, North Carolina 28640
www.mcfarlandpub.com

Acknowledgments

In 1697 Sir William Temple described a modern writer as "just a dwarf standing upon the shoulders of giants." This is an image I will cheerfully accept as describing my own pretensions as a writer and researcher. I am dependent on many, and I want to acknowledge some of those shoulders on which I stood while preparing this book.

It is likely that when the first major league pitch was thrown, a scribe was present to chronicle the event and chart the result on a card. Those chronicles and scorecards form the basis of our journey into baseball history.

And the moment the scribes discovered that the public deeply cared about the lives of those with the skill "to urge the flying ball," as the poet Gray put it, *Sporting Life*, *National Police Gazette* and ultimately *Sporting News* arrived to provide a weekly compilation of the news, opinion and gossip the public craved. These weeklies contain many a nugget for the researcher, and I am grateful to the Society for American Baseball Research for making them available.

Baseball research entered a new era in 1955 when S.C. Thompson and Hy Turkin compiled the first baseball encyclopedia. This attempt to create a record for every man who ever played major league baseball became the basis for a host of constantly updated and emended encyclopedias available in print and online today. Any foray into baseball history or research invariably begins with one or more of these encyclopedias. I believe that my own computer "falls open" to *Baseball-Reference.com*.

At times the giants on whose shoulders we stand are our contemporaries who have taken a long step ahead of us. Most of us are members of and greatly indebted to the Society for American Baseball Research. While working on this book, I didn't get far into any day without consulting the publications of fellow members. In particular, I am indebted to the work of the Biographical Research Committee. Their "find of the month" gives substance to players who were previously only a last name. It is one thing to know that a man named Jones played in a major league game in 1884; it is quite another matter to know his first name, a date and place of birth and of death. It is still another step forward when we see a photograph of him. And for this we are all indebted to the work of the SABR Pictorial Committee.

In a special way, I want to acknowledge a debt of gratitude to fellow SABR members who stepped in when I was most in need of photos. Mark Fimoff and T. Scott Brandon generously shared their photos of the 1884 players. Without their assistance, this book would have a much smaller visual presence.

And even though I am now only an emeritus, Mayville State University continues to provide technical support and assistance, and I am grateful for that.

Table of Contents

Acknowledgments v

Preface 1

Introduction 3

THE PLAYERS 9

Appendix I:
Performance of Players
by League and Team 177

Appendix II:
Birth and Mortality Summary 224

Bibliography 229

Index 231

Preface

Like its predecessor, *Major League Baseball Players of 1916*, this book focuses on a single season—the expansion 1884 season. It is a biographical dictionary of the 637 men who played on one of the National League, American Association or Union Association teams in that season. Fourteen of those men—players such as Cap Anson, Old Hoss Radbourn, King Kelly and Dan Brouthers—enjoyed stellar careers which resulted in their being enshrined in baseball's Hall of Fame. But also performing in 1884 were players named "Murphy," "Smith," "Jones," and "Scott," players without first names and whose last names may even be bogus. Such a disparity of roles is typical, for the fabric of major league baseball has always contained dominant threads of bold color and length. But the basic fabric is woven from many smaller, shorter threads with very little splash. The pitcher who struck out "Mighty Casey" is unnamed, and Casey himself would not have become the focus of the drama without the contributions of Jimmy Boyle, whose single caused "the wonderment of all," and of the "much despised" Flynn, who "tore the cover off the ball."

Because I prefer to study that whole fabric of major league baseball, my models are those biographical dictionaries that are least selective of subjects. In that regard, the standard is *Baseball Players of the 1950s* by Richard Marazzi and Len Fiorito, which includes a biographical sketch of every one of the 1,560 men who played during that decade. At some point in the future the standard will surely be the mammoth Biography Project by members of the Society for American Baseball Research. The goal of the Biography Project is nothing less than to present "high quality journal-length biographies of every player who ever played in the major leagues." At the moment this project has just passed 1,300 of the more than 17,000 biographies planned.

As I was in the final stages of researching and writing this work, McFarland published *The Complete New York Clipper Baseball Biographies (CNYCBB)*, compiled by Jean-Pierre Caillault. The two studies have much in common. Both are essentially biographical dictionaries of 19th-century baseball players. *CNYCBB* has 800 biographical sketches, each 200 or more words in length, illustrated by woodcuts. This book has 637 biographical sketches, each upward of 200 words in length, some illustrated by photographs. But the differences are significant. First, *CNYCBB* is selective. Its subjects appeared in the *New York Clipper* over a period of more than 40 years (1859–1903). Those subjects tend to be players the editors thought would interest New York readers (no Pete Browning, Charlie Ferguson or Will White). Only 192 players appear in both this book and *CNYCBB*. Second, except for an occasional obituary, *CNYCBB* focuses on the careers of active baseball figures, providing a wealth of detail about their major league careers to the time of writing as well as their minor league and amateur associations. This work provides a perspective on careers long finished and players' lives beyond baseball. In truth, the two works tend to complement rather than compete with each other.

I began researching with most of the same tools that I had used for my previous book. In the beginning, at least, I still had the ProQuest Historical Newspaper collection, giving me access to the 19th-century issues of *New York Times, Washington Post, Chicago Daily Tribune,* and *Boston Globe*—as well as *Los Angeles Times, Atlanta Constitution* and *National Police Gazette*. For obituaries, I still had available *Sporting News* and DeadballEra.com, in addition to Bill Lee's *Baseball Necrology*. My primary sources for baseball records continued to be *Total Baseball* and Baseball-Reference.com. The *SABR Baseball Encyclopedia* was the source for the pictorial record of each player.

However it would not have been possible to research this biographical dictionary without new resources. An indexed version of the *U.S. Federal Census* has become available through *Ancestry.com*. Census data provides information about nationalities, family relationships, occupations and residences—information especially valuable in working with the lesser known players. The LA Foundation has continued to expand the issues of *Sporting Life*, now available to researchers through SABR. *Sporting Life* is a chatty source of news, opinion and gossip about athletes—especially baseball players. Available issues cover the late 1880s and early 1890s—a time when many of the 1884 players were leaving the majors, moving into other baseball positions and other occupations. And finally, since some of the 1884 players are still missing, the *SABR Biographical Committee Newsletter* provides information about efforts and successes in locating those players.

The choice of 1884 as a focal year was not a random one, as it was baseball's first big expansion season. I entered this study in disbelief that a relatively small nation, as the United States was then, could increase its major leagues by 75 percent in a single season. Where were so many additional players to come from? Through this biographical dictionary, I hoped to show the source of these players.

The introductory chapter sets forth the problems that expansion created in 1884—in terms of geography, population and baseball history. An appendix summarizes the birth and mortality data contained in the biographies. Not surprisingly, it finds that the players tended to be young, Eastern, urban and Irish. And despite what seems to be a high mortality rate among young players from infectious diseases, accidents, suicides, and alcohol-related causes, the life expectancy for the players as a group was average for the time.

But through the study, I quickly discovered that transition in baseball was more than an 1884 phenomenon. The men who played in that season were a part of the evolution and development of baseball over a period of more than 40 years. The 19th century saw baseball undergo profound changes both on and off the field. When Joe Start finished third in hitting in the amateur National Association in 1862, pitchers threw underhand from 45 feet, batters could define their own strike zones, eight and two was a full count, and not even catchers wore gloves. Well before the American League emerged as a rival major league in 1901, the pitching distance was lengthened to 60' 6", the mound had appeared, three and two was a full count, and all fielders were wearing gloves.

Off the field changes were even more pronounced: over the same period the status of organized baseball changed from amateur to professional; from club based to league based; from local to national. The control of the game passed from the players to the owners. The structure changed from one league, to two leagues, to three leagues, back to two leagues, again to three leagues, again back to two leagues, and to one league before finally settling on two. The players of 1884 were a part of all these manifestations; between 1871 and 1912, they played on 110 clubs in six major leagues. So in another appendix, I try to show the part the men of 1884 played in the development of baseball by charting the contributions of each player to each club for which he played.

My own baseball experience is in the nature of a wannabe. As a result I am far more interested in major league baseball as the embodiment of a dream rather than as a sport or business. Like most in the stands, I watch those on the field, wondering what routes brought them here and where they will go from here. All have a talent denied to most of us; all have sacrificed more than most of us can imagine. For some their piece of the dream will carry them to Cooperstown; for others the dream will end after their cup of coffee. So the limits of my study are those lives—specifically the lives of those who played major league baseball in its formative years. Our knowledge of many of those lives is incomplete. What we know of some others is not pretty, but that may well have been the way life was in the 1880s.

One thing I learned from my research is that baseball cards predated major league baseball. The first set of baseball cards were issued by Peck and Snyder in 1868, one year before Harry Wright began paying the Cincinnati Red Stockings and three years before the formation of the National Association of Professional Baseball Players. The appearance of baseball cards, team photographs, and composites at that early date confirms that our interest as fans in knowing our heroes as intimately as possible has a very long standing. The more famous Old Judge baseball cards date from 1887. We are fortunate that the Library of Congress has made so many of these available so we can see how the heroes of another century appeared. I have included a number of those in this study.

Introduction

Even after a century and a quarter, the 1884 major league baseball season continues to fascinate us. Perhaps it is because the Providence Grays won the first ever World Series that season in a three-game sweep of the original New York Mets. Perhaps it is the pitching performance of Charles "Old Hoss" Radbourn or the home run record of Ned Williamson. Surely some of the cause is the presence of the Union Association. Despite Bill James' persuasive argument in *The New Bill James Historical Abstract* that the UA has dubious claim to major league status, it is nevertheless a presence in the record books and thus in baseball lore.

The 1884 season brought major league baseball's first attempt to expand to three leagues. In 1881 there had been one major league with eight teams. In 1883 there were 16 major league teams in two leagues—eight each in the seven-year-old National League and the two-year-old American Association. By the start of play in 1884 there were 28 teams—eight in the NL, 12 in the expanded AA, and eight in the brand spanking new Union Association. Before the end of the season, the total number of major league teams had reached 34 as franchises moved or were added. In 1881 there were 121 major league players; in 1883 there were 261; in 1884 there were 637. When the American League added two teams in 1961 and the National League added two in 1962, many were concerned that adding 100 major league positions—a 25 percent increase—would dilute the quality of play. Today we are apt to be stunned by the magnitude of the 1884 expansion—244 percent over 1883 and 426 percent over 1881—but hardly surprised by the results.

By today's standard the United States was a small country in 1884. The U.S. federal census for 1880 lists a population of just over fifty million; that of 1890 shows it nearing 63 million. So in 1884 the population would have been about one-sixth of today's figure. Geographically the country was even smaller. Of the twenty cities with populations of more than 100,000, only San Francisco and New Orleans were located outside the Northeast Quadrant, an area generally bounded by the Mississippi and Ohio rivers, the Atlantic Ocean and the Canadian border.

The centers of population and the difficulties of travel kept major league baseball pretty much within this quadrant for another three quarters of a century. (As late as 1924 the University of Pennsylvania football team needed three days to travel to the West Coast to play the University of California.) Earlier attempts to locate National Association clubs in "western" cities such as Peoria and Keokuk were not successful—at least partially due to higher travel costs. Later, in 1876, Philadelphia and New York City clubs in the National League found travel costs into the West more than they could afford. Kansas City, targeted for expansion by five different leagues, was not a successful major league city until air travel made it just another stop on the way to the West Coast.

Of the twenty largest cities in the United States, only San Francisco (9th), New Orleans (10th), and the New York City suburbs of Newark (15th) and Jersey City (17th) were not represented by a major league team in 1884. The National League had clubs in eight—New York City (1st), Philadelphia (2nd), Chicago (4th), Boston (5th), Cleveland (11th), Buffalo (13th), Detroit (18th), and Providence (20th). The American Association had clubs in nine of the twenty—New York City, Philadelphia, Brooklyn (3rd), St. Louis (6th), Baltimore (7th), Cincinnati (8th), Pittsburgh (12th), Washington (14th), and Louisville (16th). Three smaller Midwestern cities—Indianapolis (24th), Columbus (33rd) and Toledo (35th)—filled out the league. When the Washington franchise folded, Richmond (25th) replaced it.

The established leagues competed for fans only in the two largest cities. But where was a third league to stake out territory?

When the Union Association opened shop in 1884, it found itself competing for fans in almost every city. The Philadelphia Keystones went head to head with both the NL Quakers and the AA Athletics. The Chicago Browns and Boston Reds competed with the NL White Stockings and Beaneaters. The St. Louis Maroons, Baltimore Monumentals, Cincinnati Outlaw Reds, and Washington Unions competed for fans with the AA Brown Stockings, Orioles, Red Stockings, and Nationals. When the Chicago franchise shifted to Pittsburgh, it began competition with the AA Alleghenys. Only Altoona among the starting field and replacement clubs in Kansas City, Wilmington, St. Paul and Milwaukee had entire towns to themselves. While there are no official attendance figures for the UA, in an Internet article entitled "That's Baseball," Donald Dewey and Nicholas Acocella show that for Altoona "the average home attendance for 17 games was only slightly more than 1000," with a low of 200. They also argue that in Baltimore theMonumentals were "no match for the Orioles." Wilmington's story is even more compelling. The Quicksteps forfeited a home game, refusing to play before empty stands. Marshall Wright points out that "Boston, Cincinnati and Chicago all lost at least $5,000 each (115)." Wright also notes that the UA's founder and president, Henry Lucas, "lost upwards of $100,000 of his own money, which was used to keep the league afloat" (115).

Were there enough players of major league caliber to support 28 clubs? Strong franchises in both of the established leagues fielded teams with minimal player turnover. The National League had five clubs with winning records—Providence, Boston, Buffalo, Chicago and New York. These clubs used 86 players, an average of 17.2 per club. The American Association had seven clubs with winning records—New York, Columbus, Louisville, St. Louis, Cincinnati, Baltimore and Philadelphia. These clubs had 132 players, an average of 18.9 per club. The four most stable Union Association clubs—St. Louis, Cincinnati, Baltimore, and Boston—used 106 players, an average of 26.5 per club. The higher turnover of players suggests that even the better UA clubs were having trouble attracting solid day-to-day players.

But the struggle to find passable major league players is best viewed from the bottom teams. The Philadelphia Quakers, the least stable NL club, used 31 players in the course of the season. The Indianapolis Hoosiers, the least stable AA club, had 35 players. By contrast, the Washington Unions used 52 players, and Kansas City Cowboys had 50 in a partial season. Related to high turnover is the issue of short-term players. Of the 637 players active in the majors in 1884, 197 played only in that season. In both the NL and AA one-year players made up 20 percent of the total (34 of 167 and 59 of 294, respectively); in the UA that figure was 35 percent (121 of 343). Again, these figures suggest that the UA was being forced to rely on fringe players to fill out rosters.

Of the 197 one-year players, 34 appeared in only one game. The most famous of these was a spectator named Murphy—no first name— who came out of the stands to play when the Boston Reds needed a catcher for the day. Probably more typical is Peter Morris, whose case was researched by SABR's Peter Morris. Morris, a shortstop for the Chicago Reserves, was picked up by the Washington Unions to play one game against the Chicago Browns. This was one of ten such one-game pickups by Washington that season, and it suggests that bottom tier UA clubs were at times having difficulty even in putting lineups on the field.

The 1884 Season

In the NL, teams with "name" players did not play up to expectations. From the perspective of 2010, it is easy to say that Buffalo should have easily won the 1884 pennant. The players who will win one for Detroit in 1887—Dan Brouthers, Hardy Richardson, Deacon White, Jim O'Rourke and Jack Rowe—are all here and in the prime of their careers. O'Rourke hit .347, Brouthers .327, White .325, Rowe .315 and Richardson .301, giving the Bisons a team .262 batting average. Pitcher James "Pud" Galvin had career highs of 46 wins, 12 shutouts, 369 strikeouts, and a 1.99 ERA. Brouthers, O'Rourke and Galvin will all end up in the Hall of Fame — where White should be. The Bisons had the third highest fielding percentage in the NL—which is exactly where they finished—19½ games behind Providence.

Chicago also should have won easily. Playing in White Stocking Park with a left field fence only 180 feet away, they were the Bash Brothers of the majors in 1884, hitting 142 home runs—103 more than their closest competitor. Portly third baseman Ned Williamson set a major league record with 27 homers, a record that stood until 1919. Second baseman Fred Pfeffer (25), outfielder Abner Dalrymple (22) and first baseman Adrian

"Cap" Anson (21) gave the White Sox a sweep of the first four places. Mike "King" Kelly finished sixth with 13 homers. Kelly (.354), Anson (.335), George Gore (.318) and Dalrymple (.317) helped the club to a league-leading .281 batting average as well. Larry Corcoran won 35 games, and rookie John Clarkson, a future Hall of Famer, went 10–3. Still, a team ERA over three and the NL's worst fielding percentage dropped the White Stockings into a tie for fourth place, 22 games behind Providence.

Much also could be said for the pennant chances of the New York Gothams, a team that lined up with four future Hall of Fame members on the field. Mickey Welch smiled 39 times during the season, with 62 complete games and 345 strikeouts. Roger Connor hit .317; Buck Ewing a respectable .277, and Monte Ward, still making the transition from pitcher to position player, only .253. However, with a lineup that appears to have been pulled from a hat each day — Ewing played seven different positions, Mike Dorgan six, Ward and Connor three each — the Gothams fielded only at an .895 clip and ended up tied with the White Stockings for fourth place.

The bottom three NL teams were never in pennant contention. Sixth-place Philadelphia had one remarkable player; twenty-one-year-old rookie Charlie Ferguson pitched 99 wins in only four seasons. Cleveland's pitching star, Scottish-born Jim McCormick, who led the NL in ERA in 1883, jumped ship to the Cincinnati Outlaw Reds in mid-season, to lead the Union Association in ERA. Shortstop Ned Hanlon, who would go on to a Hall of Fame career managing Baltimore and Brooklyn, and rookie pitcher Pretzels Getzein (1.95 ERA) were not enough to keep Detroit from the cellar.

Past all these teams swept defending champion Boston. Without a single Hall of Fame candidate on the team, the Beaneaters kept a solid lineup in place, leading the league in fielding. Third baseman Ezra Sutton hit .346 and led the league in hits. Charlie Buffinton had a career year, posting 48 wins and striking out 417. Fire-balling Jim Whitney added 23 wins and a 2.09 ERA. The Beaneaters had ten wins more than they had in their 1883 pennant winner, but still finished 10½ games behind Providence.

In 1884 the Providence Grays won the National League pennant for the second time in six years. Like Boston, the Grays had a solid lineup, but few stars. Only outfielder Paul Hines hit over .300 on a team that hit only .241, and they finished second to Boston in fielding. The difference was Charley Radbourn, who had the most phenomenal pitching season ever. Working 678.2 innings, he won 59 games with 441 strikeouts and a 1.38 ERA. When Charley Sweeney (17 wins, 1.55 ERA) jumped to the St. Louis Maroons in late July, Radbourn became a one-man pitching staff for more than a month, winning 20 consecutive games. Even with the 50-foot pitching distance of the time, 73 complete games (in a 114 game schedule) is remarkable.

In a three-game series "for the championship of the United States," Providence defeated the American Association New York Metropolitans 6–0, 3–1 and 12–2. Radbourn pitched all three games for the Grays; Fellow Hall of Fame member Tim Keefe pitched the first two games for the Mets.

American Association batting champion Dave Orr (a career .342 hitter) hit .354 to lead the original New York Metropolitans to their only pennant in 1884. The "Dude," Tom Esterbrook, hit a career high .314 for the champions. Keefe (37–17) and mate Jack Lynch (37–15) combined for 74 of the Mets' 75 victories in route to a 6½ game margin over Columbus.

Only eight games separated the next six teams in the standings. Without a regular above .276, the light-hitting Columbus Buckeyes won 69 games. A stable lineup (six regulars with more than 99 games) and solid fielding (.908 percentage) helped the Columbus cause. Pitcher Ed "Cannon Ball" Morris had 34 wins with a 2.18 ERA — second lowest in the league.

Louisville's Guy Hecker had an 1884 season to rival that of Radbourn. The big right-hander led the AA with 72 complete games, 670 innings, 52 victories, 385 strikeouts and a 1.80 ERA. Not surprisingly, Louisville had the lowest team ERA in the league. The original Louisville Slugger Pete Browning, a career .341 hitter, hit .336 in 1884. The Eclipse fielded .912, highest in the AA, but finished 7½ games behind the Mets.

First baseman and manager Charles Comiskey, who later made the Hall of Fame as an executive, led the St. Louis Browns to a fourth-place finish, only half game behind Louisville and a game behind second-place Columbus. The Browns' heavenly twins — Dave Foutz (15–6) and Bob Caruthers (7–2) — who combined for a 22–8 record, debuted in 1884. Ultimately they would combine for 365 wins as pitchers and 1948 base hits as position players.

The Cincinnati Red Stockings played two more

games than the Browns, so their 68–41 record lost on percentage points to the Browns' 67–40. Second baseman Bid McPhee was one of the few American Association players later to be named to the Hall of Fame. Teammate Long John Reilly led the AA with 11 homers and finished second in batting with a .339 average; bespectacled pitcher Will White won 34 games. The slick-fielding Red Stockings, with Pop Corkhill leading AA outfielders in percentage, were second in team fielding.

Without a regular hitting over .270, and a team average of only .233, Baltimore still managed 63 wins, good for sixth place. It helped that Canadian Bob Emslie (32 wins) and 21-year-old Hardie Henderson (27 wins) led the pitching staff to a 2.71 ERA.

Led by Harry Stovey's .326 average and 10 homers, the heavy hitting Philadelphia Athletics finished seventh, just 2½ games behind Baltimore. With six regulars over .270, the team batted .267. Bobby Mathews, who, as a 19-year-old pitching for Fort Wayne, won the first major league game ever played in 1871, added 30 more to his victory totals in 1884.

The rest of the American Association teams lost more games than they won. Eighth-place Toledo featured the first and last black major league players—Fleet and Welday Walker—before Jackie Robinson. Irish-born Tony Mullane led the AA with seven shutouts, amassing 36 of his career 284 victories in 1884.

The Brooklyn Trolley Dodgers and the Richmond Virginians (which replaced Washington on August 5), both with six regulars hitting below .250, finished ninth and tenth. Dodger pitchers yielded 3.79 earned runs per game, better than the 4.52 given up by Richmond pitchers. Only Ed Swartwood (.288) hit above .250 for the 11th place Pittsburgh Alleghenys, and only Jack Nagle (3.73) had an ERA below 4.0. Larry McKeon was a 41-game loser for 12th place Indianapolis. Before folding, the Washington franchise featured five regulars hitting below .200, leading to an overall .200 batting average and a .190 winning percentage.

No team ever dominated a league as the St. Louis Maroons did the Union Association. Playing at a .832 pace, they won 25 more games than runner-up Cincinnati. Second-baseman Fred Dunlap, a career .292 hitter, hit .412; "Buttercup" Dickerson hit .365, 81 points above his career average. Billy Taylor won 25 of his career 50 victories before leaving the club in August; Charley Sweeney won 24 of his career 64 games after joining the club in July. Henry Boyle, who never again enjoyed a winning season in the majors, went 15–3 with a 1.74 ERA. The pitching staff combined for a 1.96 ERA. The best fielding team in the UA, the Maroons had four position leaders—Dunlap at second base, Dave Rowe in centerfield, George Baker at catcher, and Sweeney at pitcher.

The Outlaw Reds won 69 games, eleven more than third place Baltimore. Outfielder and pitcher Dick Burns hit .306 and won 23 games, two fewer than the veteran George Bradley. But the pitching story was the big Scot Jim McCormick, who won 21 games and led the UA with a 1.54 ERA after jumping from Cleveland in mid-season.

Of Baltimore's 58 wins, 40 came from another Sweeney—Bill—who led the UA with 538 innings pitched. Only in his second season, Sweeney never pitched again, leaving the majors with 49 wins. Outfielder Emmett Seery hit .311 on a Monumentals' team that hit .245.

The 1884 season also debuted Hall of Fame outfielder Tommy McCarthy. The 21-year-old pitched and played outfield for his hometown Boston Reds, going 0–7 and .215. Pitching star Frederick Lander "Dupee" Shaw had 21 wins with a 1.77 ERA after coming from Detroit in mid-season. He led the staff to a 2.70 ERA, helping the Reds to a fourth-place finish among teams that completed the season. Harry Moore, a one-year phenom outfielder, who hit .336 before disappearing entirely from baseball (and from public records), led Washington to a 47–65 record. Moore and second baseman Tom Evers were the only Washington players to appear in as many as 100 games.

None of the remaining UA teams played a complete season. Except for Milwaukee, these teams ranged from mediocre to downright awful. Before passing into oblivion in September, the Chicago Browns had morphed into the Pittsburgh Stogies, being mediocre in two cities. First baseman Jumbo Schoeneck hit .306 and led the UA in fielding. Hugh "One Arm" Daily struck out 483 batters (including 14 with Washington), 8.68 per game, a major league record that stood until 1960 when Sandy Koufax averaged 10.13. Before closing shop in August, the Philadelphia Keystones combined the worst fielding percentage in the majors (.841) with one of the higher ERA's (4.63). After hitting .364 for the Keystones, outfielder Buster Hoover finished the season with the NL Quakers, for whom he hit .190. Altoona won only six of 25 games before disbanding in June. Their replacement, Kansas City, need 79 games to win 16, an even lower percentage.

Among the replacement teams, Milwaukee won eight of 12 games after joining the UA in September. Ed Cushman allowed only four runs in four starts with two shutouts. St. Paul hit only .180 in compiling a 2–6 record. Wilmington hit even worse — .175 — and needed 18 games to win two.

In January 1885 the National League admitted the St. Louis Maroons to membership, replacing Cleveland. This move brought the Union Association saga to a close. Also in January the American Association reorganized into an eight-team league, eliminating Richmond, Columbus, Indianapolis, and Toledo. Major league baseball returned to the 16-club status of 1883.

THE PLAYERS

John Ake came to the Baltimore Orioles in 1884 from the semi-pro Altoona club in his home town. Used primarily at third base, Ake hit only .192 and fielded .714 in 13 games before being released. He later played with Fort Smith, Youngstown, Meridian, Indianapolis and Duluth. On May 11, 1887, the 25-year-old Ake was drowned on the Mississippi River when the boat he was rowing capsized in the wake of a steamboat. His body was recovered a month later. The son of a farmer, Ake appears as an eighteen-year-old laborer in the 1880 census. *(Total Baseball; Sporting Life; DeadballEra.com; Baseball-Reference.com; U.S. Federal Census)*

Gus Alberts had major league trials in 1884, 1888 and 1891, resulting in 120 games and a .197 batting average. He played four games with the Pittsburgh Alleghenys early in 1884 and finished that season with the Washington Unions. As a regular infielder with the Cleveland Blues in 1888, Alberts hit .206. In 1891 he played twelve games for the Milwaukee Brewers. Alberts played, managed and umpired in the minors. In 1896 *Sporting Life* describes him as "boss lemon-ade peddler at the St. Joseph [MO] grounds." In 1908 he was groundskeeper at Bartlesville, OK. In 1909 he was described as a deputy sheriff "doing a collection business." Born to German parents in Reading, PA, Alberts appears in the 1910 census as a resident of Topeka, KS, working as a baseball manager. He later worked for the Clara Exploration and Development Company, mining near Alice, ID. Contacting pneumonia, he died in Idaho Springs, CO, on May 7, 1912, at age 52. His 1887 Old Judge card brought more than $1,000 in a 2004 auction. *(Total Baseball; Retrosheet; Idaho Springs Siftings-News; Sporting Life; Baseball-Reference.com; U.S. Federal Census)*

William Henry "Nin" Alexander joined the Kansas City Cowboys when the club entered the Union Association in June, playing in nineteen games. In these games he managed nine hits, for a .138 average. Switching leagues in September, he went hitless in one game for the St. Louis Browns, giving him a .130 average for the season. Used primarily as a catcher, he fielded .895, the average for the league. Alexander, who later managed St. Joseph of the Western League, was a lifelong resident of Pana, a small town in south central Illinois. In censuses for 1900, 1920 and 1930 he is variously described as the proprietor of a butcher shop and a retail meat merchant. Bill Lee found that Alexander also served as town mayor and city councilman for Pana. He died in Pana on December 22, 1933, at age 75. *(Total Baseball; Baseball-Reference.com; Sporting Life; U.S. Federal Census; Baseball Necrology)*

Hezekiah "Ki" Allen caught one game for the Philadelphia Quakers, a home game on May 16, 1884. The 21-year-old native of Westport, CT, had two singles in three at bats and was errorless in the field. The 1900 census for Westport lists him as a "day laborer"; the 1910 census shows him as a watchman at a button factory. According to Bill Lee, Allen later became a constable in Saugatuck, CT. He died at Saugatuck on September 21, 1916, at age 53. *(Total Baseball; Baseball-Reference.com; Baseball Necrology; U.S. Federal Census)*

Gus Alberts (Library of Congress)

Ed Andrews joined the Philadelphia Quakers in 1884 from Akron, becoming the club's regular second baseman. For the next three seasons he was a regular outfielder. A career .257 hitter over eight seasons, he reached .325 in 1887. A native of Painesville, OH, Andrews had attended Western Reserve College prior to entering professional baseball. He played briefly for the Indianapolis Hoosiers in 1889, the Brooklyn Wonders in 1890 and the Cincinnati Kellys in 1891 before leaving the playing ranks. Listed by *Sporting Life* as a stenographer in 1891, Andrews was a National League umpire in 1895 and 1898-99. He then moved to South Florida in 1898 and was involved in a number of real estate developments. The 1910 census lists him as a fruit grower (*Sporting Life* says pineapples), and the 1920 census shows him as a retail salesman for mineral water. He also gained fame as a writer of yachting literature. Andrews died at West Palm Beach on August 12, 1934, at age 75. *(Total Baseball; Baseball-Reference.com; SABR Collegiate Database; New York Times; U.S. Federal Census; Sporting Life)*

Wally Andrews, a Philadelphia native, had two trials with Louisville. In 1884 the 24-year-old played in 14 games as a general utility player with the Eclipse, hitting .204. At Memphis in 1887 he led the Southern league with 218 hits, a .422 average, and 28 homers. Returning to Louisville in 1888 as a first baseman, Andrews hit .194 in 26 games. In 1896 *Sporting Life* reported that Andrews had been umpiring in the Interstate League but was now ill and destitute. Bill Lee found that Andrews "for 30 years was timekeeper for the Indianapolis City Street Commission." This is verified by the 1910 U.S. Federal Census. Andrews, a child of Scottish immigrants, is listed as a resident of Indianapolis and a "laborer" for the city street board. Andrews died at Indianapolis on Janu-

Ed Andrews (T. Scott Brandon)

Walley Andrews (Library of Congress)

ary 30, 1940, at age 80. *(Total Baseball; New York Times; Baseball Necrology; U.S. Federal Census; Sporting News; Sporting Life)*

Fred Andrus hit .306 in eight games as an outfielder for the National League champion Chicago White Stockings in the inaugural 1876 season. At the end of the season he was hired to manage the Milwaukee club for 1877. The *Chicago Daily Tribune* concludes that because of his experience under Albert Spalding, he "knows the business well." Andrus reappeared in the White Stockings lineup on July 4, 1884, to pitch against Philadelphia. His delivery was described as "slow with very little curve." Andrus left the majors with one victory and a .293 batting average. In 1889 he was described as an "incorporator" of the Chicago Baseball Club, and an 1895 note in the *Chicago Daily Tribune* described him as an employee of A.G. Spalding in Chicago. Bill Lee says that Andrus was "connected with the management of the David Whitney estate." The 1910 census confirms this. Andrus died at Detroit on November 10, 1937, at age 87. *(Chicago Daily Tribune; Boston Daily Globe; Baseball-Reference.com; Baseball Necrology; U.S. Federal Census)*

Bill Annis, from Stoneham in the metropolitan Boston area, joined the Beaneaters in May 1884. In 27 games the outfielder hit .177 and fielded .897. He had begun his professional career at Pottsville, PA, in 1873. He later played for Newark (1886-87), Omaha (1888), Worcester (1889), Hartford (1890), Providence (1891), and finished with Portland, ME, in 1892. In 1890 *Sporting Life* noted that Annis and John Henry had formed a semi-pro team in Hartford. The 1900, 1910 and 1920 censuses for Stoneham list William P. Annis as a resident and a shoe factory employee. Annis died at Kennebunkport, ME, on June 10, 1923, at age 66. *(Sporting News; Baseball-Reference.com; Total Baseball; U.S. Federal Census; Sporting Life; Retrosheet)*

Adrian "Cap" Anson played major league baseball for 27 seasons, beginning with Rockford (1871) and the Philadelphia Athletics (1872–75)

Fred Andrus (T. Scott Brandon)

"Cap" Anson (Library of Congress)

of the National Association. When the National League was formed in 1876, he began a 22-year career with the Chicago White Stockings, helping them win the initial NL championship. Beginning in 1879, he also managed the team, winning five league titles. During this career he hit .329 with four batting crowns, reaching .399 in 1881. A 200-plus pounder, he also hit with power, winning three slugging titles and leading the league in RBIs eight times. He led the NL in fielding five times—four as a first baseman. As manager he ran his club with an iron hand, enforcing a no-drinking rule. Anson had attended Notre Dame, and after leaving the playing ranks in 1897, he was involved in running a billiards parlor, managing a touring all-star baseball team, acting in vaudeville, working in Democratic Party politics and managing a golf course. He was a native of Marshaltown, Iowa — the first white baby born in the town, he said — but became a Chicago resident. He died in Chicago on April 14, 1922, and was elected to the Baseball Hall of Fame in 1939. *(New York Times; Chicago Daily Tribune; Baseball-Reference.com; Total Baseball; National Baseball Hall of Fame)*

Joe Ardner played second base for the Cleveland Blues in 1884 and for the Cleveland Spiders in 1890, holding regular status in 1890. In 110 major league games he hit .212. Ardner played at Altoona before joining Cleveland; between Cleveland engagements, he played for Kansas City in 1888 and later played for Atlanta in 1892 and Youngstown in 1896. The Atlanta newspaper said of Ardner's play at second base, "His fielding work in that position has no superior in the country." Bill Lee says that Ardner became a "theatre stageman" after leaving the majors; the census identifies him as a "stage mechanic." Born in Mt. Vernon, OH, to German parents, Ardner died at Cleveland on September 15, 1935, at age 77. *(Total Baseball; Baseball-Reference.com; Chicago Daily Tribune; Atlanta Constitution; Baseball Necrology; U.S. Federal Census; Sporting Life)*

Harry Arundel, a right-handed pitcher from Philadelphia, made his debut in the National Association with the Brooklyn Atlantics in 1875. The 20-year-old lasted only two innings, losing his only start. Seven years later he made fourteen starts for the Pittsburgh Alleghenys, compiling a 4–10 record. In 1884 pitching the last game of the season for the Providence Grays, Arundel gave up only one earned run in a win, allowing him to leave the majors with a 5–11, 4.40 ERA career record from three leagues. In 1891 *Sporting Life* noted that he had become an agent for a book company in Cleveland. The 1900 census for Cleveland lists Arundel as an insurance agent. He died at Cleveland on March 25, 1904, at age 49. *(Total Baseball; Baseball-Reference.com; Sporting Life; U.S. Federal Census)*

John "Tug" Arundel played 76 major league games — most as a catcher — spread over four seasons. As a 19-year-old, he played in one game for the Philadelphia Athletics in 1882. Returning with the Toledo Blue Stockings in 1884, he logged 15 more games. Shifting to the National League, he played for the Indianapolis Hoosiers in 1887 and the Washington Nationals in 1888. Overall, he hit .173. Playing without glove, mask or chest protector, he fielded .882. Richard Curry describes Arundel as a "comic personality" who dropped a third strike with the bases loaded while catching

"Tug" Arundel (Library of Congress)

for the Saginaw Old Golds. He chased the batters around the bases, allowing four runs to score. Born in Romulus, NY, to Irish parents, Arundel died of paralysis at Wilson State Hospital in Auburn, NY, on September 5, 1912, at age 50. *(Total Baseball; Baseball-Reference.com; Wikipedia; U.S. Federal Census; New York Times; Curry, "Saginaw Old Golds"; Sporting Life)*

Al Atkinson or **Atkisson** won 51 games (3.96 ERA) in a three-year major league career. Signed from the amateur ranks in 1884, the 23-year-old product of Clinton, IL, won 20 games—split among the Philadelphia Athletics, the Chicago Browns/Pittsburgh Stogies and the Baltimore Monumentals. Returning to the majors in 1886, Atkinson turned in a 25–17 record for the A's and pitched two no-hitters. After going 6–8 with the A's in 1887, he struck out 307 at Toronto in 1888. Atkinson then gave up baseball and went to the Missouri Ozarks to work as a carpenter and a lead and zinc miner. He taught himself to paint and carve wood, so he became an artist, painting Ozarks scenes and creating objects in wood. Atkinson died near Stella, MO, on June 17, 1952, at age 91. *(Total Baseball; Baseball-Reference.com; Baseball Almanac; Baseball Necrology; Sporting News; U.S. Federal Census)*

Jake Aydelott, a "Hoosier pitcher" from North Manchester, IN, debuted with the Indianapolis Hoosiers in 1884, when he was only 22 years old. The right hander completed 11 of 12 starts, winning five. Two years later he had a trial with the Philadelphia A's, losing both starts, giving him a 5–9, 4.79 ERA career record. According to *Sporting Life*, Aydelott was managing and pitching for Charleston of the Southern League in 1889. Jacob Aydelott appears in the U.S. Federal Census for both 1900 (Center, IN) and 1920 (Columbus, OH)—both times described as a salesman. He died in Detroit on October 22, 1926, at age 65. *(Total Baseball; Sporting News; Baseball-Reference.com; U.S. Federal Census)*

Frank Bahret was the opening day centerfielder for the Baltimore Monumentals in 1884. Five days later, on April 22, the 26-year-old again played centerfield in a game at Philadelphia. Bahret went hitless in eight at bats but handled four chances in the field without an error. Born in Poughkeepsie, NY, he was the son of a tailor and merchant from Baden-Württemberg. Bahret was only 30 years old when he died at Poughkeepsie on March 3, 1888. *(Total Baseball; Baseball-Reference.com; U.S. Federal Census)*

Edward "Jersey" Bakely (**Bakley**) turned in a 76–125 record while pitching in four major leagues. The Blackwood, NJ, product went 5–3 with the American Association Philadelphia Athletics in 1883, his debut season. He also pitched for Cleveland (25–33 in 1888), Washington and Baltimore (6–12 in 1891) in that league. In 1884 the 20-year-old right-hander went 16–30 among the Philadelphia, Wilmington and Kansas City clubs of the Union Association. In 1889 when Cleveland joined the National League, he fashioned a 12–22, 2.96 ERA in that league. *Sporting Life* praised him for his effect on team effort: "When Bakely walked in the box ... the whole Cleveland Club could get in and play ball that would astound themselves." In 1890 he stayed in Cleveland and pitched for the Players League Infants, winning 12 more games. Bakely (as Enoch Bakley) appears in the 1900 Philadelphia census, listed as a baseball player. He died in Philadelphia on February 17, 1915, at age 50. *(Baseball-Reference.com; Total Baseball; U.S. Federal Census; Sporting Life)*

"Jersey" Bakely (Library of Congress)

Charlie Baker (T. Scott Brandon)

Charlie Baker a 5′ 4″ outfielder and infielder from Stirling, MA, played in fifteen games for the Chicago Browns in August 1884, moving with the franchise to Pittsburgh. He had two doubles and a homer among his 8 hits, but settled for a .140 average. In the field he committed 9 errors for a .735 fielding percentage. Federal censuses shows Charles Baker living in Hudson, MA, working first as a shoe finisher (1900), then as a coat maker (1910) and finally as a farm laborer in New Hampshire (1920). He died in Manchester, NH, on January 15, 1937, his 81st birthday. *(Total Baseball; Baseball-Reference.com; U.S. Federal Census)*

George Baker became the regular catcher for the St. Louis Maroons in 1884, hitting .164 in 80 games but leading Union Association catchers in fielding. When the Maroons moved to the National League in 1885, Baker appeared in only 38 games. In 1883 he had played seven games for the Baltimore Orioles; after one game with the Kansas City Cowboys in 1886, Baker left the majors with a .156 average for 126 games. In 104 games as a catcher, he had fielding statistics close to the league average. *Sporting News* notes in 1886 that Baker had been very ill but that he "would make a good catcher for almost any team in the country." His post-baseball life had long been a mystery until Peter Morris discovered that Baker and George Boecke were the same person. Born in St. Louis to German parents, Boecke/Baker worked as a newspaper stereotyper for the *St. Louis Republic*. He died in St. Louis on January 29, 1915, at age 55 or 56. *(Baseball-Reference.com; Total Baseball; SABR Biographical Research Newsletter; U.S. Federal Census)*

Phil Baker caught only 50 games in the majors but that number is tenth on the list of games caught by a left-handed catcher. In three seasons, he played in three leagues. He broke in with the Baltimore Orioles in 1883, coming off the American Association's black list. In 1884 he shifted to the Washington Unions, hitting .288 in 86 games, primarily as a first baseman. With the demise of the Union Association, Baker played with the Washington Nationals in 1885 as a first baseman and outfielder, but hit only .222 in 81 games. Overall, he managed a .259 average for 195 games. In all positions he fielded .945 — above the league average. Born in Philadelphia, Baker appears in the 1880 census for Washington, DC, as a baseball player who boarded there. In 1886 he opened a cigar store in DC, but continued to play for Rochester. In 1896 there was a benefit game for him in Washington because after a spell of illness, he had "a large family and no work." Baker died in Washington, DC, on June 4, 1940, at age 83. *(U.S. Federal Census; Sporting News; Total Baseball; Baseball-Reference.com; Encyclopedia of Baseball Catchers; Sporting Life)*

Charles "Lady" Baldwin, "the best left-hander of his day," did not drink, smoke or curse — hence, the nickname. He had a short major league career, but in one season — 1886 — he made history, leading the National League with 42 wins — the single-season record for a left-hander — 323 strikeouts, and seven shutouts. He posted a 1.86 ERA in 1885, after leading the Western League in victories. Despite a mediocre 13–10 record, he led Detroit to a world championship in 1887 with a 4–1, 1.50 ERA record in the series against the Browns. Baldwin entered the majors with the Milwaukee Cream Citys, coming from the Northwestern League as an outfielder and pitcher in 1884. After three years in Detroit, he finished in 1890 with the NL Brooklyn team and Buffalo of the Players League, leaving the majors with a 73–31 pitching record and a .231 batting average. Born in Orinco, NY, Baldwin "retired to his farm" near Hastings, MI, after the 1890 season. He died at Hastings on March 7, 1937, at age 77. *(Baseball-Reference.com; New York Times; Total Baseball; U.S. Federal Census; Sporting Life)*

"Lady" Baldwin (Library of Congress)

Sam Barkley (Library of Congress)

Clarence "Kid" Baldwin debuted with the Kansas City Cowboys in 1884 as the regular catcher and maintained a more-or-less regular status throughout his seven-year career. After one game with the Pittsburgh Stogies at the end of 1884, Baldwin spent the next six seasons in Cincinnati—across the Ohio River from his Newport, KY, home — moving with the club into the National League before finishing with the Philadelphia Athletics in 1890. He managed a .253 average in 1887, but hit under .200 three times and finished at .221. He caught 392 games but also played all the other positions except shortstop — even pitching in two games. His overall fielding average was below that of the league. His dissipation — especially drinking — eventually brought his exit from the majors and, by 1894, from organized baseball. According to his obituary in *Sporting Life*, his dissipation led to near blindness, and he became a tramp. Eventually he was committed to the Longview Insane Asylum in Cincinnati, where he died on July 12, 1897, at age 32. He first appears in the 1880 census as a schoolboy in St. Louis, where he developed as a baseball player. *(Baseball-Reference.com; Total Baseball; U.S. Federal Census; Baseball Necrology; SABR Biography Project; Sporting Life)*

Charlie Barber did not enter the majors until he was thirty years old, joining the Cincinnati Outlaw Reds in 1884. As the regular third baseman, he hit .201 in 55 games. However, both his fielding average and range far exceeded the league averages for third basemen. When the Union Association folded, Barber left the majors. According to *DeadballEra.com*, Barber worked as a bricklayer after leaving baseball. He was a native of Philadelphia, and the 1900 census for Philadelphia lists Charles Barber as a mason. He died on November 23, 1910, in Philadelphia at age 56. *(Total Baseball; Baseball-Reference.com; DeadballEra.com; U.S. Federal Census)*

Sam Barkley, a second baseman from Wheeling, WV, played with the Toledo Blue Stockings in 1883 when they were a member of the Northwestern League and moved with the franchise into the American Association in 1884. That season he hit .306 and led the league with 39 doubles. The Toledo franchise dropped by the league, Barkley moved on to the champion St. Louis Browns in 1885 and then to the Pittsburgh Alleghenys in 1886, moving with that franchise into the National League in 1887. He finished his major league career with the Kansas City Cowboys as player and manager in 1889. In six seasons, Barkley hit .258 and helped the Browns tie the White Stockings in the 1885 World Series. Barkley was the son of a cigar maker, and *DeadballEra.com* says that he also became a cigar maker after leaving baseball. *Sporting Life* says that he "degenerated into a tough saloon keeper" who had "become so fat that he couldn't stop a grounder." Barkley died in Wheeling on April 20, 1912, at age 53. (*Total Baseball; Baseball-Reference.com; DeadballEra.com; U.S. Federal Census; Sporting Life*)

Bill Barnes played center field for St. Paul when the Saints moved into the Union Association. In eight games he hit .200 (on a team that hit .180) but fielded .727 (in an outfield that fielded .854). Recent research by the SABR Biographical Committee has determined that Barnes was born in Shakopee, MN, to an English father and a Dakota Indian mother — hence the designation "half-breed Canadian Indian." Barnes lived in St. Paul; the 1930 census shows him employed as a carpenter and house builder. He died in St. Paul on July 10, 1945, at age 87. (*Baseball-Reference.com; Retrosheet; Baseball-Almanac.com; U.S. Federal Census; SABR Biographical Committee Newsletter*)

Bob Barr had 62 decisions and 28 wins for the Rochester Hop-Bitters in the expansion 1890 season. That year he finished in the American Association's top five in games, starts, innings, complete games, shutouts, and wins — as well as wild pitches, walks and losses. The Washington, DC, native had joined the Pittsburgh Alleghenys in 1883, posting a 6–18 record. He divided the following season between AA clubs in Washington and Indianapolis, winning 12 and losing 34. Returning to the majors in 1886, he won three games for the National League Washington Nationals. He earned his Rochester trial after leading the International League with 29 wins in 1889. After his season with the Hop-Bitters, Barr returned to the minors. A late season 1891 trial with the Giants

Bob Barr (T. Scott Brandon)

resulted in an 0–4 record, giving him a 49–98 major league record. In 1897 *Sporting Life* noted that he was "in business" in Washington. The 1900 census lists Barr as a government clerk. Bill Lee states specifically that Barr "was the chief clerk of the Washington, DC, engineering department from 1896." Barr died of uremic poisoning in Washington on March 11, 1930, at age 73 or 74. (*Baseball Necrology; Total Baseball; Baseball-Reference.com; Sporting Life; U.S. Federal Census*)

Marty Barrett made his debut as a catcher with the Boston Beaneaters in 1884. After only three games, in which he went hitless, he was released and finished the season with Indianapolis of the American Association. In five games with the Hoosiers, Barrett managed one hit, leaving the majors with an .053 average. In seven games as a catcher, he fielded .833 — well below the league average. In the 1900 census, Martin Barrett is shown as living in Holyoke, MA, and working as a "Cutter — Envelop Shop." According to Bill Lee, Barrett "tended bar and was employed by S J Wolohan and Company." Born in Port Henry, NY, to Irish parents, Barrett died in Holyoke on January 29, 1910, at age 50. (*Baseball Necrology; Baseball-Reference.com; Total Baseball; U.S Federal Census*)

Charley Bassett was reported dead in a trail accident in 1904 and received a nice obituary in the *Boston Globe*. The following week's *National Police Gazette* reported that he was very much

Charley Bassett (Library of Congress)

alive, "holding a policeman's berth in Pawtucket." Bassett, a graduate of Brown University, began his career with National League champion Providence in 1884. From 1886 through 1892 he held regular status as a second or third baseman with Kansas City, Indianapolis, New York and Louisville — all NL clubs. Only a career .231 hitter, he hit .260 in both 1886 and 1891. A career .918 fielder, Bassett led the NL in fielding three times. He later played in the Eastern League before retiring. The 1920 census confirms the *National Police Gazette* report that he was employed as an officer in the Pawtucket police force. Bassett died on May 28, 1942, at age 79. (*Baseball-Reference.com; Boston Globe; National Police Gazette; Washington Post; U.S. Federal Census; Sporting News; Sporting Life*)

Charlie Bastian, a sure-handed middle infielder, lasted eight seasons in the major leagues despite a .189 career batting average. One of the four-league players, Bastian began with the Wilmington Quicksteps in 1884. When the club folded, he finished the season with the Kansas City Cowboys. Bastian spent the next four seasons with his hometown Philadelphia Quakers, holding regular status in both 1885 and 1886. He then played in Chicago with both the National League Orphans and the Players League Pirates. In 1891 he put in brief appearances with the American Association Cincinnati Kellys and the Philadelphia Quakers. Whether as a second baseman (.932) or a shortstop (.892), he fielded well above the league average. An 1898 note in *Sporting Life* places Bastian in the Sixth Cavalry Corps for the Spanish-American War. The 1930 census for Pennsauken, NJ, shows that Charles Bastian, at age 70, is employed as a carpenter for a gas company. Bill Lee's research shows the same information. Bastian died at Pennsauken on January 18, 1932, at age 71. (*Baseball-Reference.com; Sporting Life; Total Baseball; U.S. Federal Census; Baseball Necrology*)

Joe Battin debuted with the Cleveland Forest Citys in the National Association in 1871 when he was 19 years old. He also played with the Philadelphia Athletics and St. Louis Brown Stockings, moving with the St. Louis club into the National League in 1876. In that first NL season he hit .300 and led the NL third basemen in fielding. On August 25, 1877, he and Joe Blong were named by gamblers as "willing partners" in a St. Louis loss and as a result was "eased" out of the league. In 1882 he returned to the majors with the Pittsburgh Alleghenys, whom he managed in 1883. Released in 1884, he played for and managed the Union Association Pittsburgh Stogies, finishing that season with the Baltimore Monumentals; thus, he became the first of the four-league players. Battin made a 29-game return to the majors in 1890 with Syracuse. In ten seasons — six in the NL or American Association — he hit .218. He later played and umpired in the minors for a number of years. Battin died in Akron, Ohio, on December 10, 1937, at age 86. Bill Lee called Battin a "retired bricklayer." Lee's finding is confirmed by the 1920 U.S. Federal Census for Akron, OH. (*Baseball Encyclopedia; Total Baseball; Baseball Necrology; Charlton Baseball Chronology; Sporting Life; U.S. Federal Census*)

Al Bauer or **Bauers**, "a left-handed twirler," had a birth date variously put at 1841, 1849, 1850 and 1859. Bill Lee says that he was a Civil War veteran, suggesting one of the earlier birth dates. Bauer joined his hometown Columbus Buckeyes in September 1884, winning one game in three starts. The *Sporting News* refers to him as being among a group of "young and rising" pitchers, suggesting one of the later birth dates. Two years later he pitched for the St. Louis Maroons, going 0–4 before being released. His career totals are 1–6, 5.37 ERA. Later in 1886 he was also released by Topeka of the Western League. In December of 1887 the American Association appointed him an umpire, a position he held until 1890. Most sources say that Bauer died at Wilkes-Barre, PA, on September 6, 1913; however, *Retrosheet, SABR Baseball Encyclopedia* and *Baseball-Almanac.com* all say that he died on February 23, 1944. The censuses of 1900 and 1910 show an Albert Bauer, born to German parents in Columbus around 1860, living in Lavinia, OH, working as a watchman.

Joe Battin (Wikimedia Commons)

Bill Lee found that the ball player had been "groundskeeper of the local ballpark." *(Baseball Necrology; Baseball Encyclopedia; Baseball Page; Sporting Life; Washington Post; New York Times; Sporting News; U.S. Federal Census)*

Jack Beach was named for Civil War hero Stonewall Jackson. The 22-year-old Virginian made his debut as an outfielder with the Washington Nationals at the beginning of 1884. Playing in eight games, he collected three hits for an .097 average, and his six errors gave him a fielding average of .667. He left the club in June. In the 1880 census for Alexandria, VA, the 18-year-old Beach is listed as a carpenter. Suffering from Bright's Disease, he died at his home there on July 23, 1896. He was only 34 years old. *(Total Baseball; Baseball-Reference.com; Retrosheet; Baseball Necrology; U.S. Federal Census)*

Dave Beatle, a 20-year-old New York City product, played in one major league game with Detroit on June 17, 1884. In the game played in Cleveland, Beatle went hitless at the plate, striking out twice. Starting the game at catcher, he had two errors and a passed ball. He committed another error when switched to the outfield. The 1900 and 1920 censuses for New York City show that a David *Beadle*, born in New York in 1864 to Irish immigrant parents, worked as a policeman and later as a private detective. Dave Beatle died at New York City on September 22, 1925, at age 61. *(Baseball-Reference.com; Total Baseball; U.S. Federal Census; New York Times)*

James "Buck" Becannon joined the champion New York Metropolitans for the last game of 1884 to pitch against Indianapolis. He was also the losing pitcher in Game 3 of the inaugural World Series. The *New York Times* judged that he was "above an ordinary pitcher." At the start of 1885 the belief was that he had "created a favorable impression by his steady work." In a few weeks, however, *National Police Gazette* noted that he was "batted silly in nearly every game." He appeared in one game for the Giants as a third baseman in 1887. By May 28 of that year he was out of the majors, leaving with a 3–8 pitching record and a .244 batting average. In 1891 *Sporting Life* reported that Becannon was working as a sporting goods salesman for Spalding Brothers in New York. The U.S. Federal Censuses for New York City in both 1900 and 1910 show Becannon as a resident, working as a clerk in the U.S. Customs. He died in New York City on November 5, 1923, at age 63. *(Baseball-Reference.com; New York Times; National Police Gazette; Sporting Life; New York Mets Hall of Records; U.S. Federal Census)*

Frank Beck (Frank J. Hengstebeck) made three starts for the Pittsburgh Alleghenys in May 1884, resulting in an 0–3 record. Later in the season, he made two starts for the Baltimore Monumentals, going 0–2, for a major league record of 0–5, 6.62 ERA. Born in Poughkeepsie, NY, at the outbreak of the Civil War, Beck lived to see the beginning of World War II, dying in Detroit on February 8, 1941, at age 80. Census figures for 1900, 1910, and 1920 show him residing in Detroit and holding responsible positions in an iron yard, with a railroad, and as an auto parts dealer. *(Total Baseball; Baseball-Reference.com; Baseball-Almanac; U.S. Federal Census)*

Frank Beck (T. Scott Brandon)

Ed Begley (Edward Bagley) joined his hometown New York Gothams in 1884. The 21-year-old pitcher worked behind Mickey Welch that season, starting 30 games and posting a 12–18 record. Contemporary accounts show that while "he made every man hit the ball," his curves were "hit hard and often." In 1885 he shifted to the New York Metropolitans, starting 14 games and winning 4. Begley then left the majors with a 16–27 record. *Sporting Life* notes that he signed with Bridgeport in 1886. The 1910 U.S. Census shows that 38-year-old Edward Bagley of New York City, son of Irish parents, worked as a steamfitter; ten years later he was listed as a laborer in an apartment building. Begley died at Waterbury, CT, on July 24, 1919, at age 56. *(Total Baseball; Baseball-Reference.com; New York Times; New York Mets Hall of Records; Sporting Life; U.S. Federal Census)*

Steve Behel, a 23-year-old outfielder, entered the majors with the Milwaukee Cream Citys when they became Union Association members in September 1884. In nine games he hit .242. The Earlville, IL, product received another trial with the New York Metropolitans in 1886, hitting .205 in 59 games. His .865 fielding percentage was slightly below the league average. One *New York Times* reader in 1938 described Behel — whose parents were both born in Pennsylvania — as "the first Russian ever to play professional baseball." After leaving baseball, Behel became a "watchman superintendent for a petroleum company." This is confirmed by his California voter registration entry. Behel died in Los Angeles on February 15, 1945, at age 84. *(Baseball Necrology; Baseball-Reference.com; New York Times; Total Baseball; California Voter Registration 1900–1968)*

Steve Behel (T. Scott Brandon)

Ike Benners, a left-handed hitting outfielder, came to the Brooklyn Trolley Dodgers in 1884 from Wilmington of the Eastern League. After 49 games, in which he hit .201, he was released. Returning to Wilmington, he played in six games for the Quicksteps in their foray into the Union Association. Between the two teams, the 28-year-old hit .185 in 55 games, and he fielded .806 — thirty-seven points under the league average. Benners was a native of Philadelphia, where he worked for the city transportation system. The 1890 city directory refers to him as a "grip man"; the 1910 and 1920 censuses both call him a "motor-man" for the street car line. Benners died in Philadelphia on April 18, 1932, at age 76. *(Total Baseball; Baseball Reference.com; AmericanMemorablia.com; U.S. Federal Census; Philadelphia City Directory)*

Charlie Bennett was "almost perfect as a catcher." In fifteen major league seasons with Milwaukee, Worcester, Detroit and Boston, he led the National League in fielding seven times, and his career .942 fielding average is almost 30 points above the league average for the time. A career .256 hitter, he had consecutive seasons of .301, .301 and .305 after joining Detroit in 1881. The native of New Castle, PA, joined Milwaukee from his local club in 1878. He helped both the 1887 Wolverines and the 1892 Beaneaters win NL pennants, appearing in 13 World Series games. After leaving the playing ranks in 1893, he was run over by a train in Kansas, losing both legs. According to Bill Lee, Bennett got around on prostheses until his death. The new stadium in Detroit, which opened in 1896, was named for him, and he threw out the ceremonial first pitch each year until his death. He died in Detroit on February 24, 1927, at age 72. Bennett's wife is credited with inventing the "breast protector" for catchers. *(Total Baseball; Boston Daily Globe; Washington Post; Los Angeles Times; U.S. Federal Census; Green Cathedrals; Baseball Necrology)*

Frank Berkelbach played in six games as an outfielder for the Red Stockings in July 1884, leaving the majors with a .240 batting average and a .667 fielding average. The *New York Times* notes that he had two hits and scored a run to help Cincinnati defeat Brooklyn on July 8. *Retrosheet* gives him a July 27, 1853, birth in Philadelphia and a June 10, 1932, death in Merchantville, NJ. He appears in the federal censuses for Camden, NJ, in 1910, 1920 and 1930, living with his daughter and son-in-law. He worked as a bartender and later as a watchman at a bank. *(Retrosheet; Total Baseball; New York Times; U.S. Federal Census)*

Charlie Berry played for three clubs in the Union Association in 1884. Beginning the season with the Altoona Mountain Citys, he moved on to Kansas City when Altoona folded, then to the Chicago Browns, moving with the club to Pittsburgh. All told, he hit .224 in 43 games. Thirty-six of his games were at second base, where he fielded .971—slightly above the league average. Born in Elizabeth, NJ, to Irish parents, Berry worked for Singer Sewing Machine Company before entering the majors. Census figures for 1910, 1920 and 1930 show him living in Phillipsburg, NJ, and working as a machinist for Rand-Ingersoll Company. He died at Phillipsburg on January 22, 1940, at age 79. His son Charlie, an all–America end in football at Lafayette College, spent eleven seasons as a catcher in the American League. *(New York Times; Total Baseball; Baseball-Reference.com; U.S. Federal Census)*

George Bignell caught four games for the Milwaukee Cream Citys at the end of the 1884 season. Born in Taunton, MA, to Irish parents, Bignell first played professional baseball with Bay City of the Northwestern League in 1884 as a catcher for Henry Porter. When Bay City folded, he and Porter went to Milwaukee, and when that club joined the Union Association at the end of September, he caught four games Porter pitched before a hand injury ended his season. On October 3, he set a still standing major league record by handling 23 chances in one game. In 1885 he played for Brockton, MA, and in 1886 for Bangor, ME, and Duluth before the toll of catching ending his playing career. According to the SABR Biography Project, he "presumably worked in the textile industry." Bignell died at Providence, RI, on January 16, 1925, at age 66. *(Total Baseball;*

Charlie Bennett (T. Scott Brandon)

Baseball-Reference.com; SABR Biography Project; U.S. Federal Census)

Judson Birchall debuted in 1882 when the Philadelphia A's re-entered the majors as an American Association team. In three seasons—all as a regular outfielder with the A's—he hit .252, with a high of .263 his rookie season. While his fielding average of .832 was seventeen points below the league average, his range numbers were twenty points higher. In 1906 *Sporting Life* noted that "no player, dead or living, ever excelled Birchall ... in the matter of sliding." Only 27 years old and suffering from "pulmonary troubles," Birchall left the major leagues after the 1884 season. He played for Newark in 1885 and umpired for a time in the amateur leagues, but died on December 22, 1887, in Philadelphia at age 32. In the 1880 Philadelphia census he is listed as being 24 years of age, still living at home with an English father, and working at a woolen mill. *(Total Baseball; Baseball-Reference.com; DeadballEra.com; U.S. Federal Census; SABR Biography Project; Sporting Life)*

Frank Bishop played four games for the Chicago Browns as a third baseman and shortstop in May 1884. He managed only three hits—one a double—in 16 at bats for a .188 average. He fielded .667 with five errors in 15 chances. Born in Belvidere, IL, Bishop is registered to vote in Chicago in 1892. He appears in the 1910 Chicago census, living with his mother and working as stockyards commissioner. In the 1920 census he is married and working as a livestock buyer. Bishop died in Chicago on June 18, 1929, at age 68. *(Total Baseball; Baseball-Reference.com; U.S. Federal Census)*

Bob Black was a super utility player for the Kansas City Cowboys in 1884. As a pitcher, he started fifteen games, winning four with a 3.22 ERA. He also played every outfield position as well as shortstop and second base, fielding overall at the league average. Black also hit .247 on a team that hit .199. Born in Cincinnati, a lawyer's son, Black appears in the 1880 census as a "crab dealer." After his baseball career, he moved to Iowa—first to Le Mars and then to Sioux City. He owned a billiards parlor in Le Mars and worked as an insurance agent and a stock salesman in Sioux City. Black died at Sioux City on March 21, 1933, at age 70. *(Total Baseball; Baseball-Reference.com; U.S. Federal Census; Iowa State Census Collection)*

Howard "Dick" Blaisdell made three starts for the Kansas City Cowboys between July 9 and July 14, 1884. The 21-year-old completed all three starts, resulting in a 0–3, 8.65 ERA record. He also played one game in center field. In four games he hit .313. An April 15, 1886, note in *Sporting Life* says that he had been reinstated by the Arbitration Committee and would pitch for Haverhill of the New England League. Blaisdell was a native of Bradford, MA, the son of a shoe manufacturer. He died at Malden, MA, on August 20, 1886, at age 24. *(Total Baseball; Baseball-Reference.com; U.S. Federal Census; Sporting Life)*

Bob Blakiston (Blackstone), a product of the Bay Area, joined the A's in 1882, appearing in 78 games as an outfielder for the American Association champions. He remained with the A's for the next two years, playing in fewer games each season. At the end of 1884 he went to Indianapolis, where he finished his major league career. In four seasons he hit .239; an above average outfielder — 24 points above the league average — he was a mediocre fielder in other positions. An 1885 note in the *National Police Gazette* states that Blakiston had not distinguished himself at Newark and "with the assistance of the manager's foot went off to look for another job." In 1886 *Sporting News* notes that Blakiston was playing for the Greenhood and Moran team in San Francisco. In 1887 Blakiston led the California League with 57 hits. In 1910 the census shows that he was working as a watchman at a water plant. According to Bill Lee's research, Blakiston had worked as a janitor. Blakiston died in San Francisco on Christmas Day, 1918. He was 63 years old. *(Total Baseball; Baseball Reference.com; National Police Gazette; Baseball Necrology; U.S. Federal Census; Encyclopedia of Minor League Baseball)*

Tommy Bond was one of the great pitchers of the 1870s. The Irish-born right-hander had 195 victories in the decade, putting together 31–13, 40–17, 40–19 and 43–19 records for the Hartford Dark Blues and Boston Red Caps in the 1876–79 period. His ERA over the same period was 1.68, 2.11, 2.06, and 1.96. He led the National League twice in wins, twice in winning percentage, twice in strikeouts and twice in ERA. Only 18 years old when he began his major league career with the Brooklyn Atlantics in 1874, Bond also pitched for Hartford in the National Association. His effective pitching over at age 24, Bond made token appearances with Boston in 1881 and Worcester in 1882, and sat out 1883 before joining the Boston Reds

Tommy Bond (Wikimedia Commons)

in 1884. After a 13-win valedictory season with the Reds and Indianapolis, the 28-year-old Bond retired from the playing ranks with 234 wins. He briefly umpired in the National League and coached at Harvard before going to work in the Boston Assessor's office. Bond died in Boston on January 24, 1941, at age 84. *Sporting Life* lists him as a Holy Cross man. *(Total Baseball; Baseball-Reference.com; New York Times; Sporting Life; Sporting News)*

Henry Boyle led the National League with a 1.76 ERA while pitching for the St. Louis Maroons in 1886. The Philadelphia native had led the Interstate Association in hitting in 1883 and then posted a 15–3, 1.74 ERA record with the Maroons in his Union Association debut in 1884. This turned out to be his only winning season out of six. When the Maroons moved into the National League, they plunged into the cellar, and Boyle became a 24-game loser, though he was regarded by *Sporting News* as the "swiftest" pitcher in the league. In 1887 he moved to an Indianapolis team which replaced the Maroons in the NL cellar. Boyle lost 69 games in three seasons there, giving him a major league record of 89–111, 3.06 ERA. His strong minor league hitting did not carry over

Henry Boyle (Library of Congress)

into the majors, where he hit .219 in 291 games. Claimed by the Giants in 1890, he did not play. Two 1897 notes about Boyle in *Sporting Life* describe him as "running a hotel in Lansingburg" and as "now a commercial traveler." A Henry J. Boyle appears in the Philadelphia censuses for 1910 and 1920, listed as a wine and liquor salesman. Boyle died in Philadelphia on May 25, 1932, at age 71. *(Total Baseball; Baseball-Reference.com; Sporting News; U.S. Federal Census)*

Al Bradley played center field for the Washington Unions in a game at Altoona on May 21, 1884. He went hitless in three at bats but drew two walks. In the field he handled three chances flawlessly. Born in Brady's Bend, PA, he spent most of his life in Altoona and played for the Mountain City club. According to the *Altoona Mirror*, Bradley worked for more than 52 years as a machinist for a railroad company there. He appears in the censuses for 1900, 1910, 1920, and 1930 in that capacity. Bradley died at Altoona on February 5,

1937, at age 80. *(Total Baseball; Baseball-Reference. com; Altoona Mirror; U.S. Federal Census)*

George Bradley was one of the great pitchers in the inaugural National League season. In 1876, as a one-man pitching staff, he led the NL in shutouts (16) and ERA (1.23) while compiling a 45–19 record for St. Louis Brown Stockings. He also pitched the first no-hitter in NL history. Bradley had gone 33–26 with St. Louis in the final year of the National Association. But after 1876 his number began to decline to 18–23 (Chicago, 1877), to 18–40 (Troy, 1879), to 13–8 (Providence, 1880), to 2–4 (Cleveland, 1881). He rebounded with 16 wins for the Philadelphia A's in 1883, and closed with a 25–15 record for the Cincinnati Outlaw Reds in 1884. The following season when the NL allowed pitchers to throw overhand, *Sporting Life* noted that "Poor George Bradley would make a great pitcher under the new League rule." Overall he won 171 games in nine seasons in four leagues. But he was also a position player, appearing in 170 games as a third baseman and 93 games at other positions, hitting .228. In fact, he made appearances as a shortstop for the Athletics (13 games in 1886), for Detroit (one game in 1881) and the Orioles (one game in 1888). Born in Reading, PA, Bradley became a Philadelphia policeman after leaving baseball, retiring in 1930. The U.S. censuses for Philadelphia verify his occupation. Bradley died in Philadelphia on October 2, 1931, at age 79. *(Baseball Necrology; Baseball-Reference. com; U.S. Federal Census; Sporting Life; Baseball-Library.com)*

Steve Brady began his career with Hartford of the National Association in 1874, also playing with the Washingtons in 1875. He came to the New York Metropolitans in 1883, drafted from Rochester, and he quickly became the team captain. Originally a first baseman, he became an outfielder in 1884 when he played in the first "World Series" against NL champion Providence. Since Brady had been in organized baseball from the middle 1870s, he was rumored to have played with Methuselah. A .264 career hitter, he reached .295 in 1885. When he left the Mets after 1886, he played at Newark and managed Jersey City until he left baseball in 1895. As early as 1891 Brady is described as a "prosperous saloon keeper" in Jersey City. From an Irish family living in Hartford, Brady was still living at home in 1910. The federal census that year lists Brady and two of his brothers as bottlers with their "own place." He died at Hartford on November 1, 1917, at age 66. *(Total Baseball; Baseball-Reference.com; Sporting Life; National Police Gazette; Washington Post; New York Times; Boston Daily Globe; U.S. Federal Census)*

Jim or **Jack Brennan** (**John Gottleib Doering**) began his major league career as the utility player for the St. Louis Maroons in 1884. The 22-year-old St. Louis native appeared in 56 games—33 as a catcher—hitting .216. After playing briefly for the Maroons when they entered the National League in 1885, he returned to the majors with the Kansas City and Philadelphia American Association clubs in 1888–89. Brennan's final season was his busiest, as he played in 59 games for the Cleveland Players League Infants in 1890. For his career he hit .220 and fielded .869—34 points below the league average. He later played at Denver and Spokane before "taking up the indicator" as an umpire in the Texas and Three-I Leagues. He is listed as a baseball umpire in the 1900 census. Brennan became a resident of Philadelphia, operating the "Light Bar" saloon there. He died from neuralgia of the heart on October 17, 1914. He was 52 years old. *(Baseball-Reference.com; Total Baseball; Baseball Necrology; U.S. Federal Census)*

Charlie Briggs played in 49 games—primarily as an outfielder—for the Chicago Browns in 1884. Of his 31 hits, eleven were for extra bases, and he drove in eleven runs. Still, he hit only .170, and his work in the outfield was average; he was out of the majors by early August. A native of Batavia, IL, Briggs appears in the censuses for 1900 and 1910 as residing there. In 1900 he is listed as a machinist, living with his father. In 1910 he has his "own income" and is living with a cousin. Briggs died in March 10, 1920, in Seattle at age 59. *(Total Baseball; Baseball-Reference.com; U.S. Federal Census)*

Frank Brill (**Briell**), a 20-year-old right-hander from Astoria, NY, made twelve starts for Detroit in 1884, completing all twelve with a 2–10, 5.50 ERA record. In 1897 *Sporting Life* states that Frank Brill, "a popular minor league pitcher a decade ago is now living in retirement at Long Island City." The 1910 U.S. Federal Census lists Frank Brill as a saloon keeper and manager of a bowling alley in Chicago. The census for 1920 shows him managing a billiards parlor there. A Frank Brill, who may have been the pitcher, was also a top-flight bowler in the Chicago area. Brill died at Flushing, NY, on November 19, 1944, at age 80. *(Total Baseball; Baseball-Reference.com; Chicago Daily Tribune; U.S. Federal Census; Sporting Life)*

"Fatty" Briody (T. Scott Brandon)

Charles "Fatty" Briody played eight seasons in the majors—three as a regular catcher—hitting .228. The *National Police Gazette* noted of another player that he was "as slow a runner *nearly* as Charlie Briody," who carried 190 pounds on his 5'8" frame. In his busiest season—1884—he played in 65 games, split between the Cleveland Blues and the Cincinnati Outlaw Reds. Beginning with Troy in 1880, Briody also played with St. Louis, Kansas City and Detroit in the National League and Kansas City in the American Association. As a catcher he fielded .910, ten points over the league average for the time. Born in Lansingburg, NY, to Irish parents, Briody became a "rotund boniface of a hostelry at Troy." Later he settled in Chicago, where he "opened his own independent trucking business." Newspapers reported him dead in May of 1892, but the *Boston Daily Globe* stated that Briody "has been in hard shape, but dead never." He actually died on June 22, 1903, in Chicago at age 44. *(Total Baseball; Washington Post; Boston Daily Globe; National Police Gazette; U.S. Federal Census; Sporting Life)*

Cal Broughton, described as the first left-handed catcher in the majors, had a big league career of 40 games spread over four years, six teams and three leagues. Broughton hit .308 in 11 games

Cal Broughton (Library of Congress)

as the regular catcher for the Union Association Milwaukee Cream Citys in 1884 but only .189 for his career. However, *Sporting Life* notes, "His fine work is often lost sight of." Broughton began and ended his major league stay with National League clubs in Cleveland (1883) and Detroit (1888). Between, he played with the Baltimore, St. Louis and New York American Association clubs in addition to Milwaukee. He entered the majors directly from amateur ranks in Janesville and Beloit, WI, and played minor league ball—mostly in the Northwestern League—until 1891. Born in Magnolia, WI, Broughton in later years served as chief of police in Evansville, WI. He died at Evansville on March 15, 1939, at age 78. *(Sporting News; Baseball-Reference.com; Baseball Encyclopedia; Baseball Necrology; U.S. Federal Census; Sporting Life)*

Dan Brouthers was one of the first great power hitters of baseball and one of the first great

Dan Brouthers (T. Scott Brandon)

left-handed hitters. In nineteen seasons, fifteen as a regular first baseman, the 6' 2" 200-pound Brouthers hit .342, leading a league in hitting five times. He also led in slugging percentage seven times, in hits and doubles three times each and in homers and RBIs twice each. Along the way, he helped four teams—NL Detroit Wolverines (1887), PL Boston Reds (1890), AA Boston Reds (1891) and NL Baltimore Orioles (1894)—win league championships. After entering the majors with Troy in 1879, Brouthers became a regular with Buffalo in 1881 and finished with Philadelphia in 1896. He also played with Boston, Brooklyn and Louisville of the NL. After stints in the minors with Springfield, Toronto, Rochester and Poughkeepsie, he played briefly with the Giants in 1904 before becoming head scout for the Giants. He later became a night watchman at the Polo Grounds. Born in Sylvan Lake, NY, to Irish parents, Brouthers died of a heart attack at East Orange, NJ, on August 2, 1932, at age 74. He was elected to the Hall of Fame in 1944. *(Total Baseball; Sporting Life; New York Times; Baseball Necrology; Hall of Fame; U.S Federal Census)*

Ed Brown had two trials with American Association teams. In 1882 he played seventeen games as an outfielder for the St. Louis Brown Stockings, hitting .183. In 1884 he returned to the majors with the Toledo Blue Stockings, hitting .176 in 42 games as the team's regular third baseman. He fielded .815 at both positions—more than 30 points below the league average. He also pitched two innings in a game in 1882; in 1884 he pitched one complete game in which he was tagged with 19 hits and 9 earned runs. Little is known of his life either before or after the majors. He was from Chicago, and Peter Morris notes, "There's a strong circumstantial case that he died there on June 19, 1918. But the direct connection to baseball is lacking." *(Baseball-Reference.com; Total Baseball; petermorrisbooks.com)*

Jim Brown pitched for three clubs in 1884, compiling a 2–14 record. He started 11 of Altoona's 25 games, going 1–9; when the Altoona club folded, Brown suffered a complete game loss for the New York Gothams before he finished the season back in the Union Association with St. Paul. He had another complete game loss for the Philadelphia Athletics in 1886, leaving the majors with a 2–15 record. Brown also played 15 games as an outfielder, committing ten errors in 26 fielding chances. Born in Lock Haven, PA, Brown lived at Williamsport, where he worked as a bookkeeper for Lycoming Rubber Company, according to Bill Lee. He died at Williamsport on April 6, 1908, at age 47. *(Total Baseball; Baseball-Reference.com; Baseball Necrology; U.S. Federal Census)*

Joe Brown joined the White Stockings in August 1884, completing five of six starts and winning four. Brown also appeared in eleven games—nine in the outfield—as a position player, hitting .213. The following season he went 0–4 as a pitcher while toiling for the Baltimore Orioles, leaving the majors with a 4–6, 5.11 ERA record. All sources make Brown a native of Warren, PA. The 1880 census for Warren shows a Canadian-born Joseph Brown of the right age living there, working at a sash factory. The ball player died at Warren on June 28, 1888. He was only 29 years old. *(Baseball-Reference.com; Total Baseball; U.S. Federal Census)*

Lew Brown, "another Boston boy," became the regular catcher for the Red Caps when they entered the inaugural National League season. The 18-year-old hit .210. After helping Boston win the 1877 championship, he raised his average to .305 with Providence in 1878 and helped the Grays win the 1879 championship, a season in which he also played for the White Stockings. Out of baseball in 1880, he played for Detroit and Providence in 1881, but was then blacklisted until 1883, when he again played for Boston and the Louisville Eclipse. In 1884 he was the regular catcher for the Boston Reds, hitting .231 in 85 games. Still only 26 years old when he left the majors, Brown hit

.248 in seven seasons—five as a regular—in three leagues. Bill Lee notes that Brown "worked as a clerk in a sporting good house." His death notice in *Sporting Life* stated that he had fractured his knee cap in a friendly wrestling match and then developed pneumonia in the hospital. He died on January 16, 1889, at age 30. *(Baseball-Reference.com; Total Baseball; Baseball Necrology; Kaese, Boston Braves 1871–1953; Sporting Life)*

Tom Brown, an English-born outfielder, spent 17 seasons in the majors, hitting .265. Beginning with the Orioles in 1882, he moved through ten different clubs in three leagues: Columbus, Pittsburgh, and Boston of the American Association; Pittsburgh, Indianapolis, Boston, Louisville, St. Louis and Washington of the National League; and Boston of the Players League. Reported to be "the fastest man getting to first base that ever played base ball," Brown hit .321 in 1891 while leading the AA in runs, hits and stolen bases. He also hit .307 in 1885 with Pittsburgh and in 1897, at age 37, he hit .292. His fielding average of .890 was slightly below the league average, but his range factors were considerably above the average. After finishing his major league career as playing manager with Washington in 1898, Brown became an umpire in the New York State League, Southern League and Pacific Coast League (1899–1905). He then went into business in Washington, DC, operating a cigar store. He died of tuberculosis in Washington on October 25, 1927, at age 67. *(Total Baseball; Baseball-Reference.com; New York Times; U.S. Federal Census)*

Louis "Pete" Browning hit .341 for his 13-year major league career, thirteenth on the all-time list. Owner of the original Louisville Slugger bat, the Louisville native led the American Association with a .378 average as a rookie in 1882. In 1885 he won his second batting championship, also leading the AA in hits. Shifting to the Players League with Cleveland in 1890, Browning won a third batting title with a .373 mark, also leading with 40 doubles. In his best season, he hit .402 in 1887. Considered a "terrible fielder," he nevertheless had a fielding average only marginally below

Tom Brown (Library of Congress)

Pete Browning (Library of Congress)

the league average and range factors marginally above. Most of his career (1882–1889) was spent with the Louisville Eclipse. In the seasons following the PL, he played in the National League with Louisville twice, Cincinnati twice, Pittsburgh, St. Louis and Brooklyn, finishing in 1894. Plagued by mastoiditis from childhood, he was largely deaf, illiterate and ignorant of subjects other than baseball. The alcoholism which plagued him throughout his career was probably as an answer to mastoid pain. After leaving baseball, he tried operating a saloon and selling cigars, but ultimately looked after his mother, a "comparatively wealthy" woman. For a time Browning was committed to the insane asylum at Lakeland, KY. His death on September 10, 1905, was attributed to alcoholism, cancer and paresis. He was 44 years of age. *(Total Baseball; SABR Biography project; Baseball-Reference.com; Sporting Life)*

Charlie Buffinton, possessor of "the best drop ball ever seen up to that time," won 48 games for the 1884 Boston Beaneaters, completing 63 games and working 587 innings with 417 strikeouts. When his win total dropped to seven in 1886, he went to the Philadelphia Quakers, for whom he won 77 games in the next three seasons. He pitched for and managed the Philadelphia team in the Players League in 1890, and then led the American Association with a 29–9 record for Boston in 1891. When he closed out with the Baltimore Orioles in 1892, he had won 233 games (2.96 ERA) in 11 seasons, including seven seasons of twenty or more victories. The *Boston Globe* reported that Buffinton, a Fall River, MA resident "has been in the coal business in ... his native city." The 1900 census for Fall River lists the native-born Buffinton as a "Clerk Coal Brd." On September 23, 1907, he died while awaiting surgery. He was 46 years old. *(Total Baseball; Boston Globe; Baseball-Reference.com; New York Times; U.S. Federal Census; Sporting Life)*

Harry Buker played in thirty games for the Detroit Wolverines between June and August 1884. He was used at both shortstop and the outfield, and his fielding at either position exceeded the league average. However, he hit only .135. The Chicago native had earlier been a member of the Lake View Brown Stockings, a top-flight amateur club which played competitively against professional clubs. The 1880 census shows a seventeen-year-old Henry Buker, born in Illinois to German parents, working as a farm laborer in Madison County. Bill Lee notes that Buker "was in the real estate business" after he left baseball. Buker died in Chicago on September 10, 1899, at age 40. *(Total Baseball; Baseball-Reference.com; Boston Globe; Chicago Daily Tribune; Baseball Necrology)*

Sim Bullas, a 23-year-old catcher, played in thirteen games for the Toledo Blue Stockings in May and June 1884. In these games the Cleveland native hit .089 and fielded .911—the league average. In 1890 A.G. Spalding sent Bullas to England as a baseball instructor, and he played that year for the Derby club in the English league. *Sporting Life* says that he retired from baseball in 1892. There is a Simeon Bullas listed in the 1895–96 Cleveland City Directory, working as a molder. The 1900 federal census for Cleveland spells his name *Bullis* but also lists him as a molder. Born in England in 1863, he had immigrated in 1870. The ball player died at his home in Cleveland on January 14, 1908, at age 46. *(Baseball-Reference.com; U.S. Federal Census; Sporting Life; Cleveland City Directory)*

Ernie Burch was the regular left fielder for the Brooklyn Trolley Dodgers in 1886, hitting

Charlie Buffinton (T. Scott Brandon)

.261. He came to the majors with the Cleveland Blues in 1884, hitting .210 in 32 games. After playing with the Washington Nationals of the Eastern League in 1885, Burch moved on to Brooklyn for the next two seasons, leaving the majors with a .260 average for 194 games. A sure hand in the outfield, he fielded .891—nine points above the league average. He made headlines in 1886 by negotiating with the New York Metropolitans while waiting to hear contract terms from Brooklyn. Both his birth and death dates are confusing; his birth date, which once had only a year (1858), now is listed as September 9, 1856, in DeKalb County, IL; the 1870 census shows him residing in Paw Paw, IL, the son of a farmer from New York state. His death date, long unknown, is now listed as both November 8, 1933, in Evanston, IL, and October 12, 1892, in Guthrie, OK. *(Total Baseball; Baseball-Reference.com; Baseball Necrology; Baseball Page; U.S. Federal Census; Sporting Life)*

John "Black Jack" Burdock was a 20-year-old shortstop for the National Association Brooklyn Atlantics in 1872, so when the National League was formed in 1876, he was already a four-year veteran, having played with the New York Mutuals (1874) and Hartford Dark Blues (1875). With Hartford in 1876, Burdock moved on to Boston two years later. Shifting to second base, he led the NL in fielding five times. Only a career .244 hitter, he hit .330 for the NL champions in 1883. As a second baseman, he fielded almost twenty points above the league average. An 1885 note in *Sporting Life* stated that he had been "suspended indefinitely for dissipation." Boston wanted to unload him, but, according to the *National Police Gazette*, no distillery owner also owned a baseball franchise. In 1888 Burdock was described as being quite an artist but as being detrimental to the team because of his painting. Burdock finished his major league career with Brooklyn clubs—the American Association Bridegrooms in 1888 and the NL Bridegrooms in 1891. The 1910 and 1920 censuses show him living in Brooklyn, employed as a painter. He is listed as an inspector for an oil corporation in the 1930 census. Born in Brooklyn to English and Irish parents, Burdock died in Brooklyn on November 27, 1931, at age 79. *(Total Baseball; Baseball-Reference.com; Boston Daily Globe; New*

Ernie Burch (Library of Congress)

Jack Burdock (Wikimedia Commons)

York Times; National Police Gazette; U.S. Federal Census)

James Burke started one game for the Buffalo Bisons in both 1882 and 1883. Entering 1884 with an 0–1 major league record, Burke became a solid performer for the Boston Reds, compiling a 19–15, 2.85 ERA record and finishing in the top ten in the Union Association in wins, starts, complete games, strikeouts and ERA. He also played 13 games as a right fielder, hitting .223. He pitched for Jersey City in 1885. Burke makes Peter Morris' "Colder Cases of the Diamond" list. Born in Rhode Island, Burke moved to Attleboro, MA, and lived there as late as 1886. Morris points out that there were two Rhode Island–born men named James Burke living in Attleboro at that time. James W. Burke, committed to the Massachusetts state mental hospital in 1888, died there in 1894. James F. Burke, a jeweler, died in Providence in 1922. *(Total Baseball; Baseball-Reference.com; petermorrisbooks.com; Sporting Life)*

Dick Burns split time between the outfield and pitcher's box for the 1884 Cincinnati Outlaw Reds, and did exceptionally well both places. As a pitcher he won twenty-three games with a 2.46 ERA; as an outfielder he hit .306, leading the Union Association with twelve triples. As a 19-year-old with the Detroit Wolverines in 1883, he did neither particularly well, going 2–12 as a pitcher and hitting .186. When the UA folded, Burns returned to the National League with St. Louis. His numbers reverted to 1883 standards, and he was out of the majors before August. In three seasons he hit .267 and compiled a 25–27 pitching record. Burns was born to Irish parents in Holyoke, MA. According to Bill Lee, Burns "was connected with the Kaffit Cigar Company and later operated a cigar store in Holyoke." This assertion is supported by the 1900, 1910, and 1920 censuses for Holyoke. Burns died at Holyoke on November 16, 1937, at age 73. *(Total Baseball; Baseball-Reference.com; Baseball Necrology; U.S. Federal Census)*

Pat Burns joined the Baltimore Orioles in August 1884, playing six games at first base. He had five hits in 25 at bats for a .200 average. On September 17, he played in one game for the Baltimore Monumentals, adding two hits to his total, for a .241 average. As a first baseman he fielded .947—just under the league average. Nothing further is known of his life. That he played only seven major league games with two Baltimore teams and that his last game was in a Monumentals' home game suggest that he may have been a local player used to fill out lineups. *(Baseball-Reference.com; Total Baseball; Baseball Almanac; U.S. Federal Census)*

Thomas "Oyster" Burns played every position except catcher in eleven major league seasons. He began as a shortstop with the Wilmington Quicksteps in 1884, after leading the Eastern League in homers, and was the regular shortstop for the Baltimore Orioles in 1887. In 1886 he went 7–4 as a pitcher for the Orioles after leading the Eastern League in batting and homers. In Brooklyn (1889–95) he was primarily an outfielder and statistically a better than average one. But he made his mark as a hitter—a .300 career average. He hit .354 for Brooklyn in 1894 and .341 for Baltimore in 1887, when he led the American Association in triples. In 1890—his first season in the National League—he led the NL with 13 homers and 128 RBIs, helping the team to a league championship. However, in 16 post season games, he hit only .226. Burns finished with New York in 1895. His nickname came from his off-season job of selling shellfish. Born in Philadelphia to Irish parents, he is listed in the 1900, 1910 and 1920 censuses as a resident of Brooklyn. He worked as a saloon keeper and later as a cigar salesman and a manufacturer of cigars. Bill Lee says that Burns was a "corporation inspector for the Borough of Brooklyn." Burns died in Brooklyn on November 11, 1928, at age 64. *(Baseball-Reference.com; Total Baseball; U.S. Federal Census; Baseball Necrology)*

Tom Burns, "unquestionably the greatest third baseman of his time," was the regular shortstop or third baseman on the famous "Stonewall infield" of the Chicago White Stockings teams from 1880 to 1890, helping them to five National League pennants in seven years. A career .264 hitter, he reached .309 as a rookie and also hit .294 in 1883. His defensive statistics as a third baseman exceeded the league average. *Sporting Life* noted that Burns wore "side whiskers" in addition to his mustache. The Honesdale, PA, native came to Chicago from Albany. Released to Pittsburgh in 1892, he became playing manager, finishing the year as an umpire. Burns managed Springfield of the Eastern League from 1893 to 1897 before coming back to Chicago as manager in 1898–1899. Returning to the Eastern League, he managed Springfield and Buffalo; he was manager of Jersey City at the time of his death. Burns died of heart failure at Jersey City on March 19, 1902, just short

Tom Burns (Library of Congress)

"Doc" Bushong (T. Scott Brandon)

of his 45th birthday. *(New York Times; Baseball-Reference.com; Boston Daily Globe; Sporting Life)*

Albert "Doc" Bushong caught one game for the National Association Brooklyn Atlantics as an 18-year-old in 1875 and five games for his hometown Philadelphia Athletics in the National League a year later. Bushong attended the University of Pennsylvania Dental School and then joined Worcester in 1880. After three seasons with the Ruby Legs, he spent two seasons with Cleveland, three with the American Association champion St. Louis Browns, and three with the Brooklyn Bridegrooms, which won championships in both the AA (1889) and the NL (1890). Only a .214 hitter over his career (.167 in 24 World Series games), he hit .267 for the Browns in 1885 and led AA catchers in fielding in 1886. In 668 career games as a catcher, he fielded .916 — thirteen points above the league average. When Bushong left baseball after the 1890 season, he became a dentist in Brooklyn, practicing there until his death on August 19, 1908, at age 52. *(New York Times; Baseball-Reference.com; SABR Collegiate Database; Total Baseball; U.S. Federal Census)*

Bill Butler, an outfielder from New Orleans, went to the Indianapolis Hoosiers in 1884, along with teammates John Peltz and George Mundinger. Joining the club in late June, Butler played in nine games. He had seven hits for a .226 average; in the field he committed three errors in ten fielding chances. A William J. Butler, born in Louisiana around 1858 to an Irish father, appears in New Orleans censuses through 1930, working as a paper roller at a bookbindery. Peter Morris suggests that this person, who died in Houston on February 2, 1938, "could be" the ball player.

(Sabrneworleans.com; Total Baseball; Baseball-Reference.com; U.S. Federal Census; petermorrisbooks.com).

Frank "Kid" Butler was the regular left fielder for the Boston Reds in 1884, his only season in the majors. The 23-year-old Boston native hit only .169 in 71 games. He fielded .810 — slightly below the league average. A Frank Butler, born in 1861 to an Irish mother and a father from Massachusetts, appears in the Boston census for 1880, working as a wood splitter. According to Bill Lee, Butler worked as a ticket taker at Boston baseball parks after leaving the majors. He died in South Boston on April 9, 1921, at age 59. *(Total Baseball; Baseball-Reference.com; Baseball Necrology; U.S. Federal Census)*

Charles Cady debuted with the Cleveland Blues as a seventeen-year-old in 1883. On September 5, he pitched a complete game, giving up thirteen hits in a losing effort. In 1884 he had four complete games, a 2.83 ERA and a 3–1 record for the Union Association Chicago Browns. Cady also played as an outfielder for both the Blues and Browns. His final two appearances were with the Kansas City Cowboys in June 1884 as a second-baseman and catcher. In eleven career games, Cady hit .059 and was out of the majors while still in his teens. *Sporting Life* reported in 1886 that he was to receive a trial with Haverhill of the New England League. Born in Chicago to parents from New York state, Cady is listed as a clerk in the 1880 census. The 1900 census shows him working as a commission merchant. Cady died in Kankakee, IL, on June 7, 1909 at age 47. *(Total Baseball; Baseball-Reference.com; U.S. Federal Census; Sporting Life)*

John "Patsy" Cahill, born in San Francisco to Irish parents, played left field for the Columbus Buckeyes in 1884 as a 19-year-old. The Buckeyes had purchased him from the Philadelphia Quakers, who had signed him as a free agent. After leading the Southern League in homers in 1885, he was back in the majors as a regular with the St. Louis Maroons in 1886. Only a .199 hitter there, he finished his major league career with Indianapolis in 1887. In three seasons, Cahill hit .205 and was statistically a below-average fielder. A *National Police Gazette* notice in October 1888 indicated that he had been playing for Peoria and that he had been made into minced meat by a freight train. However, he was still playing for San Antonio as late as 1896. When the 36-year-old Cahill died from consumption in Pleasanton, CA,

John Cahill (Library of Congress)

on October 31, 1901, newspapers identified him as the original of Casey from Ernest Thayer's poem. *(Total Baseball; Baseball-Reference.com; Atlanta Constitution; Los Angeles Times; National Police Gazette; Sporting Life)*

Ed Callahan played for three Union Association teams in 1884: one game for St. Louis, three games for Kansas City and four games for Boston. He hit well (9 for 27, a .333 average), but he didn't field especially well as either an outfielder (two errors in nine chances) or as a shortstop (three errors in 17 chances). Born in Boston to Irish parents, Callahan appears in the censuses for Manhattan (1910), Los Angeles (1920) and Monmouth, NJ (1930). He is listed as a barker at a race track in 1910 and lists "none" as his occupation after that year. He died in New York City on February 5, 1947, at age 89. *(Total Baseball; Retrosheet; Baseball-Almanac.com; U.S. Federal Census; New York Times)*

Pat Callahan was born on October 15, 1866, making him the youngest major league player in 1884. The seventeen-year-old was the regular third baseman for the Indianapolis Hoosiers until the end of July, hitting .260 in 61 games. Most sources say that he was born in Cleveland, but *Baseball Almanac* and *Retrosheet* say New York City. Those sources have an open death date, but other sources say that he died on February 4, 1940, in Louisville. Bill Lee states that Callahan "owned and operated the Louisville Varnish Company, the world's largest maker of varnishes." The Cleveland birth place and the occupation are confirmed by the U.S. Federal Census, which shows him born to Irish parents; the death date is confirmed by the Kentucky death index, which shows that he died of coronary thrombosis. He would have been 75 years old at the time of his death. *(Total Baseball; Baseball-Reference.com; Baseball Almanac; Baseball Page; Retrosheet; Baseball Necrology; U.S. Federal Census; Kentucky Death Index)*

Warren "Hick" Carpenter, a product of the tiny Massachusetts town of Grafton, originated the phrase "hot corner" in 1889 when he caught seven line drives hit directly at him. Like most players at the time, he was bare handed. Carpenter began his major league career with Syracuse in 1879. After playing with Cincinnati and Worcester of the National League, he became an American Association star in Cincinnati. In 1882, his first season there, he hit .342, leading the AA in hits and third basemen in fielding. He continued with the Red Stockings through 1889. Referred to as "Old Hick," he was the object of jokes suggesting that he "has been a prominent ball player ever since Noah came out of the ark." Carpenter played one game with the St. Louis Browns in 1892, and then, according to the *New York Times*, was to "go into the service of the Pulman Company before many days." The 1900 census shows Carpenter living in Cincinnati and working as a railroad conductor. According to *Sporting Life* he received a new appointment in 1902 as "the assistant collector of the port of Ocala, Fla." The census shows him working for the U.S. Customs service at Nogales, AZ (1910), and El Paso, TX (1920 and 1930). Carpenter died at San Diego, CA, on April 18, 1937, at age 81. *(Total Baseball; Baseball Reference.com; Baseball Historian; National Police Gazette; New York Times; Washington Post; U.S. Federal Census; Sporting Life)*

Cliff Carroll joined Providence as an outfielder in 1882 and helped them win the 1884 National League championship. Born in Clay Grove, IA, he had played at Peoria, San Francisco, Oakland and Austin, NV, before joining the Grays. "One of the best baserunners in the profession," he spent eleven years in the NL, eight as a regular. After playing with Washington (1886–87), Carroll was released by Pittsburgh early in 1888 and was out of baseball in 1889. Signed by Chicago, he "improved with age," and enjoyed four more productive seasons with Chicago, St. Louis and Boston, hitting as high as .285 in 1890 — thirty-four points over his career average. Primarily a left fielder, he fielded .905 — 11 points better than the league average. *Sporting Life* notes that Carroll's career is a "shining example of what temperance can do for a player." After being released by Boston at the end of 1893, Carroll moved to Illinois "to take up farming." He is listed in the 1910 census as a resident of Linn, Oregon, working as a fruit farmer. He died at Portland, Oregon, on June 12, 1923, at age 68. *(Total*

Cliff Carroll (Library of Congress)

Baseball; Chicago Daily Tribune; Boston Globe; Washington Post; New York Times; U.S. Federal Census; Sporting Life)

Edward "Chick" Carroll was possibly the youngest player in the majors in 1884. *Baseball-Reference.com* says that he was sixteen years old on opening day 1884. *Encyclopedia of Arkansas* says he was eighteen but shows no specific birth date or place of birth. *Retrosheet* and *Baseball-Almanac* have no birth date. In four games with the Washington Unions, he had four hits for a .250 average, but committed four errors for a .500 fielding average. Replaced in the lineup, he never again played in the majors. He died in Chicago on July 13, 1908, at age 39. Since the U.S. Federal Census shows no Edward Carroll born in Arkansas, he is difficult to trace. SABR now lists him only as "Carroll" with no first name or place of birth. *(Total Baseball; Baseball-Reference.com; Retrosheet; Baseball-Almanac.com; U.S. Federal Census; SABR Baseball Encyclopedia)*

Fred Carroll averaged 94 games per season for eight years in the major leagues. After playing at St. Mary's College (1881–83), the Sacramento native played for Reading, PA, and was purchased by the Columbus Buckeyes in 1884. Sold to Pittsburgh at the end of the season, he spent the next seven seasons in Pittsburgh, playing in three leagues. The catcher-outfielder hit .288 (1886) in the American Association; .330 (1889) in the National League and .298 (1890) in the Players League, finishing with a career .284 average. A better than average catcher, he was less effective as an outfielder. Carroll was a member of the All-America team that toured the world from 1889 to 1890. Returning to California in 1891, he operated a "profitable transfer business." The 1900 census shows him as an "Express Co. owner." Carroll died of an "athletic heart" at San Rafael, CA, on November 7, 1904, at age 40. *(Total Baseball; Baseball-Reference.com; Sporting Life; SABR Collegiate Database; U.S. Federal Census)*

John "Scrappy" Carroll played right field for the St. Paul Saints when they entered the Union Association in 1884, hitting .097 in nine games. The following season the Buffalo native played in thirteen games for his hometown Bisons of the National League. In 1887, playing in the American Association with Cleveland, he had his most productive season, hitting .199 in 57 games. Carroll was able to leave the majors with a .171 average in 79 games. As an outfielder, he fielded

"Scrappy" Carroll (Library of Congress)

only .853, more than 30 points below the league average. In the minors he played with Omaha, St. Paul and Utica. Born to Irish parents, Carroll appears in the censuses for Buffalo in 1910, 1920 and 1930—each time with "none" given as the usual occupation. He died at Buffalo on November 14, 1942, at age 82. *(Baseball-Reference.com; Sporting News; Baseball Encyclopedia; U.S. Federal Census)*

Pat Carroll played in eleven games—eight as a catcher—for Altoona at the beginning of 1884. After the Mountain Citys folded, Carroll caught five games for his hometown Philadelphia Keystones in August. Between the two Union Association clubs, Carroll hit .235 and fielded .877—both below the league average. He was 31 years old at the time. In August 1885, *Sporting Life* describes him as the new catcher for Cumberland. Later that season he was secured by Springfield, OH. But in 1886 he is noted as being without a team. A Patrick Carroll of the right age was born to Irish parents in Philadelphia. He appears in both the 1900 and 1910 censuses, working as a produce dealer. The ballplayer died in Philadelphia on Valentine's Day, 1916, at age 62. *(Total Baseball; Baseball-Reference.com; U.S. Federal Census; Baseball Necrology; Retrosheet)*

Bob Caruthers joined the St. Louis Browns from Grand Rapids in 1884. The 20-year-old right-hander went 7–2 in his first year. In nine seasons he won 218 games with a .688 winning percentage — third on the all-time list. Twice he won 40 games, and three times he led a league in winning percentage. Along the line he helped four teams — the 1885–87 St. Louis Browns, and the 1889 Brooklyn Bridegrooms — win American Association championships and one team — the 1890 Brooklyn Bridegrooms — win a National League title. In the fifteen-game 1887 World Series, Caruthers had four wins with a 2.13 ERA. The 5'7" 138-pounder played almost as many games as an outfielder as he did as a pitcher, hitting .282 for his career. He hit .357 in the inflated 1887 season and .334 in 1886. By 1892 he had converted to an outfield regular with the St. Louis Browns, finishing his major league career in 1893. Caruthers played in the minors through 1898 and then became an umpire in the Three-I League. The 1910 census shows him living with his wife's parents in Peoria, IL, and working as an umpire. Born in Memphis, Caruthers died at Peoria on August 5, 1911. He was 47 years old. *(Total Baseball; BaseballLibrary.com; Peoria Transcript; DeadballEra.com; Baseball-Reference.com; U.S. Federal Census; Sporting Life)*

Dan Casey posted a 96–90, 3.18 ERA record in seven seasons in the majors. Fifty-two wins came in two seasons — 1886–87 — when he went 24–18 and 28–13 with the Philadelphia Quakers. In 1887 the left-hander led the National League with a 2.86 ERA and four shutouts. Casey, along with his older brother Dennis, had debuted with the Wilmington Quicksteps in 1884, after leading the Eastern League in winning percentage. In 1885 he joined Detroit, coming from Indianapolis, and moved on to the Quakers a year later. In 1890 — his final season — he had 40 complete

Bob Caruthers (Library of Congress)

Dan Casey (Library of Congress)

games and 19 wins for Syracuse of the American Association. After pitching in the Eastern League in 1891, he umpired in the league in 1892. Born in Binghamton, NY, to Irish parents, Casey is listed in the 1900, 1920 and 1930 censuses for Binghamton, working as a streetcar conductor. He died at Washington, DC, on February 8, 1943, at age 80. Casey was one of a number of players who claimed to be the hero of "Casey at the Bat." *(Total Baseball; Baseball-Reference.com; U.S. Federal Census; Sporting News; Sporting Life)*

Dennis Casey joined the Wilmington Quicksteps in 1884 along with his younger brother Dan. They left three days later, jumping to the Baltimore Orioles of the American Association. In the final 37 games of the season, Casey hit .248 as the regular centerfielder. The following season the left-handed hitting Casey was batting .288 after 63 games when he was released on July 24 for poor base running. He also did not field very well, his .847 average being thirty points below the league average. *Sporting Life* shows him playing for Newark in 1886 and Binghamton in 1887. Like his brother Dan, Casey was born in Binghamton, NY, to Irish parents and grew up as a farm laborer, and is so listed in the 1880 census. In 1900—his last census—he is listed as a farmer. Dennis Casey died on January 19, 1909, at age 50. *(U.S. Federal Census; Total Baseball; Baseball-Reference.com; Sporting Life)*

Ed Caskin (or **Caskins**) joined Troy in 1879, coming from "the Rochesters." He was the regular shortstop in Troy (1879–81). Blacklisted, he sat out 1882, returning as the regular shortstop for the New York Gothams (1883–84), and the regular third baseman for the St. Louis Maroons (1885). He led National League shortstops in double plays in 1884 and in errors in 1880; however, his career .883 percentage was fifteen points above the league average. A career .228 hitter, he hit .257 as a 27-year-old rookie. After leaving St. Louis, he played at Rochester and Lynn and played in one game for the Giants in 1886. Born in Danvers, MA, to Irish parents, Caskin worked in the shoe factory there both before and after his baseball career. The 1910 census lists his occupation as "laster." In 1909 *Sporting Life* describes Caskin as "hale and hearty." He died at Danvers on October 9, 1924, at age 72. *(Total Baseball; Baseball-Reference.com; Baseball Encyclopedia; Chicago Daily Tribune; Sporting News; U.S. Federal Census; Sporting Life)*

John Cassidy (Wikimedia Commons)

John Cassidy played every position in his eleven major league seasons. He began as an eighteen-year-old pitcher for the Brooklyn Atlantics in 1875, going 1–21 before finishing the season as a first baseman at New Haven. In the National League he played with the Hartford Dark Blues (1876–77), the Chicago White Stockings (1878), the Troy Trojans (1879–82), and the Providence Grays (1883) before finishing in the American Association with the Brooklyn Trolley Dodgers (1884–85), for whom he served as team captain. A career .246 hitter, he hit .378 in the inflated 1877 season. The majority of his games were played in the outfield, but across all positions his fielding percentage of .845 was well below the league average. Born in Brooklyn to Irish parents, Cassidy died of dropsy at his home in Brooklyn on July 2, 1891, at age 36. *(Total Baseball; Baseball-Reference.com; Sporting News; U.S. Federal Census; Sporting Life)*

John Cattanach, a local Providence athlete, pitched in one game for the Providence Grays on June 5, 1884. The 21-year-old "made a signal failure, although he began well" in his only National League appearance. In July he pitched in two games for the St. Louis Maroons, leaving the majors with a 1–1 record. A year later Cattanach pitched for Macon and Columbus of the Southern League. According to the 1900 census, Cattanach was still living at home with his parents—a Scots father and half–Scots mother — working as the manager of a water company. *DeadballEra* says that he later became a chemist. Cattanach died in Providence on November 10, 1926, at age 63. *(Baseball-Reference.com; Boston Daily Globe; Atlanta Constitution; Sporting Life; DeadballEra.com; U.S. Federal Census)*

Jim Chatterton played in four games for the Kansas City Cowboys in June 1884. He started one game as a pitcher, a game in which he gave up eleven hits and seven runs in five innings. Otherwise he played at first base or in the outfield. The 19-year-old Brooklyn product managed two hits — one a double — for a .133 average, and by June 15, he was out of the majors. Described by *Sporting Life* as a "good pitcher and a good fellow," Chatterton played in the New England League for Portland (1885), Salem (1887) and Dover (1891), where he also managed. He appears in the censuses of 1900 (Rockingham, NH), 1920 (Lynn, MA) and 1930 (Manchester, NH) working as a shoemaker. Chatterton died at Tewksbury, MA, on December 15, 1944, at age 80. *(Total Baseball; Baseball-Reference.com; Sporting Life; U.S. Federal Census)*

John Clarkson won 328 games in just 12 seasons, 309 of those coming in nine seasons — 1885–1893. He won 30 or more games six times topped by seasons of 53 wins (1885) and 49 wins (1889). Twice he worked more than 600 innings, leading the National League four times. Twice he had league-leading 68 complete games, and twice he struck out more than 300 batters. The Cambridge, MA, native pitched briefly for Worcester in 1882 and joined the Chicago White Stockings late in 1884, following a 34-win, 388-strikeout performance for Saginaw earlier in the season. He promptly helped the White Stockings win NL championships in 1885 and 1886. Sold to Boston for an unheard of $10,000 in 1888, he helped the Beaneaters win the 1891 NL championship. Clarkson's strengths were his control and "the headwork he put into pitching." He was also regarded as a "clean-cut, day-in and day-out athlete" who earned his stardom. After his arm went bad and he was released by Cleveland in 1894, he opened a cigar store in Bay City, MI. Later his mind began to be affected — *Sporting Life* termed him "incurably insane" in 1906. However, he died from pneumonia in a Belmont, MA, sanitarium on February 4, 1909, only 47 years old. He was named to the Baseball Hall of Fame in 1963. Two younger brothers, Arthur "Dad" Clarkson and Walter

John Clarkson (Library of Congress)

Clarkson, also pitched in the majors. *(Chicago Daily Tribune; Washington Post; Baseball-Reference.com; Curry, "Saginaw Old Golds"; Sporting Life)*

Jack Clements was the last and greatest of the left-handed catchers. In seventeen seasons (1884–1900) Clements caught 1073 games. He fielded .937, thirteen points over the league average, and led NL catchers in fielding in 1898. Extremely durable, Clements caught 399 games in the four-year period 1890–93 and caught at least 75 games eight times. He entered the majors with his hometown Philadelphia Keystones in 1884. The 19-year-old split time between the outfield and catching. After hitting .282 in 41 games, he finished the season with the National League Quakers and spent the remainder of his career in the NL with Philadelphia (1884–97), St. Louis (1898), Cleveland (1899) and Boston (1900). The

Jack Clements (T. Scott Brandon)

career .284 hitter was over .300 five times with a high of .394 in 1895. *Sporting Life* reported that the 40-year-old Clements was still catching in the semi-pro ranks in 1904. Bill Lee found that Clements worked for A.G. Reach and later for another baseball manufacturer. Clements died in Norristown, PA, on May 23, 1941, at age 76. *(Total Baseball; Baseball-Reference.com; Sporting News; U.S. Federal Census; Baseball Necrology; Sporting Life)*

Elmer Cleveland, a second cousin of President Grover Cleveland, played 80 major league games spread over eight years, four teams, and three leagues. The third baseman from Washington, DC, hit .322 in 29 games for the Cincinnati Outlaw Reds in 1884. Later trials with the New York Giants and Pittsburgh Alleghenys (1888) and the Columbus Solons (1891) were less productive, and he settled for a career .255 average. His fielding statistics are exactly at the league average. An 1896 note in *Sporting Life* says that Cleveland was "out of the game altogether." The 1900 Pittsburgh census lists Cleveland's occupation as "Mfg." The 1910 census for Johnstown, PA, states that he was a hotel owner. According to Bill Lee, Cleveland owned and operated hotels in Johnstown and Zimmerman, PA, after leaving baseball. He died at Zimmerman on October 8, 1913. He was 51 years of age. *(Total Baseball; Baseball-Reference.com; Baseball Necrology; U.S. Federal Census; Sporting Life)*

John "Monk" Cline was a regular outfielder for the Louisville Eclipse in 1884 and for the Kansas City Cowboys in 1888. His entire career spent in the American Association, the Louisville native entered the majors in 1882 with Baltimore and finished back with Louisville in 1891, hitting .235 in five seasons. Between AA engagements, the left-handed Cline was a star shortstop for Atlanta in 1886, leading the Southern League in batting and homers. In 1888 with Memphis he again led the Southern League in hitting, and added a Western Association batting crown in 1889. After umpiring in the Western League, he joined teammate Jimmy "Chicken" Wolf on the Louisville Fire Department—"a pipeman at Number Three Engine house." In this job Cline was injured by a falling wall in 1894. He died on September 23, 1916, in Louisville. The death certificate for the 58-year-old lists his profession as "Iron Molder." *(Total Baseball; Baseball Necrology; New York Times; Atlanta Constitution; Chicago Daily Tribune; Sporting Life; Kentucky Certificate of Death; U.S. Federal Census)*

Elmer Cleveland (Library of Congress)

James "Big Jim" Clinton was the regular left fielder for the American Association Baltimore Orioles (1883–4) and Cincinnati Red Stockings (1885). Born in New York City to Irish parents, the 5'8" Clinton began in the National Association with the Brooklyn Eckfords—which he also managed—in 1872, also playing for the Elizabeth Resolutes (1873), and Brooklyn Atlantics (1874–75). Making fourteen starts as a pitcher for the Atlantics in 1875, he went 1–13. When the National League was formed, Clinton played 16 games for the Louisville Grays and was then out of the majors until 1882, when he played with the Worcester Ruby Legs. In ten seasons in three leagues, he hit .256 but reached .313 for the Orioles in 1883. After finishing with Baltimore in 1886, Clinton played with and managed Nashville. The 1900 and 1910 censuses show Clinton living in Brooklyn and tending bar in a hotel. He died in Brooklyn on September 3, 1921, at age 71. *(Total Baseball; Baseball-Reference.com; U.S. Federal Census; Sporting Life)*

John Coleman went 12–48 for the last place Philadelphia Quakers in his rookie season of 1883. In that year he set still-standing major league records for losses, hits (772), runs (503) and earned runs (291). The 20-year-old right-hander was the first major league player from Syracuse University. In the following season, he made only twenty-one pitching appearances and fewer each season after that as he made the transition to outfielder. His final pitching log shows a 23–72, 4.68 ERA record. As a National League outfielder with Philadelphia (1884) and Pittsburgh (1887–90), and an American Association outfielder with the Athletics (1884–86 and 1889), and Pittsburgh (1886), he hit .257, his high being .299 in 1885. Coleman, a native of Saratoga Springs, NY, played for Lebanon and Omaha in 1891 before becoming a bowling alley employee in Detroit. A 1908 note in *Sporting Life* stated that Coleman was looking for an umpiring job. He died after being run over by a car in Detroit on May 31, 1922. He was 59 years old. *(Baseball Necrology; Total Baseball; Baseball-Reference.com; Washington Post; Sporting Life)*

William "Ed" Colgan is listed as the first-string catcher of the Pittsburgh Alleghenys in 1884, though he caught only 44 games and played in 48. The native of East St. Louis, IL, fielded .906—roughly the league average—but hit only .155 for the season, his only one in the majors. After playing for Memphis in 1885–86, Colgan operated a "paying saloon" in his home town. He later worked for Montana Central Railroad while playing for the Great Falls baseball club. On August 8, 1895, he was killed in an accident while coupling railroad cars. His obituary, appearing in the *Great Falls Tribune*, says that he was "about 34 years of age and a single man." *(Baseball Encyclopedia; Baseball Necrology; Retrosheet; Sporting Life; DeadballEra.com)*

Charles "Chub" Collins, a 26-year-old Canadian, joined the Buffalo Bisons at the beginning of 1884, coming from the Dundas Standards. Hitting only .178 after 42 games, the second baseman transferred to the American Association Indianapolis Hoosiers, for whom he hit .225 in 38 games. Collins finished his major league career the following season by playing sixteen games for the Detroit Wolverines, leaving the majors with a .196 average for 97 games. Eighty of his games were at second base, where he fielded .901, above

John Coleman (Library of Congress)

the league average of .895. Collins played for and managed the Hamilton Clippers (1885–6) and also played for Rochester (1888–9). A native of Dundas, Ontario, he helped manage the family-run hotel there while serving as mayor and later reeve of the city of Dundas. He died at Dundas on May 20, 1914, at age 56. *(Baseball-Reference.com; Baseball Encyclopedia; Chicago Daily Tribune; Dundas Star)*

Charles Comiskey was involved in baseball for more than 40 years as player, manager and club owner. Born in Chicago to an Irish father, Comiskey was signed as a free agent by the St. Louis Brown Stockings, coming from Dubuque of the Northwestern League in 1882. Immediately he became the regular first baseman — the first to play off the base to increase his fielding range. In 1883 the 23-year-old became manager of the club. He remained with the Brown Stockings through 1889, hitting .294 in 1883. In 1890 he jumped to the Players League Chicago Pirates as playing manager but was re-assigned to the Brown Stockings in 1891. In 1892 he jumped again, this time to Cincinnati, finishing his playing career with the Reds in 1894. In thirteen seasons as a player, Comiskey hit .264 and fielded .973 — marginally above the league average. However, his range factor far exceeded that of other first basemen. He led a league in putouts four times and in total chances per game three times. As a manager he led St. Louis to four consecutive American Association championships (1885–1888) and a World Championship in 1886. As owner of the Chicago White Stockings, Comiskey designed the ballpark named for him, but also instituted such penny-pinching measures in regard to his players that much of the Black Sox scandal was traced to his policies. Comiskey died at Eagle River, WI, on October 26, 1931, at age 72. He was named to the Hall of Fame as an executive in 1939. *(Baseball-Reference.com; Chicago Daily Tribune; Total Baseball; BaseballLibrary.com)*

Ed Conley made eight starts for the National League champion Providence Grays in 1884, completing all eight with a 2.15 ERA. Born to Irish parents living in Sandwich, MA, Conley attended the College of the Holy Cross and then joined Providence from the Woonsocket semi-pro team. The *Providence Journal* reported that "he twirls the sphere with swiftness and accuracy." In early 1885 *National Police Gazette* noted that Conley was "troubled with rheumatism in his arm," which might end his career. However, he was able to pitch for Bridgeport in that season. Conley died at Valley Falls, RI, on October 16, 1894, at age 30. According to his death certificate, he was a "student." *(SABR Collegiate Database; Baseball-Reference.com; New York Times; National Police Gazette; U.S. Federal Census)*

John Connor joined the Boston Beaneaters in July 1884. The 23-year-old pitcher had seven complete games and a 3.15 ERA on his way to a 1–4 record. But one of his complete games was his debut in New York in which the host Gothams "hit his delivery all over the field" in a 12–3 victory. In 1885 he pitched for the Buffalo Bisons and the Louisville Eclipse, again going 1–4, before being sold to Chattanooga at the end of August. He left the majors with a 2–8, 3.81 ERA record. Once thought to be a Scot from Glasgow, Connor now is listed as a product of Nashua, NH. Born to Irish parents, Connor appears in the 1900 census as a shoe merchant. He died at Nashua on November 14, 1905, at age 44. *(Baseball-Reference.*

Charles Comiskey (Library of Congress)

com; *Total Baseball; New York Times; U.S. Federal Census*)

Roger Connor, "the Babe Ruth of the 19th Century," hit 138 career homers, six times going into double digits, with a high of 17 in 1887. He hit 233 career triples, leading the National League twice; he also led in slugging percentage twice. A career .317 hitter over 18 seasons, he reached an NL-leading .371 in 1885. The 220-pound first baseman also led his league in fielding four times. The Waterbury, CT, product entered the NL with Troy in 1880, shifting with the franchise to New York in 1883. Except for 1892 when he played in Philadelphia, Connor played in New York with the Gothams/Giants or the Players League Giants through 1894. That year Connor went to St. Louis, where he finished his career in 1897. He played for and managed his hometown Waterbury club after leaving the Cardinals and then became a school inspector and baseball coach for Waterbury schools. In 1913 he was appointed supervisor of umpires in the Eastern League. Born to Irish parents, Connor died at Waterbury on January 4, 1931, at age 74. He was elected to the Hall of Fame in 1976. (*Total Baseball; DeadballEra.com; New York Times; U.S. Federal Census; Sporting Life*)

Joe Connors (**Joseph C. O'Connor**) played in three games for the Altoona Mountain Citys in May 1884 and three more for the Kansas City Cowboys in June 1884. His statistics for the two Union Association clubs are nearly identical. In each he had one hit in eleven at bats for a .091 average; in each he started one game on the mound and suffered a complete game loss. Most sources state that he was born in Paterson, NJ, in 1862. A Joseph O'Connor is listed as a "laborer" in the *Paterson City Directory* between 1878 and 1882. Joseph C. O'Connors is also listed in the 1890 *Denver City Directory* as a laborer for the Troy-Globe Laundry Company. The ball player died in Denver, CO, on January 13, 1891 at age 29. (*Total Baseball; Baseball-Reference.com; Retrosheet; Paterson City Directory; Denver City Directory*)

Bill Conway caught one game for the Philadelphia Quakers on July 28, 1884, going hitless at the plate. The 22-year-old had been signed from the Rollstones of Fitchburg, MA. In 1886 he along with his brother, pitcher Dick Conway, returned to the majors with the Baltimore Orioles. Bill Conway caught seven games, leaving the majors with 2 hits in 18 at bats. At the end of the 1886 season, he suffered a serious hand injury while playing for Portland and retired from baseball. Conway, son of Irish immigrants, had worked as a textile engraver prior to entering the majors and returned to that profession with Middlesex Bleachery of Somerville, MA. He died at Somerville on December 28, 1943, at age 82. (*SABR Biography Project; Total Baseball; Baseball-Reference.com; U.S. Federal Census*)

Jim Conway posted a 19–19 record for the Kansas City Cowboys of the American Association in 1889, his last season in the majors. Born in the Philadelphia suburb of Upper Darby, Conway broke into the majors with the Brooklyn Trolley Dodgers in 1884, compiling a 3–9 record as a back-up pitcher to Adonis Terry. The following season he pitched in two games for the Philadelphia A's, losing his only decision. With a 3–10 record, Conway was out of the majors for the next three seasons. After his service with the Cowboys, he left the majors with a 22–29, 3.64 ERA record. His brother Pete pitched for Buffalo,

Roger Connor (T. Scott Brandon)

Kansas City, Detroit and Pittsburgh, winning 61 games between 1885 and 1889. Sources now give Jim Conway a death date of December 21, 1912, at Clifton Heights, PA, making him 54 at the time. *(Total Baseball; Baseball-Reference.com; Retrosheet; U.S. Federal Census; SABR Biographical Committee Newsletter)*

Paul Cook of the Excelsior club of Rochester caught in three games for the Philadelphia Quakers in 1884. After catching for Washington of the Eastern League in 1885, he joined the Louisville Eclipse in 1886. A member of the Brotherhood, he caught for the Brooklyn Wonders of the Players League in 1890, finishing his major league career back in the American Association with Louisville and St. Louis in 1891. In his best seasons, he caught 89 games for Louisville in 1889 and hit .252 for Brooklyn. In seven seasons, he hit .223 and fielded .906 — just below the league average. In 1895 The *Washington Post* noted that Cook "is running a hotel at Rochester." In 1900 the *National Police Gazette* reported that he and a partner had "made a great success of their handsome hotel and restaurant." Born in Caledonia, NY, to German immigrant parents, Cook died at Rochester, NY, on May 25, 1905, at age 42. *(Baseball-Reference.com; Total Baseball; Boston Daily Globe; Washington Post; National Police Gazette)*

Jack Corcoran was the regular catcher for the Brooklyn Trolley Dodgers in 1884, his only season in the majors. The 26-year-old son of Irish immigrants hit .211 in 52 games. His .873 fielding average was well below the league average of .913. He continued to play minor league ball into the 1890s. *Sporting Life* reported that Corcoran had signed to catch for Sioux City in 1891, but he actually played for Lynn. A year later the same paper reported that Corcoran had received "two or three telegrams" about catching for clubs in the West. Born in Lowell, MA, John Corcoran is listed in the 1880 Federal Census as a resident of Lowell, working in a cotton mill; by 1900 he has married and is employed as a machinist. In the 1920 census, he is living in Jersey City and is listed as a "laborer." Corcoran died in Jersey City on December 28, 1935, at age 77. *(Total Baseball; Baseball-Reference.com; U.S. Federal Census; Sporting Life)*

Larry Corcoran, "a smart little bit of a man," won 170 games — including three no-hitters — in five seasons (1880–1884) with the White Stockings. His win totals read 43, 31, 27, 34 and 35. He led the National League in strikeouts in 1880, in wins in 1881, and in ERA in 1882. He is reported to be the first pitcher to work out signals with his catcher. The 120-pounder twice pitched more than 500 innings, throwing 2279 innings in five seasons. "Crippled by hard work," he was released in 1885, finishing his career with stints in New York, Washington and Indianapolis. His final numbers read 177–89, 2.36 ERA. One verdict on him was, "Playing ball and swilling beer and whiskey don't go together." The Brooklyn native first came to the White Stockings from Springfield, MA, where he had pitched in 1878–79. After leaving the playing ranks, Corcoran umpired until felled by ill health. Corcoran was only 32 years old when he died of Bright's disease in Newark, NJ, on October 14, 1891. *(Total Baseball; National Police Gazette; Chicago Daily Tribune; Washington Post; Sporting Life; DeadballEra.com)*

Mike Corcoran pitched one game for the Chicago White Stockings against Detroit on July 15, 1884. In a 14–0 loss he allowed 16 hits and walked seven. He was a brother of White Stockings ace Larry Corcoran. The 1860 federal census for Brooklyn lists the two-year-old Mike and ten-

Paul Cook (Library of Congress)

month-old Larry as children of Irish immigrants. Baseball historian Peter Morris describes Mike Corcoran as a "cold case," difficult to trace because he "never married," and he bears a "common Irish name." Morris says that Corcoran was still living in Brooklyn in 1920. SABR researchers have finally been able to trace Michael Corcoran. He worked in Brooklyn as a carpenter or spar maker and died at East Setauket, NY, on October 11, 1927, at the age of 69. *(Total Baseball; Charlton's Baseball Chronology: 1884; petermorrisbooks.com; U.S. Federal Census; SABR Biographical Committee Newsletter)*

Fred Corey began his professional career as a 21-year-old utility player with his local Providence club in 1878. He returned with Worcester in 1880 and moved on to the Philadelphia Athletics in 1883, where he became the regular third baseman. In 1884 he hit .276 and led American Association third basemen in fielding. Corey also made 74 career starts as a pitcher, winning ten games in 1883. At the end of the 1885 season he was involved in a "shooting accident." In May 1886 *National Police Gazette* noted that "it is doubtful if Fred Corey will ever recover the full use of his eyesight," and he was released by the A's. His seven-year career totals show a 27–46, 3.32 ERA record as a pitcher and a .246 batting average. As a third baseman he had a higher fielding percentage and greater range than the league average. Corey died on November 27, 1912, in Providence, asphyxiated by gas jets in his room. Bill Lee notes that whether this was an accident or suicide was never determined. Corey was 55 years old and unmarried. *(Total Baseball; Baseball Necrology; National Police Gazette; U.S. Federal Census; Sporting Life)*

John "Pop" Corkhill played for three consecutive seasons without dropping a flyball — a remarkable achievement in that pre-glove era.

Larry Corcoran (Library of Congress)

"Pop" Corkhill (Library of Congress)

Not surprisingly, he led the American Association in fielding four times in eight seasons as a regular outfielder with Cincinnati, Brooklyn and Philadelphia. His career .946 fielding percentage is more than fifty points over the league average. *Sporting Life* praised Corkhill's ability at forward running catches, saying that he could "skate in on his breastbone and snatch flies off the grass." After joining the Cincinnati Red Stockings in 1883, the Parkesburg, PA, native played ten seasons in the majors, which also included stops with the Brooklyn, Pittsburgh and Cincinnati National League teams. On his way to a .254 career average, he hit .311 in the inflated 1887 season but hit a solid .285 a year later. Corkhill's playing career ended in 1893 when he was hit in the head by a pitch from "Cannon-Ball" Crane. The 1900 census shows him living in Philadelphia, working as a furniture salesman. He later became a machinist in a furniture factory, according to Bill Lee. *(Total Baseball; Baseball-Reference.com; Philadelphia Enquirer; Baseball Necrology; Washington Post; Chicago Daily Tribune; New York Times; U.S. Federal Census; Sporting Life)*

Phil Corridan played second base for the Chicago Browns on July 16–17, 1884. In seven at bats, he had a single for a .143 average. In ten fielding opportunities, he had two errors for a .800 percentage. *Baseball-Almanac.com* and *Retrosheet* both now show a date and place of birth of August 19, 1858, in Hancock County, IN. If this is the case, Corridan came from an Irish family (parents born in Ireland), that had first settled in Canada (an older sister born there). By 1870 the family had moved to Indianapolis. The *Indianapolis City Directory* for 1879–81 lists Phillip Corridan as a laborer. Corridan now has a death date of July 1, 1915, in Indiana. *(Baseball-Almanac.com; Retrosheet; Baseball-Reference.com; U.S. Federal Census; Indianapolis City Directory)*

Ed Coughlin joined the Buffalo Bisons in early 1884 as an outfielder. The 22-year-old played in one game on May 15, 1884. Starting in the outfield, he went one for four and drove in a run. But Coughlin has the distinction of being a member of the "Infinite ERA Club." When called on to pitch that day, he gave up three hits, leaving the mound without recording an out. Born in Hartford, CT, to Irish parents, Coughlin was a lifelong resident of that city. The 1900 census lists him as a freight clerk; the 1910 census shows him to be a traveling salesman for provisions; in the 1930 census he is listed as manager of an electric light company. According to Bill Lee, Coughlin "worked 35 years for the Hartford Electric Light Company, retiring as traffic manager in 1946." He died at Hartford on Christmas day, 1952, at age 91. *(Baseball Necrology; Baseball-Reference.com; Baseball Encyclopedia; Baseball-Fever.com; U.S. Federal Census)*

Frank Cox played in 27 games as a shortstop for the Detroit Wolverines at the end of 1884. Captain and shortstop for Grand Rapids of the Northwestern League, he joined Detroit when Grand Rapids was dropped from the league. He hit only .127 for Detroit, and was described as "fat." In 1885 Cox returned to his native New England, playing and managing through 1887. Throughout his career he had supplemented his baseball earnings by working off-season in the mills around New Britain, CT. In 1887 he opened a saloon there, which he operated for 15 years. After working for Metropolitan Insurance Company for ten years, he opened a realty and insurance office in 1908. A child of Irish immigrants, Cox was born in Waltham, MA, and died at Hartford, CT, on June 24, 1928, at age 71. *(Total Baseball; Boston Globe; Washington Post; Encyclopedia of Minor League Baseball; SABR Biography Project; U.S. Federal Census)*

Edward "Cannon-Ball" Crane began his major league career in 1884 as an outfielder and catcher who occasionally pitched. He hit .285 as a rookie with the Boston Reds, considerably above his nine-year career average of .238. After bouncing around among Providence, Buffalo, and the minors, he had become by 1888 a pitcher who occasionally filled in as an outfielder. After hitting only .171 as a regular for Washington in 1886, he led the International League in both hitting (.428) and pitching (33 wins) in 1887. He led the American Association with a 2.45 ERA while pitching for the Cincinnati Kellys in 1891—before crossing town to pitch for the National League Reds. Winner of 16 games for the New York Players League Giants (1890), Crane duplicated the feat for National League Giants (1892). By the time he had finished with Brooklyn in 1893, Crane had compiled a 72–96 record, but had pitched for two pennant winning New York teams and gone 5–2 in post-season play. Selected to play on the All-America team that toured the world after the 1889 season, Crane developed the taste for alcohol while on that tour that led to his decline as a player. After leaving the majors, Crane pitched and umpired in the minors, getting work as he

"Cannon-Ball" Crane (Library of Congress)

Sam Crane (Library of Congress)

could. On September 19, 1896, the 32-year-old Crane, unable to pay his boarding house bill, died from drinking chloral. His death, which took place in Rochester, NY, was ruled an accident. He had been born in Boston to an Irish family. *(Total Baseball; Baseball-Reference.com; Baseball Necrology; Sporting Life)*

Sam Crane was player-manager of the Cincinnati Outlaw Reds in 1884, enjoying his best season in either role. He hit .235, more than thirty points above his career average, and the team finished third in the Union Association. The Springfield, MA, native began as a player-manager for the Buffalo Bisons in 1880, playing in only ten games and seeing his team finish seventh. Crane returned to the majors with the New York Metropolitans in 1883, and after jumping to the Outlaw Reds for 1884, he spent the remainder of his career in the National League with Detroit, St. Louis, Washington, New York and Pittsburgh. As a second baseman he fielded .878 — about ten points below the league average. According to Bill Lee, Crane then spent twenty-five years with the *New York Evening Journal*, and was regarded as the "dean of baseball writers." After a visit to Havana in 1914, he predicted that there would be a "constantly increasing demand" for Cuba players in the major leagues. Crane died in New York City on June 26, 1925, at age 71. *(Total Baseball; Baseball-Reference.com; Baseball Necrology; New York Times; Sporting News; U.S. Federal Census)*

George Creamer (**Triebel**) played on a five-man team in an exhibition game in New Orleans in 1880. Tim Keefe pitched with a catcher and first baseman. Creamer along with George Wood was "intrusted with the onerous task of filling the other six positions." The Philadelphia native entered the majors with the Milwaukee Cream Citys

George Creamer (Wikimedia Commons)

in 1878, also playing with Syracuse and Worcester of the National League. However, Creamer had his best seasons after shifting to the American Association with Pittsburgh. In 1883 he hit .255, and in 1884 he led AA second basemen in fielding. He also managed Pittsburgh for eight winless games in 1884, his last season in the majors. Brooklyn paid $400 for him at the end of that season, but he never played a game for the Bridegrooms, being "a corpse before the season was well on." In seven seasons—six as a regular second baseman—Creamer hit only .215 but fielded .901, above average for the league. He died of consumption in Philadelphia on June 27, 1886, at approximately 31 years of age. *(Baseball Encyclopedia; BaseballAlmanac; Baseball-Reference.com; Sporting Life)*

Mark Creegan (Marcus Kragen) had a nine-game trial with the Washington Unions at the beginning of 1884. The San Francisco product had five singles for a .152 batting average. In the field he was tried as a center fielder, catcher, third baseman and first baseman, but he committed eleven errors for a .750 fielding average. Marcus Kragen appears in the 1880 California census, the son of an Austrian father and German mother, himself an apprentice upholsterer. In the 1900 census he is listed as an upholsterer. In the 1910 and 1920 censuses, he has become a superior court clerk. Creegan died in San Francisco on July 29, 1920, two days before his 46th birthday. *(Total Baseball; Baseball-Reference.com; U.S. Federal Census)*

Dan Cronin, a South Boston player, appeared in two Union Association games in 1884. On July 9, he played second base for the Chicago Browns, and on July 14, he played right field for the St. Louis Maroons. Both games were in Boston against the Reds. At the plate Cronin had a single in nine at bats in the two games; in the field he bobbled six of the seven chances he received. Cronin had previously played for "a fast professional team" sponsored by a hotel in Natick, MA. The 1880 census shows him living with his brother in South Boston, working as a bartender. Born to an Irish father and Canadian mother, Cronin died at South Boston on November 30, 1885, at age 28. *(Total Baseball; Baseball-Reference.com; Baseball-Fever.com; U.S. Federal Census)*

George Crosby pitched three complete games for the Chicago White Stockings in May and June 1884. In compiling 1–2 record, the 23-year-old had eleven strikeouts and a 3.54 ERA. Born in Lyons, IA, Crosby appears in the 1880 Chicago census, living with his sister and brother-in-law, working as a flour inspector. He later married and moved to California. In the 1900 census he is a resident of San Francisco, working as a rubber salesman. The 1910 census shows him living in Oakland, working as a purchasing agent for a barber and cutlery supply company. Crosby died in San Francisco on January 9, 1913, at age 53. *(Baseball-Reference.com; U.S. Federal Census; Total Baseball)*

Clarence Cross (Crause) debuted with Altoona Mountain Cities in May 1884. After two games, he transferred to the Philadelphia Keystones, for whom he also played two games. Later that season he signed with the Kansas City Cowboys. Among the three Union Association clubs, he hit .230 in 29 games. In 1887 he returned to the majors as a member of the American Association New York Metropolitans, hitting .200 in 16 games. Used primarily as a shortstop, Cross fielded .818, just below the league average. Born in St. Louis, Cross died in Seattle on June 23, 1931, at age 75. The name change makes research difficult, but a Missouri-born Clarence Cross of about the right age was working as a hotel porter in Montana in 1920 and still resided there in 1930. *(Baseball-Reference.com; Total Baseball; U.S. Federal Census)*

Doug Crothers made three starts for the Kansas City Cowboys in August 1884, completing all three with a 1.84 ERA. With the New York Metropolitans in 1885, he completed all eighteen starts, but his ERA ballooned to 5.08. The *New*

York Times describes him as a "St. Louis amateur" who "lacks command of the ball." Released in September, Crothers left the majors with an 8–13, 4.63 ERA record. Bill Lee believes that Crothers played minor league ball in the Texas League and Southern Association. In 1888 he went 24–10 for Dallas, leading the Texas League in wins and percentage. A year later *Sporting Life* noted that his "days as a pitcher have faded and gone." In 1890 he was reported to be working in a tax collector's office. Born in Natchez, MS, the son of a carpenter, Crothers appears in the St. Louis census in 1870 and is listed as a clerk in 1880. Crothers died of tuberculosis in St. Louis on March 29, 1907, at age 47. *(Total Baseball; Baseball-Reference.com; U.S. Federal Census; Baseball Necrology; Sporting Life; New York Times)*

Joe Crotty played in 87 games—85 as a catcher—in four major league seasons. The Cincinnati native entered the majors with the Louisville Eclipse in 1882, he along with Pete Browning, Chicken Wolf and John Reccius moving with the club out of the semi-pro ranks. He also played with the St. Louis Browns in 1882 and with the Union Association Outlaw Reds in 1884, returning to the American Association with Louisville in 1885 and the New York Metropolitans in 1886. Crotty played in 39 of his 87 games in 1885 and hit .262 in 1884—eight points over his career average. As a catcher he fielded .915, fourteen points above the league average. After playing with Memphis in 1887—where he was described as the "best coacher in the Southern League"—he moved to Minneapolis and is listed in the 1910 census as a "Merchant Installment Emp." Crotty died at Minneapolis on June 22, 1926, at age 65. *(Total Baseball; SABR Biography Project; Sporting News; U.S. Federal Census; Sporting Life)*

Bill Crowley, a "model right fielder," twice had four assists in a game in the 1881 season, the only player ever to do so. He began his career as an 18-year-old with the Philadelphia White Stockings of the National Association in 1875. He was a regular National League outfielder for Louisville (1877), Buffalo (1879–80 and 1885) and Boston (1881 and 1884). On September 29, 1881, he was placed on the NL "black list." Reinstated in 1883, he split that season between his hometown Philadelphia Athletics and the Cleveland Blues. A career .266 hitter, he reached .287 with Buffalo in 1879. Statistically, he was an average outfielder for the time. The son of Irish immigrants, Crowley was only 34 years old when he died of Bright's disease on July 14, 1891, at Gloucester, NJ. *(Total Baseball; Boston Globe; Baseball-Reference.com; DeadballEra.com; U.S. Federal Census; Sporting Life)*

John Crowley caught 48 games for the Philadelphia Quakers in 1884, hitting .244. However in those 48 games, he committed 50 errors for an .832 fielding average, and had an additional 66 passed balls. The 21-year-old Crowley was a native of Lawrence, MA, and later played for that club. According to *Sporting Life,* Crowley also played for Washington, Norfolk and Portland before illness forced him to retire. The 1880 census for Lawrence shows Crowley living with his mother, an Irish-born housekeeper, and working in a woolen mill. He died of tuberculosis at Lawrence on September 23, 1896, at age 34. *(Total Baseball; Boston Globe; Baseball-Reference.com; Baseball Necrology; U.S. Federal Census; Sporting Life)*

Joe Crotty (T. Scott Brandon)

Jim Cudworth (T. Scott Brandon)

Jim Cudworth played in 32 games for the Kansas City Cowboys in 1884. Either as a first baseman (19 games) or an outfielder (12 games), he fielded far above the league average. However, he hit only .147. Tried as a pitcher, he had one complete game and one relief appearance, working 17 innings with a 4.24 ERA. In September he was out of the majors. Born in Farnham, MA, Cudworth became a resident of Lowell, where he managed the New England League team in 1888. In 1898 *Sporting Life* described him as "prospering in business" in Lowell. The 1900 census shows him working as a saloon keeper. He later worked as a steward at the Lowell Elks Club, verified by the 1910 and 1920 censuses. Cudworth died at Middleboro, MA, on December 21, 1943, at age 85. *(Total Baseball; Baseball-Reference.com; U.S. Federal Census; Sporting Life; Encyclopedia of Minor League Baseball)*

John Cuff caught three games for the Baltimore Monumentals September 11–16, 1884. Though he fielded well (a .920 average), the 20-year-old had only one hit for a .091 average. Cuff was born in Jersey City, NJ, to Irish immigrant parents. In the 1880 census he is still living at home. The *Rathmore Dennehy Family Tree* shows him living in Jersey City, working as a laborer in 1889 and 1897. In 1916, before his death, he was a watchman at the Warner Sugar Refinery. Cuff died on December 5, 1916, in Hoboken, NJ, at age 52. *(Baseball-Reference.com; Total Baseball; U.S. Federal Census; Ancestry.com)*

John Cullen played in nine games for the Wilmington Quicksteps—about half of the club's

Ed Cushman (Wikimedia Commons)

total. In those games he hit .193. Tried at shortstop, he committed six errors in three games for a .571 fielding average; tried in the outfield, he had three errors in six games for a .750 average. If *Baseball-Almanac.com* and *Retrosheet* are correct in stating that Cullen was born in New Orleans and died in Ukiah, CA, that John Cullen appears in the 1880 census for San Francisco, the 1910 census for Green Valley, CA, and the 1920 census for Ukiah. The son of Irish immigrants, he worked as a printer both before and after his major league experience. Cullen died on February 11, 1921, at age 66. *(Total Baseball; Baseball-Reference.com; Retrosheet; Baseball Almanac; U.S. Federal Census)*

Wes Curry started (and completed) two games for the Richmond Virginians on August 6 and 8, 1884, losing both. The 24-year-old Delaware product was tagged for 15 hits in sixteen innings. He later umpired 382 games in the National League in 1885–87, 1888–89 and 1898. On one occasion he created a furor by declaring a runner out when the runner preceding had crossed the plate and then interfered with the catcher. At the time there were no rules to cover the conduct of a runner after he had scored. The 1900 and 1910 censuses show Curry living in Philadelphia and working as an oiler for the city. The 1930 census lists him as a messenger for a jewelry store. Curry died in Philadelphia on May 19, 1933, at age 73. *(Total Baseball; Retrosheet; Bill Burgess; U.S. Federal Census; Philosophy and Baseball; Sporting Life)*

Ed Cushman debuted with the Buffalo Bisons in July 1883, the 31-year-old lefty going 3–3 that season. He returned to the majors in 1884 with the Milwaukee Cream Citys following a 22–1 record in the Northwestern League, and continued in the American Association for the next four seasons with Philadelphia, New York and Toledo. In his best season he had 37 complete games and a 17–20 record for the 1887 New York Mets. After leaving the majors with a 61–82, 3.96 ERA record, he pitched in the minors until 1893, finishing with Erie, PA, where he made his residence. According to his obituary, he became a "conductor on the New York Central railroad and later conducted a restaurant." The 1910 census shows him managing a billiards room. Cushman died in Erie on September 15, 1915, at age 63. *(Baseball-Reference.com; Total Baseball; U.S. Federal Census; DeadballEra.com)*

Andrew "Tony" Cusick played in 95 major league games over a five-year period. After eleven games with the Wilmington Quicksteps in 1884, Cusick jumped to the Philadelphia Quakers, with whom he played the rest of his career. He barely hit his 190-pound weight, reaching .193 for his career. In 82 games as a catcher, he committed 100 errors and allowed 95 passed balls. Some sources give Cusick a Fall River, MA, birthplace, but the census suggests that he was actually born in Limerick, Ireland, immigrating in 1875 or 1880. He appears in the censuses of 1910 and 1920 as a resident of Chicago, working as a city policeman. Cusick died in Chicago on August 6, 1929, at age 71. *(Total Baseball; Baseball-Reference.com; U.S. Federal Census; Retrosheet)*

Edgar "Ned" Cuthbert was the regular right fielder for the Baltimore Monumentals in 1884 at age 39. Born in Philadelphia in 1845, he entered organized baseball in the 1860s, predating even the National Association. As a member of the Philadelphia Keystones, he is alleged to have stolen the first base in baseball history in 1865. Already 26 years old, he entered the National Association in 1871 with the Philadelphia Athletics, for whom he hit a career high .338 in 1872. In the NA he also played with the Philadelphia White Stockings, the Chicago White Stockings, and the St. Louis Brown Stockings, entering the National League with the latter club in 1876 and playing for the Cincinnati Red Stockings in 1877. When St. Louis placed a club in the American Association in 1882, Cuthbert managed it and played outfield before jumping to the Union Association in 1884. In ten seasons he hit .254 and fielded .841— much higher than the league average. Bill Lee says that Cuthbert was "superintendent of the original Sportsman's Park before he opened a saloon in St. Louis." Cuthbert died of endocarditis in St. Louis on February 5, 1905, at age 50. *(Total Baseball; Baseball-Reference.com; Baseball Necrology; U.S. Federal Census; DeadballEra.com)*

Cornelius "Con" Daily or **Dailey** caught two games for the Philadelphia Keystones in June 1884, going hitless in eight at bats. A year later he began a career in the National League, which— with a year out for Players League service with the Brooklyn Wonders—lasted until 1896. During this time he played for Providence, Boston, Indianapolis, Brooklyn and Chicago. He hit .320 for Brooklyn in 1891 but settled for a .243 career average. In September 25, 1895, Daily suffered a "concussion of the spine" while sea bathing, ending his catching for that season; his career ended the following spring. In 550 games as a catcher,

Tony Cusick (Wikimedia Commons)

he fielded .912 — seven points below the league average. An 1897 note in *Sporting Life* indicates that Daily was "a great plunger at the races" and that he had won $1,000 the previous week. In 1902 he was given a trial as an Eastern League umpire. Born in Blackstone, MA, to Irish parents, Daily died in Brooklyn on June 14, 1928. *(Total Baseball; Baseball-Reference.com; U.S. Federal Census; Sporting Life)*

Hugh "One Arm" Daily (Harry Criss) struck out 483 batters in the 1884 season, third highest of all time. His nickname came from the fact that he had lost his left hand and part of his left arm in a hunting accident. He fielded his position by trapping the ball between a pad on the severed arm and his right hand. But at a time when a pitcher could not be removed from a game, his lack of a glove hand effectively prevented him from moving to another position. As a rookie with Buffalo in 1882, he had 15 wins, including a no-hitter against Philadelphia. In 1883 with Cleveland he struck out 19 batters in a nine-inning game, a record that stood until 1986 when Roger Clemens struck out 20 Brewers. In 1884 he compiled a 28–28, 2.43 ERA record in the Union Association — twenty-two wins for the Chicago Browns, five with the Pittsburgh Stogies and one with the Washington Unions. After that season, pitching for St. Louis and Washington in the National League and Cleveland of the American Association, he had only seven more wins, leaving the majors with a 73–87, 2.92 ERA record. With a surly personality, he had few friends in baseball, and when he left the majors in 1887, he disappeared from view. Frank Vacarro says that he pitched semi-pro ball around Pennsylvania for several years. His birth date, once listed as 1857 in Baltimore, now seems to be 1847, making him thirty-four when he entered the majors. Peter Morris contends that Daily was born in Ireland and that he was living in Baltimore as late as 1923. *(Total Baseball; Baseball-Reference.com; Retrosheet; BaseballLibrary.com; petermorrisbooks.com; "One-Arm Daily: 20 K's?")*

George Daisey played left field for the Altoona Mountain Cities in a home game against Baltimore on May 31, 1884. Going hitless in four at bats, he had an error on his only fielding play. Born into a blacksmith's family in Gloucester, NJ, Daisey lived most of his adult life in Cumberland, MD. He appears in each Cumberland census from 1900 through 1930; he is listed as a dancing teacher in 1900, 1920 and 1930. In 1910 he is listed as a collector for the electric company. Daisey died on April 27, 1931, in Cumberland at age 73 or 74. *(Baseball-Reference.com; Retrosheet; U.S .Federal Census)*

Abner Dalrymple played left field and hit leadoff for the Chicago White Stockings from

"One Arm" Daily (Wikimedia Commons)

Abner Dalrymple (Library of Congress)

1879 through 1885. Entering the National League with Milwaukee in 1878, he led the league in hitting that year with a .354 average; in 1880 he led the NL with 91 runs and 126 hits; his 11 homers were tops in 1885. A career .288 hitter, he had four seasons over .300. After helping Chicago to pennants in 1885 and 1886, he hit .234 in 13 World Series games. Illnesses began to cut into his performance in 1886, and he was released to Pittsburgh in 1887 and dropped into the minors at Denver in 1889, leading the Western Association in hits that year. His last major league action was in 1891 with the Milwaukee Brewers, for whom he hit .311 in 32 games. Becoming a conductor for the Northern Pacific railroad in 1892, Dalrymple continued to take summers off to play minor league and semi-pro ball until he was fifty years old. He is listed in the 1880 census as a "Base Ballist L.F." The 81-year-old Dalrymple died at his home in Warren, IL, on January 25, 1939. *(Total Baseball; Sporting News; "The Babe Ruth of His Day"; U.S. Federal Census)*

Charlie Daniels started and completed two games for the Boston Reds on April 18 and 26, 1884. He struck out twelve but gave up 20 hits and eight earned runs in losing both contests. Notes in *Sporting Life* show him managing Hartford and umpiring in the minors until at least 1890. Charles L. Daniels is listed in the Boston census through 1920. Like his father, he became a machinist, working for a hardware store. In both 1910 and 1920 he is shown as living with a sister in Boston. Daniels died at the Home for Aged Men in Boston on February 9, 1938, at age 76. *(Total Baseball; Retrosheet; U.S. Federal Census; Baseball Necrology)*

James "Jumbo" Davis played seven seasons as a major league third baseman — primarily in the American Association. After debuting with the Union Association Kansas City club in 1884, the 195-pound Davis played for the Baltimore Orioles, Kansas City Cowboys, St. Louis Browns, Brooklyn Gladiators and Washington Statesmen, all AA clubs. He was a regular with Baltimore in 1887 — when he hit .309 and led the league with 19 triples — and with Kansas City in 1888. For his career he was a strong .272 hitter, but his .824 fielding average was far below the league average of .858. Born in New York City to a Canadian father, he became a resident of St. Louis. The 1910 census shows him working as a general clerk; in the 1920 census he has become a real estate agent. Davis died in St. Louis on February 14, 1921, at

"Jumbo" Davis (Library of Congress)

age 59. *(Total Baseball; Baseball-Reference.com; U.S. Federal Census)*

John Henry Albert "Daisy" Davis made 24 starts for the St. Louis Browns in 1884, winning 10 games with a 2.90 ERA. Finishing that season with his hometown Boston Beaneaters, Davis found National League hitters harder to solve, as he won one game in four starts with a 7.94 ERA. After going 5–6 with Boston in 1885, he left the majors with a 16–21, 3.78 ERA record. He later pitched for Syracuse, Toronto and Rutland, VT. Born in Boston to a family that had emigrated from Nova Scotia, Davis is listed as a blacksmith in the 1880 census. He died in Lynn, MA, on November 5, 1902, at age 43. *(Total Baseball; Baseball-Reference.com; U.S. Federal Census; Sporting Life)*

Ren Deagle, a New York City product, grew up in Cincinnati and joined the Red Stockings in 1883. That year he had 17 complete games in 18 starts, finishing third in the American Association with a 2.31 ERA. Sent to Louisville in mid–1884, he left the majors at age 26 with a 17–15 career record. Slated to start 1885 with Cleveland, the 190-pound Deagle pitched "fine" in the exhibition season, but wound up at Lancaster before the regular season began. He later moved to Kansas City, where he worked for American Railway Express Co. Deagle died in Kansas City on Christmas Eve 1936 at age 78. *(Total Baseball; National Police Gazette; Washington Post; Biographies—The D's: Elmwood Cemetery's List of Honor; Sporting Life; DeadballEra.com)*

Pat Dealy debuted with the St. Paul Saints at the end of 1884. When the Union Association folded, he went to the Boston Beaneaters for 1885–86, to the Washington Nationals (1887), finishing in the American Association with the Syracuse Stars (1890). Between major league engagements, he played for Troy, Buffalo and Jamestown. Dealy played in 58 games for Washington and hit .326 for Boston in 1886. Eighty-five of his 136 games were at catcher, where he fielded .914, ten points above the league average, but set a major league record with ten passed balls in one game. Born in Vermont, Dealy appears in the 1910 census as a resident of Buffalo, NY, where he worked as foreman of a steel plant. He died on December 16, 1924, in Buffalo at age 63. *(Total Baseball; Baseball-Reference.com; U.S. Federal Census)*

John Deasley split 44 games between the Washington and Kansas City teams of the Union Association in 1884. He apparently was a sure-handed fielder—his .835 percentage is nineteen points above the league average for shortstops—but he did not hit well—.216 in 31 games at Washington and .175 in 13 games in Kansas City. Deasley was born and lived in Philadelphia. His parents are listed as Irish (1870 and 1910 census) and as German (1900 census). The 1900 census lists his occupation as a cigar dealer. At that time his older brother Pat, a former major league catcher, is listed as head of household; their positions have become reversed by 1910. John Deasley died on Christmas day, 1910, at age 49. The 1920 census shows that his widow Gertrude has continued the cigar business and is now head of the household, which includes Pat Deasley. *(Total Baseball; Baseball-Reference.com; U.S. Federal Census)*

Thomas "Pat" Deasley entered the majors with the Boston Beaneaters in 1881, coming from Rochester and the New York Metropolitans. After hitting a career-high .265 and leading the National League in fielding in 1882, he shifted to the St. Louis Browns, where he promptly led the American Association in fielding. After his wife paid $400 for his release in 1884, Deasley moved on to the New York Gothams, where he split playing time with Buck Ewing, catching Hall of Fame pitchers Tim Keefe and Mickey Welch. In eight seasons—four as a regular—Deasley hit .244. In 1888 while playing with Washington, he was hit in the head by a pitched ball, ending his career. Later reports were that he was never quite right mentally afterward and that he was being supported by his brother John, who had played in the Union League. In 1907 *Sporting Life* includes Deasley in a list of ten baseball suicides. However, Deasley actually died in Philadelphia on April 1, 1943, at age 85. *(Total Baseball; Washington Post;*

Pat Dealy (Library of Congress)

Pat Deasley (Library of Congress)

Harry Decker (Library of Congress)

New York Times; National Police Gazette; findagrave.com; Sporting News; Sporting Life)

Harry Decker developed one of the first catcher's mits—a round pillow with a glove stitched on the back. He was able to patent it as the "Decker Safety Catcher's Mit" in 1889. While still in his teens, he debuted with American Association Indianapolis in August 1884, splitting that season between Indianapolis and the Kansas City Unions. In 1886 he divided 21 games between Detroit and Washington in the National League. After a trial with the Philadelphia Quakers in 1889, Decker became a regular in 1890 when he was sold to Pittsburgh. That season the 25-year-old hit .279 in 97 games. Leaving the majors at the end of 1890, Decker finished with a .242 average in 156 games. In 1897 he was sentenced to the Illinois penitentiary for forgery, beginning what Peter Morris calls "a very long career of crime." The Lockport, IL, native is one of baseball's "cold cases." According to Morris, Decker's use of aliases has made his case difficult to trace since he was released from San Quentin Prison in 1915. *(Baseball-Reference.com; Total Baseball; petermorrisbooks.com; Sporting Life)*

Jim Dee had a two-week major league career with Pittsburgh in 1884. The 19-year-old shortstop played in twelve games for the Alleghenys, hitting .125. He fielded .860, right at the league average. *Sporting Life* reported that Dee was captain of the Bradford, PA, team in 1887. Born in Safe Harbor, PA, to Irish parents, Dee grew up in Buffalo, NY. Peter Morris found that Dee was living in Buffalo with his wife and children in 1893, but that he married again in Pittsburgh and was living there with the second wife as late as 1930. Both the 1900 and 1910 censuses for Pittsburgh show a James Dee, with roughly the same background, working as an electrician *(Baseball-Reference.com; Total Baseball; Retrosheet; U.S. Federal Census; petermorrisbooks.com; Sporting Life)*

Jerry Denny joined Providence in 1881, coming from San Francisco. He had played college ball at St. Mary's, the first Gael to make the majors. Of his thirteen major league seasons, ten were as a regular third baseman. The tall, long-armed Denny played his entire career without a glove but twice led the NL in fielding, and he holds career records for total chances per game and putouts. For his career, he fielded .882, seventeen points better than the league average for the time. A career .260 hitter, he reached .324 in the inflated 1887 season, and in 1889 he hit 18 homers and drove in 112 runs. His career took him from Providence to St. Louis, Indianapolis, New York, Cleveland, Philadelphia and Louisville. Released by Philadelphia, he played 1892 and part of 1893 in the minors before finishing with Louisville. After Denny left baseball, one report said that he "opened a saloon in Norwich"; another had him "in the gent's furnishing business." At one point we are told that he "keeps a hotel." For a time he was a club owner at New Haven. Born in New York City to Irish parents, Denny died at Houston, TX, on September 16, 1927, at age 71. (*Washington Post; Boston Globe; New York Times; Chicago Daily Tribune; Baseball-Reference.com*)

Mike DePangher, along with his fellow Bay Area resident Vincent Nava, was regarded as the first Hispanic to play in the majors. He began 1884 with the reserve team of the Chicago White Stockings. After joining the Philadelphia Quakers in August, the 25-year-old Californian caught four games, fielding .920 but hitting only .200. Returning to California after the 1884 season, DePangher played for the California League champion Stockton team for a number of years. The 1900 census shows a Mike DePangher residing in San Francisco. His parents are listed as French, but the occupation line is blank. DePangher died at San Francisco of cerebral sclerosis on July 17, 1915, at age 56. (*Total Baseball; Baseball-Reference.com; Chicago Tribune; Los Angeles Times; Runs, Hits and an Era; The Pacific Coast League 1903–1958; U.S. Federal Census; Sporting Life*)

Lewis Pessano "Buttercup" Dickerson, the first Italian-American to play in the majors, joined the Cincinnati Red Stockings as an outfielder in 1878; the following season the left-handed hitting Dickerson led the National League with 14 triples. He moved on to Troy and Worcester, and after the 1881 season, when he hit .316, he was blacklisted. Reinstated for the 1883 season, he played in the American Association for Pittsburgh and helped make the Alleghenys "The Hardest Drinking Team of All Time." In 1884 he was a regular with the St. Louis Maroons, hitting Union Association pitching at a .365 clip for 46 games before going to the Baltimore Orioles and then to the Louisville Eclipse, finishing with Buffalo in 1885. In a seven-year major league career in three leagues, he hit .284. By 1886 he was playing for Chattanooga and had "quit his convivial habits." However, later that season he was suspended for "lushing." Born in Tyascin, MD, he appears in the 1900 census for Baltimore as a real estate agent. He died in Baltimore on July 23, 1920, at age 61. Dickerson was elected to the National Italian-American Sports Hall of Fame in 1979. (*Total Baseball; Baseball-Reference.com; Atlanta Constitution; U.S. Federal Census*)

Tom Dolan had seven trials as a catcher-outfielder in three leagues, hitting .204 in 225 games. Born in New York City to Irish parents, Dolan was a product of the St. Louis sandlots. He

Jerry Denny (Library of Congress)

Tom Dolan (Library of Congress)

Jim Donnelly (Library of Congress)

entered the majors in 1879, catching one game for the Chicago White Stockings; he also had trials with Buffalo (1881) and the St. Louis Maroons (1885–86) in the National League. He was a regular with the St. Louis Browns in 1883, also playing with the Baltimore Orioles in the American Association. In mid–1884 he jumped to the Maroons when they were a Union Association club and moved with them into the NL in 1885. Dolan finished his career back with the St. Louis Browns in 1888, one source noting that he caught until he was too fat to waddle behind the plate. After a stint as an American Association umpire, Dolan joined former St. Louis Maroons teammates in the St. Louis Fire Department in 1897. He died in St. Louis on January 16, 1913, at age 59. *(Total Baseball; Baseball-Reference.com; Washington Post; National Police Gazette; U.S. Federal Census)*

James B. "Jim" Donnelly debuted as a third-baseman with the Indianapolis Hoosiers in 1884, hitting .254 in 40 games. Over the next seven seasons he played in the National League with Detroit, Kansas City and Washington — holding regular status in 1886–88 — and in the American Association with St. Louis and the Columbus Solons. Returning to the NL in 1896, Donnelly had his best year with Baltimore, hitting .328 as the regular third baseman. He finished his major league career with Pittsburgh and New York in 1897 and St. Louis in 1898. In eleven seasons he hit .229; *Sporting Life* noted that "if he could just school himself a little bit into assisting the team in their innings, he would be almost invaluable." As a third baseman he fielded .862, slightly under the league average, but "a prettier or headier fielder ... would be hard to find." Born in New Haven, CT, to Irish parents, Donnelly is still listed as a ball player in the 1900 census and is still living with his mother. He died in New Haven on March 5, 1915, at age 49. *(Baseball-Reference.com; Total Baseball; U.S. Federal Census; Sporting Life)*

James H. "Jim" Donnelly played six games as a third baseman and catcher with the Kansas City Cowboys in 1884, coming from Minneapolis and Lynn. In those six games he hit .130. In five games at third base he committed 13 errors for a .536 fielding percentage. Born in Boston to Irish parents, Donnelly returned there to play with Cambridge, Medford and Randolph and manage the semi-pro Cambridge Reds. Off-season, he worked as a bookkeeper in Boston's Clinton Market. Donnelly died in suburban Somerville in 1933 at age 65. His playing record has just been separated from that of James B. Donnelly. *(SABR Biographical Society Newsletter; Baseball-Reference.com; U.S. Federal Census)*

Jerry Dorgan played in only 131 major league games over a four-year career, despite a very strong bat. The left-handed hitting Dorgan batted .282 for his career, reaching .299 for the Indianapolis Hoosiers and Brooklyn Trolley Dodgers in 1884. His career included additional stops in Worcester, Philadelphia, and Detroit and position trials as an outfielder and a catcher. As an outfielder he fielded only .817—compared to the league average of .860. In 1885 *Sporting Life* reported that Dorgan had been indefinitely suspended by Detroit for insubordination. The 35-year-old Dorgan was found "very sick" in a stable with a whiskey bottle beside him on June 9, 1891. Taken to a lockup, he was found dead in his cell the following morning, the cause listed as alcoholism. He was a brother of major league player and manager Mike Dorgan. *(Total Baseball; Baseball-Reference.com; U.S. Federal Census; Sporting Life; DeadballEra.com)*

Mike Dorgan joined the St. Louis Brown Stockings in 1877 from Syracuse, and returned to the majors in 1879 when Syracuse entered the National League. After playing at Providence (1880) and Worcester/Detroit (1881), he sat out 1882 before joining the New York Gothams in 1883. Released by New York in 1887, Dorgan finished his career with the American Association Syracuse Stars in 1890. During his ten-year major league career, he played every position, going 8–6 as a pitcher for New York in 1884. A career .274 hitter, he hit .326 in 1885. In 1886 Boston *Globe* balloting for the best all-around player, Dorgan finished tenth. After leaving baseball, Dorgan was proprietor of a café in Hartford and later tended bar there. Still later, he was employed by American Bridge Company in Hartford. Born to Irish parents in Middletown, CT, Dorgan died at Hartford

Mike Dorgan (Library of Congress)

on April 26, 1909, at age 56. His younger brother Jerry was an outfielder and catcher in the majors. *(Total Baseball; Boston Daily Globe; Chicago Daily Tribune; National Police Gazette; New York Times; U.S. Federal Census; DeadballEra.com)*

Jerry Dorsey started one game for the Baltimore Monumentals on July 9, 1884. The 28-year-old Canadian lasted four innings, striking out three but giving up seven hits, before he was shifted to the outfield for the remainder of the game. At the plate he went hitless in three at bats. From an Irish family that emigrated from Canada to Auburn, NY, in 1865, Dorsey made his home there. The 1891–92 city directories for Auburn list Dorsey as a shoemaker. He died at Auburn on November 3, 1938, at age 72. *(Total Baseball; Baseball-Reference.com; U.S. Federal Census; Auburn City Directory)*

Charlie Dougherty was a regular as a second baseman and outfielder for the Altoona Mountain

Citys in 1884. Appearing in 23 of the team's 25 games, he hit .259. In sixteen games at second base the 22-year-old committed fifteen errors for an .854 average. Born in Darlington, WI, Dougherty became a policeman in Milwaukee. The censuses of 1900, 1910 and 1920 all show him in that capacity. Dougherty died in Milwaukee on February 28, 1925, at age 63. *(Total Baseball; Baseball-Reference.com; U.S. Federal Census)*

Clarence Dow played center field for the Boston Reds on September 22, 1884, in a home game against St. Louis. The 29-year-old local player had two singles in six at bats and handled three fielding chances without error in his only major league appearance. Born in Charlestown, MA, Dow appears in the 1860, 1870 and 1880 censuses for Charlestown and Boston. As a 25-year-old in 1880, he is listed as having no occupation. Bill Lee says that Dow was a baseball writer for the *Boston Globe*. The *New York Times* describes him as the "great baseball statistician." *Sporting Life* calls him "the greatest statistician the game ever knew." Dow died of consumption on March 11, 1893, at age 39. *(Total Baseball; Baseball-Reference.com; U.S. Federal Census; Baseball Necrology; New York Times; Sporting Life)*

Cornelius "Conny" Doyle, an Irish-born outfielder, had trials with the Philadelphia Quakers in 1883 and the Pittsburgh Alleghenys in 1884. With Pittsburgh he hit .293 in 15 games; overall he hit .254 in 31 games but fielded only .800 — 48 points below the league average for outfielders. Until the 1990s Doyle's statistics were believed to be the work of two different players — Conny Doyle with the Quakers and John Doyle with the Alleghenys. Born around 1862, Doyle appears in the 1930 census for El Paso, TX, as a lodger. He died in El Paso on July 29, 1931, at age 67 or 68. *(Total Baseball; Baseball-Reference.com; Baseball Page; U.S. Federal Census; Texas Death Index 1903–2000)*

Lyman Drake played in two games for the American Association Washington Nationals on June 29 and July 1, 1884. The 30-year-old hit well — collecting two hits in seven at bats — but made an error on the only chance he handled in the outfield. A native of Berea, OH, Drake worked in a brickyard as an eighteen-year-old. The 1880 census finds him married and working on a farm in Indiana. The 1900 census shows him living in Boonville, MO, where he was superintendent of the state training school for boys. He died in Muskegon, MI, on February 6, 1932 — just three days shy of his 80th birthday. *(Total Baseball; Baseball-Reference.com; U.S. Federal Census)*

Dave Drew hit very well in his brief major league career in the Union Association, having four hits in two games with the Philadelphia Keystones and sixteen hits in thirteen games with the Washington Unions for an overall .323 average. In the field he was tried at shortstop, first base, second base, and centerfield; he even pitched seven innings of relief for the Keystones. At this time nothing further is known about Drew after he left the majors on June 9. *(Total Baseball; Baseball-Reference.com; Retrosheet; SABR Baseball Encyclopedia; Sporting Life)*

John "Denny" Driscoll led American Association pitchers with a 1.21 ERA in the inaugural 1882 season while compiling a 13–9 record with the Pittsburgh Alleghenys. He had begun his major league career in 1880 as an outfielder and change pitcher with the Buffalo Bisons, winning one game and hitting .154. Driscoll pitched independent ball for the New York Metropolitans, the Brooklyn Atlantics and the Philadelphia A's in 1881 before joining the Alleghenys in 1882. After going 18–21 for the Alleghenys in 1883, the left-hander went to the Louisville Eclipse in 1884. His 6–6 record there allowed him to leave the majors with a 38–39, 3.08 ERA pitching record. Having difficulty in adjusting to overhand pitching, he spent 1885 with clubs below the major league level. Born in Lowell, MA, to Irish immigrant parents, Driscoll died of consumption at his home in Lowell on July 11, 1886. He was 30 years old. Another Denny Driscoll — also a Lowell resident — played second base for Buffalo in 1885, and his records are sometimes combined with those of the pitcher. *(Baseball-Reference.com; SABR Biography Project; New York Times; Total Baseball)*

Bill Dugan was born in New York City but played semi-pro baseball in Kingston, NY, before going to Richmond of the Eastern League in 1884. When the Virginians moved into the American Association in August, replacing Washington, Dugan made his major league debut. At Richmond he caught his brother Ed for nine games, hitting .107, before finishing 1884 as an outfielder for the Kansas City Unions. Between the two clubs he appeared in twelve games, hitting .088. *Baseball-Reference.com* and *Baseball Encyclopedia* list both brothers as being born in 1864. This may not be the case. John Thorn says that the Dugans came to Kingston from Brooklyn. In the 1880 census for Brooklyn, an Irish family — William and Bridget Dugan — had sons William and Edward, ages 19 and 15. Bill Dugan appears in the 1900 and 1910 censuses, living in Kingston and working as a cigar salesman. By 1920 he had become a retail hardware merchant. When he died in New York City on July 24, 1921, he was around the age of 60 or 61. Like his brother, Bill Dugan is buried in Kingston. *(Baseball-Reference.com; Baseball Encyclopedia; Thorn Pricks; U.S. Federal Census)*

Ed Dugan, born in Brooklyn, developed his baseball skills in Kingston, NY, from where he, his brother Bill, Dick Johnston and Billy Nash went to the Richmond Virginians. When Richmond moved into the majors from the Eastern League, so did they. After striking out 260 batters in the EL, Dugan compiled a 5–14 record in the American Association, with his brother as his catcher for part of the season. The AA downsized to eight teams in 1885, eliminating Richmond, and Ed Dugan was out of the majors. He pitched for Kansas City in 1885 and Portland, ME, in 1886. *Total Baseball* gives a death date of July 19, 1943, in Sea Cliff, NJ. John Thorn says that Ed Dugan "left his heart in Kingston, where he is buried." *(Total Baseball; Thorn Pricks; U.S. Federal Census; Sporting Life)*

Ed Dundon became a deaf mute at the age of two, the result of typhoid fever. A graduate of the Ohio School for the Deaf, he entered professional baseball with his hometown American Association Columbus Buckeyes in 1883–84. He pitched in 31 games over the two seasons, compiling a 9–20 record. He also played in 28 games as a position player — primarily an outfielder — hitting .151. In 1885–86 he played for Atlanta, Augusta and Nashville where, according to *National Police Gazette*, he was considered "the crack pitcher of the Southern League." Sold to Syracuse in 1887 for $160, he continued to pitch in the Eastern League until illness forced him to the sidelines. Born to Irish parents, Dundon is listed in the 1880 census as a book binder. He died of consumption at Columbus on August 18, 1893. The 34-year-old had recovered his hearing two days before his death. *(Baseball Encyclopedia; Atlanta Constitution; National Police Gazette; Baseball-Reference.com; U.S. Federal Census)*

Fred Dunlap was one of a small group of four-league players. In 1884 he managed the St. Louis Maroons to a runaway Union Association

Fred Dunlap (Library of Congress)

championship. That season he led the UA in runs (160), hits (185), home runs (13), batting average (.412) and slugging percentage (.621). A strong fielder, he also led UA second basemen in percentage. Entering the majors with the Cleveland Blues in 1880, he led the National League with 27 doubles. He continued in the NL with Cleveland (1880–1883), St. Louis (1885–86), Detroit 1886–87, and Pittsburgh (1888–90), twice leading NL second basemen in fielding and helping Detroit win the 1887 championship. He finished his career by playing one game for the Players League New York Giants in 1890 and eight games for the American Association Washington Statesmen in 1891. Injured, he was released by Washington in June 1891. In twelve seasons — ten as a regular — he hit .292 and fielded .924 — more than twenty points over the league average. *Sporting Life* noted that Dunlap was an "artist at getting the fat salaries," being paid $7,000 in 1888. Dunlap was born in Philadelphia to Scots parents. The 1900 census for Philadelphia shows him as a boarder with no listed occupation. One editorial included him in a list of alcoholics; another placed him in a list of those suffering from "mental gloom." Dunlap died on December 1, 1902, at age 43. *(Total Baseball; Baseball-Reference.com; U.S. Federal Census; Baseball Necrology; Sporting News; Sporting Life)*

Steve Dunn became a major league player on September 27, 1884, when his club, the St. Paul Saints, moved from the Northwestern League to the Union Association. Appearing in all nine games the Saints played, he hit .250. He also fielded .972, some 22 points higher than the league average for first basemen. When the UA folded, so ended Dunn's major league career. He later played in the International League for Rochester and his hometown London, Ontario, team. By 1892 *Sporting Life* reported that he had moved to Toronto and would play for a local club there, the Parkdales. In 1893, he was playing first base for the London Alerts in the Canadian championship. Dunn died in London on May 5, 1933, at age 74. *(Total Baseball; Baseball-Reference.com; Sporting Life)*

Albert Ward Dwight had a major league career of just over a month — June 19 to July 25, 1884. He played in twelve games for the Kansas City Cowboys, catching ten. During this time he hit .233 and fielded .953 — considerably above the league average. Listed in baseball records as Al Dwight, he appears in the census as Ward A. Dwight. He grew up in Binghamton, NY, and settled in San Francisco, where the 1900 census shows him to be a lumber dealer. Dwight died in San Francisco on February 20, 1903, at age 47. *(Total Baseball; Baseball-Reference.com; Baseball Necrology; U.S. Federal Census)*

Henry Easterday debuted with his home team Philadelphia Keystones as a nineteen-year-old in June of 1884. In 28 games at shortstop he hit .243 — the only one of his four major league seasons in which he topped .200. In 1888 he returned to the majors with the Kansas City Cowboys, leading American Association shortstops in fielding, but hitting only .190. As the regular shortstop for the Columbus Solons in 1889, he fielded better, but hit worse — down to .173. By 1890 his hitting fell below .150, as he moved among Columbus, the Athletics, and Louisville. In 322 major league games Easterday hit only .180 but fielded .884 — seventeen points above the league average; his range factors were also higher. He played at Rochester in 1892. Born to native Pennsylvanians, Easterday died in Philadelphia on March 30, 1895, still only thirty years old. *(Baseball-Reference.com; Total Baseball; U.S. Federal Census; Sporting Life)*

Charlie Eden, a left-handed outfielder, occasionally caught or played third base, so his name appears in the short list of left-handed players at those positions. He entered the majors with the White Stockings in 1877. With the Cleveland Blues in 1879 he hit .272 with a league-leading 31 doubles. His 41 extra-base hits made him the season record holder until 1882. After hitting .359 to lead the Northwestern League in 1883 and hitting a league-leading four homers in 1884, Eden returned to the majors with Pittsburgh late in 1884. In 1885, his final season, Eden hit .254 as a Pittsburgh regular, leaving the majors with a .261 career average. As an outfielder, he fielded more than sixty points below the league average. The Lexington, KY, native became a conductor on the New York Central Railroad after leaving baseball. He died in Cincinnati on September 17, 1920, at age 65. *(Total Baseball; Baseball-Reference. com; DeadballEra.com; Baseball Necrology; Encyclopedia of Minor League Baseball; U.S. Federal Census)*

Dave Eggler played with the New York Mutuals in 1870 and moved with them into the National Association a year later. After playing with the Philadelphia White Stockings in 1874, he shifted to the Athletics and moved with them into the National League in 1876. Eggler also played with NL clubs in Buffalo, Chicago, and with the American Association Baltimore Orioles. A strong National Association hitter (.323 average for five seasons), he tailed off to .224 in six seasons in the NL and AA. He led NA outfielders three times in fielding, and it was later said of him that he "could get under long drives as well as the modern stars." For his career he fielded .900 — 69 points over the league average. Toward the end of his career with Buffalo, he was "released at the end of each week and signed at the beginning of the next to fill some hole in the team." Born in Brooklyn to German parents, he lived in Buffalo, where, for the last eighteen years of his life, he was employed by American Express. He died after being run over by a train in Buffalo on April 5, 1902, at age 50. *(Total Baseball; Baseball Reference.com; Chicago Daily Tribune; Washington Post; U.S. Federal Census)*

Joe Ellick became a major league regular at the age of thirty with the Chicago Browns. The Cincinnati product had debuted in 1875 with the St. Louis Red Stockings of the National Association, hitting .222 in seven games, before jumping to Louisville. Trials with the Milwaukee Cream Citys (1878) and Worcester Ruby Legs (1880) added only eight games. Shifting to the Union Association in 1884, Ellick became the regular right fielder for Chicago, hitting .236, and managed the team for twelve games in which it went 6–6. He finished that season and his major league career with the Kansas City Unions and the Baltimore Monumentals. He was an NL umpire (1886) and an AA umpire (1888–89). Between times he managed the Kansas City Western League team. The 1910 and 1920 censuses show Ellick living in Kansas City, KS, working as a bookkeeper for a cigar factory. He died at Kansas City on April 21, 1923, at age 69. Before his death, he expressed great regret over his 1875 contract jumping. *(Total Baseball; Baseball-Reference.com; U.S. Federal Census; Baseball Necrology; Sporting Life)*

Fred "Bones" Ely, after ten years of bouncing around among Buffalo, Louisville, Syracuse, Brooklyn and the minors, emerged at age 31 as a solid National League shortstop with the St. Louis Browns and maintained regular status through 1902 with St. Louis and Pittsburgh. When Ely finished his major league career in the American League with Philadelphia and Washington, he had become a career .258 hitter, with a high of .306 in 1894. The tall, lanky Ely fielded .923—fifteen points above the league average for shortstops. Thirty-nine years old when he finished with the Senators, he was already being referred to as "Old Bones" and being regarded as a dangerous clutch hitter. In 1903 he went to Portland as a player and "made quite a name for himself in the Northwest." He and his brother became majority owners of the club, but he was replaced as manager in 1904. In the 1920 census he is shown as a resident of Berkeley, CA, managing a tractor company. Ely died at Napa State Hospital in California on January 10, 1952, at age 88. *(Los Angeles Times; Total Baseball; Baseball-Reference.com; finadagrave.com; U.S. Federal Census; Sporting News)*

Bob Emslie, a Canadian right-hander, joined the Baltimore Orioles in August 1883, coming from Camden, where he had led the Interstate Association in winning percentage. In the closing months of the season, he produced a 9–13 record

"Bones" Ely (T. Scott Brandon)

Bob Emslie (Wikimedia Commons)

for the last-place club. In 1884 he had 50 complete games and 32 wins for the Orioles. But throwing his curve for almost 500 innings strained his arm, so that he dropped to three wins in 1885. Traded to the Philadelphia Athletics, he went out of the majors with 44 wins at age 26. By 1887 he had returned to Canada, and the *National Police Gazette* observed, "For heaven's sake, let him stay there." In 1888 he took up umpiring by accident, and after working in the International League, Western Association and American Association, he became a National League umpire in 1891, holding his position until 1924, when he became NL chief of umpires. He was one of the umpires in the Fred Merkle game in 1908. Emslie died at St. Thomas, Ontario, on April 26, 1943, at age 84. *(Total Baseball; Baseball-Reference.com; SABR Biography Project; Sporting News; National Police Gazette)*

Thomas "Dude" Esterbrook earned his nickname through his clothing. *National Police Gazette* notes, "His new overcoat, trimmed with sealskin, is said to be the handsomest worn by any living baseball-player." Born on Staten Island to English-Scots parents, Esterbrook lasted eleven seasons in the majors — seven in New York — with seven different clubs, beginning with Buffalo in 1880 and ending with Brooklyn in 1891. In addition to the New York clubs, he played with Cleveland, Indianapolis and Louisville. Only a .261 career hitter, he hit .314 for the championship Mets team of 1884. Leading NL third basemen in fielding in 1886 while playing with the Gothams, Esterbrook fielded .923 for his career. His odd beliefs — that if he practiced the behaviors of a child, he could avoid dying, for instance — became more pronounced as he left the playing ranks. Finally, he was committed to a mental hospital. But on the way, he squeezed through a lavatory window and leaped from the train, dying from his injuries on April 30, 1901. He was 43 years old. *(Total Baseball; New York Times; National Police Gazette; BaseballLibrary.com; Sporting Life)*

Uriah "Bloody Jake" Evans was an outfielder that "old-timers still talk about the fielding achievements of." As a right fielder, he "led for many years." Beginning in 1879, Evans spent seven seasons in the majors — five as a regular National League outfielder for Troy, Worcester and Cleveland — before finishing with his hometown Baltimore Orioles in 1885. An injury to his throwing arm brought his career to an end at age 29. A career .238 hitter, he reached .259 in 1884, when he also was the fielding leader among NL outfielders. For his career he fielded .907 — more than forty points over the league average and with better than average range. In the 1900 census for Baltimore, he is shown living with his brother, working as a day laborer. His death notice in *Sporting Life* says that his final years were spent in obscurity and "poor financial circumstances." Evans died in Baltimore of "uremia and acute nephritis" on January 16, 1907, at age 50. *(New York Times; National Police Gazette; Total Baseball; DeadballEra.com; U.S. Federal Census; Sporting Life)*

Tom Evers, the uncle of Hall of Fame second baseman Johnny Evers, was himself the regular second baseman for the Washington Unions in 1884. Already 30 years old, Evers had a one-game trial with Baltimore in 1882, one in which he went hitless and committed three errors. With Washington the left-handed Evers hit .232 in 109 games and led UA second basemen in errors. Born in Troy, NY, to Irish parents, he became a resident of Washington, DC, appearing in the censuses of

"Dude" Esterbrook (Library of Congress)

1900, 1910 and 1920 as a government clerk in the War Department. Bill Lee says he worked there for 41 years. Evers died on March 23, 1925, at age 72. *(Baseball Encyclopedia; Baseball Reference.com; Baseball Necrology; U.S. Federal Census; Sporting Life)*

John "Long John" Ewing had two major league careers and is one of the few four-league players. He played one game as a 20-year-old outfielder with the St. Louis Browns in 1883. In 1884 he played one game each with the Cincinnati and Washington Union Association clubs. After going 20–6 at New Orleans in 1887 and 12–4 at Memphis in 1888, he returned to the majors as a pitcher with the Louisville Eclipse, winning 14 games over the next two seasons. Shifting to the Players League, Ewing went 18–12 with the New York Giants, and when that league folded, he went 21–8, 2.27 ERA with the National League New York Giants, leading the league in ERA and winning percentage. His pitching record overall was 53–63, 3.68 ERA. Ewing was the younger brother of Hall of Fame catcher and first baseman Buck Ewing, his teammate in 1890–91. Only 28 years old when he left the majors, John Ewing was dead from tuberculosis by age 31. *Sporting Life* reported his death in Cincinnati on May 5, 1893, but retracted it a week later. Born in Cincinnati, Ewing actually died at Denver on June 23, 1895. *(Total Baseball; Baseball-Reference.com; Baseball Necrology; Sporting Life)*

William "Buck" Ewing was considered the greatest catcher of the nineteenth century. "As complete a ballplayer as there was in the 19th Century" is the way his Hall of Fame plaque describes him. A native of Cincinnati, he entered the National League with Troy as a 21-year-old in 1880. He was with New York in 1883–89 and 1891–92, being with the New York Players League team in 1890. He played for the Cleveland Spiders in 1893–94, finishing as player-manager with Cincinnati in 1895–97. A career .303 hitter for 18 seasons, he had nine consecutive years over .300, topped by a .344 average in 1893. After leading the NL in homers in 1883, he led in triples a year later. Possessing a great arm, he was the first catcher to throw from the crouch, and led the PL in fielding in 1890; for his career he fielded more than twenty-five points higher than the league average for catchers. When he retired, he was "well to do, owning considerable property throughout the West." Only 47 years old, Ewing died of diabetes in Cincinnati on October 20, 1906. He was

Buck Ewing (T. Scott Brandon)

named to Baseball's Hall of Fame in 1939, the first catcher and — along with Cap Anson — the first nineteenth century player to be named. *(New York Times; Total Baseball; U.S. Federal Census)*

Jay Faatz, a 6'4" first baseman, led the American Association in fielding in 1888. In the following season he hit one of the shortest home runs in major league history when his line drive hit the third baseman on the foot and caromed into the stands. Faatz played with his hometown Weedsport Watsons before entering organized baseball. Joining Pittsburgh in August 1884, he played in 29 games. After a stint in the minors at Toledo, he returned to the majors with Cleveland in 1888, moving with the club into the NL in 1889. His last season was with Buffalo of the Players League in 1890. There he also served as manager, leading the club to a 9–24 record. In all he hit .241 in his four seasons in three leagues, but his fielding average of .982 was well above the league average, and his range was much greater. In 1896 Faatz became the owner of the Savoy Hotel in Syracuse and, according to *Sporting Life*, was "doing well." In 1905 he was an organizer and manager of the Lyons team in the Empire State League. After leaving baseball, Faatz became an insurance salesman. The 1920 census lists him as an insurance broker. He died in Syracuse on April 10, 1923, at age 62. *(Baseball Encyclopedia; Baseball-Reference.com; Deadball Era.com; futilityinfielder.com; Watsons; U.S. Federal Census; Sporting Life)*

Anton Falch was one of the first Wisconsin natives to play major league baseball. When the Milwaukee Cream Citys moved from the Northwestern League to the Union Association, Falch became a major leaguer. A physical giant, the 6'6", 220-pound Falch played outfield and caught in five of Milwaukee's 12 UA games, hitting .111. He played with the Milwaukee Whites of the Western League in 1885. He later went into law enforcement, being variously described as a policeman, a sergeant of police, and an inspector of police in the 1900, 1910 and 1920 *U.S. Federal Census* reports for Milwaukee. Born in Milwaukee to Prussian parents, Falch died in Wauwatosa, WI, on March 31, 1936 at age 75. *(Baseball-Reference.com; U.S. Federal Census; Anton Falch — Ballplayer, but Much More in Life; Sporting Life)*

Lawrence "Tom" Farley, a resident of Alton, IL, and a member of the defunct semi-pro Vincennes, IN, team, was signed by the Washington Nationals for a game in St. Louis on June 24, 1884. He went on to play in fourteen games as an outfielder, hitting .212 before being released on July 12. Farley later managed a team in Alton, IL. In 1892 he shot and killed his brother-in-law, a saloon keeper, in a business argument. Sentenced to life imprisonment, Farley was pardoned in 1897. Born in Seneca Falls, NY, to Irish immigrants, he appears in the 1870 census there as a farm laborer. After his release from prison, he worked as a glass blower and is so listed in the 1910 census. Farley moved to Kansas City some time prior to 1910 and died there on October 6, 1910, at age 54. *(Total Baseball; Baseball-Reference.com; SABR Biographical Committee Newsletter; U.S. Federal Census)*

Sid Farrar came to the Philadelphia Quakers from Stoneham in 1883 and became the club's regular first baseman over the next seven seasons. A career .253 hitter, he reached .282 in the inflated 1887 season. Leading National League first basemen in assists in 1884, he also led in fielding percentage in 1886. For his career, he fielded .974 — slightly above the league average — but his range greatly exceeded the average. The Quaker captain moved over to the Philadelphia team in the Players League in 1890, when he led that league in double plays. After the PL folded, he played for New Haven of the New England League. While still playing, Farrar opened a clothing business in Melrose, MA, where he resided. Since his daughter Geraldine was a famous opera singer, Farrar became a resident of Berlin, where she was a prima donna. He died in New York City on May

Sid Farrar (Library of Congress)

7, 1935, at age 75. *(Baseball Encyclopedia; Baseball-Reference.com; Boston Daily Globe; Sporting Life)*

Jack Farrell began playing with the Syracuse Stars in 1876 and moved with them to the National League in 1879, joining Providence later in that season. After helping the Grays win the 1884 NL pennant, he hit .444 in the three-game series against the New York Metropolitans. When Providence disbanded in 1885, Farrell played with the Philadelphia Quakers, Washington Nationals and Baltimore Orioles. In eleven seasons he hit .243, but hit .305 in 1883 while leading NL second basemen in fielding. Farrell managed Providence in 1885 and was captain of Washington in 1886–87. Contemporary accounts indicate that he was "a little too red headed." Released by Baltimore in 1889, Farrell then played in the minors. Born in Newark to Irish parents, Farrell is listed in the 1910 census as a widower, living in Newark, working as a "nurse." Bill Lee says that Farrell was a "hospital attendant." Farrell died at Overbrook,

Jack Farrell (Library of Congress)

Frank Fennelly (Library of Congress)

NJ, on February 10, 1914, at age 56. *(Total Baseball; Boston Globe; National Police Gazette; Chicago Daily Tribune; U.S. Federal Census)*

Joe Farrell was the regular third baseman for the Detroit Wolverines from 1882 through 1884. The Brooklyn native hit .247, 273, and .226 during those seasons. Released in 1885, he caught on with the Baltimore Orioles for 1886. After hitting .209 for Baltimore, he was again released. During his four years in the majors he fielded .840 — exactly the league average. Farrell died in Brooklyn on April 17 or 18, 1893, at age 36. His death notice in *Sporting Life* indicates that he had played with Albany, Detroit and Washington. Following his death, Brooklyn and New York teams played a benefit game for his destitute mother, from which she was thought to realize a "goodly sum." *(Total Baseball; Baseball-Reference.com; National Police Gazette; Boston Globe; New York Clipper; Sporting Life)*

Jack Farrow began his major league career with the Elizabeth Resolutes of the National Association in 1873. The 19-year-old catcher played in 12 games, hitting .167. The following season he played in 27 games for the Brooklyn Atlantics. The Verplanck, NY, native was then out of the majors until 1884, when he played in 16 games with Brooklyn of the American Association, leaving the majors with a .197 average for 55 games. He managed briefly for Newark of the Eastern League in 1885. In the 1880 census, Farrow, the son of an English father and an Irish mother, is shown as a retail milk dealer. In 1910 Farrow and his son are listed as proprietors of a saloon. Bill Lee describes Farrow as a retired hotel keeper. After a long illness, Farrow died at Perth Amboy, NJ, on December 31, 1914, at age 61. *(Total Baseball; Baseball-Reference.com; New York*

Times; Encyclopedia of Minor League Baseball; U.S. Federal Census; Baseball Necrology)

Frank Fennelly was a regular American Association shortstop for six seasons beginning as a rookie in 1884. Coming from Brooklyn, where he had led the Interstate Association in hits and homers, he hit .311 between Washington and Cincinnati in 1884 and led the AA with 89 RBIs in 1885. In seven seasons with Washington, Cincinnati, the Athletics, and Brooklyn, he hit .257 and served as captain for Cincinnati. Although he led AA shortstops three times in errors, he also led three times in double plays and twice in assists. His overall fielding statistics show him eight points below the league average in percentage and ten points above in range factors. The son of Irish parents, Fennelly was a life-long resident of Fall River, MA. In the 1889 City Directory, he is listed as a "base-ball player." *Sporting Life* shows him as a wine clerk in 1896, as a Connecticut League umpire in 1902 and as a member of the Massachusetts legislature in 1905. In 1920 Fennelly, himself, is the federal census enumerator for Fall River. Fennelly died on June 4, 1920, at age 60. *(Baseball Encyclopedia; Baseball-Reference.com; BaseballLibrary.com; U.S. Federal Census; Sporting Life)*

Bob Ferguson was the first switch hitter in professional baseball. He played "amateur" baseball with the Enterprise club of Brooklyn as early as 1865 and began his professional career as a player-manager with the New York Mutuals at the inauguration of the National Association in 1871. He played with and managed the Brooklyn Atlantics and Hartford Dark Blues before moving to the National League with Hartford in 1876. In the NL he was player-manager for Chicago, Troy and Philadelphia, in addition to Hartford. He finished as a player with Pittsburgh early in 1884, then resigned to take up umpiring. Ferguson umpired until 1891 with time out to manage New York in 1886–87. At that time, "being well fixed financially," he retired from baseball. As a player he was a regular at third base or second base for thirteen seasons in a 14-season career. Ferguson hit .351 for Chicago in 1878, much above his career .265 mark. His fielding statistics in both percentage and range far exceed those of third basemen of his era; those for second base are at the league average. Born in Brooklyn to Irish parents, Ferguson died there of an attack of apoplexy on May 3, 1894. He was 49 years old. *(Baseball Encyclopedia; Baseball-Reference.com; Sporting Life; U.S. Federal Census)*

Bob Ferguson (T. Scott Brandon)

Charlie Ferguson had 99 wins with a 2.67 ERA for the Philadelphia Quakers by age 24. The native of Charlottesville, VA, had win totals of 21, 26, 30 and 22 in his four seasons after joining the club in 1884 from a Richmond semi-pro club. In 1886 he posted a 30–9, 1.98 ERA record, helping the Quakers to a second-place finish. He also played 85 games as a centerfielder and second baseman. Overall, he hit .288, going over .300 twice. In the spring of 1888 he contacted typhoid fever and died on April 29, 1888, just a few days after his 25th birthday. While *Sporting Life* placed him in the short list of candidates for "greatest player ever," their judgment was that "he died too soon." *(Baseball-Reference.com; Chicago Daily Tribune; Baseball-Fever.com; Sporting Life; DeadballEra.com)*

Charlie Ferguson (Library of Congress)

Jim Field spent three seasons (1883–85) as a regular American Association first baseman with the Columbus Buckeyes, Pittsburgh Alleghenys and Baltimore Orioles. He also played for Rochester (1890), finishing with five games for the Washington Nationals in 1898. In all he hit .229 in five seasons, with a high of .254 in his rookie season. He fielded .956 with range factors 35 points above the league average. The big Philadelphia native played with Erie, Newark, Albany, Syracuse, and Buffalo while not in the majors. At Buffalo he served as team captain and was regarded as "one of the finest fielding first basemen in the league." He hit .344 with Erie and .341 with Newark. After leaving the playing ranks, Field operated a liquor store and later a tavern near Connie Mack Stadium. On May 5, 1953, the 90-year-old Field died in Atlantic City, NJ, from injuries received in a fall. *(Baseball-Reference.com; Total Baseball; Baseball Necrology; Sporting News; U.S. Federal Census; Sporting Life)*

John "Ted" Firth started one game for the Richmond Virginians on August 15, 1884, at Brooklyn. Tagged for 14 hits and eight earned runs, he took the loss. Firth was a native of Lowell, MA, the son of an English-born blacksmith. The 1880 census for Lowell lists Ted Firth as a 25-year-old "machine forger." *DeadballEra.com* shows his post-playing occupation as "machinist." Two sources—*Baseball Chronology* and *Baseball Necrology*—say that he was murdered in 1885. There is general consensus, however, that he died in Tewksbury, MA, on April 18, 1902, at age 46. The cause of death listed is phthisis pulmonalis. *(Baseball-reference.com; Total Baseball; Baseball Encyclopedia; Baseball Necrology; DeadballEra.com; Baseball Chronology; U.S. Federal Census)*

Charles Fisher (**Charles Fish**), a 32-year-old infielder, joined the Kansas City Cowboys in June 1884. After ten games there, he played one game for the Chicago Browns on July 7. In the eleven games, he hit .233. Primarily a third baseman, he fielded .702 with 14 errors in ten games. Born in Boxford, MA, Fisher appears in the 1900 and 1910 censuses for Eagle, AK, where he had gone as a miner. He died at Eagle on February 18, 1917, at age 64. *(Baseball-Reference.com; Total Baseball; U.S. Federal Census)*

George Fisher was the first Delawarean to play major league baseball when he had a six-game trial with the Cleveland Blues in August 1884. Used at second base, the left-handed hitter produced three singles for a .125 average. Later in the season he played in eight games as an outfielder and shortstop for his hometown Wilmington Quicksteps of the Union Association, leaving the majors with an .094 average. Fisher played for Macon in 1885 and later moved to California. He appears in the 1910 and 1930 census figures for Oakland, working in the liquor industry and later in sales. Fisher died at Oakland on January 29, 1937, at age 81. *(Total Baseball; Baseball-Reference.com; U.S. Federal Census; Sporting Life)*

J. Fisher pitched well for the Philadelphia Keystones in 1884. He had eight complete games in eight starts (3.57 ERA) but wound up with a 1–7 record. The Keystones tried him at first base for two games, but neither his hitting (.222) nor his fielding (.769) qualified him for major league service at that position. In August 1885 he returned to the majors as a pitcher, suffering a complete game loss for the Buffalo Bisons. Fisher seems to have been a native of Philadelphia; nothing further is known of his life at this time. *(Baseball-Reference.com; Total Baseball; Retrosheet)*

Frank "Silver" Flint played for the St. Louis Red Stockings of the National Association as a teenager in 1875. He was the regular catcher for the Indianapolis Hoosiers in 1878 and joined the Chicago White Stockings in 1879, remaining with them until 1889 and helping them win five league championships in seven years (1880–82 and 1885–86). Flint hit .310 in 1881 but only .239 for his career and .118 in five World Series games. Twice leading the National League in fielding, he was described as having "few equals and no superiors" as a catcher. For his career he fielded .911, some thirteen points over the league average at the time. In 1888 he contacted consumption, limiting his play to just 37 games in his last two seasons with Chicago. The years of catching with little protection also took their toll: "his fingers, owing to all the breaks and bruises, pointed in all directions." The Philadelphia native lived most of his life in St. Louis. Only 36 years of age, Flint died in Chicago on January 14, 1892. *(New York Times; National Police Gazette; Baseball-Reference. com; Chicago Daily Tribune)*

Joe Flynn was an outfielder and catcher for the Union Association Philadelphia Keystones for 52 games in 1884. Later in the season he became a catcher and outfielder for the Boston Reds of the same league. As a batter, he hit .249, above the league average. However, both as an outfielder and a catcher, he fielded well below the league average. *Retrosheet* and *Baseball-Reference.com* agree on the dates of birth and death. *Retrosheet* says that he was born in Providence. A Joseph N. Flynn, born in Providence in 1861, the son of Irish parents, is listed in the 1900, 1910 and 1920 censuses as a Providence city policeman. The ballplayer died in Providence on December 22, 1933, at age 71. *Baseball-Almanac.com* says that he was the father of Pittsburgh and Washington first baseman John Flynn. *(Retrosheet; Baseball-Reference.com; U.S. Federal Census; Baseball Almanac)*

Jim Fogarty, born in San Francisco to Irish parents, "came east" in 1884 to join the Philadel-

"Silver" Flint (Library of Congress)

Jim Fogarty (Library of Congress)

phia Quakers after leaving St. Mary's College. First a utility player who "quietly submitted to playing in every position," he became a "clever right fielder." He led the National League in fielding in 1889, being described as one who made phenomenal catches "characteristic." His career figures in fielding (.940) and fielding range (2.50) far exceeded the league average (.893 and 1.90) In seven seasons in Philadelphia with the National and Players League teams, he hit only .246, but reached .293 in 1886. He drew 82 bases on balls in 1887, and stole 99 bases in 1889 — both league-leading figures. A member of the Players League Quakers, he served as team captain and managed the club for 16 games. *Sporting Life* listed him as one with a love for "tasty dress and disposition to enjoy the best in life." Only 27 years old, Fogarty died of consumption in Philadelphia on May 20, 1891. *(SABR Collegiate Database; Total Baseball; Baseball-Reference.com; New York Times; National Police Gazette; Boston Daily Globe; Sporting Life)*

Will Foley played in three games for the Chicago White Stockings as a 19-year-old in 1875. He became the regular third baseman for Cincinnati when the National League was formed, moving on to Milwaukee (1878) and back to Cincinnati (1879). Foley played briefly with Detroit in 1881 before finishing with the Chicago Browns in 1884. In seven seasons, four as a regular, he hit as high as .271 with Milwaukee, considerably above his career .226. However, his fielding statistics were below the league average. Born in Chicago to English parents, Foley worked as a railroad agent while playing baseball. He died in Chicago — found dead in his brother's barn — on November 12, 1916, at age 60. *(Baseball Necrology; Total Baseball; Baseball-Reference.com; U.S. Federal Census)*

David "Wee Davy" Force was another player whose career spanned three manifestations of professional baseball. The New York City product played for the New York Mutuals and the Olympics of Washington prior to the establishment of the National Association. He moved with the Olympics into the NA, also playing for Troy, the Lord Baltimores, Chicago and the Athletics. Force moved with the Athletics into the National League when it was formed in 1876. In the NL Force also played for the Mutuals, St. Louis and Buffalo, before finishing with Washington in 1886. Only 5' 4" and 130 pounds, he was one of the best fielding shortstops of his time, leading his league in fielding seven times. His overall fielding average (.896) was forty-eight points higher than the league average. A strong National Association hitter (.336) he did not find National League pitching congenial, finishing with a .211 average for 10 seasons. When he retired from baseball, he received a position with Otis Elevator, which he held for 25 years. Force died on June 21, 1918, in Englewood, NJ, at age 68. *(Total Baseball; Baseball-Reference.com; Sporting News; U.S. Federal Census)*

Ed Ford, a 22-year-old local player, appeared in two home games for the Richmond Virginians on October 9–10, 1884, going hitless in five at bats. He played errorless ball as a first baseman one day and committed four errors as a shortstop the next. The Ford family were native Virginians, and Ed Ford's father was an excavator; Ford himself appears in the 1910 and 1920 censuses for Richmond, working as a contractor. In the first he is employed by the city; in the second he is listed as a house builder. Ford died in Richmond on June 8, 1931 at age 69. *(Baseball-Reference.com; Baseball-Almanac.com; U.S. Federal Census)*

Frank Foreman pitched for eleven teams in four leagues during his eleven-year major league career. He began as a 21-year-old with the Chicago Browns and Kansas City Cowboys in 1884 and ended with his hometown Baltimore Orioles, an American League entry, in 1902, when he was 39 years old. The lefty had 23 of his 96 career victories with the Orioles — then an American Association club — in 1889, one of six seasons in which he had at least ten victories. Foreman had one win in the Union Association; forty-three wins in the AA — including 18 with the Washington Statesmen in 1891; forty wins among Washington, Baltimore, New York and Cincinnati of the National League; and twelve wins between the Orioles and Boston of the AL. Foreman finished professionally with Holyoke in 1905. After retiring from baseball, he operated an ice rink and developed a reputation for his skills as a skater. As a scout he claimed to have discovered Eddie Plank. In the 1930 census for Baltimore, he is listed as a clerk in a confectionery. Foreman died in Baltimore on November 19, 1957, at the age of 94. Foreman's younger brother Brownie, also a left-handed pitcher, was a Cincinnati teammate in 1896. *(Total Baseball; Baseball-Reference.com; Sporting News; U.S. Federal Census; Sporting Life)*

Tom Forster played for the New York Metropolitans in the 1884 World Series without playing for them in the regular season, instead having played for Pittsburgh. A New York City native — son of an Irish clerk — Forster entered the majors with Detroit in 1882. The middle infielder played for the Mets in 1885–86, holding regular status both seasons; however, his light bat led to a career average of only .197 for 180 games. He also fielded 18 points below the league average for second basemen. Forster played in the minors with Milwaukee in 1887; there is a baseball card showing his gloveless fielding. In the 1900 census Forster is listed as an insurance agent. Bill Lee says that Forster worked for Consolidated Edison for a number of years. He died in New York City on July 17, 1946, at age 87. *(Total Baseball; Baseball-Almanac.com; Baseball Necrology; Curry, "Saginaw Old Golds"; U.S. Federal Census)*

Robert Foster caught four games for his hometown Philadelphia Athletics beginning June 18, 1884. In that season he also caught one game for the Union Association Philadelphia Keystones. In the five games he hit .214; in the field he had six errors. Robert Foster was long thought to be the same person as Elmer Foster, who played in New York and Chicago (1886–91). "*Bullpen*" says that Robert Foster played at Schuykill Falls with his brother and that "he was a saw maker in civilian life." This is confirmed by the 1870 census, which shows 13-year-old Robert Foster working at a sawmill, and the 1880 census which lists him as a saw maker. Foster died at Philadelphia on June 15, 1921, at age 65 or 66. *(Baseball-Reference.com; U.S. Federal Census; Total Baseball; "Bullpen")*

Dave Foutz came to the St. Louis Browns in 1884 from Bay City, MI. The tall, slim right-hander, nicknamed "Scissors," helped the Browns to three American Association championships (1885–87) going 33–14, 41–16, and 25–12. In 1886 he led the AA in wins, percentage and ERA. Sold to Brooklyn in 1888, he helped that team win an AA championship in 1889 and a National League championship in 1891. Foutz compiled a 147–66, 2.84 ERA career record. When his pitching production fell off in 1888, he became an outfielder and first baseman, hitting an inflated .357 in 1887 and .303 in 1890. Becoming the Brooklyn manager in 1893, he continued through 1896, when ill health forced him to retire, his teams going 264–257. Prior to entering baseball, the Maryland native worked as a miner in Leadville, CO, and is so listed in the 1880 census for Leadville. However, he was a recruited pitcher — "a paralyzer and make no mistake" — for the Colorado champion Leadville Blues, and this may have been his job in the mines. Foutz died from asthma in Waverly, MD, on March 5, 1897, at only 40 years old. *(New York Times; Baseball Reference.com; Sporting Life; Journal of Sport History)*

John Fox had four major league trials. The 22-year-old Roxbury, MA, native joined his hometown Boston Beaneaters in 1881, winning six and losing eight. Two years later Fox went 6–13 for the Baltimore Orioles. And with the Pittsburgh Alleghenys in 1884, he had seven complete games but a 1–6 record. Back in the National League in 1886, Fox lost his only start for Washington. Overall he compiled a 13–28, 4.16 ERA record. He may be the John Fox in the 1886 picture of John L. Sullivan's baseball team. The son of an Irish farm laborer, Fox appears in the 1880 Boston census as a "horse car driver." Only 34 years old, he died in Boston on April 18, 1893. *(Total Baseball; Retrosheet; U.S. Federal Census; Sporting Life)*

Franklin played center field for the Washington Unions in a game at Milwaukee on September 27, 1884. He was hitless in three at bats but handled two chances in the field without error. Nothing more — not even a first name — is known about this player. The circumstances suggest that he was a local Milwaukee player borrowed for the day. *(Baseball-Reference.com; Retrosheet)*

Pete Fries, a lefty from Scranton, PA, made three starts for the Columbus Buckeyes in August of 1883. His three complete games resulted in a 0–3, 6.48 ERA record. But he also hit .300 while pitching. In July of 1884 he played in one game as an outfielder for the Indianapolis Hoosiers, picking up a hit in three at bats. In later years, according to Bill Lee, Fries served as a "postal clerk at the Grand Crossing Postal Station forty years before retiring in 1926." The censuses for 1900, 1910 and 1920 all list him as a resident of Chicago and as an employee of the U.S. Postal Service in some capacity. The census of 1930 lists him as a retired civil servant. Born to a German family, Fries died in Chicago on July 29, 1937, at age 79. *(Baseball Necrology; Total Baseball; Retrosheet; U.S. Federal Census)*

Charles "Chick" Fulmer began his major league career as a 20-year-old with Rockford of the National Association in 1871. After playing with the New York Mutuals and his hometown Philadelphia White Stockings, Fulmer joined Louisville when the National League began in 1876. He also played with Buffalo (1879–80) before joining Cincinnati of the American Association. In 1882 he hit .281 and led the AA shortstops in fielding to help the Red Stockings win the league championship. Fulmer finished his major league career in 1884 with the St. Louis Browns. Overall, he hit .266 in five seasons in the NA and .257 in six NL/AA seasons. His fielding average at shortstop (.839) was fifteen points above that of the league. The son of a butcher, Fulmer appears in the 1880 census as a butcher as well. Philadelphia censuses for 1900 and 1910 show him as retired. In 1920 he is employed as a watchman for a publishing company. When Fulmer died in Philadelphia on February 15, 1940, he was the oldest major leaguer. His older brother Washington played for the Atlantics in 1875. *(Total Baseball; New York Times; Sporting News; U.S. Federal Census)*

Chris Fulmer "always claimed to have originated the idea of the type of glove used by catchers today," according to his *Sporting News* obituary. He joined the Washington Unions in August 1884, hitting .276 in the last 48 games. Returning to the majors in 1886, he played with the Baltimore Orioles through 1889, his career ended by an arm injury. For his five-year career, he hit .247. One of the better catchers in the American Association, he had a career .929 fielding percentage, higher than either Doc Bushong or Silver Flint. Born in Tamaqua, PA, to German parents, Fulmer appears in the 1900 and 1920 censuses as a widower, operating a hotel in Tamaqua. He died there on November 9, 1931, at age 73. *(Baseball Encyclopedia; Baseball-Reference.com; Total Baseball; Sporting News; U.S. Federal Census)*

Eddie Fusselback (Fusselbach), a Philadelphia-born catcher, had four major league trials with four clubs over a period of seven seasons. Breaking in with the St. Louis Browns in 1882, he hit .228 in 35 games. In his busiest season, he hit .284 as the regular catcher for the Baltimore Monumentals in 1884. Trials in 1885 and 1888 with the Philadelphia Athletics and Louisville Eclipse added only six more games. Overall he hit .268 in 109 games. Also overall, he was a .892 fielder — better than the league average. Fusselback was one of six children of a Philadelphia printer, and he followed in his father's trade. The 1890 *Philadelphia City Directory* lists him as a printer. In 1897 *Sporting Life* reported that he participated in an "old-timers" game in Philadelphia. By 1920 he had become a plumber, living with his brother and sister-in-law. Fusselback died in Philadelphia on April 14, 1926, at age 71. *(Total Baseball; Baseball-Reference.com; U.S. Federal Census; Philadelphia City Directory)*

Charlie Gagus (Charles F. Geggus) played at St. Mary's College of California with Jim Fogarty, Jim McElroy, Ed Morris, Hank O'Day and Fred Carroll; all six had major league debuts in 1884. Gagus joined the Washington Unions in August, completing 19 of 21 starts for a 10–9, 2.54 ERA record. Like most pitchers of the time, he also filled in at other positions — primarily in the outfield, hitting .247 and fielding .881 — more than forty points above the league average. When the Union Association folded, Gagus' major league career ended. He played in the Eastern League with Washington and Newark in 1885, but returned to California because his aging mother "desires his presence here." Born in San Francisco to a wealthy German father and Irish mother, Gagus (spelled *Geggus*) is found in the 1900 and 1910 censuses as a resident of San Francisco, working as a saloon keeper and a liquor merchant. He died in San Francisco on January 16, 1917, at age 54. *(Total Baseball; Baseball-Reference.com; U.S. Federal Census; Sporting Life)*

Bill Gallagher had five complete games for the Baltimore Orioles in 1883 and three complete games for the Philadelphia Keystones in 1884; in two seasons the lefty had a 1–7, 4.70 ERA record for eight starts. Although he hit only .138, Gallagher played sixteen games in the outfield, split between the Orioles and the Philadelphia Quakers in 1883. *Total Baseball*, *Retrosheet*, and *Baseball-Almanac.com* make Gallagher a Philadelphia native. There were at least two William J. Gallaghers — one a machinist and the other a lithographer — living in Philadelphia who were the right age to be the ball player. *(Total Baseball; Retrosheet; Baseball-Reference.com; Baseball Almanac; U.S. Federal Census)*

James "Pud" Galvin had a fastball that turned batters into pudding, hence the nickname. He won 361 games in 15 seasons, sixth on the all-time list. He had back-to-back 46-win seasons in 1883–84, in which he completed 143 of 147 starts, working 1292-plus innings. Galvin also enjoyed a 37-win season and seven other 20-win seasons. As an 18-year-old he pitched for his hometown St. Louis Brown Stockings of the National Association, but did his best work for the Buffalo Bisons in 1879–85. Then after he played for Pittsburgh teams in three different leagues, he finished back in St. Louis with the Browns in 1892. Second

"Pud" Galvin (Library of Congress)

behind Cy Young in career innings pitched and complete games, Galvin is also second in losses (308). Listed at 5'8" tall and 190 pounds, he ballooned to 300 pounds at points in his career. Galvin managed Buffalo for 24 games in 1885 and umpired briefly after leaving the playing ranks. When "Old Man Galvin" retired in 1892, *Sporting Life* reported that he "thinks of going into the laundry business." He actually opened a saloon in Pittsburgh, but lost money even though the place was always packed, and died penniless. Born in St. Louis to Irish parents, Galvin died at Pittsburgh of catarrah of the stomach on March 7, 1902, at age 47. Galvin was named to the Hall of Fame in 1965. *(Sporting News; Total Baseball; Baseball Encyclopedia; Baseball-Reference.com; BaseballLibrary.com; U.S. Federal Census; Sporting Life)*

Lou Galvin pitched three complete games for the St. Paul Saints in October 1884. The 22-year-old St. Paul native compiled a 0–2, 2.88 ERA record — one game ending in a tie. The son of an Irish-born policeman, Lou Galvin appears in both the 1870 and 1880 censuses living at home. The 1895 death date given by some sources may not be correct. The 1900 *U.S. Federal Census* for St. Paul shows Galvin now working as a policeman himself. The *Minnesota State and Territorial Census* of 1905 shows him still alive at that date and working as a policeman. *(Total Baseball; Baseball-Reference.com; Retrosheet; Baseball Almanac; U.S. Federal Census; Minnesota State and Territorial Census)*

Charlie Ganzel debuted with the St. Paul Saints in September 1884, hitting .217 in seven games. In 1885 he began a thirteen-year National League career with Philadelphia, Detroit and Boston. Primarily a catcher, he played every position except pitcher. As a catcher he fielded .934 — eleven points above the league average. At the plate he hit .259 with a career high of .278 in 1894. Along the way he helped two teams — the 1887 Detroit Wolverines and the 1892 Boston Beaneaters — win league and world championships. Born in Wisconsin to German parents, Ganzel appears in the censuses for 1900 and 1910,

Charlie Ganzel (Wikimedia Commons)

living in Massachusetts and working as a traveling salesman for a clothing company. *Sporting Life* says that he was "a very good salesman" for French Garment Company. Ganzel died of cancer at Quincy, MA, on April 7, 1914, at age 51. His younger brother John, a first baseman, had a seven-year major league career; his son Foster "Babe" Ganzel had two trials as an outfielder for Washington in 1927–28. *(Total Baseball; Baseball-Reference.com; U.S. Federal Census; Baseball Necrology; Sporting Life)*

Alex Gardner caught in one game for the American Association Washington Nationals on May 10, 1884. In a home game against New York, the Toronto-born Gardner went hitless in three at bats while committing six errors behind the plate. From a family of Scottish weavers that had immigrated to Danvers, MA, in 1865, Gardner continued to live in Danvers. The censuses for 1900, 1910 and 1920 all show him working as a cutter in a shoe factory there. He died in Danvers on June 18, 1926, at age 65. *(Total Baseball; Baseball-Reference.com; Baseballhistorian.com; U.S. Federal Census)*

Frank "Gid" Gardner had the stuff to be "one of the best all-round players this country ever saw." Certainly he played every position at some time in his seven-year major league career. However, *National Police Gazette* noted that "nearly every club he has played with has had to suspend him for drunkenness." As a result, he played with nine clubs during his career and averaged fewer than 30 games per season. In only one year — 1884 — did he hold regular status, and that was split time among four clubs. A native of Attleboro, MA, he entered the majors with Troy, coming from Clinton. The career .233 hitter also played with Cleveland (1880), Indianapolis (1887), Washington (1888) and Philadelphia (1888) in the National League; Baltimore (twice) in the American Association, and Chicago, Pittsburgh and Baltimore of the Union Association. After leaving the majors, he played at Worcester. Bill Lee says that Gardner had no regular employment, but *DeadballEra.com* states that he was a traveling salesman after leaving baseball. Part of the problem may be that the Frank W. Gardner listed in the 1880 census for Cambridge, MA, as a "Professional Ball Player" does not have the same parents as the Frank W. Gardner from Attleboro, MA, having the player's birth date. The 1900 and 1920 censuses show the Attleboro Frank W. Gardner as a "Bench Hand" and later as a foreman for a jewelry company. The ball player died in Cambridge on August 1, 1914, at age 65. *(Total Baseball; DeadballEra.com; Boston Daily Globe; National Police Gazette; Baseball Necrology; U.S. Federal Census)*

Ed Gastfield played in 23 games for the Detroit Wolverines as an 18-year-old in 1884. Born to German immigrants, Gastfield along with pitcher Charles "Pretzels" Getzien formed what the *New York Times* called the "German battery" for Detroit. The following season he played in one game for Detroit and one game for his hometown Chicago White Stockings, leaving the majors with six hits in 25 games, a .068 average. He later played with Oshkosh of the Northwestern League and played independent ball with West End and the Franklins in the Chicago League. Before entering professional baseball, he had been apprenticed to a cabinetmaker, but later worked as a plumber. Gastfield died of pulmonary tuberculosis in Chicago on December 1, 1899, at age 34. *(Total Baseball; Baseball Reference.com; New York Times; Chicago Daily Tribune; DeadballEra.com; U.S. Federal Census)*

William H. "Billy" Geer had seven major league trials with seven different teams in four leagues over a twelve-year period. He played two games for the Mutuals of the National Association in 1874; in 1875 he was a regular for New Haven of the same league, hitting .244 in 37 games. Three years later he debuted in the National League as the regular shortstop for Cincinnati, also playing with Worcester in 1880. After six games in the Union Association with the Philadelphia Keystones in 1884, he became the regular shortstop for Brooklyn of the American Association, finishing his major league career with Louisville in 1885. All together he hit .214. As a shortstop he fielded .858, slightly below the league average but with above-average range. Details of his life are often confusing. Some sources claim that he was only fourteen years old when he played with the Mutuals, giving an August 13, 1859, birth date. Even so, he would have been fifteen years old when he debuted in October 1874. SABR's Biographical Research Committee believes that an 1849 birth date is more likely and that he may have played at Manhattan College. Early in his career Geer was arrested for burglary of hotel rooms and later for passing bad checks. In 1897 *Sporting Life* calls him "the notorious ex-shortstop," who "is reported to be pursuing a criminal career in the West." That paper carefully separates him from another baseball-related Geer, George H. Some sources still list Billy Geer's birth name as George H. While SABR reports that Billy Geer lived for a while and married in Syracuse, the George H. Geer who appears in the Syracuse censuses for 1900, 1910 and 1920 is apparently not the ball player. *(Baseball Encyclopedia; Total Baseball; Baseball-Reference.com; Baseball Necrology; U.S. Federal Census; Sporting Life; SABR Biographical Committee Newsletter)*

Bill Geis (Geiss) was the regular second baseman for the Detroit Wolverines in 1884. He hit .177 in 75 games and fielded .862 — 28 points below the league average. Described as a "starting pitcher last year," Geis pitched five innings of relief on May 24, giving up 14 hits and 16 runs. *Baseball-Reference.com* and *Baseball-Almanac.com* now credit Bill Geis with the 1882 pitching record (4–9, 4.80 ERA for Baltimore) previously credited to German-born Emil Geis. When Bill Geis' younger brother — also named Emil — pitched a game for the White Stockings in 1887, the *New York Times* identified him as the former Detroit player who had been pitching in amateur league in Chicago. This statement is more nearly a description of the career of Bill Geis than of his brother. Born into an impoverished German family in Chicago, Bill Geis (spelled *Gise* in the 1870 census, and *Giss* in the 1880 census) is described as a "laborer" in both 1880 and 1920. He died in Chicago on September 18, 1924, at age 66. *(Total Baseball; Baseball Reference.com; New York Times; Chicago Daily Tribune; U.S. Federal Census; BaseballLibrary.com; Sporting Life)*

Joe Gerhardt began his professional career as a teenage shortstop with his hometown Washington Blue Legs of the National Association in 1873, also appearing with the Lord Baltimores and the Mutuals in that league. When the National League opened in 1876, he was the regular first baseman for the Louisville Grays, moving to Cincinnati in 1878. He also played with Detroit and the New York Giants in the NL. Disgruntled by lack of playing time, he was released to the American Association New York Mets. After an exile to the minors, he returned to the majors with the Brooklyn Gladiators and the St. Louis Browns in 1890, leading AA second basemen in fielding that season. Gerhardt finished his major league career with Louisville in 1891. In fifteen seasons he hit .227 but reached .304 in the inflated 1877 season and was called a "lightning player" in the field. His fielding average and range factors were well above those for the league. He was also manager at Louisville in 1883 and for the Browns in 1890. After leaving baseball, Gerhardt became "manager of a café in the Columbia Theater Building, New York," from which he drew a "fat salary." He later operated hotels in New York City and in Tarrytown, NY, and for a while managed a bowling alley. Born in the District of Columbia to German parents, Gerhardt died at Middletown, NY, on March 11, 1922, at age 67. *(Total Baseball; Base ball-Reference.com; Washington Post; Chicago Daily Tribune; National Police Gazette)*

Charles "Pretzels" Getzein won 145 games in nine National League seasons with Detroit, Indianapolis, Boston, Cleveland and St. Louis. Fifty-nine of those wins came in 1886–87 when he went 30–11 and 29–13 for Detroit, helping the Wolverines win the 1887 NL championship. He won four games with a 1.58 ERA in the World

"Pretzels" Getzein (Library of Congress)

Series that year against the St. Louis Browns. After six seasons of 300-plus innings, Getzein won only nine games after the 1890 season, and he was out of the majors by age 28. His nickname came from Chicago batters who described his curve ball as twisting like a pretzel. Born in Germany, Getzein made his home in Chicago, where he later played independent ball in the Chicago League. In 1897 *Sporting Life* describes him as a "type sticker." Both the 1920 and 1930 U.S. Federal Censuses describe him as a state grain inspector. Getzein died in Chicago on June 19, 1932, at age 68. (*Total Baseball; Baseball-reference.com; Chicago Daily Tribune; Boston Daily Globe; U.S. Federal Census; Sporting Life*)

Tom Gillen debuted with his hometown Philadelphia Keystones on April 18, 1884. The 21-year-old catcher went on to play in 29 games, in which he hit .155. Two years later he played two late-season games for the Detroit Wolverines. His four hits allowed him to leave the majors with a .175 batting average; he fielded at a .895 percentage. Gillen played with Macon in 1885 and Savannah in 1886, earning an 1887 trial with Detroit, but was injured and released. Born to Irish parents, he worked as a blacksmith before entering the majors. On January 26, 1889, Gillen died in Philadelphia of congestion of the lungs and heart disease. He was only 26 years old. (*Total Baseball; Baseball-Reference.com; DeadballEra.com; U.S. Federal Census; Sporting Life*)

Pete Gillespie was reported to be the first major league player to earn $2,800 in a season. Already 28 years old, the Pennsylvanian joined Troy in 1880 from Holyoke. Moving with the club to New York in 1883, he finished his major league career there in 1887, holding out for a higher salary which never came. In eight major league seasons he hit .274, with a high of .314 in 1883. The *National Police Gazette* described Gillespie's work in the outfield as the "finest and sharpest play of any player in the league." He led National League outfielders in fielding in 1885, and his career average of .903 is thirty-seven points above the league average. Gillespie played for Troy of the International League in 1888. Born in Carbondale, PA, to Irish parents, Gillespie worked as a breaker in the mines before entering professional baseball. When he left baseball, he returned to Carbondale and was listed as a miner at the time of his death. He died at Carbondale on May 5, 1910, at the age of 58. (*Total Baseball; National Police Gazette; New York Times; Baseball-*

Pete Gillespie (Library of Congress)

Reference.com; SABR Biography Project; Sporting Life)

Barney Gilligan, a 130-pound catcher, lasted eleven seasons in the majors—five as a regular. As an 18-year-old amateur, he caught two games for the Brooklyn Atlantics of the National Association in 1875. In 1879 he joined Cleveland, coming from Clinton. He played for Cleveland (1879–80), Providence (1881–85), Washington (1886–87) and Detroit (1888). In all he hit .207, but he hit .245 for the National League champion Providence Grays in 1884, when he caught "Old Hoss" Radbourn, and hit .444 in the World Series that year. Gilligan is most often praised for not being "afraid of work." His defensive statistics (.912 percentage, 6.78 range factor) are above the league average for the time. Born in Cambridge, MA, to Irish parents, Gilligan moved to Lynn, MA, where he was described as "prospering in business." Bill Lee's research showed that Gilligan worked for the sanitation department, a fact confirmed by the 1930

Barney Gilligan (Library of Congress)

U.S. Federal Census. Gilligan died at Lynn on April 1, 1934, at age 78. *(Total Baseball; Washington Post; Boston Globe; New York Times; Baseball Necrology; U.S. Federal Census)*

Pit Gilman, a twenty-year-old outfielder from Laporte, OH, played in two games for the Cleveland Blues on September 18 and 20, 1884, collecting one hit in ten at bats and handling five fielding chances without an error. A Gilman played outfield in the minors for Charleston, Toronto and Columbus in the late 1880s. The 1910 U.S. Federal Census shows Gilman living in Carlisle, OH, employed as a mercantile salesman. Bill Lee found that Gilman worked as a salesman for a candy company. He died on August 17, 1950, in Elyria, OH, at age 86. *(Baseball-Reference.com; Total Baseball; Baseball Necrology; U.S. Federal Census; Sporting Life)*

James "Buck" Gladman or **Gladmon** played for Washington clubs in both the American Association and National League. After a one-game trial with the Philadelphia Quakers in 1883, he became the regular third baseman for the AA Nationals in 1884. The twenty-year-old hit only .156 in 56 games. Returning to the majors in 1886 with the NL Nationals, he managed a .138 average for 44 games, giving him a career .147 mark. He also committed 65 errors in 101 games. *Sporting Life* reported that Gladmon had inherited George Bradley's nickname of "Fog Horn." Born in Washington, DC, to a shoemaker, Gladmon appears in the 1880 census as a 15-year-old newspaper seller. The 36-year-old Gladmon died in Washington on January 13, 1890. *(Baseball-Reference.com; Sporting News; Retrosheet; U.S. Federal Census; Sporting Life)*

Jack Glasscock, "the king of shortstops," played seventeen seasons in the majors—sixteen as a regular shortstop. Except for 38 games with the Cincinnati Outlaw Reds—for whom he hit .419 in 1884—he spent his entire career in the National League with Cleveland (1879–84), St. Louis

Jack Glasscock (Library of Congress)

(1885–86 and 1892–93), Indianapolis (1887–89), New York (1890–91), Pittsburgh (1893–94), Louisville (1895) and Washington (1895). He was playing manager at Indianapolis (1889) and St. Louis (1892). The career .290 hitter hit .352 in 1889 and led the NL with a .336 average in 1890. He led the NL in hits in both 1889 and 1890. In the field Glasscock led NL shortstops in fielding and assists six times each, in double plays four times, and in put outs three times. His career fielding average of .910 far exceeded the league average of .882. After leaving Washington, Glasscock played and managed in the minors for several years. By 1905 he is identified as "a carpenter in Wheeling, W. Va.," his home town. This is confirmed by the 1910 census. Glasscock died at Wheeling on February 24, 1947. *(Washington Post; New York Times; National Police Gazette; Total Baseball; SABR Biography Project; U.S. Federal Census)*

Bill Gleason became the regular shortstop for his hometown St. Louis Browns in 1882 and held that position through 1887, for a while playing beside his older brother Jack. A career .267 hitter, he twice hit .288 and once hit .287 in his eight seasons—all spent in the American Association and six spent as a regular. Sold to the Athletics in 1888, he finished with Louisville in 1889. Gleason later played for the Washington club of the Atlantic League (1890) and Peoria (1891). An attempt to become an umpire in the American Association was not successful, his work being termed "incompetent" by the *Washington Post*. Like his brother Jack, he joined the St. Louis Fire Department after leaving baseball and was promoted to captain in 1907. Bill Gleason died on July 21, 1932, from heat prostration, incurred while fighting a fire. He was 73 years old. *(Total Baseball; Baseball-Reference.com; Washington Post; Chicago Daily Tribune; Sporting News)*

Jack Gleason played with St. Louis teams in three different leagues. After playing on the Union Stockyards team, he had a one-game trial with the National League St. Louis Brown Stockings in l877. In 1882 he played beside his younger brother Bill in the St. Louis Browns infield, leading the American Association in bases on balls. He was also a regular with Louisville in 1883. In his best year, l884, he hit .319 as the regular third baseman for the Union Association St. Louis Maroons, moving with that club into the NL in 1885. The St. Louis native finished with the Philadelphia Athletics in l886, leaving the majors with a .269 average for six seasons. However, his fielding average of .781 was more than thirty points below the league average. Gleason then accepted an appointment with the St. Louis Fire Department. Born to Irish parents in St. Louis, he died in St. Louis on September 4, 1944, at age 90. *(Baseball-Reference.com; Total Baseball; Sporting News; U.S. Federal Census)*

Edward "Mouse" Glenn was a regular outfielder for his hometown Richmond Virginians when they entered the American Association in August 1884. The 23-year-old hit .246 that year, the best of his three seasons. A regular with Pittsburgh in 1886, he managed only a .171 average. Splitting 1888 between the AA Kansas City Cowboys and the National League Boston Beaneaters, he hit only .137, leaving the majors with a career .202 average for 137 games. He finished his professional career with Sioux City of the Western League in 1890. In the 1890 *Richmond City Directory*, Glenn is listed as a "baseballist." Only 31 years old, he died on February 10, 1892, in Rich-

Bill Gleason (Library of Congress)

mond. His death, listed as consumption, was thought to be the result of a baseball injury. *(Total Baseball; Baseball-Reference.com; Baseball Necrology; DeadballEra.com; U.S. Federal Census; Sporting Life; Richmond City Directory)*

Walt Goldsby joined the American Association St. Louis Browns as a 22-year-old outfielder in 1884. After five games, he transferred to Washington, finishing the season with Richmond when Washington disbanded. In 22 games he hit .262. Goldsby played with the Southern League champion Atlanta club in 1885, leading the league in homers, and managed Nashville in 1886, finishing that season in the National League with Washington. He also played with Baltimore in 1888, leaving the majors with a .243 average for 73 games. Goldsby later managed Birmingham and was appointed an umpire in the Southern League in 1903. Mobbed after a June game in Shreveport, Goldsby resigned. Born in Marion, LA, to Irish parents, Goldsby is listed in the 1900 census as a resident of Pine Bluff, AR, employed as a railroad clerk. By 1910 he resides in St. Louis and is listed as a railroad machinist. Suffering from "general despondency," he took his own life in a hotel in Dallas, TX, on January 11, 1914, at age 52. *(Baseball-Reference.com; Total Baseball; Atlanta Constitution; Baseball Necrology; U.S. Federal Census; DeadballEra.com; Sporting Life)*

Fred Goldsmith claimed to have been the inventor of the curve ball, usually credited to Candy Cummings. He always kept a clipping from an 1870 *Brooklyn Eagle* relating an experiment in which he proved that he could throw a baseball so that it curved around a pole. As a 19-year-old, he played one game as a second baseman for New Haven of the National Association in 1875. Then after pitching every game for the Tecumsehs of London, Ontario, for three seasons, he joined Troy in 1879 and shifted to the Chicago White Stockings in 1880. Pitching beside Larry Corcoran, he won 98 games in a four-year period (1880–1883) before injuring his arm. The NL leader in winning percentage (21–3) in 1880, Goldsmith won 28 games in 1882. After a 9–11 start in 1884, he was released to the Baltimore Orioles and then became an umpire. The *Chicago Daily Tribune* later identified him as operating a truck farm. The 1910 U.S. Federal Census lists a Fred Goldsmith matching the pitcher's background working as a salesman in Detroit. According to Bill Lee, Goldsmith became a postmaster and operator of a general store in Berkeley, MI. He died there on March 28, 1939, at age 86. *(Baseball Necrology; Sporting News; Total Baseball; Chicago Daily Tribune; U.S. Federal Census)*

George Gore is believed to be the first major league holdout. Offered $1,200 when he joined the White Stockings from Fall River in 1879, he demanded $2,500 and held out until he received $1,900. Gore led the NL with a .360 average in 1880, one of eight seasons in which he hit over .300 on his way to a .301 career average for 14 seasons. He was a regular outfielder for the White Stockings in 1879–86, helping them win five National League championships. Sold to New York in 1887, he helped the Giants win two more titles. Like many NL players, he spent 1890 in the Players League, hitting .318 for New York. Returned to the Giants in 1891, he finished as a playing manager in St. Louis in 1892. In 1897 *Sporting Life* reported that Gore was "manager of a new roadhouse … in New York City"; in 1912 the magazine reported that he was negotiating with John McGraw for a scouting job. *Bleed Cubbie Blue* says, "Reports are" that he was "mostly penniless and working odd jobs" at the end. Gore, who "made Sacarrappa, Me. famous," died at Utica,

George Gore (Library of Congress)

NY, on September 16, 1933, at age 81. *(Washington Post; Chicago Daily Tribune; New York Times; Total Baseball; bleedcubbieblue.com; Sporting Life; U.S. Federal Census)*

Jack Gorman had a one-game trial with his hometown St. Louis Browns on July 1, 1883, going hitless in three at bats. In 1884 he split 16 games between the Union Association Kansas City Cowboys and the Pittsburgh Alleghenys, playing every outfield position and third base. For 17 major league games, Gorman hit .129. Statistically a sound outfielder, he had ten errors in six games as a third baseman. In addition, he pitched three complete games for Pittsburgh, going 1–2 with a 4.68 ERA. After obtaining his release from Memphis in 1887, Gorman played at Omaha in 1888. The 1880 census for St. Louis shows three John Gormans, born around 1859, living there — a laborer, a tinsmith and a Bell Telephone employee. Missouri death records show that John Gorman, age 30, died at his home in St. Louis on September 9, 1889. He had suffered from a lung problem. *(Baseball-Reference.com; Retrosheet; Missouri Death Index; U.S. Federal Census; Baseball Necrology; Sporting Life)*

Tom Gorman, a left-handed first baseman, played 25 games for the Kansas City Cowboys between June 10 and July 25, 1884. In those games he hit .321 — fourth highest in the Union Association — and fielded .954, six points over the league average. Until recently his records have been combined with those of Jack Gorman. Like Jack Gorman, Tom Gorman was from St. Louis, where he played amateur and semi-pro baseball. *(Baseball-Reference.com; Retrosheet; Sporting News)*

John Grady joined the Altoona Mountain Citys in May 1884, hitting .306 in nine games before the club folded. The 23-year-old played first base, where he fielded .909 — below the league average. Born in Lowell, MA, to Irish parents, Grady appears in the 1880 census as a "laborer." After his baseball career, he became active in civic affairs and, according to Bill Lee, was elected to the Lowell City Council. Grady died suddenly of a stroke on July 15, 1893. He was just 33 years old. *(Total Baseball; Baseball-Reference.com; Baseball Necrology; U.S. Federal Census)*

Bernie Graham played one game for the Chicago Browns on July 11, 1884, and then went on to play regularly as an outfielder for the Baltimore Monumentals later in that season. The left-handed batter hit .267 — ten points over the league average. He committed 17 errors in 42 games for an .833 percentage — right at the league average for outfielders. Graham later played for Kansas City of the Western League and for Memphis and Mobile of the Southern League. Born in Beloit, WI, to an Irish family, Graham contracted typhoid fever and died in Mobile on October 30, 1886, at age 26. *(Total Baseball; Baseball-Reference.com; U.S. Federal Census; DeadballEra.com; Sporting Life)*

Jim Gray now has the records previously attributed to two different players — Jim Gray and Reddy Gray. The Pittsburgh native played for Pittsburgh clubs in three different leagues in his short career. In 1884 the 22-year-old infielder played in an October game for the American Association Alleghenys. In 1890 he appeared in two games for the Players League Pittsburghers and in one game for the National League Pirates. Three years later he played in two games for the Pirates. In his six games, he went 7 for 23, a .304 average. According to Bill Lee, Gray umpired in the minors before beginning a 50-year career with the city of Pittsburgh as a water assessor and chairman of the Board of Water Assessors. This is confirmed by the censuses of 1920 and 1930, which show that Gray, a son of Irish parents, was employed in those capacities. He died in Allegheny on January 31, 1938, at age 75. *(Baseball-Reference.com; Baseball Almanac; Baseball Necrology; U.S. Federal Census)*

Jim Green played ten games as a third baseman and outfielder for the Washington Unions during July and August 1884. *Retrosheet* and *Baseball-Almanac* are accepting the Windham County, CT, and May 22, 1854, birth data on Green, making him 30 years old when he debuted. He fielded .818 at third base, making him an above-average fielder for the time, but he managed only five hits in 36 at bats for a .139 batting average. There are two James Greens of the right age in the Windham County census for 1860–1880. Both are children of Irish immigrant parents. The ballplayer died in Cleveland, OH, on December 12, 1912. A Connecticut-born James Green of the right age and parentage is listed in the 1900 Cleveland census, working as a tailor. This may be the ballplayer. *(Baseball-Reference.com; Baseball Almanac; Retrosheet; U.S. Federal Census)*

Bill Greenwood, the only left-handed shortstop to participate in a triple play, led American

Association second basemen in fielding in 1887. The Philadelphia native had a trial with his hometown Athletics in 1882 and was a regular for Brooklyn in 1884. Leading the Eastern League in runs scored in 1885, he became a regular for Baltimore in 1887–88, with Columbus in 1889 and with Rochester in 1890. In six seasons—all in the AA—he hit .226. As a second baseman he fielded .912—the league average. After leaving the majors, Greenwood captained the Eastern League Lebanon team in 1891. A William Greenwood, born to English parents, appears in the 1880 census for Philadelphia as a 23-year-old worker in a woolen mill. The ballplayer died at Philadelphia on May 2, 1902, at age 45. *(Total Baseball; Baseball-Reference.com; Sporting Life; U.S. Federal Census)*

Thomas Griffin hit Union Association pitching at a .220 clip when his Milwaukee Cream Citys joined the league at the end of 1884. His hitting was actually above the league average; but in those gloveless days, the first baseman also committed nine errors in the 11 games he played; the resulting .918 percentage was below average. The UA folded at the end of the season, ending Griffin's major league career. Born in Titusville, PA, to Irish parents, Griffin went on to become a superintendent of bridge building for the Chicago and Northwestern Railroad. In the 1930 census the 74-year-old Griffin is listed as a private tutor for a family. He died at Rockford, IL, on April 17, 1933. *Retrosheet* and *Baseball-Reference.com* both give him a January 1857 birth date, so he would have been 76 at the time of death. *(Baseball-Reference.com; Retrosheet; Baseball Page; Baseball Necrology; U.S. Federal Census)*

Tobias "Sandy" Griffin had four major league trials over a ten-year period. In his only season as a regular, he hit .307 for the Rochester Hop-Bitters in 1890. He also played briefly for the Washington Statesmen—whom he managed for six games—in 1891 and the New York (1884) and St. Louis (1893) National League clubs. Overall he hit .275 in 166 games. Statistically he was a below average outfielder in both percentage and range. At one point in his career, he was crippled by a pitch from Edward "Cannon-Ball" Crane that "broke the drum of his ear." For the most part the Fayetteville, NY, product played in the Eastern League, later managing both Syracuse and Scranton. In the 1910 census, he is listed as the manager of a baseball club. When Griffin died in 1926, his obituary described him as a former "part-owner of the Syracuse club." *(Total Baseball; New York Times; Washington Post; Johnson, Encyclopedia of Minor League Baseball; U.S. Federal Census; Sporting Life)*

Emil Gross hit over .300 in three of his five major league trials with the Providence Grays, the Philadelphia Quakers and the Chicago Browns. Hitting .358 in 30 games for the 1879 Grays, he added a .307 for the Quakers in 1883 and .358 in 23 games for the Browns in his final season. Overall, he hit .295. Gross caught every game for the Grays in 1880, but his fielding did not match his hitting, as his percentage was 36 points below the league average. After the 1881 season he was among the group of blacklisted players, and so missed the 1882 season entirely. An 1886 note in *Sporting News* says that while Gross was looking for a catching job, he had "inherited $50,000 a year ago." Born in Chicago to German and French parents, Gross is listed as a proprietor of a hotel in both the 1900 and 1910 censuses. In 1907 *Sporting Life* said that he owned a plantation in Georgia. Unmarried, Gross lived with his sister and brother-in law, moving with them to Alabama. He died in Eagle River, WI, on August 24, 1921, at age 63. *(Total Baseball; Baseball-Reference.com; U.S. Federal Census; Sporting News; Sporting Life)*

Ben Guiney caught three games for Detroit in 1883–84, getting one base hit in 12 at bats. The *Chicago Daily* describes Guiney as "the Anson of amateur baseball." For more than 20 years he played on the powerful Detroit Athletic Club team which was frequently Western amateur champions. Born in Detroit to Irish parents, Guiney learned baseball while attending L'Assumption College in Sandwich, Ontario. Both the 1900 and 1910 censuses show that he was a resident of Detroit and secretary to the Detroit Water Commission. According to Bill Lee, Guiney became president of the Kelsey Wheel and Manufacturing Company, a fact confirmed by the 1920 census. Guiney died at Detroit on December 5, 1930, at age 72. *(Total Baseball; Chicago Daily; Baseball Reference.com; Baseball Necrology; U.S. Federal Census)*

Tom Gunning, a graduate of College of the Holy Cross, came to the Boston Beaneaters in 1884 from Springfield, IL, catching in 12 games that season. He caught 48 games in 1885, his most productive season. After playing for the Philadelphia Quakers in 1887, Gunning shifted to the

Tom Gunning (Library of Congress)

American Association with the Athletics in 1888 and left baseball early in 1889 because of an arm injury. In six seasons he hit .205 in 146 games—all as a catcher. His fielding percentage was below the league average, but his range factors were greater. After pursuing a medical degree at the University of Pennsylvania School of Medicine, Gunning became a full-time practicing physician and medical examiner at Fall River, MA. This is confirmed by the 1930 census. Born in New Hampshire to an English father and Irish mother, Gunning died at Fall River, on March 17, 1931, at age 68. *(Total Baseball; Boston; Washington Post; New York Times; U.S. Federal Census; SABR Collegiate Database; Sporting Life)*

Joe Gunson played in 45 games for the Washington Unions in 1884 after joining the club in June, coming from the Philadelphia sandlots. In 1889 Gunson played for Kansas City of the American Association and in 1892 with Baltimore of the National League, finishing with the St. Louis and Cleveland clubs of the NL in 1893. In his busiest season, he played 89 games for Baltimore, 67 as a catcher. Not hitting well in earlier trials, Gunson hit .268 in his final season. In 187 games as a catcher, he fielded .912, a respectable figure for the time. According to *Sporting News*, Gunson "was credited with inventing the catching glove" while playing for Kansas City. Because of aching knees late in his career, he developed a system of giving signals while standing. Born in Philadelphia to English Parents, Gunson appears in the Philadelphia census each decade. In 1900 he still lists "baseball" as his occupation. In the 1910 and 1920 censuses, he appears as a city policeman or detective. Gunson died in Philadelphia November 15, 1942, at age 79. *(Total Baseball; Baseball-Reference.com; U.S. Federal Census; Sporting News; Sporting Life)*

Mortimer "Mertie" Hackett came to Boston in 1883 from the amateur Newton club. Sharing catching duties with Mike Hines, Hackett hit .235 for the National League champions. The native of Cambridge, MA, hit .215 in five seasons with Boston, Kansas City, and Indianapolis, holding regular status only in 1884. After leaving the majors, he played for and managed Troy of the International League in 1888. Hackett joined the Cambridge police force in 1893, holding that position until 1935, when he retired because of ill health. He died in Cambridge on February 22, 1938, at age 75. His brother Walter played shortstop for the Boston Unions (1884) and Nationals (1885). He was also a cousin of the pitching Clarkson brothers—John, Dad and Walter. *(Los Angeles Times; Boston Daily Globe; Total Baseball; Baseball-Reference.com; U.S. Federal Census; Sporting News)*

Walter Hackett, a 26-year-old shortstop, led the Union Association in fielding in his rookie season with the Boston Reds in 1884. According to *Sporting Life*, "he covered as much ground as three men." In that season he hit .243 in 103 games. When the UA folded, Hackett caught on with the National League Boston Beaneaters, getting into 35 games in 1885 but hitting only .184. Born in Cambridge, MA, to Irish parents, Hackett appears in the 1880 census, working as a compositor. The 1900 and 1910 censuses show him as a printer for a newspaper. Bill Lee identifies the newspaper as the *Boston Globe*. Hackett's younger brother Mert was a National League catcher, and he was a cousin to the pitching Clarkson family. Walter Hackett died in Cambridge on October 2, 1920, at age 62. *(Total Baseball; Baseball-Reference.com; U.S. Federal Census; Baseball Necrology; Sporting Life)*

Art Hagan joined the Philadelphia Quakers in June 1883 from Worcester, MA. The *New York Times* reported that the 20-year-old "has a very deceptive curve," and that "he may develop into a good pitcher." After going 1–14 with the Quakers, Hagan arrived in Buffalo in late season, and the report was that "when well supported he could do effective work." The Providence native left the majors in May 1884 with a 2–18, 5.36 ERA record. He pitched for the Sylvan Club of New York in 1885. Bill Lee reports that Hagan was a grocer in Providence and that later he operated a funeral home. The 1930 census shows him as a caretaker of a private estate. Born in Providence to Irish parents, Hagan died at Providence on March 26, 1936, at age 73. *(Baseball-Reference.com; Total Baseball; New York Times; Boston Daily Globe; Washington Post; Baseball Necrology; U.S. Federal Census; Sporting Life)*

Jim Halpin, an English-born infielder, joined the Worcester Ruby Legs in June of 1882. At age 18, he was the youngest player in the National League at the time. Returning to the majors in 1884, he hit .185 in 46 games for the Washington Unions. When he finished his major league career by playing 15 games for Detroit in 1885, he was still only twenty-one years old. In all he hit major league pitching at only a .130 clip in 63 games, and his fielding percentage of .821 was also well below the league average for shortstops. Halpin later played for Utica, Albany and Newark of the International League. In 1888 *Outing* included him in the "prominent array of ball players" from the Boston area. Only 29 years of age, Halpin died of consumption in Boston on January 4, 1893. *(Total Baseball; Baseball-Reference.com; Retrosheet; Outing; Sporting Life)*

John Hamill, a 23-year-old right-hander, completed eighteen of nineteen starts for the hapless Washington American Association club in 1884. For this effort he was rewarded with a 2–17, 4.48 ERA record. When the club folded in August, his major league career ended. Born in New York City to Irish parents, Hamill became the owner of a small rubber company in Bristol, RI. According to Bill Lee, Hamill was "well-known as an expert in rubber." He also worked in Liverpool, England, for National India Rubber Company and in Racine, WI, for the Chicago Rubber Company. Hamill died in Bristol on December 6, 1911, just short of his 51st birthday. *(Baseball Necrology; Total Baseball; Baseball-Reference.com; U.S. Federal Census)*

Frank Hankinson entered the majors with the Chicago White Stockings in 1878. In ten seasons, eight as a regular, he also played with Cleveland, Troy, and New York of the National League and with the New York Metropolitans and Kansas City of the American Association. A career .228 hitter, he reached .267 as a rookie and .268 with the 1887 Mets. He led AA third basemen in fielding in 1885; over his career he fielded .875, twenty-four points above the league average for third basemen. Moved to the starting pitching rotation in 1879, Hankinson responded with a 15–10, 2.50 ERA record but was back at third base the following season. Born to English parents in New York City, he died at Palisades Park, NJ, on April 5, 1911, at age 54. In the 1910 Palisades Park census, Hankinson is listed as one having his "own income." *(Total Baseball; National Police Gazette; Baseball Necrology; Baseball-Reference.com; U.S. Federal Census; Sporting Life)*

Edward "Ned" Hanlon played 13 seasons in the majors, 12 as a regular outfielder. After coming to Cleveland from Albany in 1880, he played for Detroit (1881–88), the Pittsburgh Alleghenys (1889 and 1891), and the Pittsburghers (1890), finishing with Baltimore in 1892. A career .260 hitter, he reached .302 in 1885 and hit .274 for the National League champion Detroit Wolverines in 1887. His fielding statistics — especially range — exceeded the league average. He became a player-manager when he joined Pittsburgh. In 1892 he became manager of Baltimore, winning three straight pennants in 1894–96. In 1899 he shifted to Brooklyn, winning pennants there in 1899 and 1900. Hanlon finished his managerial career with Cincinnati in 1906–07. Practicing a roughhouse style of play, his teams won 53 percent of games in 19 seasons. This style of play was continued with great success by his disciple, John J. McGraw. In 1908 Hanlon became president of the Baltimore Orioles. At the time of his death, he was president of the Baltimore Park Board. One account has him making a fortune in real estate. Born in Connecticut to Irish parents, Hanlon died in Baltimore on April 14, 1937, and was elected to the Baseball Hall of Fame in 1996. *(Total Baseball; New York Times; Baseball Necrology; Chicago Daily Tribune)*

Ned Hanlon (Library of Congress)

John Hanna caught for two American Association clubs in 1884. For the first part of the season he played for Washington, hitting .066 in 23 games. When that club folded, he finished the season with the new Richmond club, hitting .194 in 22 games. Between the two clubs, he hit .126 and fielded .892. Described as a "wonderfully good little catcher," Hanna signed with Toledo a year later. He was a native of Philadelphia, born to Irish immigrant parents. After leaving baseball, he started as a shipping clerk and then became "an inspector for the Pennsylvania Bureau of Highways and the Bureau of Weights and Measures." He later served as a "tipstaff for the Quarter Sessions Court of Philadelphia." Hanna died in Philadelphia on November 7, 1930, just days after his 67th birthday. *(Baseball Necrology; Total Baseball; Baseball-Reference.com; U.S. Federal Census; Sporting Life)*

Bill Harbidge (or **Harbridge**) is supposed to be the first left-handed catcher in the National League when he caught Candy Cummings at Hartford. He began his major league career with Hartford in 1875 when the club was part of the National Association and moved with the club into the NL in 1876. He also played with Chicago, Troy and Philadelphia of the National League before finishing with the Cincinnati Outlaw Reds. In a nine-year career spent mostly as a utility player, Harbidge hit .247, finishing with a .279 average as a regular with Cincinnati. Career statistics show that he was a slightly better-than-average outfielder and a slightly below-average catcher. Earliest census reports show that his name was Harbidge, later reported as Harbridge. Born in Philadelphia to English parents, he remained a resident of that city, where he was employed as a government clerk and messenger. He also worked in U.S. Customs. Harbidge died in Philadelphia on March 1, 1924, at age 68. *(U.S. Federal Census; Total Baseball; Baseball-Reference.com; Baseball Historian)*

Lou Hardie played in 81 games—most as a catcher—in four major league trials over an eight-year period. He had a three-game trial with the Philadelphia Quakers in 1884 and sixteen games with the Chicago White Stockings in 1886. After leading the California League in average and homers in 1889, he earned a 47-game trial with the Boston Beaneaters in 1890 followed by a 15-game trial with the Baltimore Orioles in 1891. Overall he hit .223. Born in New York City to German parents, Hardie grew up in the Bay Area and returned there to play after leaving the majors. When the 64-year-old Hardie died in Oakland in 1929, the *New York Times* described him as the "man who discovered James J. Corbett ... and assisted in his development." Bill Lee asserts that Hardie managed the ball park in San Francisco. This is confirmed by 1920 census data for San Francisco. *(Total Baseball; New York Times; Baseball Necrology; U.S. Federal Census; Sporting Life)*

John "Pa" Harkins joined the Cleveland Blues in 1884 after playing at Rutgers College and leading the Interstate Association in strikeouts while pitching for Trenton. That season the 205-pound right-hander led the National League with 32 losses. In five major league seasons with Cleveland, and with Brooklyn and Baltimore of the American Association, he compiled a 51–83, 4.09 ERA record, leaving baseball in mid–1888 to open a tavern in New Brunswick, NJ, his home town. In his best season he went 15–16 with Brooklyn in 1886. The father of nine sons, Harkins later

"Pa" Harkins (Library of Congress)

coached at Yale, Princeton and Lehigh and then became sergeant-at-arms in the district court in New Brunswick. He also served as alderman there. Harkins died at New Brunswick on November 20, 1940, at age 81. *(New York Times; Total Baseball; SABR Collegiate Database; Baseball-Reference.com; Sporting News; Encyclopedia of Minor League Baseball; U.S. Federal Census; Sporting Life)*

Frank Harris was a regular for the Altoona Unions in 1884, playing either first base (seventeen games) or the outfield (seven games). At the plate he hit .263 — well above the league average; in the field he averaged .944 overall — about the league average. When the club folded at the end of May, Harris' major league career ended as well. Born in Pittsburgh, Harris was convicted of killing either his wife (Bill Lee report) or "the man" (*Sporting Life* report) in 1895 and was sentenced to death. However, his sentence was commuted, and he was released in 1911. The census of 1910 shows him as a prisoner in the Illinois State Penitentiary in Joliet, working as a tailor. The 1920 census shows Harris living in Freeport, IL, the proprietor of a tailor shop. He died at East Moline, IL, on November 26, 1939, at age 81. *(Total Baseball; Baseball-Reference.com; Baseball Necrology; U.S. Federal Census; Sporting Life)*

Charlie Hautz joined his hometown St. Louis Red Stockings of the National Association in 1875. The 23-year-old first baseman hit .301 in 19 games. In 1878 he joined his friend Silver Flint in helping Indianapolis win the International League. After umpiring in the National League in 1876, 1879 and 1882, he returned to the majors as a player, joining the American Association Pittsburgh Alleghenys for seven games in 1884. In 26-major league games, he hit .280. Hautz was born in St. Louis to German immigrant parents. In the 1870 census he is listed as a nail cutter and in 1880 as a laborer. The *St. Louis City Directory* for 1899–1900 shows him to be a bartender. In the 1920 census the 67-year-old Hautz is retired and living with his brother-in-law. Hautz died in St. Louis on January 24, 1929, at age 76. *(Total Baseball; Baseball Almanac; Baseball-Fever.com; DeadballEra.com; U.S. Federal Census; St. Louis City Directory)*

Bill Hawes hit .278 as a regular outfielder for the Cincinnati Outlaw Reds in 1884, his last season in the majors. Born in Nashua, NH, to English parents, Hawes had been a member of the Bartletts, the earliest amateur baseball club formed in Lowell, MA. After the Bartletts won the state amateur championship, Hawes joined the Boston Beaneaters in 1879, hitting .200 in 38 games. In 117 games with Boston and Cincinnati, Hawes hit .254 and fielded right at the league average. *Sporting Life* shows Hawes playing for Brockton in 1885 and managing a skating rink. *Baseball-Reference.com* notes that Hawes played professional baseball for twenty years. In the 1880 census, he is listed as a "base ballist"; later census reports show that he owned his own business — a pawnbroker shop in Lowell — for 50 years. Bill Lee notes that Hawes was a member of the board of cemetery commissioners. Hawes died in Lowell on June 16, 1940, at age 86. *(Total Baseball; Baseball-Reference.com; U.S. Federal Census; Baseball Necrology; Sporting News; Sporting Life)*

Thorny Hawkes was the regular second baseman for Troy in 1879, leading the National League in total chances per game. After working in a shoe factory, he was back in the majors in 1884 as the regular second baseman for the American Association Washington club, hitting .278, third highest on the team. For his 102 major league games, he hit .234. Both his percentage and his range in the field exceeded the league averages. *Sporting Life* shows that he continued to play for Haverhill of the New England League. A lifelong resident of Danvers, MA, Hawkes operated a drug store there; Bill Lee's research and the censuses of 1900 and 1910 confirm this. But by 1920 he is listed as a post office employee. Hawkes died at Danvers on February 2, 1929, at age 76. *(Baseball Encyclopedia; Baseball-Reference.com; Baseball Necrology; U.S. Federal Census; Sporting Life)*

John "Jackie" Hayes entered the majors as a regular outfielder with Worcester in 1882, hitting a career high .270. A year later he was the regular catcher for the Pittsburgh Alleghenys, hitting .262. In all, the Brooklyn native played seven seasons in the majors— with Brooklyn and Baltimore of the American Association and with the Washington Nationals and the Players League Brooklyn Wonders in 1890. In 1891 *Sporting Life* reported that Hayes had played for the Cuban Blues over the winter and was "now ready to talk business," but his major league career was over. His hitting fell off after the second season, and he retired with a .233 average for 300 games. He spent 218 of those games as a catcher, fielding .906, an above-average mark. Born to Irish immigrant parents, Hayes appears in the 1900 Brooklyn census as a shipping clerk. He died in Brooklyn on April 25, 1905, at age 43. *(Total Baseball; Retrosheet; Umpire Rulings in a Triple Play; U.S. Federal Census; Sporting Life)*

Guy Hecker, a big (6'1", 190 pounds) right-hander, was signed by the American Association Louisville Eclipse in 1882 as a backup pitcher and first baseman. Twenty-six years old, Heckler was married and engaged in business in Oil City, PA, playing baseball in his spare time. In 1883 he won 28 games, and in 1884 he became one of only three men ever to win 50 games when he posted a 52–20 record, leading the AA in games, complete games, innings, strikeouts and ERA. Then his arm began to go bad, and his win totals dropped to 30, 26, 18 and then into single digits. But his hitting improved so that by 1886 he led the AA with a .341 average. In 1890 he managed and played for Pittsburgh of the National League, leaving the majors with 175 wins and a .282 batting average

Guy Hecker (Library of Congress)

for nine seasons. Hecker played and managed in the minors until 1893, when he returned to Oil City and entered the oil business. In his later years he was a grocery merchant and file clerk. The 1930 census lists him as a lease adjuster for the Ohio Fuel and Gas Company. Crippled from an automobile accident, he died at Oil City on December 3, 1938, at age 81. *(Baseball-Reference.com; Baseball Necrology; SABR Biography Project; Total Baseball; U.S. Federal Census)*

James "Hardie" Henderson had logged more than 1300 major league innings before the age of 23. After one game with his hometown Philadelphia Quakers in 1883, he was sent to Baltimore of the American Association. After going 10–32, 27–23 and 25–35 with the Orioles, he "threw his arm out," and was sold to Brooklyn in 1886. Henderson finished his major league career with the

Hardie Henderson (Library of Congress)

Pittsburgh Alleghenys in 1888. Overall, he turned in an 81–121, 3.50 ERA record for six seasons. The *National Police Gazette* accused him of "sticking so close to the old booze" that he wore out his welcome. Henderson later umpired in the Western Association and in the National League (1895–96). On February 6, 1903, Henderson was killed instantly when he stepped from a Philadelphia trolley into the path of an oncoming trolley. He was 40 years old. *(Total Baseball; National Police Gazette; Washington Post; DeadballEra.com; U.S. Federal Census; Sporting Life)*

Emery "Moxie" Hengle was a second baseman with a very light bat. In his debut with the Union Association Chicago Browns, he hit .203 in 19 games—his only experience above the .200 mark. Subsequent trials with the St. Paul Saints (1884) and Buffalo Bisons (1885) left him with a career .180 average for 35 games. Hengle, born in Chicago to German immigrant parents, played and managed in the Western Association with Minneapolis in 1889 and 1890. According to a 1912 *Sporting Life* report, Hengle was "in Chicago in the insurance business earning a good income." He is listed in the 1900, 1910 and 1920 censuses, ultimately as a manager of an insurance company. The 67-year-old Hengle died on December 11, 1924, at River Forest, IL, at age 67. *(Total Baseball; Baseball Necrology; U.S. Federal Census; Stew Thornley; Sporting Life)*

John Henry, a lefthander from Springfield, MA, had trials with the Cleveland Blues (1884), Baltimore Orioles (1885), and Washington Nationals (1886), compiling a 4–14, 4.09 ERA record. He returned to the majors in 1890 as an outfielder with the New York Giants, hitting .243 in 37 games. In the 1890s Henry was one of the founders of the Connecticut State League, which became a signatory league in 1899. Bill Lee notes that when Henry left baseball, he became a policeman in Hartford, CT. The 1910 Hartford census lists him as a detective, and the 1920 census lists him as "Lieutenant Police Department." This is an ironic career choice because in 1901 *Sporting Life* reported that the police had had to rescue Henry from his friends after he had participated in a fixed foot race in which they lost money. Born to Irish parents, Henry died in Hartford on June 11, 1939, at age 75. *(Total Baseball; Baseball-Reference.com; New York Times; Baseball Necrology; U.S. Federal Census; Sporting Life)*

John Hibbard, a nineteen-year-old righthander, started and completed two home games for the Chicago White Stockings in 1884. On July 31 he shut out Detroit 4–0; On August 2, he lost to Cleveland 10–8. Hibbard then left baseball to attend the University of Michigan. Born in Chicago to parents from Vermont, he appears in the 1900 and 1910 censuses for Hyde Park, IL. In the first his occupation is listed as "plumbing supplies"; in 1910 he is listed as a bank president. Bill Lee found that Hibbard was Commissioner of the Metal Trades Association of the United States. By 1930 Hibbard was retired and living in Los Angeles. He died in Hollywood, CA, on November 17, 1937, at age 72. *(Baseball-Reference.com; Retrosheet; Baseball Necrology; U.S. Federal Census)*

Ernie Hickman made seventeen starts for the Kansas City Cowboys in June and July 1884, compiling a 4–13, 4.50 ERA record. However, his four wins represented one-fourth of the Kansas City win total for the season. Since the closure of the

Union Association ended his major league career, he later pitched for teams in the Western League. Born in East St. Louis, IL, Hickman worked in his father's office as a commission man for the National Stockyards. *DeadballEra.com* calls him a salesman. On November 19, 1891, after a "protracted spree," the 35-year-old Hickman shot his wife and then took his own life. *(Total Baseball; Baseball-Reference.com; Baseball Necrology; DeadballEra.com; Sporting Life)*

Charlie Hilsey joined the last place Philadelphia Quakers in late September 1883. The 19-year-old was described as "a West Philadelphia amateur." Though he lost all three of his starts, he was "said to be very promising." The following spring, Hilsey changed leagues, crossing town to join the Athletics, for whom he compiles a 2–1 record before his release in June. His career record shows six complete games in six starts, resulting in two wins, four losses and a 5.09 ERA. In three games as an outfielder he had errors on three of four fielding chances. Born in Philadelphia, Hilsey is listed as a ball player in the 1900 census. *Sporting Life* shows him playing for Brandywine, Oswego, Kalamazoo and Coatesville in the 1880s and '90s. By 1910 he had taken up his father's trade of carpentry. Hilsey died on October 26, 1918, at age 54. *(Total Baseball; Baseball-Reference.com; Chicago Daily Tribune; Washington Post; U.S. Federal Census; Sporting Life)*

Mike Hines, an Irish-born, left-handed catcher, joined the Boston Beaneaters in 1883 only eight years after he had immigrated to the United States. In his rookie season he caught 59 games, hitting .225. According to the *Washington Post*, he was "possessed with the faculty of being able to throw right or left handed." He was also remarkable for his ability to catch fire-balling Jim Whitney. However, in 1885 he was a given a "twenty-day notice" and released, playing briefly with the Brooklyn Trolley Dodgers and Providence Grays later that season. Released after a try-out with Washington in 1886, Hines played in the minors before finishing his major league career back in Boston in 1888. Overall he hit .202 in 120 games. In the 1900 census for New Bedford, MA, Hines is still described as a baseball player. According to Bill Lee, Hines became a painter and decorator. In 1905 he fell from a building, receiving injuries to his head, which "affected his mind." In 1909 he was adjudged insane by the district court in New Bedford. Hines died at New Bedford on March 14, 1910, at age 47. *(Washington Post; Boston Daily Globe; Total Baseball; U.S. Federal Census; Sporting Life)*

Paul Hines, "the king of out-fielders," began his career as a twenty-year-old with the Washington Nationals of the National Association in 1872. He also played with the Washington Blue Legs and Chicago White Stockings, moving into the National League with the latter club in 1876. He helped them win the inaugural championship by hitting .331 with 21 doubles and leading the NL in fielding. Shifting to Providence in 1878, Hines hit .358, leading the NL in homers, RBIs, and slugging and being credited with an unassisted triple play. The following season he led the NL with 146 hits. For the 1884 NL champion Providence team that won the first World Series over the New York Mets, Hines had a league-leading 36 doubles. Before finishing in 1891 at age 39, Hines played with Washington, Indianapolis, Pittsburgh and Boston of the National League and Washington of the American Association. In addition to four seasons in the National Association, he played 16 seasons in the majors, hitting .302. Both his fielding percentage and range were well above the league averages. Born in the District of Columbia to Irish parents, Hines invested in Washington real estate, and after leaving baseball, he received a government position in the post office of the Department of Agriculture. Blind and deaf, he died at a nursing home at Hyattsville, MD, on July 10, 1935, at age 93. *(Boston Globe; Washington Post; Total Baseball; Baseball-Reference.com; U.S. Federal Census)*

Charlie Hodnett turned in numbers similar to those of teammate Perry Werden in 1884. With the Union Association champion St. Louis Maroons, Hodnett completed 12 of 14 games, compiling a 12–2, 2.01 ERA record — including three shutouts. An earlier trial with the St. Louis Browns resulted in a 2–2, 1.41 ERA record. Much about Hodnett is now a mystery. Whether he threw with the right or left hand and exactly where and when he was born are unknown. While Hodnett was earlier thought to have been born in Iowa some time in 1861, SABR now accepts a St. Louis birthplace. A December 1886 note in *Sporting News* says that Hodnett was "hobbling around with the aid of a cane," a victim of his "old enemy" rheumatism. He died in St. Louis on April 25, 1890, at approximately the age of 28. *(Baseball-Reference.com; Total Baseball; Des Moines Register; Sporting News; SABR Baseball Encyclopedia)*

Mortimer "Ed" Hogan began his major league career with the Milwaukee Cream Citys in 1884, hitting .081 in 11 games. The club's regular right fielder, he committed six errors in those 11 games. Hogan then hit .200 in a 32-game trial with the New York Mets in 1887 and .227 as an outfield regular with the Cleveland Blues in 1888. In all he hit .207 in 122 games, and fielded almost sixty points below the league average. Hogan's records were formerly combined with those of St. Louis Browns pitcher Eddie Hogan. A native of Illinois, Ed Hogan died in Chicago on March 17, 1923, at age 61. The Mortimer Hogan who appears in the 1910 Chicago census as an electric railway motorman seems to be much younger than the ball player. *(Baseball-Reference.com; Total Baseball; U.S. Federal Census)*

Bill Holbert joined the Louisville Grays for 12 games late in 1876, coming from Wilmington. After spending 1877 with Allegheny, he reached the majors to stay with Milwaukee in 1878, also playing with Syracuse (1879), Troy (1879–82), and American Association clubs in New York (1883–1887) and Brooklyn (1888). One of the founders of the Brotherhood of Baseball Players, he was one of the former New York Mets who reformed the club as an independent cooperative club in 1889. His career totals show a .208 average for 12 seasons— in about half of which he held regular status. The big catcher holds the distinction of going 2335 times at bat in the majors without a homer. However, his career fielding average of .907 is well above the league average. In 1890 he was a regular umpire in the Players League. In later years he was "employed as a stereotyper by several New York newspapers, including the old *New York World*." Born in Baltimore, he died at Laurel, MD, on March 20, 1935, at age 80. *(Baseball-Reference.com; New York Times; National Police Gazette; Chicago Daily Tribune; U.S. Federal Census; Sporting Life)*

James "Long Jim" Holdsworth played four seasons in the National Association before participating in the inaugural National League season in 1876. The 21-year-old Holdsworth played shortstop for the Forest Citys of Cleveland and Brooklyn Eckfords in 1872 and for the New York Mutuals in 1873; shifted to third base, he played for the Philadelphia White Stockings in 1874, returning to the Mutuals as an outfielder in 1875. In four seasons in the NA, Holdsworth hit .312, winning the Silver Slugger award when he hit .340 in 1874. He enjoyed two more seasons as a regular in the NL with the Mutuals (1876) and Hartford (1877). In 1882 Holdsworth played in one game for Troy, and in 1884 he played in five games for Indianapolis of the American Association. In 1886 *Sporting Life* noted that Holdsworth had played for the Rochesters and was a candidate for State League umpire. Born in New York City with an English father, Holdsworth died there on March 22, 1918, at age 67. He appears in the 1900 and 1910 censuses as a retired New York City resident. *(Baseball-Reference.com; Total Baseball; Retrosheet; U.S. Federal Census; Sporting Life)*

William "Buster" Hoover played for four teams in three leagues over a nine year period. After debuting as a regular outfielder with the Philadelphia Keystones in 1884, he finished that season by crossing town to play for the National League Quakers. He also had trials with the Baltimore Orioles in 1886 and the Cincinnati Reds in 1892. Hoover hit .364 in 63 games with the Keystones, but the other trials resulted in .190, .217, and .176 averages, giving him an overall mark of .288. As an outfielder, he fielded .840, nineteen points below the rest of the league. Released by Cincinnati, he played with Birmingham in 1893. Born in Philadelphia to an English mother, Hoover appears in the Jersey City census as early as 1910, working as a clerk for the railroad. He died at Jersey City on April 16, 1924, at age 61. *(Total Baseball; Baseball-Reference.com; U.S. Federal Census; Sporting Life)*

Patrick "John" Horan, an Irish-born pitcher and outfielder, was a member of the Chicago Browns at the onset of the 1884 season. As a pitcher he started 10 games, completing nine for a 3–6, 3.49 ERA record. He also made 10 outfield appearances, hitting .088 and fielding .714. His last major league game was on July 14, before the Browns moved to Pittsburgh. *Total Baseball* says that he was born in Ireland around 1863. The most likely ball player among the Irish-born Patrick J. Horans came to the United States in 1865 and became a farmer in Oyster Bay, NY. He died in Brookville, NY, on April 29, 1942, at age 78. *(Total Baseball; Baseball-Reference.com; U.S. Federal Census)*

Joe Hornung, "the king of left fielders," joined the Buffalo Bisons in 1879, coming from the Tecumsehs of London, Ontario. After two seasons with Buffalo, he was picked up by Boston, for whom he played through 1888. Only a .257 career hitter, he hit .302 in 1882 and led the National

League in runs in 1883. His arm a wonder, Hornung led the NL in fielding on five occasions and revolutionized positioning for left fielders against left-handed batters. His career fielding average of .922 was forty-six points over the league average. By 1885 he began to suffer from rheumatism, thus missing most of the season. Released in 1889, he played that season for the Baltimore Orioles, finishing with the New York Giants in 1890. In 1891 he signed with Buffalo of the International League and umpired in the NL in both 1893 and 1896. In the 1880 census Hornung is called a "Ball Player" and is married and living with his father-in-law. In 1898 *Sporting Life* calls him an "assistant engineer in a New York sky scraper." In 1910 he and his wife were living in Manhattan, and he was working as a bank messenger. Born in Carthage, NY, to German parents, Hornung died at Howard's Beach, NY, on October 30, 1931, at age 74. (*New York Times; Total Baseball; Boston Daily Globe; U.S. Federal Census; Sporting Life*)

Pete Hotaling was a much-traveled major league outfielder. Chicago's Fred Pfeffer described him as "one of the old birds—good batsman, sturdy all-around player—fine type of the bygone generation." Only twice in nine seasons did he play with the team he had played with the previous season. A career .267 hitter, he reached .309 in 1881 with Worcester and an inflated .299 in 1887 with Cleveland. Hotaling's .868 fielding average and 2.05 range factor were at least average for the time, and he held regular status throughout his career with Cincinnati, Cleveland, Worcester and Boston of the National League and Brooklyn and Cleveland of the American Association. Brooklyn paid $10,000 for his contract in 1885. An 1897 note in *Sporting Life* showed that after leaving baseball, Hotaling was "keeping a saloon in Cincinnati." In the 1900 census for Cleveland, the 44-year-old Hotaling is listed as a dry goods salesman. Bill Lee found him to be a machinist. Born in Mohawk, NY, Hotaling died in Cleveland on July 3, 1928. He was 71 years old. (*Total Baseball; Baseball-Reference.com; Baseball Necrology; U.S. Federal Census; Sporting Life*)

Sargent "Sadie" Houck, a Washington, DC, product, entered the majors as an outfielder with the Boston Beaneaters in 1879, coming from the Washington club of the Atlantic League. Houck became a regular at shortstop with Providence in 1880 and Detroit in 1881. After being blacklisted for 1882, he continued as a regular with Detroit (1883), the A's (1884–85), Baltimore (1886), and

Sadie Houck (Wikimedia Commons)

the Washington Nationals (1886), before finishing his career with the Metropolitans in 1887. In eight seasons Houck hit .250; he reached .297 with the A's in 1884, the same year he led American Association shortstops in fielding. After leaving baseball, he operated a roadhouse in Rockville, MD ("doing well" with it, according to *Sporting Life*), and later was said to be "working in Chicago." A fixture in old-timers' games, Houck died in Washington on May 26, 1919, at age 63. (*Baseball-Reference.com; Total Baseball; Washington Post; National Police Gazette; Sporting Life*)

Charles F. Householder was the regular first baseman for the Baltimore (1882) and Brooklyn (1884) American Association teams. The left-handed batter hit .254 for the Orioles and .242 for the Trolley Dodgers. He fielded a sparkling .967 as a first baseman. Tried as a catcher, Householder had 56 passed balls in 34 games. He appears in the 1880 census as living in Harrisburg and working as a carpenter. The research of Al Kermisch shows that Householder was injured in a fall from a roof, but recovered to play minor league ball later. His health failing, he died at Harrisburg on December 26, 1908, at age 52. (*SABR Baseball Encyclopedia; Baseball-Reference.com; U.S. Federal Census; Baseball Necrology; Baseball Research Journal*)

Charles W. Householder is listed as the regular third baseman for the Chicago Browns in 1884, moving with the club to Pittsburgh. However, he split the season almost exactly between third base and the outfield, his fielding at either position exceeding the league average. At the plate, he hit .239 in 83 games, slightly below the league average. Householder was born in Philadelphia, the son of a carpenter. He himself is listed in both the 1900 and 1910 censuses as a resident of Philadelphia, employed, like Charles F. Householder, as a carpenter. Charles W. died there on September 3, 1913, at age 59. *(SABR Baseball Encyclopedia; Baseball-Reference.com; U.S. Federal Census; SABR Research Journal)*

Bill Hughes, a seventeen-year-old outfielder and first baseman, joined the Washington Unions at the end of August 1884. The left-handed hitter managed only a .122 average for fourteen games. In 1885 he returned to the majors with the Philadelphia Athletics as a pitcher and outfielder. He had two complete-game starts, resulting in a 0–2, 4.86 ERA record. For his 18-game career, he hit .138. Hughes was born in Blandinsville, IL, to parents from Kentucky. He appears in both the 1920 census for Maryville, MO, and the 1930 census for Santa Ana, CA. In both cases the employment column is "none." Bill Lee says that Hughes was a rancher. He died at Santa Ana on August 25, 1943, at age 76. *(Total Baseball; Baseball-Reference.com; Baseball Necrology; U.S. Federal Census)*

John Humphries, a left-handed Canadian, played in 96 games, catching 75, in two major league seasons. Coming from Cornell University, Humphries played in 29 games for the New York Gothams in the second half of 1883, hitting .112. The following season he hit .146 in 49 games for the American Association Washington Nationals. When that club folded in August, he returned to New York, hitting .094 in 20 games. His career totals show a .143 average. Behind the plate Humphries fielded .876 with 96 passed balls in 75 games. Remaining in baseball, he later managed Toronto in 1886 and Rochester in 1887. Born to English and Irish parents, Humphries taught Latin and mathematics in high schools in Pennsylvania and California. He died at Salinas, CA, on November 29, 1933, at age 72. *(Total Baseball; Baseball-Reference.com; SABR Collegiate Database; Baseball Necrology; U.S. Federal Census; Sporting Life; Encyclopedia of Minor League Baseball)*

Bill Hunter caught two home games for the American Association Louisville Eclipse on May 2 and 9, 1884. He collected one hit in seven at bats, while committing three errors. The 29-year-old was born in St. Thomas, Ontario. Prior to playing with Louisville, Hunter had played with the St. Thomas Atlantics in 1882 and the Saginaw Old Golds in 1883. Though some sources show him to be a brother of Brooklyn outfielder George Hunter, this is surely not the case. First, George Hunter is thirty years younger. Also, another Bill Hunter, a Cleveland outfielder, was, like George Hunter, born in Buffalo. *(Total Baseball; Baseball-Reference.com; Curry, "Saginaw Old Golds")*

Bill Hutchinson turned in three monster seasons for the Chicago Orphans. In 1890 he led the National League with 42 wins, 65 complete games and 603 innings. In 1891 he upped his win total to 44, again leading the NL in wins, complete games (56) and innings (561). In 1892 he added a strikeout crown (314) to his league-leading wins (36), complete games (67) and innings (622). Hutchinson had won one game for the Kansas City Unions in 1884 before joining Chicago in 1889. Remaining with Chicago through 1895, Hutchinson saw his win totals drop to 16, then to 14 and then to 13. His one win with St. Louis in 1897 gave him a career total of 183. He later pitched for Minneapolis. A *Sporting Life* note in 1898 says that Hutchinson would not "return to the diamond and the temptations concomitant to the wearing of the spangles." Born in New Haven, CT, Hutchinson lived as an adult in Kansas City. The 1900 and 1910 censuses show him working as a freight agent for the railroad. Bill Lee says he was a railroad engineer. Hutchinson died in Kansas City on March 19, 1926, at age 66. *(Total Baseball; Baseball-Reference.com; U.S. Federal Census; Baseball Necrology; Sporting Life)*

Art Irwin, a Toronto-born shortstop, began his career with Worcester in 1880, coming from the amateur ranks of Boston, where he grew up. He later played with NL clubs in Providence, Philadelphia and Washington and with Boston clubs in the Players League and American Association. Irwin helped Providence (1884), Boston Reds (PL, 1890) and Boston Reds (AA, 1891) win league championships. In thirteen seasons as a player he hit .241, with a high of .286 in 1883. Both his fielding average and range factors were above the league average. He was captain in Philadelphia and managed both the Boston PL club and Washington. Remaining in baseball, he managed four

Art Irwin (Library of Congress)

John Irwin (Library of Congress)

more seasons in the majors (Philadelphia, New York and Washington), managed in the minors, owned the Toronto club, umpired in the NL and scouted. In poor health and suffering from depression, the 63-year-old Irwin jumped or fell from a New York–Boston steamship on July 16, 1921. At the time he was manager of Hartford. After his death, it was revealed that he had maintained wives and homes in both Boston and New York. *(New York Times; Boston Globe; Boston; Total Baseball; National Police Gazette; Washington Post; Sporting Life)*

John Irwin is another of the four-league players. Following in the footsteps of his brother Art, John Irwin had had a one-game trial with the Worcester Ruby Legs in 1882. He enjoyed his first full season in the majors with the Boston Reds in 1884. After the Union Association folded, he received a three-game trial with the Philadelphia Athletics in 1886, then had a three-season run with the Washington Nationals (1887–89). When the Players League opened, Irwin played with Buffalo in 1890 and finished back in the American Association with Boston and Louisville in 1891. In eight seasons—three as a regular third baseman—he hit .246. Like his brother, he was born in Toronto with an Irish father, and grew up in Boston. At the time of his brother's death in 1921, John Irwin is described as the proprietor of the New Weymouth Hotel at Nantucket Beach. Bill Lee says that Irwin coached at Bowdon and was associated with Miah Murray in a pool and billiards parlor. Jown Irwin died at Boston on February 22, 1934, at age 72. *(Total Baseball; Baseball-Reference.com; U.S. Federal Census; New York Times; Baseball Necrology)*

Bill Johnson hit .271 as a regular outfielder for the Baltimore Orioles in 1891. He had had a one-game trial with the Philadelphia Keystones in 1884 and an eleven-game trial with the Indianapolis Hoosiers in 1887 before joining Baltimore in 1890. Johnson finished with the Orioles in 1892. He later played with Rochester before being released in 1897. In all, the left-handed hitter had a .288 average. As an outfielder he had better-than-average range, but fielded forty points below the league average. Born in New Jersey, he appears on the Chester, PA, census as early as 1880, when he is listed as a painter. The census of 1910 shows him working in a foundry; those of 1920 and 1930 show him employed as a school janitor. Johnson died in Chester on July 17, 1942, at the age of 80. *(Total Baseball; Baseball-Reference.com; U.S. Federal Census; Sporting Life)*

Dick Johnston, a 21-year-old outfielder, hit .281 in 39 games for the Richmond Virginians after they entered the American Association in 1884. Like teammate Billy Nash, he moved on to the National League Boston Beaneaters, for whom he was an outfield regular from 1886 to 1889. In 1889 he hit .296 and led the NL with 18 triples. In 1890 he jumped to the Players League, splitting time between Boston and New York, before finishing back in the AA with Cincinnati. In eight seasons he held regular status seven times, hitting .221; his .903 fielding percentage was above the league average. Teammate Tom Gunning later insisted that Johnston was "the greatest outfielder that ever lived." A native of Kingston, NY, he was employed there as a superintendent of Freeman's Job Printing Plant. Some time after 1920 Johnston moved to Detroit, where the 1930 census shows him employed as a guard at the House of Correction. Johnston died in Detroit on April 4, 1934, two days short of his 71st birthday. *(Total Baseball; Baseball-Reference.com; Baseball Necrology; U.S. Federal Census; Sporting Life)*

Jones played in four games as a left fielder for the American Association Washington Nationals July 14–18, 1884 — two games were at Cleveland and two at Pittsburgh. In those games he had five hits for a .294 average. In the field he handled six chances without error. Where he came from and where he went to are unknown, as is his first name. *Total Baseball* and *Retrosheet* give him a Johnstown, PA, birth. *(Total Baseball; Baseball-Reference.com; Retrosheet; Baseball Almanac)*

Bill Jones had an eight-game major league career as a catcher and outfielder in two leagues. In 1882 he appeared in four games for the American Association Baltimore Orioles, hitting .067. In 1884 he appeared in four games for the Union Association Philadelphia Keystones, hitting .143, giving him a career mark of .103 for 29 at bats. He fielded .857 as a catcher and .625 as an outfielder — both much below the league average for those positions. *Retrosheet* says that Jones was born in Syracuse. The common name creates daunting research problems. *(Total Baseball; Baseball-Reference.com; Retrosheet)*

Charles F. Jones played in 25 games for the 1884 Brooklyn Trolley Dodgers. A utility infielder, the 22-year-old played in thirteen games at second base and twelve games at third base, hitting .178 and fielding .870 — both below the league average. *Retrosheet* and *Total Baseball* both say that he was a New York City product. If this is the case, then the Charles F. Jones who resided in Manhattan in 1910, working as a policeman, may be the former Dodger. The ballplayer died in

Dick Johnston (Library of Congress)

Charles W. Jones (Wikimedia Commons)

New York City on September 15, 1922, at age 60. *(Total Baseball; Baseball-Reference.com; Retrosheet; U.S. Federal Census)*

Charles W. Jones (Benjamin Wesley Rippy), a colorful player of the 1880s, is one of the lost players. Born in North Carolina in 1850 — the first major league player from North Carolina — he entered the majors with Keokuk of the National Association in 1875, also playing with Hartford after Keokuk disbanded. For the next three seasons he toiled for the Cincinnati Red Stockings in the National League, jumping to the White Stockings for two games in 1877. In 1879 with Boston he led the NL in runs, home runs, RBIs and fielding, one of six times he hit over .300. Blacklisted in 1880, he was forced to sit out 1881–82, playing independent ball, before returning to Cincinnati. He rejoined the Red Stockings, now an American Association club, in 1883–1887. Purchased and released by the New York Mets in 1887, he finished his career with the Kansas City Cowboys in 1888. A career .299 hitter, he was a regular outfielder for 11 of his 12 major league seasons. In 1890 *National Police Gazette* stated that Jones had gone "into business for himself" in New York City. In 1900 the *Washington Post* noted that Jones "has a political job under the Tammany regime." Peter Morris found that Jones was "living in Staten Island in 1909 in very poor health; apparently still alive in December 1910." *(Total Baseball; Baseball-Reference.com; National Police Gazette; Washington Post; petermorrisbooks.com; U.S. Federal Census)*

Frank Jones, a 25-year-old native of Princeton, IL, played in two home games for the Detroit Wolverines in the first week of July 1884. Playing one game at shortstop and one game in the outfield, the left-handed hitter had one base hit in eight at bats and one error at each fielding position. In the 1900 census for Marietta, OH, Jones is shown living with his mother-in-law and operating a saloon. By 1920 he is operating a restaurant there, and by 1930 he is described as a "Poultry Man." Jones died at Marietta, OH, on February 4, 1936, at age 77. *(Total Baseball; Baseball-Reference.com; U.S. Federal Census)*

Henry Jones, a 27-year-old utility player, joined the Detroit Wolverines in August 1884, playing in 34 games the rest of the season. He had been a member of Grand Rapids club of the Northwestern League and had led the league in runs scored in 1883. The New York native was used primarily as a second baseman but also played at shortstop and in the outfield. Peter Morris credits him with being a pioneer in realizing the advantages of being able to hit from the opposite side of the plate from the pitcher's delivery. The switch-hitting Jones hit only .220 in 127 at bats but drew 16 walks and scored 24 runs. On the birth of his child, he decided to forego baseball for a full-time job as an engineer of the Grand Rapids and Indiana Railroad. Despite repeated offers from Detroit, he remained with the railroad until a fall from a locomotive forced him to seek other employment. In later years he operated a photography studio and worked as a stationary engineer and as a carpenter. Jones died at a Manistee, MI, nursing home on May 31, 1955 at age 98. *(Total Baseball; Baseball-Reference.com; SABR Biography Project)*

Uriah "Jack" Jones debuted with the Louisville Eclipse in 1883, going hitless in two games. In 1884 he became the regular shortstop for the Cincinnati Outlaw Reds, hitting .261 in 69 games. *Retrosheet* and *Baseball-Almanac.com* now give him a birthdate of February 4, 1859, in Ohio. He apparently was born Uriah L. Jones in Cincinnati and played under the names Jack Jones and Ryerson Jones — the latter perhaps a longer form of "Ri." Both the 1900 and 1910 censuses list a Uriah Jones born in Ohio in 1859. That Uriah

Jones was a resident of Columbus and employed as a switchman for the railroad. *Retrosheet* and *Baseball-Almanac.com* show him dying in Fresno, CA, on November 29, 1936, at age 77. (*Baseball-Almanac.com; Retrosheet; U.S. Federal Census; Total Baseball*)

Aloysius "Pop" Joy played 36 games as a first baseman for the Washington Unions in 1884. The local DC product fielded .966, higher than league-leader Jumbo Schoeneck, but he hit only .215. Joy is listed as a confectioner in the 1900 census. Bill Lee says that Joy became prosperous and gave "large amounts of money to charity." The census of 1920 lists Joy as secretary of the Knights of Columbus, and that of 1930 as manager of an office building. Joy died in DC on June 28, 1937, at age 77. (*Baseball-Reference.com; Baseball Encyclopedia; U.S. Federal Census; Baseball Necrology*)

Charlie Kalbfus played right field for the Washington Unions on opening day 1884. The nineteen-year-old local went one for five at the plate and handled no fielding chances. This was the extent of his major league experience. Kalbfus is listed in the 1890 *Washington City Directory* as a post office clerk. The federal censuses for 1900 and 1910 both show him with that occupation. In the 1930 census, he is listed as a government accountant. Born to a Canadian father and an Irish mother, Kalbfus died in Washington, DC, on November 18, 1941, at age 76. (*Total Baseball; Baseball Reference.com; Washington City Directory; U.S. Federal Census*)

Joe Kappel, a 27-year-old Philadelphia native, caught in four games for the Quakers in May of 1884, collecting one hit in fifteen at bats. Six years later he played in 56 games for the Athletics, hitting .240. For the A's he played every position except pitcher and first base but fielded well below the league average. In the 1890 *Philadelphia City Directory*, he is still listed as a baseball player. In 1896 *Sporting Life* reported that Kappel was coaching the South Jersey Institute team. Kappel came from a skilled artisan background. The 1880 census shows that, like his German-born father, Kappel worked as a gun maker. By 1900 he and his father were both working as machinists—as is his younger brother Henry (Heinie), who had played shortstop for the American Association Cincinnati and Columbus clubs (1887–89). Joe Kappel died in Philadelphia on July 8, 1929, at age 72. (*Total Baseball; Baseball-Reference.com; U.S. Federal Census; Philadelphia City Directory; Sporting Life*)

Tom Kearns played in two games with the Buffalo Bisons as a 20-year-old catcher in 1880. Shifting to second base, the Rochester native played in four games with the Detroit Wolverines in 1882 and twenty-one games with the same club in 1884, coming from Grand Rapids when that club folded. On the Detroit reserved list, Kearns was released in 1885. In 27 Major league games, he hit .202. Back in the minors, Kearns played until 1892 with stops in Toledo, Syracuse, Portland, Toronto, Hamilton, Omaha, Providence and Memphis. The 1900 and 1910 censuses for Buffalo show him residing there, working as a locomotive engineer. Born to Irish immigrant parents, Kearns died in Buffalo on December 7, 1938, at age 79. (*Total Baseball; Baseball-Reference.com; Washington Post; Sporting News; U.S. Federal Census; Sporting Life*)

Tim Keefe joined Troy in August 1880 from Albany, winning the first six of his 342 career victories that season. In 1883 he went from Troy to the American Association New York Metropolitans, helping them to the AA championship in 1884. Using an effective changeup, Keefe averaged 31 wins each season between 1883 and 1889. Shifting to the National League, Keefe and fellow Hall of Fame member Mickey Welch pitched side by side in 1885–1889, helping the New York Giants to NL championships in 1888 and 1889. He led

Tim Keefe (T. Scott Brandon)

the AA or NL in wins twice — including a 42-win season in 1886 — in ERA three times, and in strikeouts twice, including 361 in 1883. In a remarkable run in 1888, Keefe won nineteen consecutive games. He pitched for the Players League Giants in 1890 before finishing with the Phillies in 1893. For his career, Keefe pitched 554 complete games, third on the all-time list. He then worked as an NL umpire in 1894–96. Bill Lee notes that Keefe became involved in Cambridge, MA, real estate, a fact confirmed by the 1920 census. Born in Cambridge to Irish parents, Keefe died at Cambridge on April 23, 1933, at age 76. He was elected to the Hall of Fame in 1964. (*Total Baseball; New York Times; Baseball Necrology; U.S. Federal Census*)

Jim Keenan was barely seventeen years old when he played in five games for his hometown New Haven club in the National Association in 1875. After playing briefly with Buffalo in 1880 and being blacklisted in 1881, Keenan moved to the American Association. He played twenty-five games for Pittsburgh in 1882 before becoming a regular with Indianapolis in 1884, leading the club with a .293 average. When Indianapolis folded at the end of the season, he signed with Detroit and then jumped to Cincinnati, where he played the remainder of his major league career, moving with the club into the National League in 1890. A .240 hitter over 11 seasons, he reached .287 in 1889. While generally sharing catching duties in Cincinnati — fielding 23 points over the league average — he also played about a fifth of his games at first base. Bill Lee says that Keenan operated a tavern in Cincinnati and once served on the city council. In the 1920 census Keenan is listed as a storekeeper. He died in Cincinnati on September 21, 1926, at age 68. (*Baseball-Reference.com; Baseball Encyclopedia; Baseball Necrology; Retrosheet; U.S. Federal Census*)

John F. Kelly debuted with the Cleveland Blues as a 20-year-old in 1879, collecting a single and committing three errors behind the plate. From 1882 through 1884 he played with five clubs in three leagues — the National League Blues and Philadelphia Quakers, the American Association Baltimore Orioles and the Union Association Cincinnati Outlaw Reds and Washington Unions; he is listed as the regular catcher for Cincinnati. In all, he hit .226 in 122 games. In 109 games as a catcher, he fielded .831 — more than sixty points below the league average. Kelly was born in Paterson, NJ, into a family headed by an Irish father. The 1900 Paterson census shows him living there with his mother and working as a bartender. Bill Lee found that Kelly opened a cafe in Paterson. Kelly died in Paterson on April 13, 1908, at age 49. This is not John O. "Kick" Kelly, also a catcher who debuted in 1879. "Kick" or "Honest John" Kelly went on to become a leading major league umpire and later a boxing referee. (*Total Baseball; Baseball-Reference.com; BaseballLibrary.com; Baseball Necrology; U.S. Federal Census; Sporting Life*)

Michael "King" Kelly played sixteen seasons in the majors, beginning with the Cincinnati Red Stockings in 1878. He came to the White Stockings in 1880 and enjoyed seven seasons in Chicago, playing on six National League champions, and hitting .346 in the 1885 World Series. His Hall of Fame plaque describes him as a "colorful player and audacious base-runner." The latter trait prompted a popular song, "Slide, Kelly, Slide." Sold to Boston for $10,000 in 1887, he stole 84

"King" Kelly (Library of Congress)

bases that season. A career .308 hitter, he led the NL in doubles and runs scored three times, and in batting once, hitting .388 in 1886. As a player-manager Kelly hit .326 in the Players League, helping Boston win the championship. Kelly once jumped from the bench to catch a foul popup, announcing himself as a substitute as he did so. After a season in the American Association with Cincinnati — where he also served as manager — and Boston, he finished his major league career back in the NL with Boston and New York in 1892. Kelly played in the minors in 1893, and he died of pneumonia in Boston on November 8, 1894. He was only 37 years old. He was named to the Baseball Hall of Fame in 1945. *(Total Baseball; Wright, Nineteenth Century Baseball; New York Times)*

Rudy Kemmler (Rudolph Kemler) caught two games for Providence in 1879, coming from the Northwestern League. He had subsequent trials with the National League Cleveland Blues (1881), and American Association clubs in Cincinnati (1882), Pittsburgh (1882), Columbus (1883–84), Pittsburgh (1885), and St. Louis (1886), finishing with Columbus (1889). A regular in two seasons, Kemmler played in 84 games in 1883. In his eight trials, he hit .195. In 227 games as a catcher, he fielded .894, slightly below the major league average. In 1885 *Sporting Life* termed Kemmler an "everyday catcher"; in 1886 *Sporting News* termed his defensive work as usually "disastrous to his team." The Chicago native was appointed an election commissioner of the Third Ward in 1899. In the 1900 census for Chicago, a Rudolph Kemmuler, born in Illinois in 1860 to German parents, is listed as a clerk. *DeadballEra.com* says he was a laborer. Kemmler died in Chicago on June 20, 1909. He was 49 years old. *(Total Baseball; Baseball-Reference.com; Washington Post; Chicago Daily Tribune; U.S. Federal Census; Sporting News; DeadballEra.com)*

Ed Kennedy appeared in thirteen games as a utility player for the Cincinnati Outlaw Reds in 1884. Splitting time between third base and shortstop, he hit .208 before being released in August. Born at Belleview, KY, the son of a printer, he is listed as a "pressman" in the 1880 Belleview census. The 1910 census shows him living in Beaver, KS, working as a farmer. Bill Lee says that Kennedy operated a newspaper in Nebraska and that he was on his way to take a position with a Wyoming newspaper when he died of a heart attack at Cheyenne, WY, on December 22, 1912. He was 51 years old. *(Total Baseball; Retrosheet; Baseball Necrology; U.S. Federal Census)*

Edward Kennedy joined the American Association New York Metropolitans in 1883 from Rochester. Although offered large sums by the St. Louis Maroons to jump his contract, he remained with the Mets through 1885 as a regular left fielder. According to *Boston*, his "judgment on fly balls is nearly perfect." His career .878 fielding average is almost twenty points higher than the league average. In four seasons with the Mets and Brooklyn Trolley Dodgers, Kennedy hit only .204 (and only .190 for the 1884 AA champions). But in 1887 he led the New England League in homers while playing with Lowell, and a year later he led the league in hits. Kennedy was born in Carbondale, PA, to Irish parents; the 1870 census shows him working as a breaker in the mine at age thirteen. According to *Sporting Life*, Kennedy retired after 1887 "to devote himself to private business in New York City." An Edward Kennedy born in Pennsylvania to Irish parents is listed as a gardener's assistant in the 1900 Manhattan census. The ball player died at New York City on May 20, 1906, at age 50. *(Total Baseball; Boston; Encyclopedia of Minor League Baseball; Washington Post; U.S. Federal Census; Baseball-Reference.com; Sporting Life)*

Ed Kent, a 25-year-old right-hander, started a game for the American Association Toledo Blue Stockings on August 14, 1884. Giving up fourteen hits and six earned runs, he took the loss that day, leaving the majors with a 0–1, 6.00 ERA record. Kent later pitched for Peoria and Omaha. *Retrosheet* lists his birth place as New York City, his height as 5'6½" and his weight as 152 pounds. Peter Morris says that Kent was born in 1859 and that he was living in Rutherford, NJ, and working in New York City in 1931. The 1910 census shows Kent working as a commercial traveler; that of 1920 as an estimator for a metal company. *(Total Baseball; Baseball-Reference.com; Retrosheet; petermorrisbooks.com; U.S. Federal Census; Sporting Life)*

John Kerins debuted as the regular first baseman for his hometown Indianapolis Hoosiers in 1884, leading the league in fielding that season. When the Hoosiers folded, he moved on to Louisville in 1885, where he led the league in errors. In 1887 he hit .294 while leading the American Association with 19 triples. While the majority of his games were at first base, he served as the

John Kerins (Library of Congress)

regular catcher for the Eclipse in 1886. As Kerins finished his major league career, he played briefly for Baltimore in 1889 and for the Browns in 1890. In seven seasons, he hit .252 and fielded .963 as a first baseman — the league average. He also served as an interim manager for both Louisville and the Browns. *Sporting Life* says that he umpired in the American Association in 1908. Kerins died in Louisville "unfriended and without funds," according to Bill Lee. His death certificate lists his occupation as "House Man" at a hotel and the cause of death as "Syphilis of Brain." After his death on September 8, 1919, "a fund drive was set up to give him a Christian burial." *(Total Baseball; Baseball-Reference.com; Baseball Necrology; Kentucky Certificate of Death; Sporting Life)*

Bill Kienzle was the regular centerfielder for the Philadelphia Keystones in 1884, hitting .254 in 67 games. He had played in nine games for the American Association Athletics in 1882. Between the two teams, he hit .262, but his fielding average of .781 was almost forty points below the league average. In 1886 *Sporting Life* judged from his play with the Athletics, Atlantic City and Wilmington that he was a "heavy left-handed batter" and "above the average" in the field. Kienzle went on to play at Rochester, Oswego, New Orleans and Galveston. Born in Philadelphia to a barber from Wurttemberg, Kienzle died in Philadelphia on April 16, 1910, at age 48. *(Baseball-Reference.com; Total Baseball; U.S. Federal Census; Sporting Life)*

John Kiley appeared in fourteen games as an outfielder for the Washington Nationals in 1884, hitting .214. In the field he committed 12 errors in 28 chances for a fielding average of .571. Kiley returned to the majors seven years later as a left-handed pitcher for the Boston Beaneaters. Making one start, he gave up thirteen hits and six earned runs in taking a loss on May 2, 1891. He was still pitching for the Boston Reds of the New England League in 1893 and, according to *Sporting Life*, was one of the best in the league. Born in Dedham, MA, to Irish immigrant parents, Kiley spent his adult life in Norwood, MA. Censuses show him working as a machinist in a car shop and as a retail merchant. According to Bill Lee, Kiley served as town clerk for Norwood. He died on December 18, 1940, at age 81. *(Total Baseball; Baseball-Reference.com; Baseball Necrology; U.S. Federal Census; Sporting Life)*

Sam Kimber pitched the first extra-inning no-hitter in major league history. On October 4, 1884, he no-hit Toledo for ten innings in a game called because of darkness with the score tied 0–0. Kimber won 28 games for Brooklyn of the Interstate Association in 1883 and moved with the club into the American Association. The 31-year-old right-hander had 41 complete games in 41 starts for an 18–20 record for the Trolley Dodgers in 1884. In 1885 he gave up fifteen hits in his only start for Providence, leaving the majors with an 18–21, 4.07 ERA record. In the minors he later pitched for Atlanta, Wheeling, Newark and the Virginias. Born in Philadelphia, Kimber appears in the 1880 Philadelphia census as a blacksmith. In later censuses he is shown as a watchman for the railroad. In explaining the demands of his job, Kimber told *Sporting Life* that "special policemen at railroad stations are not there for the sole purpose of preventing people from taking the trains." Kimber died in Philadelphia on November 7,

1925, at age 73. *(Total Baseball; Baseball-Reference.com; U.S. Federal Census; Sporting Life)*

Sam King, a 32-year-old first baseman, played twelve games for the Washington Nationals in May of 1884. The left-handed batter hit only .178; in the field he committed twelve errors for a .912 average and was out of the majors by the end of May. He had earlier played for the Lynn (MA) Live Oaks and in 1909 was described as "still living in New England, hale and hearty." A lifetime resident of Peabody, MA, King appears in the 1870 census as a farm laborer — his father being a Massachusetts-born farmer. By 1880 he was married and was listed as a retail grocer; by 1900 he had become a widower and returned to farming. King died on August 11, 1922, at age 70. *(Baseball Encyclopedia; Baseball-Reference.com; Retrosheet; U.S. Federal Census; Sporting Life)*

Walt Kinzie, who "has been playing third-base this season for Spalding's amateurs," joined the Detroit Wolverines in July 1882. However, he hit only .094 in thirteen games. The Chicago resident came back to the majors with the White Stockings in 1884 but hit only .159 in 19 games as a utility infielder; he finished that season playing two games for the St. Louis Browns. Kinzie played for Kansas City of the Western League in 1887 and was back with Spaldings in the Chicago Commercial League in 1888. An 1891 note in the *Daily Tribune* says that Kinzie's work as an umpire in a Chicago semi-pro league was "satisfactorily to all." The 1880 census shows him working in the U.S. Post Office in Chicago; in the 1900 census he is shown as a stockyards worker. Born in Kansas, Kinzie died in Chicago on November 5, 1909, at age 51. *(Total Baseball; Baseball-Reference.com; Chicago Daily Tribune; U.S. Federal Census; Sporting Life)*

John Kirby went 18–50, 4.09 ERA in five major league seasons in three leagues. After debuting with the Kansas City Unions in 1884, the right-hander pitched for the National League St. Louis Maroons in 1885–86, going 5–8 and 11–26 in those seasons. Splitting 1887 between the Indianapolis Hoosiers and Cleveland Blues, he went 1–11. *Sporting News* reported that Kirby had worn out his welcome in Indianapolis for "lushing." In 1888 Kirby finished his career back in Kansas City with the American Association Cowboys, posting a 1–4 record. Born in St. Louis to an Irish father, Kirby is listed in the 1900 and 1910 censuses for St. Louis; he is shown to be married and employed as a city policeman. He died in St. Louis on October 6, 1931, at age 66. *(Total Baseball; Baseball-Reference.com; U.S. Federal Census; Sporting News; Sporting Life)*

Joe Knight started six games for the Philadelphia Quakers in 1884, winning two with a 5.47 ERA. He had played earlier at Bay City of the Northwestern League before that club disbanded. After playing at Toronto, he was signed by the Cincinnati Red Stockings as an outfielder for 1890. As a regular outfielder he hit .312 that season and fielded .925, an above-average mark. He went on to an extended minor league career with Providence and Wilkes-Barre of the Eastern League. Though the 39-year-old Knight's arm was so bad that he "couldn't break a pane of glass," *Sporting Life* reported in 1898 that his "batting will keep him in the game." He was a native of Port Stanley, Ontario, and died at Lynhurst, Ontario, on October 16, 1938. *(Total Baseball; Baseball-Reference.com; Washington Post; Sporting News; Sporting Life)*

Lon Knight was born Alonzo Letti and changed his name while attending Girard College where, like a later Philadelphia A's great Harry Davis, he was trained as an accountant. Knight began with the National Association Athletics in 1875, continuing with the club into the National League. In 1880 Knight returned to the majors with Worcester, moving on to Detroit (1881–82), to the American Association Athletics (1883–85), and finally to the Providence Grays in 1885. Primarily a pitcher early in his career, Knight made 32 starts with a 10–22, 2.62 ERA in 1876 and was 16–28 for his career. As an outfield regular for four seasons, he hit .245, reaching .271 in both 1881 and 1884. His .887 fielding average was almost thirty points higher than the league average for outfielders. Knight managed the A's in both 1883 and 1884. After leaving the playing ranks, he umpired in all three major leagues through 1890. Later he worked for the city of Philadelphia as a highway inspector. On April 23, 1932, he died in Philadelphia of gas poisoning, the result of a gas line rupture. He was 78 years old. *(SABR Biography Project; Total Baseball; Baseball Necrology; Baseball-Reference.com; U.S. Federal Census)*

Jimmy Knowles began his major league career as the regular first baseman for Pittsburgh and Brooklyn of the American Association in 1884. After leading the Eastern League with 120 hits in 1885, he became the regular second baseman for the Washington Nationals in 1886, and, after leading the Central League in homers in 1888, he became the regular third baseman for the Rochester Hop Bitters in 1890. His fielding averages at each position are approximately the league averages. Knowles was a utility player in New York for the Mets in 1887 and the Giants in 1892. The Toronto native hit .281 for Rochester, forty points above his five-year career figures. Knowles managed Atlanta in 1895–96 and umpired in the Eastern League in 1897. Most sources say he died in Jersey City on February 11, 1912. However, *Sporting Life* published a death notice — identifying him as a former Rochester third baseman — for March 1, 1904, in Chicago. *(Total Baseball; Baseball Almanac; Baseball-Reference.com; U.S. Federal Census; Sporting Life)*

Harry Koons began 1884 with the Altoona Mountain Citys. The third baseman hit .231 in 21 games and fielded a solid .866 — almost ninety points above the league average. After the Altoona club folded, he played a final major league game for the Chicago Browns in a game in Philadelphia on July 5. Koons continued to play in the minors, catching and playing first base for Reading as late as 1892. He was a native of Philadelphia, appearing in the 1910 census for that city and the 1920 and 1930 censuses for Camden, NJ, just across the Delaware River. These censuses show that he was employed by the Express Company, first as a sorter, then as a shipper and finally as a teamster. The 70-year-old Koons was struck by a bus in Camden on August 18, 1932, and died from the injuries. *(Total Baseball; Baseball-Reference.com; U.S. Federal Census; Sporting Life)*

Frank Kreeger started one game for the Kansas City Unions on July 28, 1884. Against the powerful St. Louis Maroons, Kreeger gave up eight runs — none of which were earned — in seven innings and took the loss, ending his major league career. Until recently he had no known first name. *Retrosheet* says that he died on July 14, 1899, in Shelby County, IL. There is a Frank Kreeger born in Wisconsin in 1861 to German parents who might be the ball player. However, that Frank Kreeger was still living in Chicago in 1900, working as a stone cutter. *(Baseball-Reference.com; Total Baseball; Retrosheet; Baseball Almanac; U.S. Federal Census)*

Charles Krehmeyer, a left-handed outfielder and catcher, joined his hometown St. Louis Browns in 1884. The 20-year-old played in 21 games. In 1885 he played in seven games for the Louisville Eclipse as a change catcher and finished his major league career with one game for the National League St. Louis Maroons in that same season. In his 29 major league games, he hit .221. As an outfielder he had 12 errors in 17 games for a .571 fielding average. Krehmeyer continued to play in the minors — primarily in the Western and Texas leagues — as late as 1896. The son of Prussian parents, he appears in the 1880 federal census and the 1890 *St. Louis City Directory* as a carpenter. Bill Lee found that he was a "sawyer in a planing mill" in St. Louis. Krehmeyer died on February 10, 1926, at age 62. *(Baseball Encyclopedia; Baseball Page; Baseball Necrology; U.S. Federal Census; St. Louis City Directory; Sporting Life)*

Bill Krieg debuted as the regular catcher for the Chicago Browns in 1884, moving with the club to Pittsburgh in August. The 25-year-old from Petersburg, IL, hit .247 in 71 games. After brief trials with the Chicago White Stockings and the Brooklyn Trolley Dodgers in 1885, he finished his major league career as a back-up first baseman with the Washington Nationals in 1886–87. In four seasons in three leagues he hit .237 in 141 games. In the 65 games he caught, he fielded more than thirty points over the league average. Bill Lee

Bill Krieg (T. Scott Brandon)

notes that Krieg managed in the minors before going to work for the Santa Fe Railroad in Chillicothe, IL. His 1901 Terre Haute team won the Three-I League. *Sporting Life* terms him "one of the most widely known players and umpires in this league." The census of 1920 confirms his railroad employment. Krieg, whose father was German, died at Chillicothe on March 25, 1930, at age 71. *(Total Baseball; Baseball-Reference.com; Baseball Necrology; U.S. Federal Census; Encyclopedia of Minor League Baseball; Sporting Life)*

Bill Kuehne (Knelme), a German-born third baseman, played ten seasons in the majors—all as a regular. Beginning with the American Association Columbus Buckeyes in 1883, he played with Pittsburgh teams in three different leagues (1885–1890), Columbus and Louisville AA teams (1891) before finishing with Louisville, and Cincinnati and St. Louis National League teams in 1892. A career .232 hitter, he reached .299 in the inflated 1887 season. He also fielded thirteen points over the league average at third base. After leaving the majors, he played in the Eastern league with Erie and later in the Western League with Minneapolis. An 1898 note in *Sporting Life* states that he had been released as player, captain, and acting manager of the St. Thomas club of the International League (despite a .359 batting average) and later signed by Chatham. Kuehne died at Sulphur Springs, OH, on October 27, 1921, at age 63. *(Total Baseball; Baseball-Reference.com; Chicago Daily Tribune; National Police Gazette; New York Times; Sporting Life)*

George "Chappy" Lane was a regular in both his major league seasons with the Pittsburgh Alleghenys and the Toledo Blue Stockings. Most sources list him as a Pittsburgh native who joined his local American Association club in 1882. Splitting time between first base and the outfield, he hit .178 in 57 games. In 1883 he played with Toledo of the Northwestern League and moved with that franchise into the AA in 1884. Against AA pitching he hit .228. Toledo was dropped from the league for 1885, and Lane left the majors with a career .203 average. As a first baseman he fielded .961, slightly above the league average. Bill Lee says that Lane was a painter who died in Pittsburgh in 1896. *Retrosheet* and *Baseball-Reference.com* now say that Lane died in Philadelphia in 1901. The 1900 census for Philadelphia shows a 41-year-old glass blower named George Lane living there with his mother and wife. This George Lane, a native Pennsylvanian, might be the ballplayer. *(Total Baseball; Baseball-Reference.com; Retrosheet; Baseball Necrology; U.S. Federal Census)*

Larkin played 17 games at third base for the Washington Unions between May 31 and July 16, 1884. His .243 batting average was above the team average; however his .726 fielding percentage was much below the league average for a third baseman. His record has just recently been separated from that of National League pitcher Terry Larkin. *(Baseball-Reference.com; Total Baseball; Retrosheet; Baseball Page)*

Frank "Terry" Larkin debuted with the New York Mutuals in 1876, starting and losing one game on May 26. However, he won 89 games in a three-year period (1877–1879) pitching for Hartford and the White Stockings. In that period

Bill Kuehne (Library of Congress)

he worked 1520 innings with win totals of 29, 29 and 31. His arm began to go bad in 1879, so he was sent to Troy in 1880, where he lost five starts and was out of baseball. In 1883 he shot and wounded his wife and a police officer, but was released from jail when his wife failed to press charges. In 1884 he returned to the majors as a second baseman for the Richmond Virginians, hitting .203 in forty games. In 1894 Larkin was institutionalized in Brooklyn after threatening to shoot a former employer and his father. There he committed suicide by slitting his throat with a razor. His date and place of birth are unknown, though *SABR Baseball Encyclopedia* gives him a Brooklyn birth place. He died on September 16, 1894; presumably he was about 45 years of age. *(Baseball-Reference.com; DeadballEra.com; BaseballLibrary.com; Bill James Historical Abstract)*

Henry "Ted" Larkin was a heavy hitting outfielder and first baseman for the Philadelphia Athletics, Cleveland Infants and Washington Nationals. A .303 hitter over a ten-year career, he went over .300 six times, with a high of .330 in 1890. He led the American Association twice in doubles and once in on-base percentage. Either as a first baseman or an outfielder, Larkin had more range than the league average, but a slightly lower fielding average. When he joined the Players League in 1890, he became playing manager of Cleveland, returning to the Athletics a year later. After finishing with Washington in 1893, he played with Allentown of the Pennsylvania State League. An 1896 note says that Larkin might not play because he was on the "foorce" as "one of the finest" in Reading. The censuses show that after leaving baseball, Larkin worked first as a boilermaker or ironworker and later as a laborer in City Parks. Born in Reading, PA, to Irish parents, Larkin died at Reading on January 31, 1942, at age 82. *(Total Baseball; Baseball-Reference.com; Baseball Necrology; New York Times; U.S. Federal Census; Sporting Life)*

Arlie Latham was the first New Hampshire native to play in the majors. As a 20-year-old, he

Henry Larkin (Library of Congress)

Arlie Latham (Library of Congress)

had a trial with Buffalo in 1880 and returned to the majors as a regular third baseman for the American Association St. Louis Browns in 1883. Helping the Browns to four straight AA championships, the "Dude" hit .301 in 1886, leading the AA in runs scored, and .316 the following season with 129 stolen bases. In 1890 he played part of the season with the Players League Chicago Pirates and then shifted to Cincinnati, for whom he played through 1895, hitting .313 in 1894. He effectively ended his major league career as manager of the St. Louis team in 1896, though he made appearances for Washington in 1899 and the Giants in 1909. In seventeen seasons—thirteen as a regular—Latham hit .269. His fielding average and range exceeded the league average. He was brought back into the majors by John McGraw in 1909 to coach the Giants (for whom he played two games), and after World War I he spent seventeen years in England teaching baseball to the locals. Latham later operated a deli in New York City and then became press box attendant for the Yankees and Giants. He died at Garden City, NY, on November 19, 1952, at age 92. *(Total Baseball; Baseball-Reference.com; New York Times; SABR Biography Project; U.S. Federal Census; Sporting News)*

George "Juice" Latham began his career with Boston and New Haven of the National Association in 1875. Two years later he became the regular first baseman for the National League Louisville Grays, hitting .291. When the Philadelphia Athletics entered the American Association in 1882, he was playing manager, hitting .285 and leading first basemen in fielding. Latham finished his major league career with the Louisville Eclipse in 1883 84 with a batting average of .248 for five seasons. A notorious umpire baiter—described as "carrying his mouth around with him"—Latham twice served as a minor league umpire, in the American Association in 1880 and in the Central League in 1888. He played with his hometown Utica team after leaving the majors and was last seen playing for Richfield when he was well past forty years of age. According to the 1900 census, Latham was a resident of Utica, working as a motorman for the railroad. He died at Utica on May 26, 1914, at age 61. *(National Police Gazette; New York Times; Chicago Daily Tribune; Baseball-Reference-com; U.S. Federal Census)*

John "Chuck" Lauer joined his hometown Pittsburgh Alleghenys as a 19-year-old in 1884. Appearing in 13 games, primarily as an outfielder, he hit .114. He played in four games—three as a

Chuck Lauer (Library of Congress)

catcher—for the Alleghenys in 1889, before finishing with Chicago in 1890. Overall he hit .147 in 19 games. Lauer continued to play in the minors at least through 1896. *Sporting Life* describes Lauer as "quite a chubby fellow," and "an apparently clumsy fielder," but noted that he "has developed into an A1 guardian of the third bag." Born of German parents, Lauer worked as a blacksmith before entering the majors. The 1910 census shows him to be a resident of Buffalo, NY, working as a livestock commissioner. Lauer died on May 14, 1915, in Buffalo. He was 50 years old. *(Total Baseball; Baseball-Reference.com; U.S. Federal Census; Baseball Page; Sporting Life)*

Johnny Lavin played in sixteen games for the St. Louis Browns at the end of 1884. The centerfielder hit .212 and fielded .750, both marks well below the league average. He was carried on the club's reserve list for 1885. *Sporting News* shows him playing for Milwaukee in 1886 and a team in Madison, WI, at the end of that season. *Sporting Life* shows him playing for Binghamton of the Eastern League in 1888. *Total Baseball, Baseball-Almanac.com* and *Retrosheet* give Lavin a Troy, NY, birthplace. The 1880 census for Troy shows John Lavin, born in New York in 1856 to Irish parents, living with his sister and brother. His occupation is "ball player." *(New York Times; Chicago Daily Tribune; Baseball-Reference.com; Total Baseball; Baseball Encyclopedia; Retrosheet; Baseball-Almanac.com; Baseball Page; Sporting News; U.S. Federal Census)*

Mike Lawlor debuted as a catcher with his hometown Troy Trojans in 1880. In four games he had one hit and suffered 19 passed balls. Four years later, he caught two games for the Washington Unions, going hitless in seven at bats, giving him a career .063 average. Lawlor played for Utica in 1886 and Bradford of the Pennsylvania League in 1887. Born in Troy to Irish parents, he was married and working as a wool sorter the year he entered the majors. The 1900 and 1910 censuses show him to be a resident of Troy, working as a shirt ironer in a collar shop. He died in Troy on August 3, 1918, at age 64. *(Total Baseball; Baseball-Reference.com; U.S. Federal Census)*

Jack Leary hit .292 in 60 games for the Pittsburgh Alleghenys in 1882 as the highlight of his four years in the majors. Overall, in 129 games with seven teams in three leagues, he managed only a .232 average. Playing in every position— including pitcher—Leary did not reach the league average as a fielder in any position, fielding just .725 overall. Beginning his major league career with the Boston Beaneaters in 1880 and Detroit Wolverines in 1881, he finished in the Union Association in 1884 with Altoona and Chicago. Between he played for Pittsburgh, Baltimore and Louisville of the American Association. *Sporting Life* reported that he had signed with Augusta in 1885. Born in New Haven, CT, to Irish parents, Leary appears in the 1880 census for New Haven as being married; his occupation is listed as a professional baseball player. In the 1900 census, he is still living in New Haven, working as an oyster digger. *Baseball-Reference.com* and *Baseball-Almanac.com* agree that he died in New Haven on December 6, 1905, at age 44. *(Total Baseball; Baseball-Reference.com; U.S. Federal Census; Baseball Almanac; Sporting Life)*

Tom Lee debuted with the Chicago White Stockings on June 14, 1884, a week after his twenty-second birthday. He won one of five starts with Chicago; in the latter part of the season, he shifted to the Baltimore Monumentals, for whom he had 12 complete games, five wins and a 3.39 ERA. Lee signed with Milwaukee as a shortstop and change pitcher for 1885 and went to Memphis later in the season. According to Bill Lee, Tom Lee contracted malaria while playing in the South, and this led to his early death in Milwaukee on March 4, 1886. Some sources give Lee a Philadelphia birth, but *Sporting Life* twice lists him as a local Milwaukee player, and the census shows a Thomas Lee born in Milwaukee in 1862. Lee was only 25 years old at the time of his death. *(Baseball Necrology; Total Baseball; Baseball Page; Wisconsin Deaths, 1820–1907; Sporting Life; U.S. Federal Census)*

James Lehan played in three games for the Washington Unions in 1884. The 28-year-old native of Connecticut banged out four hits in twelve at bats. But he fielded only .688 with five errors at shortstop. Until recently his statistics have been included in those of Mike Lehane, an infielder with Columbus in 1890–91. Lehan, born to Irish parents who had migrated to Hartford from Canada, later worked as a machinist for Remington Firearms factory. The 1920 census shows him to be a chauffeur for a florist shop. Lehan died in Hartford on July 18, 1946, at age 90. *(Baseball-Reference.com; Retrosheet; U.S. Federal Census)*

Charlie Levis, a 23-year-old St. Louis native, became the regular first baseman for the Baltimore Monumentals in 1884, hitting .228 in 87 games. Before that season was over, he had also performed for the Washington Unions in one game and the Indianapolis Hoosiers in three games. In 1885 Levis played in one game with a fourth club—the Baltimore Orioles—after leading the Southern League in homers. Among the four clubs he hit .226 in 92 games. In both percentage and range, his fielding exceeded the league average. Levis managed Chattanooga in 1886–87. In 1896 *Sporting Life* notes that he was employed in a wholesale house in St. Louis. Levis appears in the St. Louis censuses for 1900, 1910, and 1920, listed as a clerk and later as a recorder of deeds. He died in St. Louis on October 16, 1926, at age 66. *(Total Baseball; Retrosheet; U.S. Federal Census; Sporting News; Encyclopedia of Minor League Baseball; Sporting Life)*

Fred Lewis, a Buffalo native, played five seasons—three as a regular—as a major league outfielder with five different clubs in three leagues. A career .296 hitter, he had big seasons in 1884, when he hit .323 in St. Louis between the American Association Browns and Union Association Maroons, and 1886, when he hit .318 for Cincinnati. Lewis had debuted with the Boston Beaneaters in 1881 and later played for National League clubs in Philadelphia and St. Louis. He had a reputation as a hard-drinking, quarrelsome player. The *National Police Gazette* noted that the Browns' owner made a habit of expelling him from the team for disorderly conduct and then hiring him back at a higher wage. The *Gazette* later noted that Lewis "had made a perfect ass of himself." After finishing with the Red Stockings in 1886, Lewis lived in Utica, where, according to Bill Lee, he worked for Foster Brothers and later for the city of Utica. The 1900 census lists Lewis as a worker in a bed spring factory. He died in Utica on June 5, 1945 at age 86. *(Total Baseball; Retrosheet; National Police Gazette; Baseball Necrology; U.S. Federal Census)*

Jim Lillie joined the Buffalo Bisons in 1883, serving as a utility player that season. The son of Irish immigrant parents, Lillie became a regular outfielder over the next two seasons. In 1886, after the breakup of the Buffalo club, he was awarded to the Kansas City Cowboys, for whom he also served as an outfield regular, though he hit only .175. His four-year totals show a .219 average. His fielding range was fifteen points above the league average; his fielding percentage was thirteen points below the average. In 1888 a gasoline stove exploded in his home, killing his wife and burning him so badly that he had to have his right hand amputated. On November 9, 1890, Lillie died in Kansas City of peritonitis. He was 29 years old. *(Total Baseball; Baseball-Reference.com; National Police Gazette; Washington Post; New York Times; U.S. Federal Census; Sporting Life)*

Marshall Locke, a 27-year-old outfielder, played in seven games for the Indianapolis Hoosiers in July 1884. In these games he hit .241 and handled eight of ten fielding chances. Born in Ashland, OH, Locke appears as a resident of Indianapolis in the 1860, 1870 and 1880 censuses. In the last he is listed as a law student. In the 1930 census, he is back in Ashland, retired and living in the home of his brother-in-law. Locke died in Ashland on March 6, 1940, at age 82. *(Total Baseball; Baseball-Reference.com; U.S. Federal Census)*

Milo Lockwood made ten starts for the Washington Unions in April and May 1884, compiling a 1–9, 7.45 ERA record. The 26-year-old Solon, OH, product also played as an outfielder and third baseman. Overall he hit .209 in 20 games while fielding .809. Bill Lee calls Lockwood a "barred attorney." The 1886–88, 1888–90, and 1890–92 city directories for Cleveland list him as a salesman for Lockwood-Taylor Hardware Company (of which his father was president). Despondent over ill health, he shot himself at a motel in Economy, PA, on October 9, 1897. He was 39 years old. *(Baseball-Reference.com; Total Baseball; Baseball Necrology; U.S. Federal Census; New York Times; Cleveland City Directory)*

Thomas Loughran had, until recently, no known first name, birth date or death date. A "change catcher," he played in nine games for the New York Gothams in 1884, hitting .103. The New York City native had attended Manhattan College. During his time in the majors, the *New York Times* alternated between praise, "bids fair to become a strong back-stop" (June 7), and censure, "played miserably" (June 12). Born to Irish parents, Loughran died at New York City on August 7, 1917, at age 54. *(Baseball-Reference.com; New York Times; National Police Gazette; SABR Collegiate Database; U.S. Federal Census)*

Dick Lowe, a 30-year-old catcher, played in one game for the Detroit Wolverines on June 26, 1884. The Evansville, WI, native collected one hit in three at bats. Lowe played in the Northwestern League with Eau Claire in 1887 and Milwaukee in 1888. The 1895 Wisconsin State Census and the 1900 U.S. Federal Census both show Lowe living in Janesville and working as a painter and paper hanger. Those for 1910 and 1920 show him working for the railroad. Lowe died at Janesville, WI, on June 28, 1922, at age 68. *(Total Baseball; Baseball-Reference.com; U.S. Federal Census; Wisconsin State Census)*

Henry Luff is another of the four-league players. In a major league career covering ten years, the Philadelphian played for six teams. He began in the National Association with New Haven in 1875, hitting .271 in 38 games. After a three-game career with Detroit in the National League in 1883, he played for Cincinnati and Louisville of the American Association. In 1884, he hit .270 in 26 games for the Philadelphia Keystones of the Union Association before finishing with the Kansas City team of the same league. Overall he hit .232 in 68 games. In the field he played every position except catcher at some point in his career. But at no position did his fielding statistics approach the league average. On the mound, Luff started seven games at New Haven, completing five, but ended with a 1–6 record. After leaving the majors, Luff was on the 1885 Albany roster. He is listed in the 1880 census and also in the 1890 *Philadelphia City Directory* as a civil engineer. The 1870 and 1910 censuses show him as a clerk. Luff died in Philadelphia on October 11, 1916, at age 60. *(Total Baseball; Baseball-Reference.com; U.S. Federal Census; Philadelphia City Directory; Sporting Life)*

Jack Lynch, a product of Fordham University, began his professional career with Buffalo in 1881, winning 10 games. In 1882 he joined the New York Metropolitans, an independent team, and moved with them into the American Association in 1883. In 1884 the right hander had 53 complete games for the AA champions, compiling a 37–15 record. When the Mets' fortunes declined, so did Lynch's. He had two more 20-win seasons before the club disbanded in 1887. He pitched for Lowell in 1888–89 and returned briefly with the Brooklyn Gladiators in 1890, leaving the majors with a 110–105, 3.69 ERA record. The *Washington Post* identifies Lynch as a member of a group of former players who are out of work because of being "demoralizers and drinkers." *Sporting Life* identifies him as a "boiler inspector" in 1902. In 1904 *National Police Gazette* states, "Jack Lynch became a policeman." The 1910 census for the Bronx verifies this assertion. He was later identified with attempts to reorganize the old Mets. Lynch, born to Irish immigrant parents, died in the Bronx on April 20, 1923, at age 66. *(Baseball-Reference.com; National Police Gazette; New York Mets Hall of Records; Washington Post; U.S. Federal Census; Sporting Life)*

Thomas J. Lynch debuted as an outfielder and catcher with the Wilmington Quicksteps in 1884. Hitting .276 when the Quicksteps folded, he moved on to the Philadelphia Quakers to finish the season. In 1885 he was hitting .313 after 13 games, when he was released, giving him a .258 mark for 42 major league games. While his catching statistics are mediocre, he was an above-average outfielder in both percentage and range. He umpired in the New England League, the National League (1888–1898) and the Connecticut League. Born in Bennington, VT, to Irish parents, Lynch finally settled in Cohoes, NY. In the 1910 census he is listed as an operative in the knitting mill. The 1920 and 1930 censuses show him to be a laborer in the Cohoes public works. When Lynch died on March 28, 1955, at age 94, he was believed to be the oldest living former major league player. *(Total Baseball; Baseball-Reference.com; U.S. Federal Census; Baseball Necrology; Sporting Life)*

Thomas S. Lynch was the second deaf person to play major league baseball. He pitched in one game for the Chicago White Stockings on August 5, 1884. The 21-year-old lasted seven innings, giving up two earned runs and leaving without a decision. This was his only major league experience. Lynch was born in Peru, IL, the son of Irish immigrants. He died there on May 13, 1903, at age 40. *(Total Baseball; Baseball-Reference.com; U.S. Federal Census)*

Malcolm "Mac" MacArthur, a Scottish-born right-hander, made six starts for the Indianapolis Hoosiers in 1884. He completed all six, winning one game. Only twenty-two years old when he made his debut, he went on to pitch for Toledo of the Western League in 1885, for Hamilton of International League in 1886 and with Savannah of the Southern League in 1887. MacArthur had immigrated to the United States in 1864, living in Detroit. Bill Lee's research on MacArthur found that "for 30 years he was an inspector for the Department of Public Works." This is confirmed by the censuses for 1910 and 1920 (both of which misspell MacArthur's name). MacArthur died in Detroit on October 18, 1932. He was 70 years old. *(Total Baseball; Baseball-Reference.com; Baseball Necrology; U.S. Federal Census)*

Jimmy Macullar was a left-handed shortstop for the Baltimore Orioles 1884–86. While Macullar's obituary describes him as "one of the greatest pitchers ... of his time" and as the first left-hander to throw a curve ball, he pitched only three innings in the majors. Joining Syracuse as an outfielder in 1879, he returned to the majors as an outfield regular with Cincinnati in 1882 and moved on to Baltimore in 1884. The career .207 hitter reached .234 in 1882. His overall .865 fielding average was slightly below the league average; however, as an outfielder, he displayed a higher average (.910) and better range than his contemporaries. Macullar played and managed in the Western Association, leading that league with a .464 average in 1887. He later umpired in the American Association (1891) and the National League (1892). After leaving baseball, he "became a guard in the Maryland penitentiary." The 1910 census describes him as a deputy warden in the Baltimore city jail. Born in Boston to Scots and English parents, Macullar died in Baltimore on April 8, 1924, at age 69. *(Total Baseball; Baseball-Reference.com; Washington Post; New York Times; Chicago Daily Tribune; Encyclopedia of Minor League Baseball; U.S. Federal Census)*

Fergy Malone, an Irish-born catcher, spent five seasons in the National Association with Philadelphia and Chicago teams. Playing for the champion Athletics, he hit .343 in the inaugural season and led NA catchers in fielding in 1872. Malone also played with the Philadelphia White Stockings (1873 and 1875) and the Chicago White Stockings (1874). Already 34 years old, Malone played in only 22 games for the Athletics in the first National League season, before injuring his arm. Eight years later he managed the Philadelphia Keystones in the Union Association, getting a hit in the only game he played. In all, Malone hit .274; the left-handed catcher fielded .845, nineteen points higher than the league average. In the 1880 census for Philadelphia he is listed as a grocer. The 1900 census shows him working for the government in customs. Bill Lee says that Malone became a special agent for the treasury department, stationed at Puget Sound, WA. Born in 1842, Malone was a Civil War veteran. He died at Seattle on New Year's Day 1905 at age 62. *(Total Baseball; Baseball-Reference.com; U.S. Federal Census; Baseball Necrology; New York Times)*

Charlie Manlove debuted with the Altoona Mountain Citys on May 31, 1884, playing one game as an outfielder and one as a catcher. When Altoona closed, Manlove played in four games with the New York Gothams, finishing on June 17. Going hitless in New York, he converted his three Altoona hits into a .176 season average. He fielded .880 as a catcher, but had an error on his only outfield chance. Manlove went on to play for the Altoona team in the Pennsylvania State Association and the Boston Blues. Born in Philadelphia, he married a woman from Altoona and appears in the 1900 census there, working as a "gang boss" for the railroad. In the 1910 census Manlove has become a "segar" merchant, and in the 1930 census, he is a machinist for a steam railroad. He died in Altoona on February 12, 1952, at age 89. *(Retrosheet; Baseball-Reference.com; U.S. Federal Census; New York Times; Sporting Life)*

Fred Mann spent six seasons in the majors—five as a regular outfielder, hitting .262. Beginning with the Worcester Ruby Legs in 1882, he played with the Athletics, Columbus, Pittsburgh, and Cleveland of the American Association. After hitting a career-high .293 in 1887, the left-handed hitter was sold to St. Louis, but since there was "not enough snap about him," he was "turned ... out to pasture" at age 30. Mann later played in the minors at Charleston, Columbus and Hartford. The 1900 and 1910 censuses show him as a resident of Springfield, MA, working as a bartender and operating a retail liquor store. Born in Sutton, VT—the first Vermont native to play in the majors—Mann died at Springfield on April 16, 1916, at age 58. *(Total Baseball; Baseball-Reference.com; National Police Gazette; Atlanta Constitution; Baseball Necrology; U.S. Federal Census; Sporting Life)*

Jack Manning entered the majors with Boston of the National Association in 1873 when he was nineteen years old (seventeen, he said). In 1876 he moved with Boston into the National League. In all, Manning had three seasons in the NA and nine in the NL–American Association, hitting .257. Career stops include the Lord Baltimores and Hartford in the NA, Cincinnati, Boston, Buffalo and Philadelphia of the NL, and Baltimore of the AA. Career highlights include a .346 average in 1874, a .317 average in 1878, and hitting three homers in one game in 1884. Primarily one of the "greatest right fielders that ever caught a ball," he also pitched, going 18–5 with the 1876 Bostons, leading the league with 5 saves. In 1887 when he had finished in the majors, he claimed to be 33 years old, but the *National Police Gazette* doubted this figure, asserting that by his grey hair he had to be fifty. *Boston Daily Globe* identified him as "superintendent of Congress st. grounds," but Bill Lee says that Manning was a "theatrical mechanic in the performing arts business." This is confirmed by the 1910 census. In 1900 he is listed as a clerk and in 1920 as a janitor. Born in Braintree, MA, to Irish parents, Manning died in Boston on August 15, 1929, at age 75. *(Total Baseball; Boston Daily Globe; National Police Gazette; U.S. Federal Census; Baseball Necrology)*

Jim Manning played outfield for the 1884 Boston Beaneaters as a 22-year-old rookie, hitting .241, his best season. He had come to Boston from Springfield, IL, of the Northwestern League. Over a five year career—three as a regular—with Boston and the Detroit Wolverines of the National League and the Kansas City

Cowboys of the American Association, he hit .215. But he fielded .903, almost twenty points above the league average. Manning remained in baseball managing at Birmingham (1892) and Savannah (1893) of the Southern League and Kansas City (1894–1900) of the Western Association. As club president of the Kansas City Blues, he brought them into the American League as the Washington Senators in 1901. A 1907 note in *Sporting Life* describes Manning as "prospering in business in Kansas City." Manning was born in Fall River, MA, to Irish parents; he died on October 22, 1929, at Edinburg, TX, at age 67. Bill Lee notes that Manning had moved to Texas "as a land appraiser for the Gulf Coast Lines division of the Missouri Pacific Railroad." *(Total Baseball; Baseball-Reference.com; Boston Daily Globe; Baseball Necrology; Washington Post; Sporting Life)*

Tim Manning, an English-born second-baseman, immigrated to the United States in 1870. After beginning his major league career with Providence in 1882, he shifted to Baltimore of the American Association in 1883. He was a regular there in 1884, hitting .205. After splitting 1885 between the Orioles and Providence, Manning left the majors with a .189 average for four seasons. His .911 fielding average as a second baseman was fifteen points above the league average. Manning played for Aurora in 1889 and later for Garden Cities of the Chicago City League. In the 1900 census he is still listed as a "ball player." In 1909 *Sporting Life* reported that Manning was "engaged in business" in Chicago. Later censuses for Chicago show Manning as a porter and as a clerk for a wholesale grocery. He died in Oak Park, IL, on June 11, 1934, at age 80. *(Total Baseball; Baseball-Reference.com; Chicago Daily Tribune; U.S. Federal Census; Sporting Life)*

Mike Mansell, the middle of three baseball-playing brothers from Auburn, NY, played five seasons in the majors—all as a regular outfielder with Syracuse, Cincinnati, Pittsburgh, the Athletics and Richmond. He entered the majors in 1879 when Syracuse was admitted into the National League. After he and his brothers Tom and John formed the outfield for Albany in 1881, he returned to the majors with Pittsburgh, leading the American Association in doubles and triples while hitting .277 in 1882. When he finished with Richmond in 1884, he owned a .239 career batting average; his .854 fielding percentage and range factors exceeded the league average. After playing in the minors with Hamilton and Syracuse, Mansell became a "keeper in Auburn prison." The 1900 census lists him as a "saloon keeper." Mansell died of pneumonia on December 4, 1902, at age 44. *(Total Baseball; Baseball-Reference.com; U.S. Federal Census; Sporting News; DeadballEra.com)*

Tom Mansell was the oldest of three brothers, born to Irish parents, who advanced from the Auburn, NY, sandlots to the major leagues. He entered the majors with Troy in 1879; dropped to Albany in mid-season, he finished the year with Syracuse. In 1883 he hit .305 split between the Detroit Wolverines and St. Louis Browns. A regular outfielder with Cincinnati in the first part of 1884, Mansell finished his major league career that season with Columbus. In 191 games as an outfielder, he fielded only .751—much below the league average. At the plate he managed a .259 average. In 1887 he joined Kansas City of the Western League, beginning a 44-year relationship with that city. His baseball career over, he became a policeman and later chief of detectives in Kansas City, KS, holding that position until 1931. Mansell died back in Auburn on October 6, 1934, at age 79. His younger brother Mike was an outfielder—primarily with Pittsburgh; another younger brother, John, played with the Athletics in 1882. *(Total Baseball; Baseball-Reference.com; Washington Post; Chicago Daily Tribune; U.S. Federal Census; DeadballEra.com)*

Leech Maskrey was 28 years old when he and his brother joined the American Association Louisville Eclipse in 1882, coming from Akron. He played five seasons in the AA—four as a regular—before finishing with Cincinnati in 1886. A career .225 hitter, he reached .250 in 1884. A very sure-handed outfielder, he fielded .910—forty-seven points above the league average. In 1890 Maskrey was a member of the touring American team which spent a year teaching baseball in England. In 1891 he managed Tacoma, shifting to Atlanta in 1892, where he was termed the "best manager in the South." When his baseball career ended, Maskrey went into the hotel business with his brother, managing hotels at Kent and Warren, OH. Born in Mercer, PA, with an English father, he is listed as a resident of Mercer in the 1910 census. At that time he was proprietor of a billiards parlor. The 68-year-old Maskrey died at Mercer on April 1, 1922. *(Baseball-Reference.com; Atlanta Constitution; Chicago Daily Tribune; U.S. Federal Census; DeadballEra.com)*

Leech Maskrey (Library of Congress)

Bobby Mathews (T. Scott Brandon)

Bobby Mathews, a 5'5", 140-pounder, is credited with throwing the first spitball and the first outcurve. With Ft. Wayne in 1871, the 19-year-old won the first six of his 131 National Association victories, to be followed with 25 victories for the Lord Baltimores and 29-, 42- and 29-win seasons for the New York Mutuals. In 1875 he threw 69 complete games and 625 innings. Moving with the Mutuals into the National League in 1876, he had a 21–34 record for a second division club that folded at the end of the season. Over the next six seasons he sat out two while winning only 39 games among Cincinnati, Providence and Boston. Then in 1883 he joined the Philadelphia Athletics and enjoyed a renaissance in the American Association, winning 90 games in three seasons, finishing in 1887 with 166 NL/AA victories. His 297 victories are the most for any pitcher not found in the Hall of Fame. He umpired in the AA as a substitute in 1888 and as a regular in 1891. A Baltimore native, Mathews died in Baltimore on April 1, 1898, of diseases associated with syphilis. He was 46 years old. *(Total Baseball; Baseball Reference.com; David Zingler; Baseball Necrology)*

Clifford Virgil "C.V." Matteson debuted as the starting pitcher with the St. Louis Maroons on June 13, 1884. Tagged for nine hits and 11 runs (six earned) in 6 innings, he retired to the outfield, but received credit for the victory. With that outing, his major league career was over. *Sporting News* shows a Matteson pitching for Augusta in 1886. Most sources now agree that the Maroon was a product of Seville, OH, and that he was 22 years old when he pitched in the majors. Clifford V. Matteson appears in the 1880, 1900 and 1930 censuses for Seville. In the last two he is described as a clothing merchant and a dry goods merchant. Matteson died in Seville on December 18, 1931, at age 68. *(Total Baseball; Baseball-Almanac.com; Retrosheet; U.S. Federal Census; Sporting News)*

Steve Matthias was the regular shortstop for the Chicago Browns for the first part of 1884. In 37 games he hit .275, second highest among the team's regulars. His fielding percentage of .840 far exceeded the league average for shortstops. However, he did not accompany the team when it relocated to Pittsburgh. Matthias continued to play in the minors with Norfolk, Chattanooga, Nashville and Hartford to 1890. Born in Mitchellville, MD, Matthias died in Baltimore on July 29, 1891, at around the age of 31. He does not appear in the census for 1870 or 1880. *(Total Baseball; Baseball-Reference.com; U.S. Federal Census; Sporting Life)*

Al Maul pitched one game for the Philadelphia Keystones in 1884 — a complete game loss— as an 18-year-old. In 1898 at age 32 he became a twenty-game winner for Baltimore with a 2.10 ERA; in 1895 he led the National League with a 2.45 ERA while pitching for Washington; in 1890 he went 16–12 for the Pittsburgh Burghers. But overall his major league play was spotty: in eight of his 15 seasons, he won two or fewer games, and only five times did he work as many as one hundred innings. Maul played in both the Union Association and the Players League; otherwise his career was spent in the National League with Philadelphia, Pittsburgh, Brooklyn and New York, and he was one of a handful of the 1884 players to perform in the twentieth century. A career .241 hitter, he played 187 games in the outfield, where he performed much better than the average. A native of Philadelphia, "he scouted for the Athletics" after leaving the playing ranks. He "also worked in the ticket department of the A's and Phillies." Maul died on May 3, 1958, at age 92, the last surviving member of the Union Association. *(Sporting News; Total Baseball; Baseball-Reference.com; U.S. Federal Census)*

Tommy McCarthy had four mediocre major league trials with the Boston Reds, the Boston Beaneaters and Philadelphia Quakers. But after leading the New England League in hitting in 1886, McCarthy emerged at age 24 as a premier performer with the St. Louis Browns. From 1888 through 1896 with St. Louis, Boston, and Brooklyn, he hit .290 or higher seven times— with highs of .350 (1890), .349 (1894), and .346 (1893). He led the American Association with 83 steals in 1890 and stole 93 in 1888. He was considered an innovator who invented or perfected the hit and run, runner-batter signals, and the outfield trap. He helped the Browns win the AA championship in 1888 and the Beaneaters win the NL championship in 1892, hitting .381 in the 1892 World Series. McCarthy was named to the Hall of Fame in 1946 — more for his innovations than his .292 career batting average. After leaving the playing ranks, he coached baseball at Holy Cross and scouted. In addition, he and Hugh Duffy operated a bowling alley and a saloon. Born in Boston to Irish parents, he died there on August 5, 1922, at age 59. *(Total Baseball; Baseball-Reference.com; Baseballlibrary.com; U.S. Federal Census; Sporting Life)*

Al McCauley joined his hometown Indianapolis Hoosiers in 1884 as a left-handed pitcher and first baseman. As a pitcher he went 2–7, 5.09 ERA; as a first baseman he hit .189 for the hapless American Association club. McCauley returned to the majors in the expansion 1890 season as the regular first baseman of the Philadelphia Quakers, hitting .244 in 112 games. His 25 doubles placed seventh in the league. In 1891 he had his best season, hitting .282 as he shared first base duties for the AA Washington Statesmen. He is still listed as a ball player in the 1893–94 Indianapolis city directories. McCauley died in Wayne Township, IN, on August 24, 1917, at age 54. *(Baseball Encyclopedia; Baseball-Reference.com; Indiana Deaths; Indianapolis City Directory)*

Al Maul (Library of Congress)

Jim McCauley played two years at Union College before joined the St. Louis Browns for one game in September 1884. In 1885 he split 27 games between the Buffalo Bisons and Chicago White Stockings; in 1886 he played eleven games for the Brooklyn Trolley Dodgers, leaving the majors with a .189 batting average for 39 games and fielding statistics slightly below the league average. In 1891 *Sporting Life* noted, "Catcher McCauley ... is now running a grain elevator in Ithaca [NY]." Born in Stanley, NY, McCauley appears in the 1920 census as a resident of Canandaigua, NY; his occupation is listed as "Merchant — Produce dealer." McCauley died at Canandaigua on September 14, 1930, at age 67. *(Total Baseball; SABR Collegiate Database; Baseball Necrology; U.S. Federal Census; Sporting Life)*

Bill McClellan, a left-handed middle infielder, hit .242 in eight major league seasons. Primarily a second baseman, he also played shortstop and third base. According to the *National Police Gazette*, "Short field play is his forte." He entered the majors with the Chicago White Stockings in 1878, coming from St. Paul. After two years in the minors with Washington, he returned with Providence in 1881 and Philadelphia in 1883–84. Shifting to the American Association, he played with Brooklyn (1885–88) before finishing with Cleveland in 1888. McClellan hit .267 in 1885 and fielded .907 in 1886, but overall fielded 11 points below the league average. Later on he played with Denver, where, according to *Sporting Life*, he enjoyed his "second time on earth." The 1900 census for Chicago shows a 44-year-old William McClellan working as a shipping clerk. Born in Chicago to a Scots father and Canadian mother, McClellan died in Chicago on July 3, 1929, at age 73. *(Total Baseball; Baseball-Reference.com; New York Times; National Police Gazette; U.S. Federal Census; Sporting Life)*

Bill McCloskey, a thirty-year-old outfielder and catcher, played in half of the Wilmington Quicksteps' games in 1884. As a catcher he had six errors and thirteen passed balls in five games. As an outfielder he had seven errors in five games. At the plate he managed three hits for a .100 average. *Baseball-Reference.com* says that he also may likely be the McCloskey who caught 11 games for the National Association Washington team in 1875. That McCloskey hit .175 and committed 17 errors in 11 games. Bill McCloskey continued to play in the minors at Trenton, Syracuse, Binghamton and Portland. He was born in Philadelphia to Irish parents. Both the 1900 and 1910 censuses show him as a Philadelphia resident working as a cigar maker. He died in Philadelphia on July 9, 1924, at age 70. *(Total Baseball; Baseball-Reference.com; U.S. Federal Census; Sporting Life)*

James "Jerry" McCormick was the regular third baseman for the Baltimore Orioles in 1883 and for the Philadelphia Keystones and Washington Unions in 1884. Remarkably consistent at the plate, he hit .262 for the Orioles and .261 in the Union Association. In 1884 he led UA third basemen in fielding with an .806 mark. In 1888 *Sporting Life* reported that McCormick was tending bar in Philadelphia and that he had signed to play with Easton. Two years later, he was "enjoying his second wind," playing for Harrisburg. Born in Philadelphia around 1860, McCormick died on September 11, 1905, at about age 45. A James McCormick born to Irish parents in 1862 resided in Philadelphia in 1900, living with his sister and working as a bartender. This is likely to be the ball player. He does not appear in the 1910 census. *(Total Baseball; Baseball-Reference.com; U.S. Federal Census; Sporting Life)*

Jim McCormick saw his name become an adjective for a rising fastball as "a Jim McCormick upshoot." The 215-pound right-hander won 265 games in 10 seasons, twice topping the 40-win barrier. Breaking in with Indianapolis in 1878, he twice led the National League in victories while pitching for Cleveland, topped by a 45–28 mark

Bill McClellan (Wikimedia Commons)

Jim McCormick (Library of Congress)

Jim McDonald had three major league trials with three teams in three leagues. In 45 games McDonald managed only 24 hits—one in two games with the Washington Unions and 23 in 38 games with the Pittsburgh Alleghenys in 1884, and none in five games with the Buffalo Bisons in 1885—for a .145 average. He played at least one game at every field position. McDonald then served as a National League umpire in 1895 and 1897–99. A 1904 note in *Sporting Life* said that he had been umpiring in the California State League, where he was still active in 1909. In 1905 the paper noted that a benefit game had been played to help pay expenses for his illness. McDonald was from San Francisco. A James McDonald of roughly the right age is listed in the 1910 Federal Census for San Francisco, working as a clerk in the sheriff's office. The ballplayer died on September 14, 1914, in San Francisco at age 54. *(Total Baseball; Baseball-Reference.com; Baseball Necrology; U.S. Federal Census; Sporting Life)*

in 1880. McCormick also led the NL three times in complete games, twice in ERA, and twice in innings pitched. In 1884 he jumped from the Cleveland Blues after winning 19 games, finishing the season with the Cincinnati Outlaw Reds, for whom he won 21 games, seven by shutouts with a 1.54 ERA the rest of the season. Starting 1885 with Providence, he then went 20–4 with Chicago, helping the White Stockings win the championship. He went 31–11 in 1886 to help win another championship and posted a 3–3 record in World Series play. He was only thirty years old when he finished with Pittsburgh in 1887. McCormick "forsook the diamond for the bangtails," alleging that he "could make more money at horse-racing in a month than in baseball in a year." Born in Glasgow, Scotland, he grew up in Paterson, NJ, where he died on March 10, 1918, at age 61. *(Baseball-Reference.com; Total Baseball; National Police Gazette; Chicago Daily Tribune; Baseball Page)*

Jim McElroy, a graduate of St. Mary's College of California, joined the Philadelphia Quakers in May 1884. He made 13 starts, compiling a 1–12 record before being released in August. Before leaving the majors, McElroy pitched one game for the Wilmington Quicksteps of the Union Association, adding one more loss to his career statistics. In 1885 McElroy pitched for Norfolk of the Eastern League. He began 1886 with Memphis and then pitched for Topeka of the Western League before being released in August. According to Bill Lee, McElroy, a native of Napa, CA, committed suicide by injecting himself with morphine on July 24, 1889, in Needles, CA. He was only 26 years old. *(Baseball Reference.com; Washington Post; Baseball Necrology; Sporting Life)*

Chris McFarland began the 1884 season as an outfielder for the Baltimore Monumentals. In three games he had three hits for a .214 average and had committed three outfield errors. Tried as a pitcher, he started one game in which he gave up nine hits and 10 runs, five of which were earned, in three innings. He went on to play with Binghamton in 1885 and the Delaware Club of New York in 1886. McFarland was born in Fall River, MA, into a family that had emigrated from Nova Scotia. The 1880 federal census and the *Fall River City Directory* both list him as a clerk. Bill Lee says that McFarland was "prominent in the dry goods business." This is confirmed by the 1900 federal census, which lists him as a "partner in dry goods store." McFarland died on May 24,

1918, at New Bedford, MA, at age 56. *(Total Baseball; Baseball-Reference.com; Baseball Necrology; U.S. Federal Census; Fall River City Directory)*

James "Chippy" McGarr enjoyed a 10-year major league career—seven as a regular—in three leagues. The 20-year-old Worcester, MA, product debuted with the Chicago Browns in 1884, hitting .157 in 19 games. He returned to the majors in 1886 as the regular shortstop for the Philadelphia Athletics. After brief stops in St. Louis, Kansas City and Baltimore of the American Association, he became the third-base regular for the Boston Beaneaters in 1890, leading the National League in fielding. In 1895 and 1896 he helped Cleveland win back-to-back championships. The career .268 hitter reached .295 with the Athletics. As a third baseman, he fielded .903—twenty points over the league average.

"Chippy" McGarr (Library of Congress)

After leaving the majors, he coached baseball at Holy Cross and helped Cleveland sign Native American star Louis Socksalexis. In 1898 he was a candidate for a position as a National League umpire, and he actually umpired in 1899. Born to Irish parents in Worcester, he was listed as a teamster in the 1880 census. In the 1900 census, he is listed as an inmate of the Massachusetts Insane Asylum, where he died on June 6, 1904, at age 41. According to Bill Lee, McGarr suffered from paresis. *(U.S. Federal Census; Baseball Necrology; Total Baseball; Baseball-Reference.com; Sporting Life)*

George "Jumbo" McGinnis won 77 games in his first three seasons in the majors. Joining the American Association Browns in 1882, the 197-pounder posted records of 25–18, 28–16 and 24–16, leading the AA in shutouts in 1884. Already 28 years old when he entered the majors, McGinnis saw his win total drop to six in 1885. Traded to the Baltimore Orioles in 1886, he went 16–18. McGinnis finished his major league career with Cincinnati in June 1887, leaving with a 102–79, 2.95 ERA record. Failing eyesight forced his retirement, but his eyesight recovered, and he became an umpire, serving in the AA and the Inter-State League. He had worked as a glass blower before entering professional baseball and returned to that profession afterward. *Sporting Life* reported in 1896 that he also had opened a saloon in St. Louis. McGinnis died at St. Louis on May 18, 1934, at age 80. *(Total Baseball; Baseball-Reference.com; National Police Gazette; Chicago Daily Tribune; Sporting News; U.S. Federal Census; Sporting Life)*

John McGuinness, an Irish-born first baseman, debuted with the New York Mutuals on May 6, 1876. The nineteen-year-old went hitless at the plate and committed four errors in the field. Three years later, in 1879, he hit .294 in twelve games for the Syracuse Stars. In 1884 he played in 53 games as the regular first baseman for the Philadelphia Keystones. For his career he hit .244 in 66 games and had a fielding average of .954, marginally higher than the league average. Born in 1857, McGuinness came to the United States in 1865. In the 1910 census, he is listed as a New York City resident, working in a factory. McGuinness died at Binghamton, NY, on December 19, 1916, at age 69. *(Total Baseball; U.S. Federal Census; Baseball-Reference.com)*

James "Deacon" McGuire began his major league career in 1884 as a backup catcher to Fleet

"Deacon" McGuire (Library of Congress)

Walker at Toledo. He finished it on May 18, 1912, when, as a 48-year-old Detroit coach, he helped replace striking Tiger players for a game in Philadelphia. Between, he played for Rochester, Washington and Cleveland of the American Association; Detroit, Philadelphia, Washington and Brooklyn of the National League; and New York, Boston, and Cleveland of the American League. In twenty-six seasons with eleven clubs he hit .278 and set a record for career assists by a catcher. His greatest years were with Washington (1891–99). Seven times in his career he caught more than 100 games with a high of 132 games in 1895. Five times he hit over .300 with a high of .343 in 1897. He served as player-manager with Washington (1898), as manager of the Red Sox (1907–08) and Cleveland (1909–11) and as a coach for the Tigers (1912–17). He later scouted for the Tigers and coached at Albion College. When he retired from baseball, he became a chicken farmer at Duck Lake, MI. He died there on October 31, 1936, at age 72. *(Total Baseball; Baseball-Reference.com; U.S. Federal Census; Sporting News)*

Frank McKee played in four games for the Washington Unions in 1884, managing three singles for a .176 average. In three games in the outfield he committed errors on four of five fielding chances. He also caught and played third base. In 1885 Alexandria was hoping to sign a player named McKee from Washington. This could be the player. *Retrosheet* lists McKee as a Philadelphian by birth. *(Retrosheet; Baseball-Reference.com; Sporting Life)*

Jim McKeever, a 23-year-old catcher and outfielder, hit .136 in 16 games for the Boston Reds at the beginning of 1884. He continued to play in the minors for Waterbury, the Boston Unions, Minneapolis and Easton. The son of an Irish iron worker who had immigrated to South Boston from New Brunswick, McKeever appears in the 1880 census as a 19-year-old who "Works in Iron Mill." In the 1890 *Boston City Directory*, he is still listed as a "ball player." At age 36 McKeever contacted brain fever and died in Boston on August 19, 1897. *(Total Baseball; Baseball-Reference.com; Baseball Necrology; U.S. Federal Census; Sporting Life; Boston City Directory)*

Ed McKenna had three major league trials eleven years apart. He played first base for the Philadelphia White Stockings of the National Association on July 29, 1874, going hitless but performing flawlessly at first base. Three years later he played center field for the St. Louis Brown Stockings in the National League, getting a hit and fielding his position without error. In 1884 he played in 32 games for the Washington Unions. At the plate he hit .188. Tried as a catcher, he suffered 47 passed balls and committed 22 errors in 23 games. Most sources give him a St. Louis birthplace. The censuses of 1880 and 1910 show a brick mason named Edward McKenna, born to Irish parents, living in St. Louis. However, Peter Morris believes that the Ed McKenna records may actually have been the work of three different players — including a Philadelphian named F. McKenna and a St. Louis policeman named Patrick McKenna. *(Baseball-Reference.com; Retrosheet; petermorrisbooks.com; U.S. Federal Census)*

Larry McKeon pitched 512 innings as an 18-year-old rookie in 1884. A product of New York City, he debuted with Indianapolis, going

18–41. This constituted sixty-two percent of the Hoosiers' wins for the season. According to the *New York Times*, McKeon had "a very slow delivery." The *Times* explained that he "handles the ball nearly a minute before he delivers it." In 1885 McKeon led the Western League with an 11–2 record. When the league folded in June, he signed with Detroit but jumped to Cincinnati of the American Association. In the remaining days of 1885, McKeon threw 290 innings and won 20 games for the Red Stockings. After an 8–8 start in 1886, he went to Kansas City, where he finished with an 0–2 record, leaving the majors at age 20 with 46 victories. In 1896 *Sporting Life* said that McKeon had become a "Cincinnati drink-mixer." Two years later the same paper noted that he had been arrested for "highway robbery" in Indianapolis, adding that "booze" was at the bottom of it. McKeon died in Indianapolis on July 18, 1915, from "Pulmonary pneumonia and excessive drinking," according to Bill Lee. *(Total Baseball; Baseball-Reference.com; New York Times; Baseball Necrology; Sporting News; Sporting Life)*

Alex McKinnon joined the New York Giants in 1884, hitting .272 as the regular first baseman. Already 27 years old, he had played professionally since 1876 but had been out of baseball since 1879. Under contract with Philadelphia in 1883, he did not play because of illness. In 1885 McKinnon shifted to the St. Louis Maroons, where he hit .294 and .301 and led the league in fielding in 1885, when he also served as manager for 39 games. In December 1886 McKinnon may have been part of the first National League trade when the Maroons sent him to the Pittsburgh Alleghenys for Otto Schonburg and $400. He was hitting .340 for the Alleghenys in 1887 when he was stricken with typhoid in July. The 30-year-old Boston native died at his home in Charlestown on July 27, 1887. *Sporting Life* writers in both Syracuse and Philadelphia hold McKinnon's work at first base as the standard by which younger players are to be measured. The career .296 hitter was described as a "terrific hitter but a very slow runner." *(Baseball Reference.com; New York Times; Chicago; Boston Daily Globe; DeadballEra.com; Sporting Life)*

Bernard "Barney" McLaughlin played three seasons in the majors with three teams in three leagues. In 1884 the Irish-born McLaughlin is listed as a regular outfielder for the Kansas City Unions, but he also filled in as a middle infielder and even pitched seven games. In 1887 he played fifty games as a second baseman for the Philadelphia Quakers; and in the expansion 1890 season, he was the regular shortstop for the American Association Syracuse Stars, hitting .264. In all, he hit .243 in 178 games. In 1884 he played beside his brother Frank on the Unions. In 1896 *Sporting Life* reported that Barney was on the verge of suicide. His friends had sent him to an institution to cure him of alcoholism, but "the love for drink returned." McLaughlin died in Lowell, MA, on February 13, 1921, at the approximate age of 59. A Barney McLaughlin played shortstop for Lowell in 1904 and later managed a café in Manchester. But since Boston considered that Barney McLaughlin to be a "comer," he is probably not the 1884 player. *(Total Baseball; Baseball-Reference.com; U.S. Federal Census; Sporting Life)*

Frank McLaughlin played 107 major league games for five teams in three leagues. The Lowell, MA, native played 15 games for the Worcester Ruby Legs in the second part of 1882. He appeared in 29 games for the Pittsburgh Alleghenys in 1883, and split 1884 among three Union Association clubs in Cincinnati, Chicago and Kansas City. Overall, he hit .228 while playing shortstop, second base and some outfield. His fielding statistics — except for second base play — are below the league average. The 1870 census for Lowell shows an Irish family of laborers named McLaughlin with sons Frank, age 13, and Bernard, age 8. That census shows Frank to have been born in Ireland; he is already employed at the cotton mill. The 1910 census for Lowell also shows Frank McLaughlin to be working in a cotton mill. He died in Lowell on April 5, 1917, at age 61. *(Total Baseball; Baseball-Reference.com; U.S. Federal Census)*

James (or William) McLaughlin was the shortstop for the Washington Unions in the first part of May 1884. In ten games he hit only .189. In nine games at shortstop he had 14 errors for a .696 fielding average. Tried at third base for one game he had even more difficulty, booting three of four balls hit to him. Born in San Francisco "around 1861," McLaughlin later became a Sacramento policeman, disappearing in 1893. Peter Morris asserts that McLaughlin "likely died then or shortly thereafter." Latest findings from the SABR Biographical Committee show that he moved to the state of Washington and played baseball around Tacoma in the 1890s. He died in 1936 at Gig Harbor, WA. *(Total Baseball; Baseball-Reference.com; petermorisbooks.com; SABR Biographical Committee Newsletter)*

Jim McLaughlin, a twenty-three-year-old lefty, made three starts for the Baltimore Orioles at the beginning of 1884. He went 1–2, 3.68 ERA in these games and finished on July 14. The Cleveland native died on November 16, 1895, when a Cleveland streetcar on which he was riding plunged into the Cuyahoga River. He was just two days from his 35th birthday. Bill Lee says that McLaughlin was a printer. *(Total Baseball; Retrosheet; Baseball Necrology; DeadBallEra.com)*

Tom McLaughlin joined the American Association Louisville Eclipse in 1883 and by 1884 had become the regular shortstop, shifting to second base in 1885. Acquired by the New York Mets in 1886, he served as the team captain. Despite the belief that he was one of the "cleverest all-round players in the American Association," he hit only .136 and was sent "back to the farm." McLaughlin finished his major league career by playing fourteen games for Washington in 1891. While he hit only .192 for his five seasons, both his range and his .920 average far exceeded those of shortstops of his time. McLaughlin later played in the minors with St. Paul and Syracuse. Bill Lee found that McLaughlin "worked for the Standard and Sanitary Manufacturing Company in Louisville." His death certificate lists him as a "brass finisher." Born in Louisville to Irish immigrant parents, he died there on July 21, 1921, at age 61. *(Total Baseball; National Police Gazette; New York Mets Hall of Records; Baseball Necrology; Kentucky Death Records; U.S. Federal Census)*

John "Bid" McPhee played eighteen seasons in the majors (1882–1897), all with Cincinnati and all as a second baseman. He joined the Red Stockings as a free agent in 1882, having played at Akron in 1881. A trained bookkeeper with a position in Akron, he was reluctant to leave the business world for baseball, which he played at a Hall of Fame level. A career .271 hitter, he was over .300 three times, leading the American Association in homers in 1886 and in triples in 1887. In that season he also stole 95 bases. But it was as a fielder that he made his Hall of Fame reputation, leading the AA or NL in fielding 8 times, in putouts eight times, in assists five times, and in double plays eleven times—all without benefit of a glove until he was 39 years old. His career .944 fielding average is twenty-five points higher than the league average, and his range factors are sixty points higher. He was much praised for his leadership and his sportsman-like behavior throughout his career. After retiring as a player in 1899,

"Bid" McPhee (Library of Congress)

he came back to manage the Phillies for a season and a half, leading the club to a fourth place finish in 1901. After that, he scouted for nine years, and then retired to California. He died at San Diego on January 3, 1943, at age 83. McPhee was elected to the National Baseball Hall of Fame in 2000. *(Total Baseball; Baseball Encyclopedia; SABR Biography Project; New York Times; Sporting News)*

William "Mox" McQuery debuted with the Cincinnati Outlaw Reds in August 1884, hitting .280 in 35 games. When the Union Association folded, McQuery became a National League player with Detroit (1885) and Kansas City (1886). He came back to the majors with the Syracuse Stars of the American Association in 1890, hitting a career high .308, before finishing with the Washington Statesmen in 1891. In five seasons he hit .271. The 6'4" McQuery had great range as a first baseman, fielding .973, slightly above the league average. A native of Gerrard County, Kentucky,

McQuery became a policeman in Covington, KY, after leaving baseball. On June 10, 1900, he was shot on a Cincinnati streetcar while trying to arrest two men wanted for murder. McQuery died two days later on June 12, just short of his thirty-ninth birthday. *(Total Baseball; Baseball-Almanac; Greater Cincinnati Police Historical Society; DeadballEra.com)*

McRemer played right field for the Washington Unions on June 20, 1884, in a game at Boston. In the 6–1 loss he was hitless in three at bats, but handled two chances in the field without error. It is likely that he was a local Boston player recruited for the day. *(Baseball Almanac; Total Baseball)*

John "Trick" McSorley, a tiny infielder who stood only 5'4", played with his hometown St. Louis Red Stockings in the National Association in 1875 when he was 23 years old. According to *Baseball-Fever.com*, McSorley was "removed from the team for crooked play." In 1884 he returned to the majors for twenty-one games with Toledo of the American Association. He also played two games for the St. Louis Maroons in 1885 and five games with the St. Louis Browns in 1886. Counting his year in the NA, he had a major league career of 43 games over twelve years, in which he hit .233. McSorley played and umpired in the minors into the 1890s. The census of 1900 shows him living with his mother in St. Louis, working as a plumber. The 1920 census lists him as a police officer. According to Bill Lee, McSorley joined the St. Louis police force in 1903, retiring in 1931. He died on February 9, 1936, at age 83. *(Total Baseball; Baseball-Reference.com; Baseball-Fever.com; Baseball Necrology; U.S. Federal Census; Sporting Life)*

Pete Meegan, a 21-year-old pitcher from the Bay Area of California, won seven and lost twelve for the American Association Richmond Virginians in 1884. Described as "a pitcher of more than ordinary ability," Meegan pitched for Reading and then joined the Pittsburgh Alleghenys in 1885, winning seven more games, his most "elusive" pitch being a drop ball. When he left the majors, he had compiled a 14–20, 3.90 ERA record. Meegan pitched for the powerful Haverly club of San Francisco both before and after his major league experience. He appears in the 1880 census for San Francisco; the son of Irish parents, he was working as a clerk in a leather store. The 1900 census shows him as a saloon keeper. Following a "brief illness," Meegan died at San Francisco on March 15, 1905, at age 42. *(Baseball-Reference.com; Professional Baseball in Pittsburgh; U.S. Federal Census; Baseball Page.com; Sporting Life)*

Frank Meinke pitched and played shortstop for the 1884 Detroit Wolverines. The 21-year-old Chicago native posted an 8–23, 3.18 ERA record as a pitcher; as a shortstop he hit .164. After the first game in 1885, he developed a sore arm and was "laid off." *National Police Gazette* predicted that he would make a rapid recovery since the layoff was "without pay." However, he left the majors at that time. In 1886 *Sporting Life* reported that Meinke had been pitching for Denver and had signed with the Chicago Blues, a strong independent team. The 1910 census shows Meinke living in Chicago, working as an agent for a brewery. His son Bob, who would later play for the Reds, is listed as a "baseball player." Bill Lee identifies Meinke as a "street department foreman"; this is confirmed by the 1920 census. Meinke, born to German immigrant parents, died in Chicago on November 8, 1931, at age 68. *(New York Times; National Police Gazette; Total Baseball; Baseball-Reference.com; Baseball Necrology; U.S. Federal Census; Sporting Life)*

John B. "George" Meister, a German-born third baseman, joined the American Association Toledo Blue Stockings in August 1884. The 1900 census shows that Meister had immigrated to the United States in 1883, so his mastery of baseball skills must have been very rapid. The twenty-year-old hit .193 and committed 15 errors in 34 games for a .817 percentage. Both marks were well below the league average. A player named Meister — possibly the same person — played for Allentown of the Atlantic League in 1888. The 1900 census lists Meister as a Pittsburgh resident and a saloon keeper. According to Bill Lee, Meister also operated a hotel in Pittsburgh. The 44-year-old Meister died at Pittsburgh on August 24, 1908. *(Baseball-Reference.com; Baseball Necrology; U.S. Federal Census; Baseball Encyclopedia; Sporting Life)*

Ed Merrill, a Maysville, KY, product, played one game as an outfielder for the American Association Louisville Eclipse in 1882, before his twenty-second birthday. Later that season, he played two games for the National League Worcester Ruby Legs as a third baseman. After further seasoning at Fort Wayne, he returned to Indianapolis as a regular second baseman in 1884, hitting .179 in 55 games before being released in July. The 1880 census shows that Merrill, the son of a Methodist bishop, was already living in Chicago.

The 1900 census shows him as a post office clerk; subsequent censuses show that he had become a bookkeeper for an insurance company. Merrill died in Elmwood Park, IL, on January 29, 1946, at age 85. *(Total Baseball; Baseball-Reference.com; Retrosheet; U.S. Federal Census)*

Levi Meyerle was more than thirty years old when the National League was formed in 1876. He had been a National Association regular for five years—four in Philadelphia with the Athletics and White Stockings— hitting NA pitching at a .365 clip, twice leading the league in hitting, and once in homers. In the inaugural 1871 season he hit .491 for the Athletics. In 1874, playing for the Chicago White Stockings, he hit .394. His strong hitting continued for the first two years of the NL, as he hit .340 for the Athletics and .327 for the Cincinnati Red Stocking before an ankle injury ended his NL career. In 1884 the 38-year-old Meyerle played in three games for the Union Association Keystones, managing one hit. In his eight-year career, he played every position except catcher, but was used mostly at third base. Labeled "not a star defensively," he fielded .796 for his entire career, seventeen points below the league average. Born in Philadelphia, Meyerle is listed as a plasterer in the 1870 census. In 1890 the *Philadelphia City Directory* gives his profession as "lather." Meyerle died in Philadelphia on November 4, 1921, at age 76. *(Total Baseball; Baseball-Reference.com; U.S. Federal Census; Philadelphia City Directory)*

Lou Meyers caught two games for his hometown Cincinnati Outlaw Reds in the spring of 1884—the season opener against Altoona on April 17 and a home game against Baltimore on May 10. He was hitless in three at bats. Nicknamed "Crazy Horse," Meyers was 24 years old at the time. Bill Lee found that Meyers worked as a porter after leaving baseball and that he died in Cincinnati from self-administered strychnine poisoning on November 30, 1920. Both his first name, "Louis" or "Lewis," and his last name, "Meyers" or "Myers," create problems in searching the census. *(Total Baseball; Baseball-Reference.com; Baseball Almanac; Baseball Necrology; U.S. Federal Census; DeadballEra.com)*

Ed Miller played outfield for the Toledo Blue Stockings in July and August 1884. In eight games he hit .250, but in the field he committed five errors for a .615 average. *Retrosheet* gives a birthplace of Tecumseh, MI. *Baseball-Almanac.com* says that he attended Lebanon Valley College. *(Baseball-Reference.com; Retrosheet; Baseball Almanac)*

George Miller caught eleven games for the National League Cincinnati Red Stockings in 1877. Seven years later he caught six games for the American Association Red Stockings, leaving the majors with 11 hits, good for a .193 average. His fielding percentage for those seventeen games was .938, 49 points above the league average. In 1885 *Sporting Life* refers to him as "one of the finest little backstops in the country" and regrets that he is "without engagement." Born to German parents in Newport, KY, across the Ohio River from Cincinnati, Miller appears in the 1900, 1910 and 1920 censuses as a resident of the Cincinnati suburb of Norwood, OH. According to Bill Lee, Miller worked as a machinist for Allis-Chalmers. The census describes him as an electric machinist and later as a trunk maker. Miller died in Norwood on July 24, 1929, at age 76. *(Total Baseball; Baseball Necrology; Baseball-Reference.com; U.S. Federal Census; Sporting Life)*

George "Doggie" Miller was used primarily as a catcher throughout thirteen major league sea-

"Doggie" Miller (Library of Congress)

sons with Pittsburgh, St. Louis and Louisville. However, he was the regular rightfielder for Pittsburgh during his rookie season of 1884 and played every position except pitcher during his career. Miller moved with the Alleghenys into the National League in 1887, and spent the remainder of his career in the NL. A career .267 hitter, he hit .339 in 1894, the year he served as playing manager for the St. Louis Browns, leading them to ninth place. There he is credited with the statement that he "couldn't throw hard enough to dent a pane of glass." After finishing his major league career with Louisville in 1896, he hit .336 while managing Minneapolis in 1897. He later managed at Fort Wayne and Saginaw. Miller was born and later lived in Brooklyn. However, there are a number of George Millers of the right age, which makes identifying the ballplayer difficult. He died at Ridgewood, NY, on April 6, 1909, at age 44. (*Baseball Encyclopedia; Retrosheet; Stew Thornley; Baseball Historian; Encyclopedia of Minor League Baseball; Sporting Life; Complete New York Clipper Baseball Biographies*)

Joe Miller moved with the Toledo franchise from the Northwestern League to the American Association in 1884. The regular shortstop for the Blue Stockings, he hit .239 in 105 AA games. After Toledo was dropped from the league, Miller moved on to Louisville in 1885. Once again the regular shortstop, he hit only .183 and left the majors in September with a career .214 average for two seasons. However, his .876 fielding average exceeded the league average for shortstops. He played in 1886 with Savannah. His father a German immigrant, Miller was born in Baltimore and moved to Wheeling, WV. He appears in the 1900, 1910 and 1920 censuses for Wheeling, living there with his sisters and working as a stoker for a coal gas company and later as an engineer for Wheeling Water Department. He died at Wheeling on April 23, 1928, at age 67. (*Total Baseball; Baseball-Reference.com; SABR Baseball Encyclopedia; Baseball Necrology; Atlanta Constitution; U.S. Federal Census*)

Joseph "Cyclone" Miller pitched for three clubs in 1884. After pitching one game with the Chicago Browns, he shifted to the Providence Grays, finishing with the Philadelphia Quakers. Among the three clubs he compiled four wins and a 3.25 ERA. After pitching for Macon in the Southern Association, he returned with the A's in 1886, going 10–8, 2.97 ERA. Despite the *Atlanta*

"Cyclone" Miller (Wikimedia Commons)

Constitution's judgment that he "has great speed and all the curves," he went out of the majors that season and was judged by the *National Police Gazette* to a "very short lived" phenomenon. Miller pitched at Lincoln of the Western League in 1887. A native of Springfield, MA, he lived in New London, CT. The 1910 census shows him working at the paper mill. He died at New London on October 13, 1916, at age 57. (*National Police Gazette; Atlanta Constitution; Total Baseball; Baseball-Reference.com; U.S. Federal Census; Sporting Life*)

John "Jocko" Milligan, a product of Girard College in Philadelphia, joined the A's from Pottstown in 1884 and immediately led American Association catchers in fielding. Over the next ten years he hit a solid .286 with three seasons over .300. He hit .366 in 1889 and led the AA in doubles in 1891. Traded to St. Louis in 1888, he helped the Browns win the AA championship and hit .400 in the World Series. Milligan also played with the Players League Philadelphia club, and with National League clubs in Washington, Baltimore, and New York, before leaving the majors in 1893. In 585 games behind the plate he fielded .930 — sixteen points above the league average. After playing and managing in the minors at Reading, he invested in real estate and later became a tipstaff for the city of Philadelphia. Born in Philadelphia to Irish parents, Milligan died on August 29, 1923, at age 62. (*Total Baseball; Baseball-Reference.com; SABR*

"Jocko" Milligan (Library of Congress)

Biography Project; U.S. Federal Census; Sporting Life)

Joe Moffett joined the Toledo Blue Stockings in 1884, appearing in 56 games. Used primarily at first base, he hit .201 and fielded his position at .957 — almost exactly the league average. Toledo was dropped from the American Association at the end of the season, ending Moffett's major league career. The Wheeling, WV, native was the younger brother of Sam Moffett, who debuted with Cleveland the same year. Joe Moffett had mined in Montana prior to playing professional baseball, and he is listed in the 1880 census for Butte and the 1900 census for Madison, working as a copper miner. Born to Irish parents, Joe Moffett died in San Bernardino, CA, on February 24, 1935. He was 75 years old. *(Baseball-Reference.com; Retrosheet; SABR Baseball Encyclopedia; U.S. Federal Census)*

Sam Moffett joined the Cleveland Blues in 1884 as a 27-year-old pitcher and outfielder. The Wheeling, WV, native went 3–19 as a pitcher and hit .184. Moffett had later trials with the Indianapolis Hoosiers in 1887 and 1888. Playing for seventh and eighth place teams, he left the majors with a 6–29 pitching record and a .169 batting average. Older brother James had gone to Montana earlier as a copper miner. Younger brother Joe, who played for Toledo, had also worked as a copper miner in Montana. Samuel appears in the 1880 census as working in an iron mill. Presumably he joined his brothers in Montana. In 1889 *Sporting Life* reported that Moffett had struck "pay dirt," as his Montana lead mine had made $40,000. Moffett died at Butte, MT, on May 5, 1907, at age 50. *(Baseball-Reference.com; Chicago Daily Tribune; New York Times; U.S. Federal Census; Sporting Life)*

Frank Monroe, an outfielder and catcher from Hamilton, OH, joined the Indianapolis Hoosiers in July 1884. He played in two home games on the 18th and 20th against Toledo and Cincinnati — one as an outfielder and one as a catcher. He was hitless in eight at bats and allowed eight passed balls in his effort as a catcher. In May of 1885, he was dismissed as manager of the Chattanooga club. Nothing more is known of his life at this time. *(Total Baseball; Baseball-Reference.com; Retrosheet; Sporting Life)*

Henry S. "Harry" Moore played outfield and shortstop for the Washington Unions in 1884. His 155 hits and .336 average placed him third in the Union Association in both categories. His .820 fielding percentage placed him among the better outfielders in the league. Even with these statistics, he is essentially lost. Peter Morris says that Moore was born in California "around 1862." He married in 1890, and his wife remarried in 1906; it isn't clear whether Moore died or divorced in the interim. Morris speculates that Moore died in San Francisco around the turn of the century when death records were mostly lost because of the earthquake. *(Total Baseball; Retrosheet; Baseball-Reference.com; petermorrisbooks.com; U.S. Federal Census)*

Jerrie Moore, a left-handed hitting Canadian, was a regular catcher and outfielder for the Altoona Unions in early 1884. He hit .313 in 20 games before the club folded. Later in the season he played in nine games for the Cleveland Blues and six for the Detroit Wolverines in 1885. However, he found National League pitching harder to solve and ended with a .263 average for his 35 major league games. With 35 errors and 54 passed balls in 27 games, his catching was below the league average. Moore went on to play for the

Hamilton Clippers until 1888. He died in Wayne, MI, on September 26, 1890, at age 34 or 35. *(Baseball-Reference.com; Total Baseball; Sporting Life)*

Bill Morgan, a 29-year-old catcher and outfielder, entered the majors with the Pittsburgh Alleghenys in 1882 when the American Association became a major league. In that season he got into 17 games, hitting .258. Returning to the AA with Richmond in 1884, he played in six more games before moving over to the Baltimore Monumentals for a final two games. In all, he hit .221 in 25 major league games. His .779 fielding percentage over three positions was more than 100 points below the league average. *Baseball-Reference* and *Baseball Page* give him an 1853 birthdate in Washington, DC. *Retrosheet* says that he was born in Brooklyn. *(Total Baseball; Baseball Almanac; Baseball-Reference.com; Baseball Page; Retrosheet)*

Bill Morgan played outfield for the Washington Nationals for the first 45 games of 1884, hitting .173. He had entered the majors with the Pittsburgh Alleghenys in August 1883, hitting .158 in 32 games. His page sponsor for *Baseball-Reference.com* notes that Morgan is "the only player in major league history to play all four up-the-middle positions every season." Morgan fielded below the league average in all four positions. *Retrosheet* and *Baseball-Almanac* now give Morgan a birthplace (Brooklyn), a birth year (1856), and a date and place of death (September 7, 1908 in New York City). *(SABR Baseball Encyclopedia; Baseball-Reference.com; Retrosheet; Baseball Almanac)*

Gene Moriarity became an outfielder for the Boston Beaneaters in June 1884, when he was only 19 years old. After four games in Boston, he finished the season with the Indianapolis Hoosiers. Between the two clubs he hit .170 in 14 games and lost two starts as a pitcher. Sold to the Detroit Wolverines in 1885, he committed 9 errors in 12 games and hit .052. Moriarity's best season was 1892 when he returned to the majors to play 47 games as an outfielder with the St. Louis Browns. In three seasons he hit .152 in 72 games. Moriarity was born in 1865 to Irish parents in Holyoke, MA. He "works in scissors shop," according to the 1880 census. The last record of Moriarity was in 1893, when he was still an active player. Peter Morris places him on the "Hot cold cases" list. *(petermorrisbooks.com; Total Baseball; Baseball-Reference.com; U.S. Federal Census)*

John "Honest John" Morrill joined the Boston Red Caps in the inaugural 1876 National League season, coming from Lowell. He spent the next 13 seasons in Boston, primarily as a first baseman, being judged "pre-eminent at that position" by the *National Police Gazette*. A .260 career hitter, he reached .319 for the NL champions in 1883 — when he also led NL first basemen in fielding. Field captain for a number of seasons, Morrill also became manager in 1883, holding that position through 1888. Released to Washington in 1889, he also managed that team. In 1890 he became "head of the Brotherhood scheme to establish a club in Boston," finishing his career with the Players League Boston Reds. After leaving the playing ranks, he wrote sporting news for the *Boston Journal* and later was described as "doing well" in the sporting goods business, from which he retired in 1931. Born in Boston to Irish parents, Morrill died in Boston on April 2, 1932, at age 77. *(Boston Daily Globe; Washington Post;*

John Morrell (*sic*) (Library of Congress)

National Police Gazette; Chicago Daily Tribune; Baseball-Reference.com)

Ed "Cannon-Ball" Morris, a Brooklyn-born lefthander, attended St. Mary's College in California and came east with his battery mate Fred Carroll. Joining Columbus in 1884, he went 34–13 with the Buckeyes, leading the American Association in winning percentage. Purchased by Pittsburgh at the end of the season, he spent the remainder of his career pitching for Pittsburgh teams in three leagues. In 1885 he led the AA in starts, innings and strikeouts while winning 39 games. The following season he led the AA with 41 wins and 12 shutouts — for which he received a salary of $2,500. For his career he won 171 games, completing 297 of 307 starts. By 1889 he is described as a piece of "worn out machinery — too badly used up to admit of repair." When Fred Carroll died in 1904, his obituary noted that Morris "now runs a pool room at No. 22 La Cock Street, Allegheny, Pa." The 1900 census shows Morris as a saloon keeper; in 1910 he is described as a liquor dealer. Morris died in Pittsburgh on April 12, 1937, at age 74. *(Baseball-Reference.com; Washington Post; Sporting Life; SABR Collegiate Database; U.S. Federal Census; Sporting Life)*

James Morris played in one major league game, a home game for the Baltimore Monumentals, on September 11, 1884. Starting in center field against Cincinnati, he went hitless in three at bats and had no fielding chances. In the 11–2 loss he pitched one inning, giving up two hits and one earned run. *Retrosheet* and *Total Baseball* give him a Trenton, NJ, birthplace. There actually was a James Morris living in Trenton in 1880, a 19-year-old son of English parents, working as a puddler. *(Total Baseball; Baseball-Reference.com; U.S. Federal Census; Retrosheet)*

Peter Morris played shortstop for the Washington Unions on May 14, 1884. He was hitless in three at bats and handled three of four fielding chances at his position. Baseball historian Peter Morris did extensive research on the baseball player and found that he was a Welsh-born resident of Ixonia, WI, and a member of the Milwaukee Reserves baseball team. While his club was in Chicago for games with the Chicago Reserves, Morris was borrowed for the day by the Unions to complete a lineup against the Chicago Browns. Working as a freight conductor, the 30-year-old Morris was killed while coupling railroad cars in December of 1884. *(Baseball-Reference.com; petermorrisbooks.com)*

Jon Morrison led the International League in batting average (.346), runs, and hits while playing for Toronto in 1886. Entering the majors with Indianapolis in August 1884, he became the club's regular outfielder for the remainder of the season. In 44 games, he hit a respectable .264. After his Toronto experience, Morrison returned to the majors in 1887, playing in nine games for the New York Mets, but hitting only .118. For his 53 major league games, Morrison hit .241 and fielded .756 — ninety-eight points below the league average. While most sources make him a native of London, Ontario, *Baseball Historian* gives him a Port Huron, MI, birthplace. Two Canadian sources do not place him in the all-time list of Canadian major leaguers. Peter Morris says that Morrison married in Utica, NY, in 1887. His name is too common to make tracing reliable.

"Cannon Ball" Morris (Library of Congress)

(Baseball-Reference.com; Total Baseball; Encyclopedia of Minor League Baseball; Baseball Historian; petermorrisbooks.com)

Tom Morrissey hit only .170 as the regular third baseman of the Milwaukee Cream Citys for their 12 games in the Union Association in 1884. He also committed nine errors at third base, giving him a .710 fielding average, lowest for any regular in the league. Earlier he had played two games as a third baseman for the Detroit Wolverines in 1882, games previously assigned to his brother John, who had played third base for Buffalo in 1881. Tom Morrissey continued to play in the high minors with Milwaukee and St. Paul. An 1896 note in *Sporting Life* mentions "Old Tom Morrissey" as the first baseman for Columbus. Born in Janesville, WI, to Irish parents, Tom Morrissey became a policeman there after leaving baseball, and he held that position for 27 years. After a long illness, he died at Janesville on September 23, 1941, at age 81. *(Baseball Encyclopedia; Baseball-Reference.com; Retrosheet; Baseball Necrology; U.S. Federal Census; Sporting Life)*

Charlie Morton entered the majors in 1882 as an outfielder and infielder, splitting time between Pittsburgh and St. Louis of the American Association. In 1883 he managed Toledo to a Northwestern League title, returning to the majors as playing manager of the Blue Stockings in 1884. In that season he won a showdown with Cap Anson over the use of Fleet Walker in an exhibition game. In 1885 he also served as a playing manager for Detroit, leaving the majors with a .194 batting average for 88 games and a 121–153 record as manager. In later years, Morton managed Toledo (1890) and the Minneapolis Millers (1892–93); he founded the Ohio-Pennsylvania League, serving as its president (1905–1912) and umpiring. In the census of 1910, Morton is listed as a resident of Akron and a baseball manager. The native of Kingston, OH, died at the Massillon State Hospital on December 5, 1921, at age 67. Bill Lee notes that his death was the result of "generalized paralysis of the insane." *(Total Baseball; Baseball-Reference.com; Encyclopedia of Minor League Baseball; Baseball Necrology; U.S. Federal Census)*

William "Sparrow" Morton made two home starts for the Philadelphia Quakers in 1884. On July 15 he lost to New York 4–3; on July 26 he lost to Providence 16–3. The left-hander gave up sixteen hits and ten earned runs in the two games. In 1885 Morton managed and pitched for Defiance, "a first-class, semi-professional club." *(Baseball-Reference.com; Total Baseball; Sporting Life; SABR Baseball Encyclopedia)*

Frank Mountain compiled a 49–50 record in 1883–84 with the American Association Columbus Buckeyes, working more than 860 innings. The Union College product pitched briefly with Troy in 1880 and with Detroit in 1881. In 1882 he was a combined 4–22 between Worcester and the Philadelphia Athletics — to whom he was loaned for part of the season — before going to Columbus. Sold to Pittsburgh in 1885, he won only one more major league game, finishing with a 58–83, 3.47 ERA record. After leaving the playing ranks, he served as "assistant fire chief of the General Electric Company in Schenectady for two-score years." Born in Ft. Edward, NY, to Irish parents, Mountain died at Schenectady on November 19, 1939, at age 79. *(Total Baseball; Baseball-Reference.com; Sporting News; SABR Collegiate Database; U.S. Federal Census)*

Bill Mountjoy, a Canadian right-hander, joined the Cincinnati Red Stockings in late September 1883, losing his only start. In 1884, pitching behind Will White, he posted a 19–12, 2.93 ERA record. In the following season he went 12–11 between the Red Stockings and Baltimore Orioles. But since he did "not come up to expectations as a pitcher," he was released with a 31–24, 3.25 ERA career record. Mountjoy later pitched in the Southern League for Nashville and for Birmingham. A cryptic note in *National Police Gazette* states that he was "taking a little turn at Sulphur Springs.... If you will dance, you will have to pay the fiddler." Montjoy died of consumption at his hometown of London, Ontario, on May 19, 1894. He was only 35 years old. *(Total Baseball; National Police Gazette; Washington Post; Baseball Necrology; Sporting News)*

Mike Moynahan, a left-handed hitting infielder whose batting was described as "very strong," joined Buffalo from Milwaukee in 1880. In four seasons he hit .294 among Buffalo, Detroit, Cleveland and the Athletics, hitting .330 in 27 games in 1880 and .310 in 95 games for the A's in 1883. He was the regular shortstop for the American Association champions in 1883 but committed 75 errors, and his fielding average (.836) was below the league average. In 1887 *Sporting Life* noted that Moynahan was "in retirement." Born in Chicago to Irish parents, Moynahan died in Chicago on April 9, 1899, at age 43. *(Baseball Encyclopedia; Baseball-Reference.com; Chicago Daily Tribune; U.S. Federal Census; Sporting Life)*

Mike Muldoon spent five seasons in the majors as a regular third baseman, first for Cleveland (1882–84) and later in the American Association with Baltimore (1885–86). For his career, he hit .233 but reached .251 in 1885. He fielded .846 as a third baseman — right at the league average. Muldoon played for Jersey City in 1887. Born in Westmeath County, Ireland, he grew up in Hartford, CT, where he was listed in the 1880 census as a "base ballist." According to Peter Morris, Muldoon left Hartford in 1890 and is "hard to trace after that." *National Police Gazette* says that as a player Muldoon "once stole a base and then told his manager he would never do it again." Richard Barbieri placed Muldoon at third base on his all-Irish team — after acknowledging that he was a poor hitter, whose career highlight was a six-homer season in 1882. *(National Police Gazette; Baseball-Reference.com; New York Times; U.S. Federal Census; hardballtimes.com; Sporting Life)*

Tony Mullane entered the majors with Detroit in 1881, coming from Akron. In 1882 with Louisville, the Irish-born Mullane started 55 games, won 30, led the league with 170 strikeouts, while compiling a 1.88 ERA. That season he threw the first no-hitter in American Association history. The following season he won 35 games for the St. Louis Browns while leading the AA in winning percentage. After a 36-win, seven-shutout season with Toledo in 1884, he jumped to Cincinnati but was suspended for the entire 1885 season. With Cincinnati (1886–93) he won 163 games — fourteen by shutouts — and saved seven games. Finishing his career with Baltimore and Cleveland in 1894, he amassed 284 career victories — third among pitchers not in the Hall of Fame. An injured right arm forced him to become a left-handed pitcher for a part of his career. Not wearing a glove, he was able to pitch with the hand appropriate for each batter. A .243 career hitter, Mullane played 265 games in a field position. After leaving the majors, he pitched briefly in the minors; then in 1903 he became a Chicago policeman, holding that position until he retired in 1924. Mullane died in Chicago on April 25, 1944, at age 85. *(New York Times, Chicago Daily Tribune, Baseball-Reference.com. BaseballLibrary.com; Sporting News)*

John Mulligan played third base for the Washington Unions on June 14, 1884. In the game in Philadelphia against the Keystones, he had a base hit and scored twice. In the field he handled seven chances without error. *Baseball Almanac* gives his birthplace as Philadelphia, and it is likely that he was a Philadelphia sandlot player filling in for the day. Unfortunately, *Mulligan* is a common Irish family name, and there were no fewer than four twenty-year-old John Mulligans listed in the 1880 federal census for Philadelphia. *(Baseball Almanac; Total Baseball; U.S. Federal Census)*

Henry Mullin, a Canadian-born outfielder, had a 36-game major league career in two leagues in 1884. Joining the Washington Nationals in June, he hit .142 in 34 games as the regular centerfielder. After the club folded, he caught on with the Boston Reds, going hitless in two games. An excellent defensive player, he fielded .882 — almost forty points over the league average for outfielders — and had above-average range. He played for the independent Boston Unions in

Tony Mullane (Library of Congress)

1885. Mullin lived most of his adult life in Beverly, MA; until the 1930 census, he listed his birthplace as Massachusetts. The 1900 and 1910 censuses show him working as a machinist. Those of 1920 and 1930 list him as a tender of a county draw bridge and a courthouse janitor, respectively. Born to Irish parents, Mullin died on November 8, 1927, in Beverly. He was 65 years of age. *(Total Baseball; Baseball-Reference.com; Baseball Historian; U.S. Federal Census; Sporting Life)*

Joe Mulvey began his major league career with his local Providence Grays in 1883. After three games there, he was shot by a fan who was trying to shoot another player. Shifting to Philadelphia later in the season, he played with the National League Quakers and Phillies, the Players League Quakers and the American Association Athletics through 1892. When he was signed by Washington in 1893, he was described as "the best third baseman ever engaged by a local club." Finishing with Brooklyn in 1895, he owned a .261 mark for 12 seasons—eight as a regular. In his best seasons he hit .289. His fielding average of .871 was slightly above the league average. He continued to play with Rochester but is described as "in town idle" in 1898. Born to Irish parents in Providence, Mulvey became a Philadelphia resident; the 1900 census shows him operating a pool hall; in 1910 he is working as a bartender; by 1920 he is "employed at the [baseball] park as a watchman." Mulvey died in Philadelphia on August 21, 1928, at age 69. *(Total Baseball; Washington Post; New York Times; U.S. Federal Census; Baseball-Reference.com; Sporting Life)*

John Munce played in seven games for the Wilmington Quicksteps in August and early September 1884. At bat he managed four hits for a .190 average. In the outfield he had three errors in nine fielding chances for a .667 average. Munce later played for Portland of the New England League. Born in Philadelphia, his father an Irish laborer, Munce was himself a resident of that city. He appears in the 1900 and 1910 censuses as a post office clerk. He died in Philadelphia on March 15, 1917, at age 59. *(Total Baseball; Baseball-Reference.com; U.S. Federal Census)*

George Mundinger became one of the first players from New Orleans to enter the majors when he, along with John Peltz and Bill Butler, joined the Indianapolis Hoosiers in 1884. Between May 9 and May 20 the 29-year-old caught three games, hitting .250. Later that season the 6'2" 200-pound Mundinger was the regular catcher for Minneapolis of the Northwestern League. In 1902 he was appointed a substitute umpire in the Southern Association. After leaving baseball, he became a "crop planter" back in Louisiana. Born in New Orleans to German parents, Mundinger died at Covington, LA, on October 12, 1910, at age 55. *(Baseball-Reference.com; Retrosheet; sabrneworleans.com; DeadballEra.com; Stew Thornley; U.S. Federal Census; Sporting Life; SABR Baseball Encyclopedia)*

Tim Murnane began his major league career as a 20-year-old first baseman with the Middletown Mansfields of the National Association in 1872, hitting .359 in 24 games. After playing for Philadelphia teams—the Athletics and White Stockings—in the NA, he entered the National League with Boston in 1876, moving on to Providence in 1878. By 1879 he was playing part time in the minors, and by 1881 he was out of baseball to open a saloon and billiards parlor. He came back in 1884 as player-manager of the Boston Reds, directing them to a fifth-place finish in the Union Association. In eight seasons in three leagues he hit .261 and once led the NA in stolen bases. Murnane later served as president of the New England League, of the Eastern League, and of the National Board of Professional Baseball Clubs. For the last 30 years of his life, he was baseball editor for the *Boston Daily Globe*. Born in Naugatuck, CT, to Irish parents, Murnane died in Boston on February 7, 1917, at age 64. In 1939 he was one of the twelve writers honored by the Hall of Fame. *(Total Baseball; Baseball-Reference.com; New York Times; Rich Eldred)*

Murphy, a spectator "who claimed to have caught before," entered a game for the Boston Reds on August 16, 1884, to replace an injured catcher. After two errors and a passed ball, he was banished to left field for the remainder of the game. He went hitless in three at bats. Peter Morris notes that "looking for a man named Murphy in Boston without any additional information is worse than trying to find a needle in a haystack, since at least if you find the needle you know that you've found it." *(Baseball-Reference.com; petermorrisbooks.com)*

Cornelius "Con" Murphy, a Worcester, MA, native, made three late-season starts for the Philadelphia Quakers in 1884, going 0–3, 6.58 ERA. He had earned this trial by leading the Eastern League with 21 wins. For the next five seasons he pitched in the New England and International leagues, leading the IL with a 2.19 ERA in 1887 while pitching for Syracuse. A year later he led the league with 34 wins and a 1.27 ERA. In 1890 he returned to the majors with the Players League Brooklyn team. After going 4–10 for the Wonders, he returned once again to the minors. In 1892 he jumped his Syracuse contract to play with the local Worcester team. In 1897 *Sporting Life* noted that Murphy was "behind Worcester club matters" when they attempted to gain entrance to the Eastern League. Murphy operated a bar for a year; later, according to Bill Lee, he became a "salesman for the Thomas Ward Company of New York." Murphy died in Worcester on August 1, 1914, at age 50. *(Baseball-Reference.com; Total Baseball; Encyclopedia of Minor League Baseball; Baseball Necrology; Sporting Life)*

Francis "Tony" Murphy caught in one game for the New York Metropolitans on October 15, 1884. The 25-year-old catcher, borrowed from the Hartford club for the last game of the season, had a single in three at bats. Born in Brooklyn in 1859, he now has an established death date of December 15, 1915, in New York City. A Francis J. Murphy appears in the census for New York City for both 1900 and 1910. Son of Irish parents, he worked as a butcher. *(New York Mets Hall of Records; Baseball-Reference.com; Total baseball; U.S. Federal Census)*

John Murphy appeared in 23 of the 25 games played by the Altoona Mountain Citys. He had ten complete games in ten starts as a pitcher, plus four relief appearances, giving him a 5–6, 3.87 ERA record. In addition he played ten games as an outfielder and second baseman, hitting .149. The Mountain Citys disbanding, Murphy shifted to the Wilmington Quicksteps, for whom he went 0–6, 3.00 ERA as a pitcher and hit .065. Richard Malatzky of SABR was able to track Murphy by using information from *Sporting Life* that he was a shoemaker in Philadelphia. Using the Philadelphia city directories, Malatzky was able to find his obituary. Murphy died in Philadelphia on March 7, 1905. *(Baseball-Reference.com; Total Baseball; SABR Biographical Committee Newsletter)*

William "Gentle Willie" Murphy played in 42 games as a 20-year-old outfielder for the Cleveland Blues in 1884, coming to the majors from Holyoke. He finished that season — and his major league career — in the American Association with Washington. In 47 total games, the 5'11", 198-pound Murphy hit .254 but committed 31 errors in the field for a .728 percentage — 140 points below the league average. He continued to play in the minors as a heavy-hitting outfielder. However, in 1898 *Sporting Life* reported a rumor that Murphy had made $50,000 in the gold fields of South Africa but suggested that fifty cents was more likely. The 1870 census lists a William Murphy, son of an Irish immigrant who operated a rag shop in Springfield, MA. However, the common name makes census searches difficult. *(Baseball-Reference.com; Chicago Tribune; U.S. Federal Census; Sporting Life)*

Jeremiah "Miah" Murray played in 34 major league games over a period of eight seasons, beginning as a substitute catcher for Providence in 1884. He had played earlier for Reading; later

Miah Murray (Library of Congress)

he played for the Louisville Eclipse (1885) and Washington clubs in the National League (1888) and the American Association (1891). Over his career he hit .142. Murray operated a bar in South Boston in 1885 and later opened a pool and billiards parlor there, "doing famously" according to *Sporting Life*. A consummate sportsman, he umpired National League and college baseball games; he was president of the Public Alley bowling league; he was a boxing promoter, and he was involved with amateur baseball. Born in Boston to Irish parents, Murray died at Boston on January 11, 1922, at age 57. *(Total Baseball; Boston Daily Globe; Washington Post; New York Times; U.S. Federal Census; Sporting Life)*

Al Myers began his major league career when the Milwaukee Cream Citys moved from the Northwestern League to the Union Association in 1884. The 20-year-old hit .326 in 12 games. He went on to be a regular National League second baseman for the next seven seasons with Philadelphia, Kansas City, and Washington. Only a .245 career hitter, he reached .277 in both 1886 and 1890. Myers' 78 errors led National League second basemen in 1889; a year later he led the league in double plays. In October 1891, he announced that since his parents were aging and his wife wanted him to quit, he was leaving baseball to go into business. He was a native of Danville, IL, and died at Marshall, IL, on Christmas Eve, 1927. He was 60 years old. *(Baseball Encyclopedia; Baseball-Reference.com; 19cbaseball.com; Sporting News; Sporting Life)*

George Myers joined his hometown Buffalo Bisons in 1884 as a 23-year-old catcher. When that club disbanded after 1885, he joined the St. Louis Maroons for 1886 and finished his major league career with the Indianapolis Hoosiers in

Al Myers (Library of Congress)   George Myers (Library of Congress)

1889. In six seasons—all in the National League—he hit .203 with a high of .238. The *Washington Post* describes him as a "good all-round player" and as "a splendid catcher." In September 1889 Myers was part of a National League tug of war. Sought by Washington and Chicago, he actually signed with Cleveland, and was awarded by the league to New York; he ended his baseball career at age 28 without playing for any of the clubs competing for his services. In 1888 he was described as a "provident" man, owner of five houses in Buffalo, one purchased at the end of each season. In 1912 *Sporting Life* noted that Myers was a contractor and builder in Buffalo and that he had "gotten rich." Myers died in Buffalo on December 14, 1926, at age 66. *(Total Baseball; Baseball-Reference.com; Washington Post; New York Times; Sporting Life)*

Henry Myers played in one game with the Providence Grays in 1881 and then became a 24-year-old playing manager for the Baltimore Orioles in 1882. Batting leadoff, he hit .180, fielded .822 at shortstop (70 errors in 68 games) and led the team to a 19–54 record. He even tried his hand at pitching that season, losing two decisions. Two seasons later, he played shortstop in six games for the Wilmington Quicksteps, making him a three-league player in three seasons. Born in Philadelphia, Myers appears in the 1880 census for Baltimore, listed as a "base ball player." He died in Philadelphia on April 18, 1895, at age 36. *(Baseball-Reference.com; Total Baseball; U.S. Federal Census)*

Billy Nash joined his local Richmond Virginians as a 19-year-old in 1884. When the club moved into the American Association, Nash hit .199 in 42 games as the regular third baseman. When Richmond was dropped from the league, Nash was signed by Boston, and by 1886 he was the regular third baseman there. In Boston he played on four straight league champions—the 1890 Players League Reds and the 1891–93 National League Beaneaters. A career .275 hitter, he reached .295 in the inflated 1887 season. He had ten homers in both 1893 and 1895, driving in more than 100 runs each season. Nash led third basemen in fielding, putouts, and double plays four times each, and his career fielding average of .897 is twenty points higher than the league average. Traded to Philadelphia in 1896, he served as team captain and as playing manager that season. In 1906 *Sporting Life* reported that Nash lived at Plainfield, NJ, and worked as a "traveling sales-

Billy Nash (Library of Congress)

man for a Perth Amboy wholesale tobacco firm." Bill Lee says that Nash worked as a hospital attendant. He died of a heart attack at East Orange, NJ, on November 15, 1929, at age 64. *(Baseball Necrology; Baseball Encyclopedia; Total Baseball; Baseball-Reference.com; DeadballEra.com; U.S. Federal Census; Sporting Life)*

Vincent "Sandy" Nava (Irwin Sandy) was described in 1907 as "the only Spaniard ever in a big league." *Sporting Life* stated that Nava was "from Cuba." David Quinn Voigt says that Nava "passed" the color barrier. The San Francisco native came to Providence in 1882 from Oakland. For three years he was the "change" catcher, catching when Charlie Sweeney pitched, doing so without a mask. Only a .177 hitter over five seasons, he hit .240 in 1883. After helping Providence win the National League championship in 1884, he finished his career with the Baltimore Orioles in 1886. He was released without a trial by Danbury in 1887. Nava is listed in both the 1890 *Baltimore City Directory* and the 1900 federal census as an unmarried resident, working as an upholsterer. He died at Baltimore on June 15, 1906, at age 46. *(Total Baseball; Baseball Reference.com; New York Times; Boston Globe; Atlanta Constitution; U.S. Federal Census; Sporting Life; America Through Baseball)*

Jack Neagle is number nine on "The Biggest Loser" list of players who spent their careers on teams with losing records. In three major league seasons, he won 16 games while losing 50 with a 4.59 ERA. After going 0–1 in his debut with Cincinnati in 1879, the 25-year-old Syracuse native lost 23 games while winning only five in 1883, a season he split among three teams—Philadelphia Quakers, Baltimore Orioles and Pittsburgh Alleghenys. In addition, he made the record books by yielding Harry Stovey's record-breaking tenth home run that season. A year later the 5'6" right-hander finished his major league career by going 11–26 for Pittsburgh. In Neagle's defense, one could note that his winning percentage exceeded that of his team in 1884. Out of the majors, he pitched for Macon in 1885. The 1900 census shows him living in Syracuse with his wife and daughter, working as a telephone lineman. He died at Syracuse on September 20, 1904, at age 46. *(Total Baseball; Baseball-Reference.com; U.S. Federal Census; Sporting Life; "Biggest Loser")*

Bill Nelson joined the Pittsburgh Alleghenys in September 1884. The 20-year-old right-hander made three starts, completing all three for a 1–2 record. An 1885 note in *Sporting Life* says that he had "fully recovered his health" and was hoping to sign with one of the "first-class nines." According to Bill Lee, Nelson umpired in the minors for several years before losing a leg in an accident. Born in Terre Haute, IN, to a Norwegian father and an Irish mother, Nelson worked as a blacksmith before entering baseball. The 1900 census for Terre Haute shows him working as a typesetter; that of 1910 shows him as a grocery salesman. By 1920 he had become a clerk and manager at a hotel. Nelson died at his residence hotel in Terre Haute on June 23, 1941, at age 77. *(Total Baseball; Baseball-Reference.com; Baseball Necrology; U.S. Federal Census; Sporting Life)*

John "Candy" Nelson began his professional career as a 23-year-old infielder with Troy of the National Association in 1872. He also played with the Brooklyn Eckfords and New York Mutuals between 1872 and 1875. He had National League trials with Indianapolis, Troy and Worcester before joining the New York Mets in 1883. He hit a career high .305 that season as the regular shortstop, led the American Association in walks in 1884, and helped the Mets win the championship. After playing one game with the NL Giants in 1887, he finished with the AA Brooklyn Gladiators in 1890. In 13 seasons—seven as a regular—he hit .254, and as a shortstop, he fielded .872, nine points above the league average. When he retired in 1890, he was 41 years old ("the oldest player in active and continuous service"). Both *Sporting Life* (1893) and *Washington Post* (1895) reported that Nelson "owns a milk route in Brooklyn." But in the 1900 census, he still lists his occupation as "ball player." In that census he gives his birthplace as Maine; he died in Brooklyn on September 4, 1910, at age 61. *(Baseball-Reference.com; Total Baseball; Washington Post; U.S. Federal Census; Sporting Life)*

Hugh Nicol holds the major league record of 138 stolen bases, set in 1887. Hitting only .215, the

Hugh Nicol (Library of Congress)

5'4" Nicol drew 86 walks, giving him an on-base percentage of .341. After trials with the White Stockings in 1881–82, he became an outfield regular with the St. Louis Browns, helping them win the 1885 American Association championship. After a down year in 1886, he again became a regular with the Cincinnati Red Stockings, finishing with that club in 1890, when it entered the National League. In Cincinnati Nicol and 6'2" teammate John Reilly formed the long and short of major league baseball, according to *Sporting Life*. For his ten seasons Nicol hit .235 but fielded .912, thirty-two points over the league average for outfielders. Born in Scotland, Nicol remained in baseball; he managed the St. Louis Browns briefly in 1897; he managed the Rockford and Peoria clubs in the Three-I League. In 1906 he became athletic director at Purdue University. During the summer months he scouted for the Reds and Dodgers. The 1920 census shows him as an agent for stocks and bonds. Nicol died at Lafayette, IN, on June 27, 1921, at age 63. (*Total Baseball; Baseball-Reference.com; New York Times; Encyclopedia of Minor League Baseball; U.S. Federal Census; Sporting Life*)

George Noftsker played in seven games as an outfielder and catcher for the Altoona Mountain Citys in 1884. The 135-pounder was an average fielder at either position, but at the plate he managed only one single in twenty-five at bats for an .040 average. Noftsker was a lifelong resident of Shippensburg, PA. He is listed in the 1880 census as a wagon-maker, and after his baseball career, he appears in the 1900 and 1910 censuses as a manufacturer of carriages. By 1920 he has become a mechanic in his own shop; in 1930 he is listed as an insurance salesman. Noftsker died at Shippensburg on May 8, 1931, at age 71. (*Baseball-Reference.com; Total Baseball; U.S. Federal Census*)

Edward "The Only" Nolan compiled a 23–52, 2.98 ERA career record with five different teams over an eight-year period. As a twenty-year-old he went 13–22 with the 1878 Indianapolis Hoosiers, but was blacklisted from the league over a brothel visit and a drinking spree. In 1881 he was 8–14 with Cleveland and was again blacklisted for drinking. In 1883 he was winless in Pittsburgh and began operating a saloon in Paterson, NJ. In 1884 he returned to the majors, gaining one of Wilmington's two wins in the Union Association, before closing his career in Philadelphia with the Quakers in 1885. He was released by both Jersey City and Savannah in 1886. Born in Paterson to Irish parents, Nolan was a life-long resident there. The 1900 and 1910 censuses both list him as a city policeman. His obituary shows that he had reached the rank of sergeant. Nolan died in Paterson on May 18, 1913, at age 55. (*Total Baseball; Baseball-Reference.com; U.S. Federal Census; New York Times; Sporting Life*)

William Nusz, a 24-year-old from Frederick, MD, played left field for the Washington Unions on April 26, 1884. Described by *Baseball-Reference.com* as a minor league and semi-pro player, Nusz went hitless in four at bats. In the field he had two errors in four fielding chances. William Nusz is one of the more recently revealed major leaguers. Recent research by SABR Bibliography Committee members Peter Morris and Richard Malatzky have established that William should receive credit for a major league game previously awarded to his brother Emory. Born in 1859 to native Maryland parents, William E. Nusz is listed in the 1900 census as a married resident of Frederick, MD, working as a shoemaker. He died on July 26, 1903, in Baltimore, at age 43. (*Baseball-Reference.com; Daily News of Frederick Maryland; petermorrisbooks.com; U.S. Federal Census; SABR Biographical Committee Newsletter*)

Henry Oberbeck had trials with four clubs—two in the American Association and two in the Union Association—in two years. He started 1883 with the Pittsburgh Alleghenys, but after two games, he went to the St. Louis Browns for four games. He started 1884 with the Baltimore Monumentals and was transferred to the Kansas City Cowboys. In all he played in 66 major league games—most as an outfielder—hitting .176. Whether as an outfielder, a third baseman or a first baseman, he fielded well above the league average. He also pitched in the Union Association, compiling an 0–5 record for Kansas City. Oberbeck was a native Missourian, born to German parents living in St. Louis. Also a St. Louis resident, Oberbeck worked for the U.S. Postal Service as a letter carrier. He died at St. Louis on August 26, 1921, at age 63. (*Total Baseball; Retrosheet; findagrave.com; U.S. Federal Census; Sporting News*)

Billy O'Brien debuted with the St. Paul Saints on September 27, 1884. In eight games as a third-baseman and pitcher he hit .233 and won a game in relief. Finishing the season with the Kansas City Cowboys, he hit .235. In 1887, after hitting

Billy O'Brien (Library of Congress)

in 1882, when he also led American Association catchers in fielding. He was Bobby Mathews' catcher for the AA champions of 1883. After playing for Brooklyn in 1887 and Baltimore in 1888, he finished back with the A's as a regular first baseman in 1890. In eight seasons, he hit .266. His fielding averages as a catcher and as a first baseman are the league averages. O'Brien died in Philadelphia on November 20, 1910, at age 50. His obituary in *Sporting Life* says that he had worked as a teamster before and after his baseball career and suffered from dropsy. *(New York Times; Total Baseball; Baseball-Reference.com; Sporting Life)*

John O'Brien, a 32-year-old outfielder, played in eighteen games for the Baltimore Monumentals in April and May of 1884, his only major league experience. The centerfielder hit .247 (on a team that collectively hit .245) and fielded .865—forty-nine points above the league average. O'Brien was born in Columbus, OH, to an Irish family and grew up in Fall River, MA. The 1870 census shows him working in a cotton mill there. According to the 1910 census, O'Brien was still a resident of Fall River, a widower, and a fireman. The 63-year-old O'Brien died at Fall River on the last day of 1914. *(Total Baseball; Baseball-Reference.com; U.S. Federal Census)*

Tom O'Brien debuted with the Worcester Ruby Legs in 1882. The big Salem, MA, product hit .202 in 22 games, mostly as an outfielder. The following season he shifted to second base and to the American Association with Baltimore. When the Union Association was founded in 1884, he came back home as the regular second baseman with the Boston Reds. He then became a first baseman, playing in the AA with Baltimore in 1885, with New York in 1887, finishing with the Rochester in 1890. In all, he hit .231 in 270 games. O'Brien continued to play in the minors with Rochester in 1891. The 1910 census lists him as living in Worcester, MA, working as a "baseball player" and "scout." Bill Lee says that O'Brien managed in the minors and scouted for Cleveland and the Red Sox. A 1912 note in *Sporting Life* says that O'Brien was resigning as a scout for the Athletics "to settle down in business life in his home city." Born to Irish parents, O'Brien died in Worcester on April 21, 1921, at age 60. *(Total Baseball; Baseball-Reference.com; U.S. Federal Census; Baseball Necrology; Sporting Life)*

a league-leading .362 at Denver, he returned to the majors as the regular first baseman with the Washington Nationals. Hitting .278, he led the National League with 19 home runs. His hitting fell off to .225 in 1888, and he was out of the majors for most of 1889. Enjoying another solid year with the Brooklyn Gladiators in 1890, O'Brien hit .278, before finishing his career back with Denver in 1891. Born in Albany, NY, to Irish immigrant parents, O'Brien settled in Kansas City, MO. The 1900 census shows him working for the railroad; the 1910 census lists him as a police officer. He died in Kansas City on May 26, 1911, at age 51. *(Baseball-Encyclopedia; Baseball-Reference.com; U.S. Federal Census; DeadballEra.com)*

Jack O'Brien (**John K. Bryne**) was another Philadelphia native who contributed to the success of his hometown Athletics (1882–86 and 1890). The 22-year-old hit .303 as a rookie catcher

Hank O'Day is the only man to play, manage and umpire in the National League (George Mo-

Hank O'Day (Library of Congress)

He worked in ten World Series before retiring after the 1927 season. In 1908 he was the umpire who called out Fred Merkle for failing to touch second base. O'Day died in Chicago on July 2, 1935, at age 73. *(Total Baseball; New York Times; Deadball Stars of the National League; Baseball Reference.com; U.S. Federal Census)*

John O'Donnell caught a home game for the Philadelphia Keystones on July 16, 1884. In a 19–4 loss to the Outlaw Reds, he committed five errors behind the plate — in addition to allowing seven passed balls. More successful at bat, O'Donnell had a single in four times up. *SABR Baseball Dictionary* and *Baseball-Almanac.com* give him a birthplace of Littlestown, PA. *(Baseball-Reference.com; Retrosheet; Baseball Almanac)*

Dan O'Leary appeared on major league rosters for five seasons, in which he played in 45 games. The Detroit-born outfielder, son of Irish parents, played for Providence, Boston, Detroit and Worcester of the National League before finishing as player-manager for the Cincinnati Outlaw Reds in 1884. In 181 plate appearances he hit .243. His .843 fielding percentage was 21 points over the league average. As a manager he led Cincinnati to a 20–15 record. O'Leary remained in baseball until World War I. *Baseball-Reference.com* says that he organized clubs in the Pennsylvania State League in 1886. He managed Davenport to a Three-I pennant in 1914. The 1900 Chicago census lists O'Leary as a reporter. Bill Lee says that he was a police reporter for 35 years. O'Leary died in Chicago on June 24, 1922 at age 65. *(Total Baseball; Baseball-Reference.com; Baseball Necrology; U.S. Federal Census; Sporting Life; Encyclopedia of Minor League Baseball)*

Frank Olin participated in baseball, track, and rifle at Cornell before entering the majors in 1884 with the Washington Nationals. The outfielder and second baseman hit .386 in 21 games before the club folded in August. After one game with the Washington Unions, Olin finished the season with Toledo Blue Stockings, hitting .256 in 26 games. He appeared in one game with the Detroit Wolverines in 1885, collecting two hits but making two errors in the field. So his major league career ended with a .316 average for 49 games. After graduating from Cornell with an engineering degree in 1886, Olin began managing businesses which made gunpowder for mining and military uses. In Alton, IL, he became one of the most suc-

riarty did so in the American League). A right-handed pitcher, born to Irish parents in Chicago, O'Day began with Toledo in 1884 and finished with the Players League New York Giants in 1890. He supposedly threw so hard that his catcher — Deacon McGuire — put a beef steak in his mitt to catch him. Major league appearances for Pittsburgh (1885) and Washington (1886) were interspersed with strong minor league performances — an Eastern League–leading 0.74 ERA in 1885 and a Southern League–leading 26 wins in 1886. Traded to the New York 1889, he went 9–1 for the Giants and won two games in the World Series that fall. In his last season he went 22–13 in the Players League. In seven major league seasons he compiled a 73–110, 3.74 ERA record. He had managerial stints with the Reds (1912) and the Cubs (1914), but is best remembered for 35 years as a National League umpire, beginning in 1895.

cessful businessmen of his day, forming the Olin-Mathison Chemical Company and ultimately the Olin Corporation. These ventures made him one of the wealthiest men in America. He died in St. Louis on May 21, 1951, at age 91. *(Baseball Reference.com; SABR Biography Project; U.S. Federal Census; Sporting News)*

James "Tip" O'Neill, a Canadian-born pitcher and outfielder, was regarded as "the finest natural hitter who ever faced a pitcher." In ten seasons he hit .326 and led the American Association in hitting twice. Believed to be "too lazy to live" while pitching for New York in 1883, he developed into a very good hitter when he shifted to the outfield in St. Louis. By 1887 when a walk was as good as a hit, he hit .435 leading the AA in runs, hits, doubles, triples, homers, RBIs and slugging. In 1888, without the benefit of the walk rule, he hit only .335 in winning his second batting title. His play helped the Browns to four consecutive AA championships in 1885–88. In 1890 O'Neill played with the Chicago Pirates of the Players League but returned to the Browns in 1891, finishing with Cincinnati in 1892. An average pitcher (16–16), O'Neill was an excellent outfielder whose fielding percentage (.917) was more than twenty points above the league average. A note in *Sporting Life* suggests that after leaving the majors, he and his brother operated "Maison de Booze" in Montreal. In 1897 he is described as having "a thriving cigar business" in Montreal. Returning to baseball, O'Neill umpired in the Eastern League in 1899. He died in Montreal on December 31, 1915. *(Total Baseball; Washington Post; National Police Gazette; Baseball Almanac; Sporting Life)*

James "Orator" O'Rourke joined the Middletown Mansfields of the National Association as a 21-year-old shortstop and catcher in 1872. He joined Boston the following season, moving with that club into the National League in 1876. After helping the Providence Grays win an NL championship in 1879, he then became a player-manager for Buffalo in 1881. From 1885 through 1892 he played in New York with the NL or Players League Giants before finishing with Washington in 1893. In 23 seasons—18 as a regular—he hit .310, leading the NL three times in homers; he led in hits and average in 1884, and in walks and runs in 1877 (when he hit a career-high .362). The son of illiterate Irish immigrants, O'Rourke graduated

"Tip" O'Neill (Library of Congress) Jim O'Rourke (Library of Congress)

from Yale Law School. His nickname came from his verbal skills. One obituary noted, "Words of great length and thunderous sound simply flowed out of his mouth." O'Rourke later was an NL umpire and playing manager and club owner in the Connecticut League, playing until he was 58 years old. In 1904, at age 52, he caught a 9-inning game for the Giants, going one for four at the plate. O'Rourke died at Bridgeport, CT, his native city, on January 8, 1919, at age 68 and was elected to the Hall of Fame in 1945. *(Total Baseball; Baseball-Reference.com; New York Times; Encyclopedia of Minor League Baseball)*

Dave Orr, after 1883 trials with the New York Gothams and Metropolitans, became a star first baseman over the next seven seasons for the Mets (1884–87), Brooklyn Bridegrooms (1888), Columbus Solons (1889) and Brooklyn Wonders (1890). Even carrying 250 pounds, he was a first baseman of "exceptional grace," leading the American Association in fielding in 1886. However, the *National Police Gazette*, commenting on his weight, noted, "A man cannot be pussy and play good ball." However, Orr was a .342 hitter over his career, twice leading the AA in hits, slugging, and triples. In his final season, he had a career-high .371 average, good for second place in the Players League. The New York City product suffered a paralytic stroke at the end of the 1890 season when he was 31 years old and never played again. He was promised an umpiring job but accepted a position as special policeman at the Brooklyn ballpark and later managed the bleachers. He was described as a "helpless paralytic" in 1905, but in 1907 he is described as a "watchman in New York." The son of Irish parents, Orr died at Richmond Hills, NY, on June 2, 1915 at age 55. *(Total Baseball; National Police Gazette; Boston Daily Globe; Chicago Daily Tribune; New York Times; Sporting Life; SABR Biography Project)*

Henry Oxley began 1884 with Lynn, MA. The American Association New York Metropolitans tried to sign him, but he was acquired in late July by the National League New York Gothams, coming "well recommended." After two games, in one of which he injured his hand, he said that he would "confine his attention to the Metropolitan club." He caught one game for the Mets, leaving the majors hitless in seven at bats. The following season he played for Portland, ME. Born in Prince Edward Island to a blacksmith who settled in Somerville, MA, Oxley followed in his father's footsteps, also becoming a blacksmith. This is confirmed by the census of 1920. Oxley died at Somerville on October 12, 1945, at age 87. *(Total Baseball; Boston Daily Globe; New York Times; National Police Gazette; U.S. Federal Census; Sporting Life)*

George Pattison played two games as an outfielder for the Philadelphia Keystones on April 24 and 26, 1884. In home field losses to the Baltimore Monumentals, he had a single in seven at bats. In the field he had one putout, one assist and two errors. A George H. Pattison who was a Philadelphia resident of about the right age appears in the censuses for 1880, 1900, 1910 and 1920. In the first he is working as a ship joiner, in the second as a lecturer and in the last two as a municipal court clerk. *(Baseball-Reference.com; U.S. Federal Census; SABR Baseball Encyclopedia)*

Elias Peak played one game as a right fielder for the Boston Reds. Picked up for a game in Philadelphia on April 19, 1884, he had two hits in three at bats. Later in the season, he played in 54 games for his hometown Philadelphia Keystones, 47 as a second baseman. In all he hit .202 in 55 games and committed 70 errors in the field for a .808 average — 59 points below the league average. Peak continued his association with baseball. As late as 1897, *Sporting Life* reported that he was seeking "a chance to re-enter the diamond" as a player or umpire. However, the 1900 and 1910 federal censuses show Peak living in Philadelphia and being employed as a letter carrier by the U.S Postal Service. He died in Philadelphia on December 17, 1916, at age 67. *(Total Baseball; Baseball-Reference.com; SABR Baseball Encyclopedia; U.S. Federal Census; Sporting Life)*

John Peltz was among the earliest major league players from New Orleans. The regular left fielder of Indianapolis in 1884, Peltz hit only .219, but his seventeen triples were fourth best in the league. He also led American Association outfielders with 38 errors. Except for one game with Baltimore in 1888, he was out of the majors until 1890, when he hit .228 in 123 games split among the Brooklyn, Syracuse and Toledo AA clubs. Overall, he hit .224 in 230 major league games. Born to German parents in New Orleans, Peltz appears in the 1900 census, living at home, and working as a grocery clerk. He died of consumption in New Orleans on February 27, 1906, at age 44. *(Baseball Necrology; Baseball Encyclopedia; sabrneworleans.com; Baseball-Reference.com; U.S. Federal Census)*

Jim Peoples spent six seasons in the majors, primarily as a catcher. However, as a 20-year-old rookie in 1884, the 5'8", 200 pound Peoples played shortstop for the Cincinnati Red Stockings. He moved on to Brooklyn in 1885 and finished his major league career with Columbus in 1889, his career cut off by the failure of his throwing arm. In his busiest season, he caught 76 games for Brooklyn in 1886. He umpired while playing (1888–89) and was a regular American Association umpire in 1890. In 1913 *Sporting Life* describes him as a "good ringer for Adolph the fat cherub." Born in Big Beaver, MI, to an Irish father, Peoples died at Detroit on August 29, 1920, at age 56. According to Bill Lee, Peoples was involved in real estate sales in Detroit; this is confirmed by the 1920 census. *(Total Baseball; Baseball-Reference.com; Chicago Daily Tribune; Baseball Necrology; U.S. Federal Census; Sporting Life)*

John Peters hit .351 to help the Chicago White Stockings win the first National League championship in 1876. He was in his third season with Chicago, being a veteran of the National Association White Stockings. In eleven seasons — eight as a regular shortstop or second baseman — he led the league in fielding, double plays, putouts, and chances twice each; his .874 percentage was seventeen points higher than the league average for shortstops. Going over .300 three times, Peters settled for a career .278 batting average. In addition to the White Stockings, he saw service with Milwaukee, Providence and Buffalo before finishing with the American Association Pittsburgh Alleghenys in 1884. *Sporting Life* reported that Peters was "without an engagement" in 1885 and was looking to "re-enter the diamond" in 1886. Both the 1880 and 1910 censuses show Peters working as a fish merchant. *Sporting News* says that he was an employee of the St. Louis Park Department. Born in Louisiana, MO, to German parents, Peters died in St. Louis on January 4, 1924, at age 73. *(Baseball Encyclopedia; Baseball-Reference. com; Retrosheet; New York Times; U.S. Federal Census; Sporting News)*

Fred Pfeffer is identified as the best second baseman in Chicago before Johnny Evers. The 22-year-old joined Troy in 1882 and lasted sixteen seasons in the majors. In an eight-year period (1884–91), he led the league eight times in putouts and seven times in double plays and chances per games. Clark Griffith credited Pfeffer with developing the cut-off throw to prevent a double steal. The first of three stints with the White Stockings began in 1883, lasting through 1889. A

Fred Pfeffer (Library of Congress)

member of the Brotherhood, he joined the Players League, playing with and managing the Chicago Pirates in 1890. After returned to the White Stockings in 1891, Pfeffer played with Louisville (1892–95) and the New York Giants (1896) before finishing back with Chicago in 1897. A career .255 hitter, he hit .308 for Louisville in 1894. Pfeffer continued to play independent ball until 1902 when he was 42 years old. The 1910 census lists him as the proprietor of a buffet. After 1920 he was "in charge of the press boxes at Chicago race tracks." Born in Louisville to German parents, Pfeffer died in Chicago on April 10, 1932, at age 72. *(Boston Daily Globe; Chicago Daily Tribune; Baseball Encyclopedia; U.S. Federal Census; Sporting Life)*

Dick Phelan hit .246 as the regular second baseman of the Baltimore Monumentals in 1884, coming from the Leadville Blues. The 29-year-old from Towanda, PA, was third on the team in games and at bats. When the Union Association folded at the end of the season, Phelan tried to gain a position in the National League, but trials with Buffalo and St. Louis in 1885 amounted to only six games and a .150 average. He played for Des Moines in 1887 and then moved to the Southern Association as an umpire and player. Phelan was a member of an Irish Family that moved from Pennsylvania to Wichita to San Antonio. He is listed as a ballplayer in the 1880 census and as an assistant notary in the 1910 census. Phelan died in San Antonio on February 13, 1931, at age 86. *(U.S. Federal Census; Baseball-Reference.com; Baseball Encyclopedia; Sporting Life)*

Bill Phillips, a product of New Brunswick, was the first Canadian to play major league baseball. He lasted ten seasons — all as a regular — with Cleveland of the National League and Brooklyn and Kansas City of the American Association. The massive first baseman — a 200-pounder — was a career .971 fielder, leading the AA in fielding in both 1885 and 1887. His fielding percentage exceeded the league average, and his range was far greater. Phillips hit .302 for Brooklyn in 1885, his only .300 season, and finished with a .266 average. His lack of speed caused *National Police Gazette* to joke that he "could run a mile an hour." After being dropped by Kansas City, Phillips played in the International League in 1889. In 1890 *Sporting Life* noted that he was "still a policeman in Chicago." Phillips died in Chicago on October 7, 1900 of locomotor ataxia — a form of syphilis — at age 43. *(Total Baseball; National Police Gazette; SABR Biography Project; Sporting Life)*

Marr Phillips came to Indianapolis along with Ed Merrill in 1884 from Fort Wayne of the Northwestern League. The 26-year-old rookie shortstop hit .269 in 97 games. The club folding, he moved on to Detroit for 1885, finishing that season at Pittsburgh. After playing at Hamilton of the International League, he finished his major league career with 64 games at Rochester in 1890. Overall he hit .239 in 198 games, but his .884 fielding percentage and range factors were much above the league average. At Rochester he started an all-tag triple play by letting a bases-loaded pop-up drop and fielding it on the bounce. In 1897 when he was 40 years old, Phillips led Canadian League shortstops in fielding. The Pittsburgh native is listed as a gatekeeper at the new Forbes Field in 1909. He died in Pittsburgh on May 1, 1928, at age 70. *(Baseball-Reference.com; Sporting News; Sporting Life)*

Grayson "Gracie" Pierce played for five clubs during a three-year major league career — Louisville and Baltimore (1882), Columbus and the New York Gothams (1883) and the New York Mets (1884). When Pierce joined the Mets, *National Police Gazette* described him as "a jewel at second base." However, he played only five games that season, leaving the majors with a .186 average for 84 games. He also committed 82 errors in 57 games as a second baseman. *Sporting News* shows him umpiring in the National League in 1886. Born around 1862, he died at New York City on August 28, 1894. *(Baseball-Reference.com; National Police Gazette; New York Mets Hall of Records; New York City Deaths 1892–1902; Sporting News)*

Maurice Pierce played third base for the Washington Unions for the first two games of the 1884 season. At the plate he had one hit in seven at bats. In the field he had two errors in nine chances, placing him right on the league average. Most sources give him a March 1859 birth date in Maryland. There is a 21-year-old Preston M. Pierce living at home in Washington, DC, in the 1880 census. One source provides a death date of January 1900. *(Total Baseball; Retrosheet; Baseball-Reference.com; SABR Baseball Encyclopedia)*

George Pinkney "made a very good impression" when he reached Cleveland in 1884 from Peoria of the Northwestern League. When the Blues folded at the end of the season, he went to Brooklyn in 1885, playing for the American As-

George Pinkney (T. Scott Brandon)

sociation team (1885–89) and moving with the team into the National League (1890–91) before finishing with St. Louis (1892) and Louisville (1893). He became a regular third baseman in 1885 and maintained regular status throughout his career, leading the AA in fielding twice. A career .263 hitter, Pinkney hit .309 in 1890 and .313 in 36 games as a rookie. In 1888 he led the AA with 134 runs scored. He helped Brooklyn win pennants in two leagues and hit .289 in 13 World Series games. Both the 1910 and 1920 censuses show Pinkney working as a clerk and bookkeeper in a railroad office. Bill Lee says that he was an auditor for the Union Railroad in Peoria. Pinkney died on November 10, 1926, in Peoria. *(Total Baseball; National Police Gazette; New York Times; Baseball Necrology; U.S. Federal Census)*

Tom Poorman came to the majors as a pitcher with Buffalo in 1880. His obituary describes him as "one of the first successful curve pitchers." But after giving up two home runs to Charley Jones in one inning, he took his 1-8, 4.13 ERA record to the outfield. In six seasons with Buffalo, Chicago, and Boston of the National League and Toledo and Philadelphia of the American Association, he was a regular four times. A career .244 hitter, Poorman reached .265 in the inflated 1887 season with the A's when he led the AA with 19 triples. His .885 fielding percentage was the league average. Bill Lee found that Poorman had been in the dry goods business at Cortland, NY. The 1900 census for Cortland calls him a machinist. A native of Lock Haven, PA, Poorman died there of consumption on February 15, 1905, at age 47. *(Total Baseball; Baseball-Reference.com; U.S. Federal Census; Sporting Life)*

Henry Porter began his major league career with the Milwaukee Cream Citys in 1884, completing all six starts for a 3–3 record, including a game in which he struck out 18 Boston hitters in a losing cause. This record stood until Steve Carlton struck out 19 in a losing effort in 1969. The 142-pound Porter went on to a solid career in the American Association with Brooklyn and Kansas City. Over the next four seasons, he won 93 games, topped by a 33–21 record with Brooklyn in 1885. With the last place Kansas City Cowboys of 1888, Porter had 53 complete games, leading to an 18–37 record. His major league career behind him, he pitched in London, Ontario, with the Tecumsehs in 1890. Porter, from Vermont, died in Brockton, MA, on December 30, 1906, at age 48. Bill Lee shows that Porter worked in a shoe factory in Brockton. *(Baseball Encyclopedia; Baseball-Reference.com; Baseball Necrology; Sporting Life)*

Matt Porter managed the Kansas Unions for sixteen games from June 14 to July 14, 1884. For three of those games he played center field. In these he had one hit for a .083 batting average and made two errors in eight fielding chances for a .750 fielding average. *Retrosheet* says that Matthew Sheldon Porter was born in New York in 1859. A Matthew S. Porter of that age, born in New York, resided in Kansas City in 1880. The son of a federal tax assessor, he was working at that time as a store clerk. *(Baseball-Reference.com; Retrosheet; U.S. Federal Census; Baseball Encyclopedia)*

Abner Powell came to the Washington Unions from Peoria of the Northwestern League in 1884 as an outfielder and pitcher. The 23-year-old Powell hit well—.283 in 48 games. On the mound he started 17 games, winning 6 with a 3.43 ERA. In the American Association in 1886 he hit only .212 between Baltimore and Cincinnati, while

Tom Poorman (Wikimedia Commons)

going 2–6 on the mound. In all, he hit .257 in 78 games and compiled an 8–18, 4.00 ERA pitching record. In 1887 Powell began a long career as a manager and club owner that took him from New Orleans to Spokane, Seattle, and Atlanta. He is credited with three inventions that changed professional baseball: the use of a tarpaulin to cover the infield in rain; the issuing of a rain check for incomplete games, and the observance of Ladies Days to attract females to games. Powell also operated an automobile agency, and in later years managed an apartment. Born in Shenandoah, PA, to Welsh parents, Powell died in New Orleans on August 7, 1953, at age 93. *(Sporting News; Baseball-Reference.com; Baseball Necrology; U.S. Federal Census; Sporting Life)*

Jim Powell, a local Richmond player, moved into the major leagues when the Virginians replaced the Washington Nationals in the American Association in August 1884. As the regular first baseman, the 24-year-old Powell hit .245 in the last 41 games of the season. The following year, when Richmond was dropped from the AA, he played 19 games for the Philadelphia Athletics, hitting .160. Those games had previously been credited to Martin Powell. Jim Powell migrated to Montana, where he appears in the 1900 census as a farm laborer in Ravalli County. In 1902 *Sporting Life* describes him as a "prosperous rancher in the Bitter Root Valley of Montana." The 1920 census shows him working as a retail merchant in Jefferson, MT. He died in Butte, MT, on November 20, 1929, at age 70. *(Baseball-Reference.com; Total Baseball; U.S. Federal Census; Sporting Life)*

Martin Powell played four seasons in the majors — all as a regular first baseman. The left-handed hitter began with the Detroit Wolverines in June 1881, hitting .338 for the remainder of that season. While his average plunged to .240 and .273 over the next two seasons, he maintained his position. In 1884 he jumped to the Cincinnati Outlaw Reds, hitting .319 until his career came to a close in August. Overall he hit .283 for 279 games. However both his fielding percentage and range factors were below the league averages for first basemen. By 1886 he had to give up baseball because of ill health. Powell was born in Fitchburg, MA, to Irish parents, and the 1880 census lists him as a baseball player. Bill Lee notes that Powell later worked with his brother "in the wood and coal business." He died from consumption on February 5, 1888, only 31 years old. *(Baseball-*

Jim Powell (Library of Congress)

Reference.com; Retrosheet; Baseball Necrology; U.S. Federal Census; Sporting Life)

Phil Powers was signed by the White Stockings in 1879 from the Tecumsehs. He also had trials with Boston (1879), Cleveland (1880), and the Red Stockings (1882–85) before finishing with Baltimore (1885). In his busiest seasons, Powers played in 37 games for Boston and 35 games for the Red Stockings in 1884. Used primarily as a catcher in the time before the catcher's mitt had been developed, he was known as "leather fist" because of his ability to handle hot throws. Overall he hit .180 in seven seasons, and his .877 fielding average was more than twenty points below the league average. He served as a National League umpire in 1881, 1883, and 1886–92. Between umpiring jobs he also tried managing at London, Ontario. The *National Police Gazette* praised his work as an umpire because he "has the backbone." However the *Chicago Daily Tribune* noted of his career that he was "not a particularly good player, [and] failed as a manager and umpire." After 1892 Powers worked as "messenger in the Manhattan Bureau of Buildings." Born in New York City, he died of pneumonia on December 22, 1914, in Manhattan. He was 60 years old. *(Total Baseball; National Police Gazette; Chicago Daily Tribune; New York Times; Boston Daily Globe)*

Walter Prince played four games as a first baseman and outfielder with the Louisville Eclipse in 1883. In 1884 he split the season among the Detroit Wolverines (seven games), Washington Nationals (43 games as the regular first baseman) and Washington Unions (one game). In all he played in 55 major league games in three leagues, hitting .208. As a first baseman he fielded .935, 21 points below the league average. Prince was a native of New Hampshire, the son of a foundry worker. In the censuses of 1900, 1910, and 1920 Prince himself is variously described as a foundry worker, as an iron molder and as a superintendent of a brass foundry. He died in Bristol, NH, on March 2, 1938, at age 76. *(Total Baseball; Baseball-Reference.com; Washington Post; U.S. Federal Census)*

William "Blondie" Purcell, a much-traveled outfielder and pitcher, spent 12 seasons in the majors with Syracuse, Cincinnati, Cleveland, Buffalo, Philadelphia and Boston of the National League and Baltimore and Philadelphia of the American Association. Primarily a pitcher when he debuted with Syracuse, he went 7–34 in his first two seasons and rarely pitched thereafter. Over his career he hit .267 but reached .316 as a 35-year-old in 1889. He served as a team captain in both Philadelphia and Baltimore and was a playing manager for the Quakers in 1883. In 1886 he took time off to manage Atlanta to a Southern League pennant, also leading that league in homers. In 1885 the *National Police Gazette* describes him as a "royal kicker" who "puts a mule to a blush" when he attacks an umpire. He was born in Paterson, NJ, to Irish parents; his death date is not listed, though Bill Lee and *CNN/SI.com* both list it as February 20, 1912. Lee calls him a "retired cabinet maker." The 1900 and 1910 censuses show a William Purcell, born in 1854, living in Newark, NJ, working as a telegraph operator. In 1908 *Sporting Life* reported that a benefit baseball game in the Southern Association netted Purcell "something over $100." *(Baseball-Reference.*

"Blondie" Purcell (Library of Congress)

com; National Police Gazette; New York Times; Atlanta Constitution; Baseball Necrology; Encyclopedia of Minor League Baseball; U.S. Federal Census; sportsillustrated.cnn.com; Sporting Life)

Harry Thomas "Shadow" Pyle, a lefty from Reading, PA, made one start for the Philadelphia Quakers at the end of 1884. He pitched for Richmond in 1885, leading the Eastern League with 37 wins, and returned to the majors in 1887 with the Chicago White Stockings. After five starts and a 1–3 record, he was released, leaving the majors with a 1–4 record. In 1888 he went 18–4 with Jersey City, leading the Central League in percentage. The 1900 census for Reading shows him unemployed and living with his brother-in-law. Pyle died at Reading on December 26, 1908, at age 47. His death notice in *Sporting Life* says that he had pitched for the Reading Actives and Minneapolis. Bill Lee says that Pyle had been ill for some time. *(Baseball-Reference.com; Washington Post; Chicago*

Daily Tribune; Baseball Necrology; U.S. Federal Census; Sporting Life)

Joe Quest first entered the majors as an 18-year-old with the Cleveland Forest Citys of the National Association in 1871. In 1878 he returned as a regular second baseman for Indianapolis, going from there to Chicago the following season. With the White Stockings he twice led National League second basemen in fielding and also posted the highest batting average of his career (.246) in 1881. Quest played with Detroit in both 1883 and 1885; in the American Association he played with the Browns and Pittsburgh before finishing with the Athletics in 1886. Over his nine-year career he batted .217, but his fielding percentage and range were above the league average. After umpiring in 1887, Quest was to be the Los Angeles captain in 1888. Claimed instead by St. Paul, he was promptly cut from the team. His career as minor league umpire was shortened by the onset of consumption. For a number of years the New Castle, PA, native lived on a plantation in Alabama to recover, and was reported near death in 1912. Quest actually died in San Diego on November 14, 1924, two days short of his 66th birthday. *(Total Baseball; Chicago Daily Tribune; National Police Gazette; Los Angeles Times; Washington Post; Baseball-Reference.com)*

Joe Quest (T. Scott Brandon)

Joe Quinn was the first Australian to play in the major leagues, when at age 19 he became the regular first baseman for the St. Louis Maroons in 1884. He went on to play 17 seasons in the majors with eleven different teams in four leagues—most seasons as a regular and most as a second baseman—leading the National League in fielding three times at that position. Moving with the Maroons into the NL in 1885, he also played with Boston (twice), the St. Louis Browns/Cardinals (three times), Baltimore, the Cleveland Spiders, and Cincinnati in that league, before finishing in the American League with Washington in 1901. In 1890 he played with Boston of the Players League. In all he hit .261, and his .946 fielding percentage was sixteen points over the league average for second basemen. Quinn also managed in St. Louis (1895) and Cleveland (1898), where his depleted ranks finished with a 12–141 record. He managed Des Moines of the Western League in 1902–03. Quinn was a mortician in off season, and in retirement he "conducted an undertaking establishment on Union Avenue, St. Louis." Born in Sydney to Irish immigrant parents, Quinn died in St. Louis on November 12, 1940, at age 75. *(Sporting News; Total Baseball; BaseballLibrary.com; Baseball-Reference.com; U.S. Federal Census)*

Marshall Quinton was 32 years old when he entered the majors with the Richmond Virginians in 1884. Used primarily as a catcher, he also played the outfield and shortstop, hitting .234 in 26 games. The following season the Philadelphia native caught seven games for the A's, leaving the majors with a .228 average for 33 games. He also played for Portland in 1885. The son of an Irish shoe factory worker, Quinton appears in the 1880 census for Albany, NY, as a boarder who "Plays B Ball." Long listed as a missing player by the SABR Biographical Committee, he now has a death date and place—Trenton, NJ, June 19, 1904, at age 56. *(SABR Biographical Committee Newsletter; Total Baseball; Baseball Almanac; U.S. Federal Census)*

Charles "Old Hoss" Radbourn won 309 games in eleven seasons in the majors. He is best remembered for his monster 1884 season in which he helped Providence win a league title. Radbourn led the NL with 59 wins, a .831 winning percentage, 73 complete games, 678 innings, 441 strikeouts and a 1.38 ERA. He pitched the last 17 games of the season, winning 14. In the first ever World Series that year, he did not yield an earned run in defeating the New York Mets three times. In his career Radbourn also had a 48-win season, a 33-win season and six more seasons with at least twenty victories. An outfielder and second baseman before his release by Buffalo in 1880, he became a pitcher at Providence in 1881. When Providence disbanded, he moved on to Boston (1886–89) and the Boston Players League Reds (1890), before finishing with Cincinnati in 1891. Radbourn then invested in a saloon and billiards

Charley Radbourn (Mark Fimoff)

Paul Radford (Library of Congress)

parlor in Bloomington, IL. In 1895 he lost an eye in a shooting accident. Born in Rochester, NY, to English parents, Radbourn died of paresis at Bloomington on February 5, 1897. He was 47 years old. Radbourn was elected to the Hall of Fame in 1939 *(Total Baseball; Boston Daily Globe; New York Times; DeadballEra.com)*

Paul Radford played with nine clubs in twelve major league seasons—all as a regular outfielder or shortstop. He debuted with Boston in 1883, coming from Hyde Park. Called "Lucky Paul," he regularly played on winners—including the 1884 league champion Providence Grays—and was considered a team's mascot. He also played with Kansas City, Cleveland and Washington in the National League; New York, Brooklyn and Boston of the American Association; and Cleveland of the Players League. Only 5'6" in height, he drew a league-leading 106 walks in 1887 and was regarded as a very fast base runner, one who "travels around the bases at a terrific rate of speed." A career .242 hitter, he hit .292 with Cleveland in the PL. After finishing with Washington in 1894, he played with Scranton and as late as 1906 was playing second base "like a youngster" for Lynn of the New England League. A resident of the Boston suburb of Hyde Park, Radford appears in the 1900, 1910, 1920 and 1930 censuses as a machinist or foreman in a machine shop. He died at Boston on February 21, 1945, at age 83. *(Total Baseball; Boston Globe; New York Times; Washington Post; Sporting News; U.S. Federal Census; Sporting Life)*

Phil Reccius joined his older brother John on the Louisville Eclipse in 1882. After two trials, the Louisville native played in 73 games as a pitcher-third baseman in 1884, and became the team's regular third baseman in 1885. Remaining with Louisville until 1887, he became a regular with the Cleveland Blues in that season. Brief trials with Louisville again (1888) and Rochester (1890) ended his major league career. In eight seasons he hit .231, and his fielding at third base was just under the league average. For the next four seasons, Reccius pitched in the minors—and also with the Kentucky champion Deppens. While pitching for Spokane in 1894, he was hit in the head by a batted ball, fracturing his skull. In the 1900 census, Reccius, son of German immigrants, is shown unemployed and living with his brother in Louisville. In 1902 the *Washington Post* noted that as a result of the head injury, Reccius "is now demented." Institutionalized, the 40-year-old Reccius died in the Kentucky insane asylum on February 15, 1903. *(Total Baseball; Baseball-Reference.com; Washington Post; Chicago Daily Tribune; Baseball Necrology; U.S. Federal Census)*

Edward "Icicle" Reeder, a local Cincinnati product, played three games for the Red Stockings in 1884, beginning in late June; shifting to the Washington Unions, he played in three more games, finishing August 5. In all, he hit .154 in 26 at bats. In the minors, he is listed as a Toledo player in 1888, and he played in the Western Inter-State League in 1890, when he instigated a walkout of Indianapolis players over back pay. The *Washington Post* identifies him as having been arrested for picking pockets outside a church in 1902. In the 1900 census he is shown as a "day laborer," still living with his mother. According to the Heritage Foundation, he died at Longview Hospital in Cincinnati on January 15, 1913, of "dementia paralysis" at age 60. *(Total Baseball; Baseball-Reference.com; Washington Post; Chicago Daily Tribune; Springgrove.org)*

Billy Reid, a left-handed hitting Canadian, had two major league trials. In 1883 he hit .278 in 24 games for Baltimore, primarily as a second baseman. In 1884, after leading the Northwestern League in hits, he appeared in 19 games for Pittsburgh, primarily as an outfielder. In a 43-game major league career he hit .263. Neither as a second baseman nor as an outfielder did he field within 24 points of the league average. Returning to the minors, he led the Northwestern League in runs scored in 1886. Reid was from London, Ontario. The 1911 Canadian census shows the 53-year-old Reid living in London with his wife and six children. He died there on June 26, 1940, at age 83. *(Total Baseball; Retrosheet; Baseball-Reference.com; Encyclopedia of Minor League Baseball; Census of Canada)*

Charlie Reilley (Charles O'Reilly) was hitless in 11 at bats for the Boston Reds in 1884. He had begun in the majors with Troy in 1879, hitting .232 in 62 games. He also played with National League clubs in Cincinnati (1880), Detroit and Worcester (1881) and Providence (1882). Overall he hit .210 in 119 games. Used primarily at catcher, Reilley played virtually every field position, with an .866 fielding percentage. Born to Irish parents in Providence in 1856, he appears in the 1880 census for Providence as a baseball player. His death on November 4, 1904, is also noted. He would have been 48 years old. *(Baseball-Reference.com; Retrosheet; U.S. Federal Census; Rhode Island Deaths 1630–1930)*

John "Long John" Reilly played his entire major league career in Cincinnati. Apprenticed to Strobridge Lithographing Company, he became a first baseman because he felt that catching might damage his art career. He played for the National League Red Stockings in 1880 but hit poorly. He returned to the majors with the American Association Red Stockings in 1883, remaining with the team through 1889. In 1884 he hit a career high .339, leading the AA with 11 homers and a .551

Long John Reilly (Library of Congress)

slugging percentage. In 1888 he hit .321 with a league-leading 13 homers, 103 RBIs and a .503 slugging percentage. In 1890, at age 32, he hit 26 triples. According to the *New York Times,* the 6'2" Reilly revolutionized first base play, being the first to play off the bag; he led first basemen in fielding in 1889, and his career range factors were more than a point higher than the league average. In 1890 he returned to the NL, when the Red Stockings changed leagues, finishing his major league career in 1891 with a .289 average. He lived his entire life in Cincinnati, where he worked as a commercial artist. Reilly died on May 31, 1937, at age 78. *(Total Baseball; SABR Biography Project; New York Times; Baseball-Reference.com)*

Charlie Reipschlager split playing on the Metropolitans with Bill Holbert, Holbert catching Tim Keefe and Reipschlager catching Jack Lynch. When the Mets were formed as an independent club in 1882, they acquired Reipschlager from the Brooklyn Atlantics. He caught 72 games in 1883, hitting .243. When the Mets disbanded after the 1886 season, Reipschlager went to Cleveland, where he finished his major league career in 1887. In five seasons, he hit .222 and fielded .900 as a catcher — just under the league average. Continuing in the minors, he played for Jersey City in 1888. Born to German parents in New York City in 1854, he would have been 29 years old when he first entered the majors. The 1890 *City Directory for Jersey City,* New Jersey, lists him as a ball player and that of 1892 lists him as a laborer. The 1900 census for Atlantic City, NJ, shows him as a mechanical engineer. He died in Atlantic City on March 16, 1910, at age 56. *(Baseball-Reference.com; National Police Gazette; Retrosheet; U.S. Federal Census; City Directory for Atlantic City; City Directory for Jersey City; Sporting Life)*

Charlie "Pop" Reising came from the village of Lanesville, IN, to play outfield for the Indianapolis Hoosiers in 1884. After two games against the Toledo Blue Stockings on July 19–20, games in which he went hitless, the 22-year-old ended his major league career. A Charlie Reising pitched for Hastings of the Western League in 1887 and signed with Davenport of the Western Association in 1888. Born to German parents, Reising became a "saloonist" in Louisville, according to the 1900 census. Kentucky death records show that the 53-year-old Reising died of pulmonary tuberculosis in Louisville on July 26, 1915. He is listed as a retired saloon keeper. *(Total Baseball; Baseball Almanac; Sporting News; U.S. Federal Census; Kentucky Death Records; Sporting Life)*

Jack Remsen played with the Chicago White Stockings in 1878–79, wearing a full beard. The Brooklyn native began his professional career in 1872 with the Brooklyn Atlantics of the National Association. He also played with the New York Mutuals and Hartford Dark Blues, moving with Hartford into the National League in 1876. With St. Louis in 1877, Remsen moved on to Chicago, Cleveland (1881) and Philadelphia (1884) before finishing with the Brooklyn Trolley Dodgers (1884). A big, speedy player, he led NL outfielders in fielding in 1878. But his career .233 batting average prompted the *Chicago Daily Tribune* to note that "but for his inability in bat [he] would be one of the most desirable ball-players in the country." He continued to play in the minors with Hartford; Ottawa, IL; and Lewiston, ME. A John J. Remsen who seems to fit the ballplayer's age and background appears in the 1900 Brooklyn census, working as a "conductor." The same person is listed in the 1920 census as a building superintendent for a real estate company in Manhattan. *(Total Baseball; Baseball-Reference.com; Chicago Daily Tribune; Boston Daily Globe; U.S. Federal Census)*

Richardson played second base for the Chicago Browns in a game at Boston on July 10, 1884, going hitless in four at bats. In the field he handled three plays resulting in one putout, one assist and one error. *SABR Baseball Encyclopedia* says that Richardson was from Boston and that he was 5'4" and 136 pounds. Marshall Wright gives him the

Charlie Reipschlager (T. Scott Brandon)

first name of "Art." *Sporting Life* notes in 1885 that a player named Richardson from the Boston Beacons was considering a move to the professional ranks. The 1880 census for Boston actually shows a 19-year-old Arthur Richardson, living with his brother-in-law, working as a silverplater *(Baseball-Reference.com; Retrosheet; Nineteenth Century Baseball; U.S. Federal Census; Sporting Life)*

Danny Richardson joined the New York Gothams from the amateur ranks after a tryout in 1884. By 1887 he had became a regular second baseman, praised as a "ground coverer," and later as being "very tidy." In 1888 he led the National League in fielding and for his career he fielded .940 — 18 points over the league average. A career .254 hitter, he reached .280 for the NL champions in 1889. An articulate spokesman for the Brotherhood, he jumped to the Players League New York Giants in 1890. In 1892 Richardson became captain of the Washington Nationals, moving on to Brooklyn in 1893. After being suspended for a part of that season for "intemperate" habits, he finished as the regular shortstop for Louisville in 1894. Only 31 years old, he left baseball to become a "dry goods merchant" in his native Elmira, and is later described as "well-to-do." Born to Irish parents, Richardson died in New York City while lunching with a buyer on September 12, 1926. He was 63 years old. *(Total Baseball; Boston Daily Globe; New York Times; Chicago Daily Tribune; National Police Gazette; Sporting Life)*

Hardy Richardson hit .299 in fourteen major league seasons as an outfielder and second baseman. Along with Jack Rowe, Deacon White, and Dan Brouthers, Richardson was a member of the so-called "Big Four" which formed in Buffalo in 1881 and then helped Detroit win the National League championships in 1887. Richardson, a Clarksboro, NJ, product, began his career with Buffalo in 1879 and was sold to Detroit in 1886. In 1888 he began a three-year stay in Boston, playing in three different leagues before finishing his career in 1892 with Washington and New York. Richardson hit over .300 seven times, leading the NL in hits and homers in 1886 while hitting .351,

Danny Richardson (Mark Fimoff)

Hardy Richardson (Library of Congress)

and in 1890 he led the Players League with 146 RBIs. Either as an outfielder or a second baseman, he posted fielding numbers superior to his contemporaries. Richardson lived in Utica, NY, where he was an avid trap shooter. According to Bill Lee, he "worked for a number of years for Remington Typewriter Company." This is confirmed by the employment line in the 1920 census. Richardson died at Utica on January 14, 1931, at age 75. *(Total Baseball; Baseball-Reference.com; Baseball Necrology; Washington Post; National Police Gazette; U.S. Federal Census)*

John Richmond hit .283 and led American Association shortstops in fielding while playing with the Columbus Buckeyes in 1883. The Philadelphia native began with his hometown Athletics in the National Association in 1875, hitting .200 in 29 games. He returned to the majors with Syracuse in 1879. In that season the *Chicago Daily Tribune* included him in a list of former major leaguers "dropped because of inefficiency." Richmond ultimately had trials with Boston (1880–81), Cleveland (1882) and the Athletics (1882) before landing with the Buckeyes in 1883–84. He finished with Pittsburgh in 1885. In all Richmond hit .238 in 8 seasons, three spent as a regular. His .866 fielding percentage was ten points over the league average. Richmond died in Philadelphia on October 5, 1898, at age 53. *Baseball Almanac* says January 1, 1900. *(Baseball-Reference.com; Chicago Daily Tribune; Washington Post; National Police Gazette; Baseball Almanac)*

Chris Rickley played shortstop for the Philadelphia Keystones for six games in June, 1884. He had five hits—two doubles—for a .200 batting average. His assist figure suggests that he had above average range, but his nine errors gave him a .757 fielding percentage. He later played for Toronto of the International Association. Rickley was a Philadelphia native; the 1900 census says that he had German parents. In 1900 he was employed as a hosteler; ten years later he is listed as a laborer in a chair factory. Rickley died in Philadelphia on October 25, 1911, at age 52. *(Total Baseball; Baseball-Reference.com; U.S. Federal Census; Sporting Life)*

Frank Ringo played in 60 games—primarily as a catcher—for the Philadelphia Quakers in 1883, his rookie year. Over the next three seasons he played for the Quakers, Detroit and Kansas City of the National League and the A's and Pittsburgh of the American Association. Overall he hit .192 in 139 games and his .844 fielding average was more than fifty points below the league average. The *National Police Gazette* described Ringo as a "good ball player, but a better drinker." Born in Parkville, MO, to Kentucky parents, Ringo is listed in the 1880 census as a store clerk. On April 12, 1889, at age 28, he took his own life in Kansas City, injecting himself with morphine. *(Total Baseball; National Police Gazette; Los Angeles Times; Washington Post; Baseball-Reference.com; Sporting Life)*

Charlie Robinson, a left-handed hitting catcher, had two major league trials. In 1884 the 28-year-old Robinson hit .284 in 20 games for the Indianapolis Hoosiers. A year later he appeared in 11 games for the Brooklyn Trolley Dodgers, hitting only .150, giving him a major league average of .242. He fielded .919—higher than the league average. Born in Westerly, RI, to a livery stable keeper from New York, Robinson followed in his father's footsteps; the 1900 census shows him living at home and working as a livery stable keeper. In the 1910 census, he has become a "Pedler." Robinson died in Providence on May 18, 1913, at

John Richmond (Wikimedia Commons)

age 56. *(Baseball Encyclopedia; Baseball-Reference.com; Retrosheet; U.S. Federal Census)*

Fred Robinson, the older brother of Hall of Fame manager Wilbert "Uncle Robby" Robinson, had a three-game tryout at second base for the Cincinnati Outlaw Reds at the beginning of the 1884 season. The South Acton, MA, native collected three hits for a .231 average, and had three errors for a .727 fielding average. The censuses of 1910 and 1920 show him living in Hudson, MA, working in a shoe factory, as his father had done. In the 1930 census he is listed as a caretaker for real estate property. Bill Lee says that Robinson was doing janitorial work at a bank and was at his job shoveling snow when he died on December 18, 1933, at age 77. *(Baseball-Reference.com; Retrosheet; Baseball Necrology; U.S. Federal Census)*

William "Yank" Robinson began and closed a ten-year major league career in the National League, hitting .179 at both Detroit (1882) and Washington (1892). Between NL engagements he was a regular infielder in three leagues. He led the Union Association in walks while playing for the Baltimore Monumentals in 1884; he twice led the American Association in walks with the St. Louis Browns, helping them win four consecutive championships; in the Players League he drew more than one hundred walks while playing for Pittsburgh in 1890. A career .241 hitter, he reached .305 with St. Louis in the inflated 1887 season, and .316 in the 1886 World Series, won by St. Louis, but in four of his ten seasons he hit under .200. Over the four-year period 1887–90, the 5'6" Robinson drew 427 walks, resulting in a league-leading on-base percentage of .400 in 1888. Suffering from pulmonary problems, the 32-year-old Robinson left the playing ranks in 1892. Born in Philadelphia to English-Irish parents, he died two years later in St. Louis on August 25, 1894. *(DeadballEra.com; Total Baseball; Baseball-Reference.com; U.S. Federal Census; Sporting Life)*

Bill Rollinson (William Henry Winslow) caught one game for the Washington Unions on June 17, 1884. In the 11–1 loss to the Reds in Boston, the 28-year-old went hitless in three at bats. He also had a difficult time behind the plate with four errors and a passed ball for a .714 fielding average. Rollinson was born in Fairfield, ME, into a farm family. He appears under his birth name in both the 1860 and 1870 censuses. In 1910 he is a superintendent of schools in New Hampshire; in 1920 he is farming in Florida; in 1930, at age 74, he is teaching at Shaw University in Virginia. Winslow died at Bristow, VA, on 28 September, 1938, at age 82. *(Total Baseball; Baseball-Reference.com; U.S. Federal Census; Ancestry.com)*

James "Chief" Roseman began his major league career with Troy in 1882, coming from Springfield. He spent four years with the Metro-

"Yank" Robinson (Library of Congress)

"Chief" Roseman (T. Scott Brandon)

politans (1883–86), helping them to an American Association championship in 1884, when he hit a career high .298. He split 1887 among the Athletics, the Mets and the Trolley Dodgers; in 1890 he served as playing manager of the St. Louis Browns before finishing with Louisville. For his seven seasons in the majors, Roseman held regular outfield status in six, hitting .263. Roseman played for Lowell of the New England League in 1891. Later notes show that he was "thinking of organizing a colored team" in 1892 and that he had closed his "Mountain dew depot" in New York City in 1896. Bill Lee found that Roseman worked for 36 years in the Department of Sewers in New York City. The 1910 census shows that he was a driver for that department. Born in New York City to Irish parents, Roseman died in Brooklyn on July 4, 1938, at age 84. *(Baseball Necrology; Total Baseball; Chicago Daily Tribune; Washington Post; National Police Gazette; U.S. Federal Census; Sporting Life)*

Dave Rowe has the dubious distinction of pitching a complete game for Cleveland in 1882 in which he was tagged for 29 hits and 35 runs— 12 of which were earned. In better days he played outfield for seven seasons. He hit .313 for the Baltimore Orioles in 1883 and .293 for the St. Louis Maroons in 1884. He was second in the Union Association with 11 triples that season. Rowe had entered the majors with the White Stockings in 1877 and returned to the majors with Cleveland in 1882. When St. Louis moved to the National League in 1885, Rowe's average dropped to .161. He was player-manager in Kansas City for the NL Cowboys in 1886 and the American Association Cowboys in 1888, leading the clubs to seventh and eighth place finishes. He later became a club owner at Denver and Lincoln, being described as one who was "in baseball business for the money to be made from it, with no local pride attached." Born in Harrisburg, PA, to a Scottish father and Canadian mother, Rowe appears in the 1900 census for Denver with a listed occupation of "mining & milling." He died at Glendale, CA, on December 9, 1930, at age 76. *(Sporting News; Baseball-Reference.com; Total Baseball; U.S. Federal Census; Sporting Life)*

Jack Rowe joined Buffalo in late 1879 from Rockford. He soon became a part of Buffalo's "Big Four," a group that moved en masse to Detroit in 1886 and helped the Wolverines win the 1887 championship. When Detroit folded in 1888, Rowe and Deacon White tried to buy their own

Jack Rowe (T. Scott Brandon)

contracts but eventually played with Pittsburgh before forming the Players League club in Buffalo in 1890, Rowe's last major league stop. Originally a catcher, Rowe became a shortstop when he moved to Detroit and was described as "a fair fielding shortstop and a great batter." In twelve seasons he hit .286, but hit .333 in 1881 (leading the NL in triples), .318 in 1887 and .315 in 1884. He led NL catchers in fielding in 1884 and PL shortstops in fielding in 1890. Married to an heiress, Rowe remained in baseball until 1898 playing in the Western Association. Rowe's obituary in *Sporting Life* noted that he "kept a cigar store on Main and North Division streets" in Buffalo. This is confirmed by the 1900 census. Rowe died in St. Louis on April 25, 1911, at age 54. The cause of death was leakage of the heart. *(Total Baseball; Baseball Reference.com; Atlanta Constitution; Boston Globe; New York Times; Sporting Life; U.S. Federal Census)*

Ed Rowen joined the Boston Beaneaters in 1882, playing regularly as an outfielder or catcher that season while hitting .248. In 1883 he jumped to the Philadelphia Athletics and saw his playing time reduced to 49 games and his average drop to .219, but he helped the team to a second place finish in the American Association. After four games in 1884, he left the majors with a .242 batting average and a .862 fielding average — more than thirty points below the league average. A baseball note says that he had signed with the New York club but did not make the team due to a lame arm. Born in Bridgeport, CT, to Irish parents, he died there of internal hemorrhaging on February 22, 1892, at age 34. (*Total Baseball; Baseball-Reference.com; National Police Gazette; Washington Post; DeadballEra.com; Baseball Magazine*)

Jim Roxburgh was the first player from Santa Cruz County, CA, to make a major league team. Growing up in San Francisco, he moved from local teams to the Baltimore Orioles in May 1884, catching two games and making two hits. In 1887 he caught two games for the Philadelphia A's, leaving the majors in August 1887 with three hits and an .840 fielding average. He caught for and managed Jamestown of the New York–Pennsylvania League in 1890–91. The son of a Scottish father and Irish mother, Roxburgh had worked in a printing office before entering the majors. The 1900 census shows him working as a pressman in San Francisco, that of 1910 as a laundry driver, and that of 1920 as a school janitor. According to Bill Lee, Roxburgh died on February 21, 1934, from injuries suffered when he was struck by a car in Santa Cruz, CA. He was 76 years old. (*Total Baseball; Baseball-Reference.com; Baseball Necrology; U.S. Federal Census; DeadballEra.com*)

John Rudderham played left field for the Boston Reds on September 18, 1884. In a home 13–7 loss to the Outlaw Reds, the 20-year-old had a single in four at bats, but committed errors on both balls hit to him. His family — a Canadian father and an English mother — had migrated to Quincy, MA, from Prince Edward Island. In the 1910 census Rudderham is shown as living in Randolph, MA, and working as a college baseball trainer. Bill Lee notes that Rudderham trained boxers, the Philadelphia Phillies, and the University of Illinois football and track teams. Rudderham also umpired in the New England League and trained the Montreal team. By 1920, his occupation is listed as "none." Bill Lee says that Rudderham was in failing health for a number of years. He died in Randolph on April 3, 1942, at age 78. (*Total Baseball; Baseball-Reference.com; U.S. Federal Census; Baseball Necrology; Sporting Life*)

John A. Ryan started six games for the Baltimore Monumentals in early 1884, coming from Dayton. With five complete games and a 3.35 ERA, he compiled a 3–2 record. Ryan also played a game in the outfield, but managed only an .080 batting average before leaving the majors in August. *Sporting Life* reported that Ryan had suffered blood poisoning from an injury, which ended his season. In 1885 he helped Raleigh win the championship of the North Carolina League. *Sporting Life* called him an "excellent, sober, steady player." *SABR Baseball Encyclopedia* gives him a Birmingham, MI, birth. (*Total Baseball; SABR Baseball Encyclopedia; Baseball-Reference.com; Sporting Life*)

John M. Ryan (Daniel Sheehan) played seven games for the Washington Unions and two games for the Wilmington Quicksteps in 1884. In those nine games he had 5 hits — one a triple — for a .147 average. As an outfielder and third baseman, he committed five errors in seventeen chances for .706 fielding average. *Retrosheet* gives him a Washington, DC, birthplace; the 1880 census for Washington, DC, shows that an Irish immigrant couple — Patrick and Ellen Sheehan — were parents of a son Daniel, born around 1860. Daniel is listed as a laborer in that census. (*Baseball-Reference.com; U.S. Federal Census; Retrosheet*)

Tom Ryder enjoyed a major-league career of two weeks in mid-1884. In eight games, the left-handed hitting outfielder had seven hits — including a double — for the St. Louis Maroons, leaving the majors with a .250 average. In the field he committed seven errors in twenty chances for a .650 average. *Retrosheet* lists his birth as May 9, 1863, in Dubuque, Iowa. This would make him 21 years old when he entered the majors. His death is listed as July 18, 1935, also in Dubuque, making him 72 years old at the time of his death. The federal census shows him born to Irish parents, his father a wagon maker. Ryder was apprenticed to this trade and is listed as a wagon maker in the 1885 state census. Later censuses show him working as a fireman, and finally as a janitor for a gas company. (*Total Baseball; Baseball-Reference.com; Retrosheet; U.S. Federal Census; Iowa State Census Collection*)

Ed Santry, a Chicago native, began his career with the Chicago Reserves in 1884. When that club disbanded, he played six games with the Detroit Wolverines. Despite the report that he was "doing well," he hit only .182. Santry played for Memphis in 1885 but left because of the heat. He played for Oshkosh in 1886 before retiring to join Picketts, a top-flight Chicago City League club. Born in Chicago to Irish parents, Santry died in Chicago on March 6, 1899, at age 38. *(Total Baseball; Baseball-Reference.com; Chicago Daily Tribune; U.S. Federal Census)*

Jimmy Say had trials with five major league clubs over a six year period. In 1882 he hit .209 in 23 games between Louisville and Philadelphia of the American Association. In 1884 he hit .224 in 18 games between Wilmington and Kansas City of the Union Association; in 1887 he hit .375 in a sixteen-game trial with Cleveland of the AA. Statistically he was a good fielding shortstop (.884 for 22 games) and a mediocre third baseman (.690 for 35 games). Born in Baltimore to native Maryland parents, Say is the younger brother of Louis Say. Following a long illness, Jimmy Say died in Baltimore on June 23, 1894, at age 32. *(Baseball-Reference.com; U.S. Federal Census; Baseball Necrology)*

Lou Say was one of the four-league players. Allegedly the inventor of the hidden ball trick, he began as a 19-year-old shortstop with his hometown Baltimore Marylands of the National Association in 1873, also playing with the Lord Baltimores and Washington of that league. After playing with the National League Cincinnati Red Stockings in 1880, Say played with Philadelphia and Baltimore of the American Association before finishing with Baltimore and Kansas City of the Union Association in 1884. In seven seasons—two as a regular—Say hit .232 and fielded .812, twenty-four points below the league average for shortstops. In the 1880 census he is listed as a "base ballist." He is still listed as a "ball player" in the 1890 Baltimore city census. *Sporting Life* reported in 1893 that Say would "confine his abilities to the management hereafter." The 1900 census shows him living in Baltimore as a boarder and working as a blacksmith. Say died on June 6, 1930, at Fallston, MD. He was 76 years old. His younger brother Jimmy was also a major league shortstop. *(Total Baseball; Baseball-Reference.com; U.S. Federal Census; Bill James' Historical Register; Baltimore City Census; Sporting Life)*

Patrick Scanlan debuted for the Boston Reds on Independence Day 1884. The 23-year-old Canadian played left field for six games, hitting .292 but fielding .800; he played his last game on July 11. He was from an Irish family that had immigrated to Massachusetts from Nova Scotia. The 1900 census shows a Patrick Scanlan, born in 1862, who had immigrated in 1863. He was living with his family at Ludlow, MA, and working as a blacksmith. Scanlan died on July 17, 1913, in Springfield, MA, at age 52. *(Total Baseball; Baseball-Reference.com; U.S. Federal Census)*

Bill Schenck hit .260 as the regular third baseman for the Louisville Eclipse in 1882. In 1884 he was the regular shortstop for the Richmond Virginians when they entered the American Association, hitting .205 in 42 games. He finished his major league career by playing one game for the Brooklyn Trolley Dodgers in September 1885. In all, he hit .236 for 103 games. Statistically he was a better-than-average third baseman and a mediocre shortstop. *Retrosheet* gives him a Brooklyn birthplace and an 1854 birth date. That William G. Schenck is still listed as a ball player in the 1900 census, when he was 45 years old. He is listed again in the 1930 census, still living in Brooklyn, working as an elevator operator at age 75. Schenck died on January 29, 1934, in Brooklyn at the age of 79. *(Retrosheet; Baseball-Reference.com; U.S. Federal Census)*

Lewis "Jumbo" Schoeneck led Union Association first basemen in fielding in 1884. The 6'3" 223-pounder debuted with his hometown Chicago Browns, finishing the season with the Baltimore Monumentals. Between the teams he hit .308, sixth highest in the UA. He found National League pitching more difficult, so subsequent trials with Indianapolis in 1888 and 1889 dropped his career mark to .283, but his fielding percentage (.964) and range factor (10.51) exceeded the league average. Schoeneck played for New Haven in 1889–90; he was released by Seattle in 1892. The son of German immigrants, Schoeneck is listed in the 1900 and 1910 censuses for Chicago, working as a solicitor for an express company. He died in Chicago on January 20, 1930, at age 67. *(Baseball-Reference.com; Total Baseball; Retrosheet; U.S. Federal Census; Sporting Life)*

William "Pop" Schwartz caught two games for the Columbus Buckeyes as a 19-year-old in 1883. When the Union Association opened in 1884, he joined Cincinnati's Outlaw Reds, catching 29 more games. When he left the majors in August, he had 26 hits for a .236 average and an .819 fielding average — 67 points below the league average for catchers. He caught for Memphis in 1885. Schwartz was born in Kentucky of German parents. Both the 1920 census and his death certificate identify him as a resident of Newport, KY, and a store clerk. Schwartz died at Newport on December 22, 1940, at age 76. Bill Lee notes that Schwartz had been crippled from injuries received while catching. (*Total Baseball; U.S. Federal Census; Kentucky Certificate of Death; Baseball Necrology*)

Scott played thirteen games as the right fielder for the Baltimore Monumentals in July and August 1884. At the plate he collected 12 hits in 53 at bats for a .226 average. In the field he handled ten of eleven chances for a .909 average. (*Retrosheet; Baseball Encyclopedia*)

Milt Scott, a Chicago native, played one game at first base for the White Stockings as a 16-year-old in 1882. In 1884 he became a regular at Detroit, where, according to the *National Police Gazette*, he "is playing a great game at first base." He split 1885 between Detroit and Pittsburgh of the American Association. In 1886, to avoid a lawsuit, he was shifted to Baltimore, where he finished his major league career at age 25. In four seasons, three as a regular, he hit only .228, but his range and fielding percentage were well above the league average. Scott played in the minors at Kansas City in 1887. The son of a Scottish merchant father who had emigrated from Canada, Scott appears in the 1920 and 1930 censuses as resident of Baltimore, working as an insurance solicitor. He died at Baltimore on November 3, 1938, at age 72. (*Total Baseball; Baseball-Reference.com; Chicago Daily Tribune; National Police Gazette; Sporting News; U.S. Federal Census*)

Emmett Seery entered the majors with the Baltimore Monumentals in 1884. Playing left field, the 23-year-old Seery hit .311, the highest mark among the Monumentals. At the end of the season, he played one game for the Kansas City Unions. After leading the Western League in runs in 1885, he went on to spend six more seasons as a regular with St. Louis and Indianapolis of the National League, with Brooklyn of the Players League, and with the Cincinnati Kellys of the American Association, making him one of the four-league players. He finished with the NL Louisville Colonels in 1892. Only a .252 career

Emmett Seery (Library of Congress)

hitter, he reached an inflated .314 with Indianapolis in 1887 and .285 with Cincinnati in 1891. He was also an .896 fielder — somewhat above average. Born in Illinois to an Irish father, Seery appears in the 1920 census as a farmer living in Jensen, FL. An 1897 note in *Sporting Life* calls it an orange plantation. Seery died at Saranac Lake, NY, on August 7, 1930, at age 71. (*Total Baseball; Baseball-Reference.com; U.S. Federal Census; Retrosheet; Sporting Life*)

Billy Serad won 16 games as a rookie with Buffalo in 1884, but after the first week the *Boston Globe* declared him "not a success as a pitcher." In 1886 he won thirty games with an 0.96 ERA and 260 strikeouts for Utica of the Eastern League. The "little Frenchman" pitched four seasons in the majors, winning 35 games, but never enjoying a winning season with either Buffalo or the Cincinnati Red Stockings. Serad then pitched in the minors until 1892, when he became a Western League umpire; he later umpired in the Southern League. Born in Philadelphia, he lived in Chester, PA, where he worked for a pipe company and later a tube company, according to Bill Lee. In 1907 *Sporting Life* reported that Serad had been struck by a trolley and that he had suffered a brain injury. He died at Chester on November 1, 1925. *(Total Baseball; National Police Gazette; Boston Daily Globe; Washington Post; Baseball Necrology; Sporting Life)*

Tom Sexton was a nineteen-year-old starting shortstop when Milwaukee entered the Union Association on September 27, 1884. In 12 games the left-handed hitting Sexton hit .234. His .853 fielding percentage was much higher than the league average for shortstops. After that season, he went on to play for Toledo and Eau Claire. Born in Rock Island, IL, to an Irish father, Sexton was employed at a saw mill in 1880. He next appears in the 1910 census, living with his brother at Rock Island, working for the federal government as a blacksmith. Sexton died at Rock Island on February 8, 1934, at age 68. *(Total Baseball; Baseball-Reference.com; Retrosheet; U.S. Federal Census; Sporting Life)*

Taylor Shafer is now credited with the records once thought to be those of two players — Frank Shaffer and Taylor Shaffer. As a 17-year-old, he debuted with the Union Association Altoona Mountain Citys in 1884, hitting .284 in 19 games. When Altoona folded, Shafer moved on to Kansas City — the team that replaced Altoona — but hit only .171 as a Cowboy. He finished that season with the Baltimore Monumentals. In the expansion 1890 season, Shafer played for his hometown Philadelphia Athletics, but again hit poorly — .172 in 69 games — and left the majors with a .186 batting mark. In 70 games at second base, his .920 average was pretty much the league average. In 61 games in the outfield, he fielded twenty points below the league average. Born in Philadelphia, Shafer was the younger brother of Orator Shaffer. Taylor Shafer appears in the censuses for both 1900 in Coatesville, PA, and 1930 in Los Angeles. In the first case he is listed as "retired." In the second, his occupation is "none." California death records give him a death date of October 27, 1945, and a birth date of July 13, 1866. *(Baseball-Reference.com; U.S. Federal Census; California Death Records; Retrosheet; Sporting Life)*

George "Orator" Shaffer (Shafer) spent 13 seasons as a major league outfielder — ten as a regular. In 1879 he recorded 50 outfield assists, a still-standing major league record. Over his career he hit .282 with a high of .360 with the Union Association St. Louis Maroons in 1884. He also hit .338 and .304 in 1878–79 but dropped to .214 in 1882 and .195 in 1885. A much traveled player — some suggest because he was an outstanding talker — he began with Hartford of the National Association in 1874. Along the way, he played with 10 clubs, finishing with his hometown Philadelphia Athletics of the American Association in 1890, making him one of the four-league players. Stops include the Philadelphia White Stockings and the New York Mutuals of the National Association and Louisville, Indianapolis, Chicago, Cleveland, St. Louis and Buffalo of the National League. His younger brother Taylor played shortstop with the Philadelphia A's in Shaffer's last season. Born in Philadelphia, Shaffer died there on January 21, 1922, at age 71. *(Total Baseball; Baseball-Reference.com; BaseballLibrary.com; SABR Baseball Encyclopedia)*

Gus Shallix (August Schallick), a German-born right hander, went 11–10 with the Red Stockings in 1884, completing all 23 of his starts. In 1885 he went 6–4 before leaving the majors. In August 1885 *National Police Gazette* noted that his "arm is 'gone' completely" and so he was released by Nashville. Actually, his "twirling days were over" when he took an "inshoot" from Cyclone Miller at Nashville. In 1894 the *Chicago Daily Tribune* reported that Shallix "has an idea that his arm has been born again," and he received a tryout with the White Stockings. Bill Lee says that Shallix was a policeman in Cincinnati for 29 years. The 1910 and 1920 censuses for Cincinnati — listing him by his German name — indicate that he had immigrated in 1869, and agree that he was a member of the city police force. Shallix died in Cincinnati on October 28, 1937. *(Total Baseball; National Police Gazette; Chicago Daily Tribune; Baseball Necrology; U.S. Federal Census; Sporting Life)*

Frederick "Dupee" Shaw, a lefthander, was "one of the first pitchers to use the 'wind-up.'" His gyrations on the mound attracted a large following, and he was for a time quite successful. After compiling a 10–15 record for Detroit in 1883, he jumped from the club in mid–1884 to the Boston Reds, going 30–33 with 451 strikeouts between the two clubs. Reinstated in 1885, he won 23 games for Providence, and when that club folded, he went to Washington in 1886, finishing there in 1888. In all, he won 83 games with a 3.10 ERA in six seasons. A native of Charlestown, MA, he appears in the census for 1900, living in Boston and working as a bartender. In the 1910 census, he is working as a grocer. However, an 1897 note in *Sporting Life* shows that Shaw was fined $300 for operating a "policy shop." Shaw died at Wakefield, MA, on June 11, 1938, at age 79. *(Total Baseball; Baseball-Reference.com; Washington Post; U.S. Federal Census; Sporting Life)*

John Shoupe played fourteen major league games in three leagues over a six-year period. Already 27 years old, he broke in as a middle infielder for Troy in 1879, hitting .091 in eleven games. In 1882 he played errorless ball in two games as a second baseman for the St. Louis Browns. On May 28, 1884, the 32-year-old Shoupe played center field for the Washington Unions. His three hits that day allowed him to leave the majors with a .127 career average. Shoupe later played with Oswego and McKeesport. A native of Cincinnati, Shoupe died in Cincinnati on February 13, 1920. *Sporting Life* notes that a Jack Shoupe who played in an 1896 all-star game in Cincinnati had played for the Memphis Reds in 1872. *(Baseball-Reference.com; Total Baseball; U.S. Federal Census; Sporting Life)*

John Siegel played third base for the Philadelphia Keystones for eight games in June 1884. He managed eight hits—including two doubles—for a .226 batting average. But at a time when the average third baseman in the league fielded .777, Siegel committed fourteen errors in those eight games for a .533 average. According to *Sporting Life*, a Siegel played shortstop for Chattanooga in 1885. *Retrosheet* and *Total Baseball* assert that Siegel was born in York, PA. In 1900 there were two John Siegels of the right age living in Philadelphia—one, the son of German immigrants, working as a baker, and one, the son of native Pennsylvanians, working as a carpenter. *(Baseball-Reference.com; Retrosheet; Total Baseball; U.S. Federal Census; Sporting Life)*

Frank Siffell, a German-born catcher, played in 10 games for the Philadelphia A's over a two-year period. Joining the club in June of 1884, he had three hits in seven games. In 1885 he got into three games, one as an outfielder. In all, he hit .148 in 27 at bats. In 1886, *Sporting Life* refers to him as an "excellent, young catcher," but reports that he is working in a cotton mill. Siffell resided in Philadelphia where, according to Frank Russo, he died on October 26, 1909, of "a sexually transmitted disease." He was 49 years old and a bachelor. *(Total Baseball; Baseball-Reference.com; Findagrave.com; SABR Baseball Encyclopedia)*

Ed Sixsmith caught in one major league game for his home town Philadelphia Quakers on September 11, 1884. In a home 16–6 loss to Chicago, the 21-year-old went hitless in two at bats and was errorless behind the plate. Sixsmith caught for Augusta of the Southern Association in 1885, later playing for Bridgeport, San Antonio and Canton. An 1888 note in *National Police Gazette* shows that he had been released as a result of putting his arm "out of gear" in a throwing contest. In 1900, according to the census, Sixsmith was living in Philadelphia and working as a "baseball sticher." By the 1920 census Sixsmith has become a clerk in a publishing office. He died in Philadelphia on December 12, 1926, at age 63. *(Baseball-Reference.com; Atlanta Constitution; National Police Gazette; U.S. Federal Census; Sporting Life)*

Alexander Skinner played in one game for the Baltimore Monumentals, a home game against St. Louis on July 12, 1884. Four days later he appeared in the lineup of the Chicago Browns in a road game at Washington. The Chicago-born outfielder went one for three at the plate and handled two fielding chances flawlessly in each game. In 1886 A.S. Skinner of Baltimore was one of the substitute umpires of the American Association. There are conflicting views of Skinner's life outside baseball. Peter Morris suggested that Skinner was a Richmond native, who was born in 1846 and died June 3, 1893. *Baseball-Reference.com* and *Total Baseball* both put his birth at 1856 in Chicago and his death at March 5, 1901, in Washington, MA. The *U.S. Federal Census* doesn't seem to support either case. *(Total Baseball; Baseball-Reference.com; U.S. Federal Census; petermorrisbooks.com)*

Art Sladen played two games as the right fielder of the Boston Reds—one on April 22 and one, a home game against Wilmington, on August 25, 1884. He went hitless in seven at bats but handled two fielding chances without an error. Born in Dracot, MA, to an English father, he was a resident of Lowell, MA, and worked at a carpet mill before playing professional baseball. The 1890 *Lowell City Directory* lists him as a "second hand," an assistant foreman, at U.S. Cord Co. The 1910 census shows him as a printer. He died at Dracut on February 28, 1914, at age 53. *(Total Baseball;*

Retrosheet; U.S. Federal Census; Lowell City Directory)

Mike Slattery was the regular center fielder for the Boston Reds in 1884, when he was just seventeen years old. A local boy, the left-handed swinging 210-pounder hit .208. After stealing 112 bases and scoring 134 runs for Toronto in 1887, he returned to the majors in 1888, helping New York win the National League, hitting .246 as the regular center fielder. Slattery played in only 12 games in 1889 but hit a career high .307 for the New York Players League club in 1890. After splitting 1891 between the NL Cincinnati Reds and Washington Statesmen, be became one of two players to play in four major leagues in five seasons. Overall, he hit .251 and fielded .883 — the league average. In 1896 *Sporting Life* notes that Slattery is "still employed in that Boston clothing store." The 1900 census supports this by noting that Slattery, born in Boston to an Irish family, was living at home and working as a clothing salesman. Suffering from "some stomach trouble," the 38-year-old Slattery died in Boston on October 16, 1904. *(Baseball Encyclopedia; Baseball-Reference.com; Baseball Necrology; Before the Curse; U.S. Federal Census; Sporting Life)*

Smith started a game for the Baltimore Monumentals against Boston on June 5, 1884, in Baltimore. Lasting six innings, he gave up 12 hits and 9 runs—six earned. Baltimore rallied but lost the game 15–12. Smith finished the game in right field. He had a hit in five times at bat. *(Baseball-Reference.com; SABR Baseball Encyclopedia)*

Bill Smith played left field for Cleveland on September 17, 1884, going hitless in three at bats and having no fielding chances in a 9–1 loss to the New York Gothams. He is described as being from the local Forest City club, filling in for a sick Ernie Burch. According to the *New York Times*, in 1886 Smith was "injured while bathing at Toronto on Sunday." The injury, which *DeadballEra.com* and Bill Lee both describe as a broken back while diving, led to his death on August 9, 1886. He was 26 years old. *(Baseball Necrology; Total Baseball; New York Times; DeadballEra.com; Baseball-Reference.com)*

Charles "Pop" Smith entered the majors in 1880 as the regular second baseman for Cincinnati. After playing with five clubs over the next

Mike Slattery (Library of Congress)

"Pop" Smith (Library of Congress)

two seasons—including Cleveland, Worcester, the Athletics, Louisville and Buffalo—he emerged in 1883 as a regular with the Columbus Buckeyes, hitting .262 and leading the American Association in triples. By 1886, playing with the Pittsburgh Alleghenys, he was leading the AA in fielding, moving with the Alleghenys into the National League in 1887. He became team captain at Boston in 1889 and then finished a 12-year career with Washington in 1891. Despite a career .222 batting average, he held regular status nine years. As a middle infielder, he had superior range and an average fielding percentage. After leaving Washington, he played at Omaha and Atlanta. Smith was born in Digby, Nova Scotia. A Charles M. Smith born in Canada around 1856 appears in the U.S. census for Boston in 1910 and 1920. In both cases he is employed as a motorman for street cars. Smith died in Boston on April 18, 1927. *(Total Baseball; Atlanta Constitution; Boston Daily Globe; Washington Post; U.S. Federal Census; Baseball-Reference.com)*

Edgar Smith joined his hometown Providence Grays in 1883, coming from Yale University. Over the next seven seasons he had four trials as an outfielder and pitcher—with Philadelphia and Cleveland of the National League and Washington of the American Association. As a pitcher he threw 82 innings for a 2–7, 5.05 ERA record. As a batter he hit .184 in 26 games. As an outfielder he fielded 30 points below the league average. Smith had left Yale early, and "not long afterwards he was stricken with chronic mental derangement." He died in Providence of pulmonary hemorrhage on November 3, 1892, at age 30. *(Baseball-Reference.com; Total Baseball; Baseball Necrology; SABR Baseball Encyclopedia)*

Frank Smith joined the Pittsburgh Alleghenys in August 1884. The Canadian-born catcher and outfielder hit .250 in 10 games, and he fielded above the league average at both positions. A Frank Smith participated in a roller rink baseball championship game in 1885. Since five 1884 major league baseball players also participated in the game, this may be the former Allegheny. Born in Fonthill, Ontario, to an English father, Smith was a baby when the family immigrated in 1859. The 1910 census shows him living in Canandaigua, NY, working as a painter; in the 1920 census he is shown as an insurance agent. He died in Canandaigua on November 11, 1928, at age 70. *(Total Baseball; Baseball-Reference.com; U.S. Federal Census; Sporting Life)*

George "Germany" Smith began a fifteen-year major league career with the Altoona Mountain Citys in 1884. In twenty-five games at shortstop, Smith led the team with a .315 average. When Altoona folded at the end of May, Smith shifted teams (Cleveland), leagues (National) and positions (second base). In 1885 he began a six-year stay in Brooklyn, moving with the club from the American Association to the National League in 1890 and helping the club win pennants in both leagues. In 1891, Smith began another six-year run with Cincinnati before finishing with Brooklyn (1897) and St. Louis (1898). He hit only .243 for his career but reached .300 in 1895 and .294 in the inflated 1887 season A fine defensive shortstop, he twice led a league in fielding. For his career, he fielded .911, fifteen points over the league average. Smith continued to play independent ball in Altoona until 1905. Born in Pittsburgh, Smith worked as a crossing guard for the railroad in later years. Bill Lee found that he was a watchman. The 1920 census calls him a machinist. Smith died at Altoona on December 1, 1927, after being struck by an automobile. He was 69 years old. *(Total Baseball; Baseball-Reference.com; U.S. Federal Census; Baseball Necrology)*

John "Phenomenal" Smith (**John Francis Gammon**) compiled a major league record that bears little resemblance to his nickname. With eleven clubs in eight seasons, the lefty went 57–78 with a 3.87 ERA. In his best year, he had 54 complete games and 25 wins for Baltimore in 1887. His win total dropped to 16 the following season; in no other year did he exceed nine wins. He had entered the majors with the Baltimore Monumentals as a 19-year-old in 1884; in 1886 he led the Eastern League with 317 strikeouts. He also pitched for American Association clubs in Philadelphia (three times), Pittsburgh, Brooklyn and Baltimore, and with National League clubs in Detroit, Philadelphia (twice) and Pittsburgh. Released by the Phillies in 1891, Smith pitched for Milwaukee and Omaha that season. He managed and played in the minors through 1904. As a scout, he is credited with discovering Christy Mathewson for the Giants. Born in Philadelphia, Smith spent most of his adult life in Manchester, NH, where he worked as a policeman after leaving baseball. He died in Manchester on April 4, 1952, at age 87. *(Sporting News; Baseball-Reference.com; Baseball Encyclopedia; U.S. Federal Census)*

"Phenomenal" Smith (Library of Congress)

John Sneed, a left-handed hitting outfielder, debuted with the Indianapolis Hoosiers as a 23-year-old in 1884. After starring at New Orleans and Memphis, he returned to the majors in the expansion 1890 season, hitting .286 between To-

John Sneed (T. Scott Brandon)

ledo and Columbus. He also was a regular in 1891, hitting .257 in 99 games. For his career he hit .268 but fielded .879 — well below the league average. Sneed left baseball after the 1891 season. *Sporting Life* first reported that he was scalping baseball tickets for a living but later described his operation as a "prosperous business in the ticket brokerage line." His first name is variously listed as Jonathon and John Law; his place of birth is both Shelby County, TN, and Columbia, OH. Sneed died in Memphis on January 4, 1899, at age 38. *SABR Baseball Encyclopedia* accepts the Tennessee birth. *(Total Baseball; Baseball-Reference.com; Retrosheet; Baseball-Almanac.com; sarbrneworleans.com; Sporting Life; SABR Baseball Encyclopedia)*

Charles "Pop" Snyder, a Washington, DC, product, began his professional career while still a teenager with the Washington club of the National Association, also playing with the Lord Baltimores and Philadelphia White Stockings. After leading NA catchers in fielding in 1875, he joined the Louisville Grays of the National League in 1876–77. He played with Boston (1878–81) before becoming a playing manager of the Cincinnati Red Stockings in 1882, leading them to a league championship. Remaining with the Red Stockings through 1886, he then played with three Cleveland entries — the American Association Blues (1887–

"Pop" Snyder (Wikimedia Commons)

88), the NL Spiders (1889) and the Players League Infants (1890), finishing back with Washington in 1891. In eighteen seasons he caught at least 50 games twelve times, hitting .236. He hit .291 with the 1882 AA champions. A .893 fielder, he was a dozen points higher than the league average for catchers. After leaving the playing ranks, he umpired in both the AA (1891), and the NL (1892–93 and 1898–1901). He also umpired in the Eastern League. Born to a German father, Snyder appears in both the 1910 and 1920 censuses for DC, living with his brother-in-law, and having his own income. Snyder died at Washington, DC, on October 29, 1924, at age 70. *(Total Baseball; Baseball-Reference.com; Washington Post; Chicago Daily Tribune; U.S. Federal Census)*

Emanuel Sebastian "Redleg" Snyder (Schneider) had two major league trials with two of the worst teams in baseball. In 1876 the 21-year-old Snyder was the regular left fielder for the last place Cincinnati Red Stockings, a team which won only nine games all season. In 1884 he was the regular first baseman for the Wilmington Quicksteps, a team which won two of eighteen games. Snyder didn't help either cause with his hitting—.151 with Cincinnati and .192 with Wilmington. However, his fielding as a first baseman (.976) far exceeded the league average. Born in Camden, NJ, to German parents, Snyder is listed in the 1930 census for Camden as a railroad conductor. Bill Lee says that Snyder died by inhaling illuminating gas on November 24, 1932, at age 76. *(Baseball Necrology; U.S. Federal Census; Baseball Encyclopedia; Baseball-Reference.com)*

Joe Sommer grew up in Covington, KY, across the river from Cincinnati, and began his career with the National League Red Stockings in 1880. Returning to the majors with the American Association Red Stockings in 1882, Sommer hit .288 for the league champions and led outfielders in fielding. He spent 1884–89 with Baltimore, going to Cleveland in 1890 after leading the Atlantic Association in batting. Released in May, he finished back with the Orioles. In ten seasons, he was a regular eight times. A career .248 hitter, he fielded .901, more than 20 points above the league average. *National Police Gazette* described him as "the best outfielder and finest baserunner in the world." Following his stay in Cleveland, Sommer played in the Eastern League with New Haven in 1891. Born to a German father and a Dutch mother, Sommer made his home in Covington. The 1900 census lists Sommer as a hotel clerk, which agrees with Bill Lee's research. The 1920 census shows Sommer to be a pilot for the railroad. He died at Cincinnati on January 16, 1938, at age 79. *(Total Baseball; Baseball Reference.com; National Police Gazette; Boston; Baseball Necrology; U.S. Federal Census)*

Joe Stanley played six games as an outfielder for the Baltimore Monumentals at the beginning of 1884. His hits (five for a .238 batting average) matched his errors (five for a .444 fielding average). *Retrosheet* and *Baseball-Almanac.com* say that Stanley was born in New Jersey. *Baseball-Reference.com* and *Retrosheet* list him as the brother of John "Buck" Stanley, who pitched for Philadelphia in 1911. But that Joe Stanley is more likely to be a much younger major league outfielder, born—like Buck Stanley—in Washington, DC. The Monumentals outfielder would likely have been born around 1860. Nothing more is known about him at this time. *(Total Baseball; Baseball-Reference.com; Baseball-Almanac.com; Retrosheet)*

Joe "Old Reliable" Start had a career that spanned three manifestations of professional baseball. Born in New York City in 1842, Start played for the powerful Brooklyn Atlantics in 1860–70 before the formation of an organized league. Already 29 years old when the National Association was formed, Start hit .360 for the New York Mutuals in the inaugural season. When the National League formed, he played with the Mu-

Joe Start (T. Scott Brandon)

tuals (1876), Hartford (1877), Chicago (1878), and Providence (1879–85), finishing with Washington (1886) at age 43. A .300 hitter for the eleven NL seasons, he hit .351 and led the NL in runs in 1878 and hit .329 as late as 1882. Start led the NA or NL first basemen in fielding six times, finishing with a .963 percentage — eleven points above the league average. He was captain at both Hartford and Providence, helping Providence to their World Series championship in 1884. When Start left baseball, he "went into the hotel business [and] amassed a small fortune," so that he became a "retired capitalist." He died at Providence, RI, on March 27, 1927, at age 84. (*Total Baseball; Baseball-Reference.com; Boston Daily Globe; New York Times*)

Dan "Ecky" Stearns entered the majors with his hometown Buffalo Bisons as an 18-year-old in 1880. He also played for Detroit of the National League and Cincinnati of the American Association before becoming a regular first baseman for the Baltimore Orioles in 1883, maintaining regular status through 1885, when he was traded back to Buffalo. After leading the Western League in runs and homers while playing for Topeka, he returned with Kansas City in 1889, enjoying his best season with a .286 batting average. In his seven seasons in the majors, Stearns hit .242 and played at least three games at every field position. After playing in the minors at Scranton, Des Moines and Birmingham, Stearns appears in the 1900 census for Buffalo, working as a policeman. The 1920 census shows him as a federal court officer. By 1930 he and his wife are retired and living in Glendale, CA. Stearns died at Glendale on June 18, 1944, at age 82. (*Total Baseball; Baseball Reference.com; Washington Post; U.S. Federal Census; Sporting Life*)

Len Stockwell played in six major league games over a 12-year period — two games as a 19-year-old with the Cleveland Blues in 1879, two with the Louisville Eclipse in 1884 and two with the Cleveland Spiders in 1890. In 22 at bats he managed three hits for a .136 career average. Stockwell also had a trial with the White Stockings in 1882, but did not play in any league games. The *Washington Post* notes in 1887 that he was transferred from St. Paul to Los Angeles. On the West Coast he also played for San Francisco and Stockton. An 1890 note identifies him as a California player signed by Cleveland "to cover left field and substitute catcher." In 1892 the *Chicago Daily Tribune* says that he is "still playing." In 1895 he is listed as umpire for a Los Angeles–Oakland playoff series. Born in Cordova, IL, Stockwell was still living there with his father and working as a photographer at the time of the 1900 census. He died at Niles, CA, on January 28, 1905, at age 45. (*Baseball-Reference.com; Chicago Daily Tribune; Washington Post; Los Angeles Times; U.S. Federal Census; Sporting Life*)

Harry Stovey (Stowe) was the Mickey Mantle of his day, leading the National League, American Association or Players League five times in homers and twice in stolen bases. His career 122 home runs included six seasons of ten or more, with a high of 19 in 1889. In the PL, he stole 97 bases in 1890, part of his career 509. Contemporary accounts credit him with 156 in 1888, a figure now reduced to 87. When Stovey retired in 1893,

Harry Stovey (Library of Congress)

he was career leader in both home runs and stolen bases. The .289 hitter went over .300 four times in 14 seasons, with a high of .326 in 1884. A Philadelphian, Stovey began with Worcester in 1880, coming from New Bedford. He played in the AA with the Athletics from 1883 through 1889. After playing with the PL Boston Reds in 1890, he moved to the NL Beaneaters in 1891, finishing with the Orioles and Brooklyn. He served as playing manager at both Worcester and Philadelphia. After retiring from baseball Stovey became police captain in New Bedford, MA, "pursuing violators of the liquor law." He died at New Bedford on September 20, 1937, at age 80. *(New York Times; Baseball-Reference.com; BaseballLibrary.com; U.S. Federal Census; Sporting Life)*

Joe Strauss (Strasser) debuted with the Kansas City Cowboys on July 27, 1884, going on to hit .200 in sixteen games that season. After playing briefly with the American Association Louisville Eclipse in 1885, he split 1886 between the Eclipse and Brooklyn Trolley Dodgers, hitting .219 in 83 games. For his major league career, he hit .216 in 101 games. Ninety-one career games were in the outfield, where his fielding percentage was slightly below the league average, but he was regarded as the "fastest catcher Cincinnati ever turned out." These three seasons were only a brief part of Strauss's career in baseball. Beginning with the Muldoons in 1876, he played 25 years in "nearly every league." Strauss was highly regarded as a base coach: "Few could do it better than he." Born to German parents, Strauss was in the "house painting business" after leaving baseball. He died in Cincinnati on June 24, 1906, at age 47. *(Total Baseball; Baseball-Reference.com; Sporting Life; U.S. Federal Census)*

John "Cub" Stricker (Streaker), a Philadelphia native, entered the majors with his hometown A's in 1882, holding regular status through 1885, when he was sold to Atlanta. Returning to the majors with the Cleveland Blues in 1887, he again held regular status through 1892 with the Blues, the NL Cleveland Spiders, St. Louis Browns, Boston Beaneaters and Baltimore Orioles, and the Players League Cleveland Infants. He finished as a major league player with Washington in 1893, but as late as 1905 he was described as "still playing ball, and playing well, with local teams." Over his eleven seasons, he hit .239, with a high of .273 in 1883. Only 5'3", he was regarded as a fine second baseman though his .907 fielding percentage was average for the time. The 1910 cen-

"Cub" Stricker (Library of Congress)

sus lists him as a real estate agent in Philadelphia. At age 70 he was still working as a ticket taker at the ball bark. Stricker died in Philadelphia on November 17, 1937, at age 77. *(Total Baseball; Baseball-Reference.com; National Police Gazette; Atlanta Constitution; U.S. Federal Census; Sporting Life)*

George Strief was a regular second baseman twice in his five-year major league career with six clubs in three leagues. He debuted with the National League Cleveland Blues in 1879, also playing with Pittsburgh, St. Louis and Philadelphia of the American Association and with Kansas City and the Pittsburgh Stogies of the Union Association. Only a .207 hitter for his career, he is one of two men who hit four triples in one game, accomplishing this feat with the Philadelphia A's in 1885. He also had a double in that game. After leaving the A's at the end of 1885, he played in the

Southern League for Savannah and was considered to be "the best third baseman in the league." He had worked as a substitute umpire in 1880; in 1890 he was appointed an NL umpire. Born in Cincinnati, Strief lived in Cleveland, where, according to the 1910 census, he worked as a city patrolman. The 1920 census lists him as a policeman employed by a steel plant. Strief died at Cleveland on April 1, 1946, at age 89. *(Total Baseball; Baseball Necrology; Chicago Daily Tribune; Washington Post; Atlanta Constitution; U.S. Federal Census)*

Al Strueve played in two games for the St. Louis Browns, home games against Washington on June 22 and 24, 1884. He caught in one game and played in the outfield in one game, going two for seven as a batter. *Retrosheet* gives his birthplace as Cincinnati and his birth date as June 26, 1860. The same source gives a death place as Ross County, OH, and a death date of January 28, 1929. An Albert Strueve appears in the 1920 census for Buckskin, OH, in Ross County. Born to a German father, Strueve is listed as a foreman for a general farm. *Baseball Almanac* gives a burial site as Greenfield, OH, which squares with that death place. *(Total Baseball; SABR Baseball Encyclopedia; Retrosheet; Baseball Almanac; U.S. Federal Census)*

Tony Suck (Charles Anthony Zuck) had a two-game trial with Buffalo in 1883 and 56 games split between the Chicago Browns and Baltimore Monumentals in 1884. He divided these games among catcher, all outfield positions, shortstop and third base, fielding .894. At the plate he hit .151. Signed by Chicago in 1886 to catch Jim McCormick, Suck did not play but appears in the box scores for Augusta in that season. At the end of 1886 he was appointed an umpire in the Southern Association and was still umpiring in 1890. Suck was born in Chicago to Norwegian immigrant parents and is listed in the 1880 census as a laborer. He died in Chicago on January 29, 1895, at age 36. *(Total Baseball; Baseball-Reference.com; U.S. Federal Census; Sporting News; Sporting Life)*

Dan Sullivan joined the Louisville Eclipse in 1882, becoming the regular catcher. That season he hit a career-high .273 in 67 games, 40 points over his career average. Described as a "huge catcher," the 5'11", 194 pound Sullivan was arrested for assaulting a Louisville sports writer in 1885; he finished that season with the St. Louis Browns. In April 1886, he finished his major league career by playing in one game with Pittsburgh; in August the *National Police Gazette* contained the cryptic note that Sullivan "has finally brought up in Memphis." In five seasons—two as a regular—he hit .233, but fielded .909—twelve points over the league average. Sullivan, a Providence native, died of consumption in Providence on October 26, 1893. He was 36 years old. *(Baseball-Reference.com; National Police Gazette; New York Times; Chicago Daily Tribune; Rhode Island Deaths 1630–1930)*

Florence "Fleury" Sullivan yielded a major league record 206 earned runs with the Pittsburgh Alleghenys in 1884. In that season he completed all 51 starts in compiling a 16–35, 4.20 ERA record, the 35 losses being a Pittsburgh record. Like battery mate Ed Colgan, he was a native of East St. Louis, IL, born to Irish parents there. Also like Colgan, the 22-year-old Sullivan had a one-line major league career. An arm injury forced him from the professional ranks, but he became a catcher for an independent team in East St. Louis. He was murdered in his home town on February 15, 1897, "shot during a political argument." Sullivan was approximately 36 years old. *(Total Baseball; DeadballEra.com; U.S. Federal Census; Sporting Life)*

Pat Sullivan, a 23-year-old Milwaukee native, hit .193 in 31 games for the Kansas City Cowboys in 1884. Used mostly at third base—a .767 fielder—he was a better outfielder—an .895 percentage. Starting one game as a pitcher, he gave up nine earned runs in seven innings. *Sporting Life* reported that Sullivan had signed with Omaha for 1885. Born to Irish parents, Sullivan is listed in the 1900 census as a railroad clerk. He died in Milwaukee on April 14, 1901, at age 39. *(Baseball-Reference.com; Retrosheet; U.S. Federal Census; Sporting Life)*

Thomas "Sleeper" Sullivan was called "Old Iron Hands" because he caught Charley Radbourn without a mitt. But he enjoyed a major league career of only 97 games—90 as a catcher. The St. Louis native joined Buffalo for 35 games in 1881. Except for a game with Louisville in 1883, Sullivan spent the remainder of his career in St. Louis with the Browns (1882–83) and Maroons (1884). Overall, he hit .184; his fielding was 43 points below the league average. T.J. Sullivan appears in the 1880 St. Louis census as a 24-year-old baseball player, living with his aunt and uncle. His parents had been born in Ireland. According to Bill Lee, Sullivan became a well-known bartender in Camden, NJ, and died there on September 25,

1899. SABR says that he died in St. Louis in 1909. *(Baseball-Reference.com; Baseball Necrology; SABR Baseball Encyclopedia; Sporting News)*

Timothy "Ted" Sullivan is credited with coining the word "fan" to describe baseball supporters. While managing the Kansas City Cowboys to an eighth-place finish in 1884, he played in three games on July 9–12. In nine at bats he produced three hits. In two games in the outfield he was errorless, but his trial at shortstop resulted in four errors. Earlier he had managed the St. Louis Browns to a second-place finish in 1883, and the St, Louis Maroons to a breakaway 28–3 record early in 1884 before shifting to Kansas City, where his team went 13–46. Sullivan also managed the Washington Nationals to an eighth-place finish in 1888. In 1907 *Sporting News* listed him as one of the best known people in baseball. He managed Memphis in 1885 and Nashville in 1893 and founded both the Texas League and the Northwest League. Sullivan was also among the earliest to see the potential of Cuban baseball. Born in County Clare in Ireland, Sullivan died in Washington, DC, on July 5, 1929, at age 78. *(Baseball-Reference.com; Total Baseball; Sporting News; Encyclopedia of Minor League Baseball; SABR Baseball Encyclopedia)*

Tom Sullivan had four trials in the American Association. Joining Columbus in September 1884, he had four complete games and two wins. After leading the Southern League with a 21–6 record while helping Atlanta win the Southern League in 1885, he won two more games for Louisville in 1886. After a 36-win season at Topeka in 1887 and a 13-win start for Birmingham in 1888, he returned to the majors, going 8–16 and 2–8 for the Kansas City Cowboys over the rest of 1888 and 1889; overall he compiled a 14–33, 4.03 ERA record. Born in New York City to Irish parents, Sullivan became a resident of Cincinnati. In the censuses of 1900 and 1910, a Thomas Sullivan is shown operating his own saloon. The 70-year-old Sullivan reappears in the 1920 census as a publishing solicitor—"on Central avenue," according to *Sporting Life*. On April 12, 1947, he died in Cincinnati, as a result of injuries from an automobile accident; he was 87 years old. *(Baseball Necrology; Baseball-Reference.com; Chicago Daily Tribune; Sporting Life)*

Billy Sunday was signed by Cap Anson from the Marshalltown, IA, semipro ranks. From Ames, IA, Sunday had attended Northwestern

Billy Sunday (T. Scott Brandon)

University. The speedster served as a utility outfielder for the Chicago White Stockings from 1883 through 1887, hitting .291 in 50 games in 1887. Over the next three seasons Sunday was a regular with Pittsburgh and Philadelphia. Despite hitting only .236, he stole 71 bases in 1888 and reached a career-high 84 in 1890 from a .258 average. Overall, Sunday hit .248 in eight seasons. He was only a .883 fielder, but his range factors were 18 points over the league average. After undergoing a religious conversion in 1886, Sunday left baseball at the end of the 1890 season to work for the YMCA. He went on to become "the greatest high-pressure and mass conversion Christian evangelist America ... has ever known." In ill health, Sunday died at Chicago on November 6, 1935. He was 71 years old. *(Total Baseball; Chicago Daily Tribune; New York Times; Baseball-Reference.com)*

Elmer "Sy" Sutcliffe was a rarity—a regular catcher who threw and batted left-handed. He had trials with Chicago, St. Louis, Detroit, Cleveland and Baltimore of the National League, Cleve-

Sy Sutcliffe (Library of Congress)

land of the Players League, and Washington of the American Association. In seven seasons he hit .288, reaching .329 in 99 games in the PL. In 1891 Sutcliffe was described as being "handy with the stick," hitting .353 before being released in October. About half of Sutcliffe's games were as a catcher, though he finished his playing career as a first baseman with Baltimore in 1892 and he filled in at shortstop for 24 games at Detroit in 1888. Across all positions, his career .887 fielding mark was 19 points below the league average. Born in Wheaton, IL, to an English father, the 30-year-old Sutcliffe died of Bright's disease at his home in Wheaton on February 13, 1893. *(Chicago Daily Tribune; Washington Post; Total Baseball; U.S. Federal Census)*

Ezra Sutton hit the first home run in major league history and led National Association third basemen in fielding as a 21-year-old in 1871. Beginning with the Cleveland Forest Citys, he moved to the Athletics in 1873 and continued with them into the National League in 1876. When that club folded at the end of the season, he transferred to Boston, where he finished his major league career in 1888. The career .288 hitter was over .300 four times in NL play, topped by a .346 mark in 1884, when he led the league in hits.

Ezra Sutton (Library of Congress)

His fielding percentage of .849 is twenty-eight points higher than the league average for third basemen. In 1888 he was released to Rochester of the International League and later played for Hartford and Milwaukee. After he left baseball, his story is not a happy one. His business venture into an ice plant failed in 1890. At this time Sutton came down with locomotor ataxia, a disease which crippled him. A product of Palmyra, NY, he died at Braintree, MA, on June 20, 1907, at age 56. Harold Seymour says that Sutton died destitute. *(Total Baseball; Baseball-Reference.com; Baseball: The Golden Age; U.S. Federal Census)*

Andy Swan joined the Washington Nationals in July 1884, hitting .143 in five games as a first or third baseman. After the Washington franchise disbanded in August, Swan played in three more games with the replacement Richmond club. Between the two, he hit .258. Most sources now credit him with being born in Falls, Pennsylvania, in 1858, with no time or place of death. The 1860 census for Falls shows two-year-old Andrew Swan born to an inn-keeper from Connecticut. The 1870 census shows that the family has moved to Mercer, NJ. Both *Baseball Necrology* and *DeadballEra.com* make Swan a murder victim in 1885. However, that Andy Swan, an investment banker from Lawrence, MA, was forty years old at the time of his death; the ball player would have been only twenty-seven in 1885. *(Total Baseball; Baseball-Reference.com; Baseball Necrology; DeadballEra.com; U.S. Federal Census)*

Ed Swartwood hit over .300 three times in a nine-year career — six as a regular outfielder. The .299 career hitter led the American Association in runs (86) and doubles (18) in 1882 and in hits (147) and average (.356) in 1883. Swartwood began with Buffalo in 1881, coming from the Akrons. The Peoria, IL, native went on to AA clubs in Pittsburgh (1882–84), Brooklyn (1885–87), and Toledo (1890) and to the National League Pittsburgh Pirates in 1892. Weighing nearly 200 pounds, he had a fielding percentage 24 points below the league average. Swartwood played with Hamilton in 1887–88 and with Sioux City in 1891. He was an NL umpire in 1894 and from 1898 to 1900. *Sporting Life* reported that he had good judgment behind the plate but was too heavy and slow as a base umpire. Later as a deputy sheriff, Swartwood became "the official hangman for Allegheny County." He died in Pittsburgh on May 12, 1924, at age 65. *(Total Baseball; Baseball-Reference.com; Baseball Necrology; U.S. Federal Census; Sporting Life)*

Ed Swartwood (T. Scott Brandon)

Bill Sweeney turned in a monster 1884 season for the Baltimore Monumentals, leading the league with 40 wins, 538 innings, and 58 complete games. The right-hander made 60 starts that season and compiled a 2.59 ERA. He had entered the majors in 1882 with the Philadelphia Athletics, when the American Association became a major league. After the 1884 season, when the Union Association folded, Sweeney left baseball, leaving behind a 49–31 record and 76 complete games in 80 starts. *Baseball Historian* says that Sweeney went to work in Paterson, NJ, and Bill Lee records him dying there on April 13, 1908. Sources give him an 1858 Philadelphia birth; in the 1880 census for Philadelphia, a 21-year-old William Sweeney is listed as working — like his Irish-born father — as a teamster. Sweeney died in Philadelphia on August 2, 1903, according to other sources. He would have been approximately 45 years of age. *(Baseball-Reference.com; Baseball Necrology; Baseball Historian; U.S. Federal Census; Retrosheet)*

Charlie Sweeney was, according to the *Los Angeles Times*, "the first man to make a success of the curved ball." Born in San Francisco to Irish parents, Sweeney came east as a 20-year-old in 1883 to join the Providence team. In 1884 he pitched 19 of the first 23 games of the season and in one game struck out 19 Boston batters. With a 17–8 record, Sweeney left the club over a disputed $50 fine. Joining the St. Louis Maroons, he went 24–7 the rest of the way, finishing with a 41–15 record and 53 complete games. When the Maroons entered the National League in 1885, Sweeney's win total dropped to eleven and then to five. He finished with Cleveland in 1887, leaving the majors with a 64–52 record. According to *Sporting Life*, his only fault was "too great a love for good company." After returning to California, Sweeney shot a "notorious San Francisco dive keeper" in a saloon brawl, for which he served a term in San Quentin Prison. When he was released, his health was impaired so that he died of consumption on April 4, 1902, at age 38. *(Los Angeles Times; Total Baseball; National Police Gazette; Boston Daily Globe; U.S. Federal Census; Sporting Life)*

Jerry Sweeney was the regular first baseman for the Kansas City Cowboys in 1884. In 31 games Sweeney hit .264, second highest on the team; his .958 fielding percentage was higher than the league average. In 1887 *Sporting Life* reported that Sweeney, "late of the Salems," had signed with Lynn of the New England League. In 1889 *Sporting Life* reported that Sweeney "is now living in Boston" and that he "is a member of the Atlantic Yacht Club and fond of the briny deep." Born in

Boston to Irish parents, Sweeney died in Boston on August 25, 1891, at age 31. *(Baseball-Reference.com; U.S. Federal Census; Retrosheet; Sporting Life)*

John "Rooney" Sweeney, one of the most colorful players in history, enjoyed a major league career of 76 games in three leagues in three years. He worked as a backup catcher for the American Association Baltimore Orioles in 1883, for the Union Association Baltimore Monumentals in 1884 and for the National League St. Louis Maroons in 1885. Overall he hit .215 and fielded .905. In his busiest season, he hit .226 in 48 games for Baltimore. Before leaving St. Louis, Sweeney barely escaped punishment at the hands of a mob for mistreating a team of livery stable horses. In 1890, while playing with the Tecumsehs, he spent time in a Canadian jail for theft from a teammate. Sweeney was born in 1858 in New York City. On September 25, 1897, *Sporting Life* reported that Sweeney had suffered an epileptic fit and fallen while assisting boatmen at Battery Park. The resulting concussion placed him "on his deathbed," according to that paper. Other sources do not show a death date. *(Baseball-Reference.com. Retrosheet; U.S. Federal Census; Sporting Life)*

Lou Sylvester played on an amateur Waltham Watch Company team in Waltham, MA, with five future major leaguers. He debuted with the Cincinnati Outlaw Reds in 1884, hitting .267 as an outfield regular. When the Union Association folded, Sylvester played in the Southern League with Memphis and Augusta in 1885. Returning to the majors, he split 62 games between Louisville and Cincinnati American Association teams in 1886, before finishing with the St. Louis Browns in 1887. Overall, the 5'3" Sylvester hit .243 in 173 major league games and fielded .854, the league average for outfielders. Born in Springfield, IL, to Portuguese parents, he appeared in the 1910 census as a resident of San Diego, where he worked as a house painter. Sylvester died in Brooklyn in 1936 at age 81. *(Total Baseball; Baseball-Reference.com; SABR Biography Project; U.S. Federal Census)*

Billy Taylor emerged at age 29 as one of the top pitchers in baseball. Splitting the 1884 season between the St. Louis Maroons and the Philadelphia Athletics, he completed all 59 starts for 523 innings, 43 wins, and a 2.10 ERA. He went 25–4 for St. Louis, finishing second in winning percentage in the Union Association. Taylor, a Washington, DC, product, began his major league career as an outfielder, infielder and catcher with Worcester and Cleveland of the National League and the Pittsburgh Alleghenys, pitching very little. After his monster 1884 season, he pitched little in three seasons with the Athletics and the Baltimore Orioles, winning only three more games, to leave the majors with a 50–36 pitching record and a .277 batting average. Only 45 years old, he died at Jacksonville, FL, on May 14, 1900. *(Baseball Encyclopedia; Total Baseball; Retrosheet; Sporting Life)*

Edward "Live Oak" Taylor was, as late as 1990, thought to be two different players — Edward S. Taylor, who played two games for the 1877 Hartford Dark Blues, and George E. Taylor, who played 41 games for Pittsburgh in 1884. However, since both were born in Belfast, ME, and died on the same day in San Francisco, they are now believed to be the same person. Taylor hit .219 for his 43-game career and .211 as the regular center fielder for the Alleghenys. His family had moved to San Francisco by 1870, so Taylor returned to the Bay area. Suffering from a lung condition, he died at San Francisco on February 19, 1888. He was 37 years old. *(Baseball Encyclopedia; Total Baseball; Retrosheet; Baseball Necrology; U.S. Federal Census; Ancestry.com)*

"Live Oak" Taylor (T. Scott Brandon)

Fred Tenney played right field for the Washington Unions at the start of 1884. The twenty-four-year-old Brown University product hit .235 in 32 games and fielded .867 — well above the league average. When he shifted to the Boston

Reds in mid-season, he pitched exclusively, completing all four starts for a 3–1, 2.31 ERA record. He finished the season by starting (and losing) one game for the Wilmington Quicksteps. Tenney, a native New Hampshireman, appears in the censuses of 1900 and 1910, first as a book salesman in Massachusetts and later as a manager of a publishing company in New Jersey. He died at Fall River, MA, on June 15, 1919, at age 69. *(Total Baseball; Baseball-Reference.com; U.S. Federal Census; SABR Baseball Encyclopedia)*

William "Adonis" Terry is the first Dodger pitcher in history. In 14 seasons, the Westfield, MA, native won 197 games for the Dodgers, Baltimore, Pittsburgh and Chicago. He began his professional career with the Brooklyn Grays and moved with the club into the American Association in 1884. In the two Brooklyn championships of 1889 (AA) and 1890 (National League), he won 22 and 26 games, starting eight World Series games. He won at least 12 games ten times in his career, three times going over 20. A good athlete, he played 248 games as a position player—primarily as an outfielder, hitting .347 in 1894 and .300 in 1889 and a career .247. After leaving the Chicago Colts in 1897, he pitched for Milwaukee of the Western Association and then went into business in Milwaukee, operating a bowling alley, the Second Street Alleys. Only fifty years old, Terry died of pneumonia in Milwaukee on February 24, 1915. *(Total Baseball; Baseball-Reference.com; New York Times, Complete New York Clipper Baseball Biographies; Sporting Life)*

Art Thompson pitched for the Washington Unions on June 17, 1884. In an 11–1 loss to the Reds in Boston, Thompson struck out eight and walked three, but gave up ten hits and six earned runs. Game circumstances suggest that Thompson was a local Boston player, recruited by Washington for the day. *(Baseball-Almanac.com; Baseball-Reference.com)*

John "Tug" Thompson was the first major league player from London, Ontario. His major league experience consisted of 25 games. In 1882, he played in one game for Cincinnati. In 1884 he returned with Indianapolis, appearing in 24 games. Overall, he hit .206. As an outfielder he committed 13 errors in 22 fielding chances. The outfielder-catcher played minor league ball in Michigan. The 1911 census for London shows a 55-year-old John P. Thompson living there with his wife and five children. Thompson died in Guelph, Ontario, on August 1, 1938, at age 79. *(Baseball Encyclopedia; Baseball-Reference.com; SABR Biographical Committee Newsletter; Retrosheet; Canadian Census)*

Bill Tierney had a two-game major league career spread over three seasons. In May 1882 the 24-year-old debuted as a first baseman for the Cincinnati Red Stockings, going hitless in five at bats. In April 1884 he returned as an outfielder for the Baltimore Monumentals, collecting a single in three at bats and handling his only fielding chance. Tierney was born in Boston; the 1890 *Boston City Directory* lists him as a "base-ball player." The William J. Tierney in the 1894 directory is a plumber. He died in Boston on September 21, 1898, at age 40. *(Baseball-Reference.com; Total Baseball; U.S. Federal Census; Boston City Directory)*

John Tilley played in parts of two seasons in the majors as an outfielder. He debuted with the Cleveland Blues in 1882, hitting .089 in 15 games. In 1883 he played with Toledo and moved with the team from the Northwestern League to the American Association in 1884. After 17 games, he jumped to St. Paul of the Northwestern League and moved with that club into the Union Association. In all he played in 41 major league games, hitting .138. His fielding average of .818 was twenty-five points below the league average. *Retrosheet* and *Total Baseball* list him as a New York City product. *(Total Baseball; Baseball-Reference.com; Retrosheet; SABR Baseball Encyclopedia)*

Bill Traffley caught two games for the Chicago White Stockings as a teenager in 1878. After four seasons with the Union Pacific semipro club of Omaha, Traffley returned to the majors with the Cincinnati Red Stockings in 1883 and moved on to Baltimore in 1884. In 1885, his best season, Traffley led American Association catchers in fielding. In five seasons he hit only .175 but was regarded as a particularly fine throwing catcher, and his .927 fielding percentage was twenty points higher than the league average. He later played for and managed Des Moines and Quincy of the Western Association, and for a time he operated a restaurant in Baltimore. The Staten Island product died in Des Moines on June 23, 1908, a victim of tuberculosis. He was 48 years old. His brother John played in one game for Louisville in 1889. *(Total Baseball; Washington Post; Chicago Daily Tribune; Baseball-Reference.com; U.S. Federal Census; Sporting Life)*

Jim Tray was on the Indianapolis roster for a two-week period in September 1884. The catcher and first baseman from Jackson, MI, appeared in 6 games, hitting .286. He later coached and managed his hometown Jaxons in 1887 and 1888. In 1893 he was promised the management of Saginaw of the Ohio-Michigan League, but did not receive it. Born to Irish parents, Tray is listed in the 1900 census for Jackson, living with his mother. His occupation is listed as "Saloon." The 45-year-old Tray was found dead in Jackson from a heart attack on July 28, 1905. *(Total Baseball; Baseball-Reference.com; Encyclopedia of Minor League Baseball; SABR Biography Project; U.S. Federal Census; Sporting Life)*

Sam Trott, a left-handed catcher and second-baseman, lasted eight seasons in the majors. He joined Boston in 1880, coming from the Nationals. With Detroit in 1881–83, Trott finished with Baltimore in 1884–85 and 1887–88. In his best season he played in 85 games for the 1887 Orioles, hitting .257 — seven points above his career average. His .906 fielding percentage placed him in the upper half of catchers (*Sporting Life* termed him "pronouncedly successful"); his .883 percentage placed him in the bottom half of second basemen. After leaving the playing ranks, Trott managed Washington for 12 games in 1891 and scouted for the Orioles. Then he was hired by H. L. Mencken's father to sell cigars for the family factory and remained in the cigar business until his death. A 1897 notes says that he was living "on the sunny side of Easy Street." A native of Maryland, he died in Catonsville on June 5, 1925, at age 66. *(Total Baseball; Baseball-Reference.com; H.L. Mencken's Legacy; Washington Post; Sporting Life)*

John "Dasher" Troy, born to Irish parents in "the Swamp" in New York City, began his major league career with the Detroit Wolverines in 1881, moving to the New York Gothams in 1882. He was a regular second baseman in New York with the Gothams in 1883 and the American Association Metropolitans in 1884, helping the latter win the pennant. In five seasons Troy hit .243, and his .873 fielding percentage was well below the league average. After leaving the Mets in 1885, Troy played with Binghamton, Scranton, Manchester, Troy and Wilkes-Barre. After 1890 he operated a saloon in Manhattan, and the 1910 census lists him as a bartender. Troy died at Ozone Park, NY, on April 1, 1938, at age 83. *(Baseball-Reference.com; New York Times; Baseball Necrology; Boston Daily Globe; U.S. Federal Census; Sporting Life)*

Ed Trumbull (Edward J. Trembly) split 25 games between the outfield and pitchers' mound for the 1884 Washington Nationals. The 23-year-old had ten complete games, resulting in a 1–9, 4.71 ERA record. Between pitching duties, Trumbull hit .116 in 15 games as an outfielder. When the Washington club disbanded in August, Trumbull left the majors. He was born in Chicopee, MA, to a Canadian father and an Irish mother. The 1900 census shows him to be married and living in Holyoke, MA, working as a brass molder. He died at Kingston, PA, on January 14, 1937, at age 75. *(Baseball-Reference.com; Retrosheet; U.S. Federal Census; SABR Baseball Encyclopedia)*

Jerry Turbidy played shortstop for the Kansas City Cowboys for thirteen games in July and August 1884. While he hit only .224, he was a capable shortstop. He fielded .830 — fourteen points above the league average — and his range factors far exceeded those of his contemporaries. An 1885 note in *Sporting Life* refers to him as the "sprint runner of last year's Saginaws" and tells that he has signed with Springfield. Born in Dudley, MA, to Irish parents, Turbidy lived in Webster, MA. According to the 1880 census, he was married and "works on shoes." By 1910 the 58-year-old Turbidy had his "own income." He died at Webster on September 5, 1920, at age 68. *(Total Baseball; Baseball-Reference.com; U.S. Federal Census; SABR Baseball Encyclopedia)*

Gene Vadeboncoeur, the first Quebec-born player in the majors, caught in four games for the Philadelphia Quakers in July 1884, coming from Akron. He managed three hits in fourteen at bats for a .214 average before being released and signing with York. He later played with Lawrence and Haverhill. According to Bill Lee, Vadeboncoeur farmed and was a shoe worker. The federal censuses for 1900, 1910 and 1920 and the 1894 Haverhill city directory all show him as a Haverhill resident and a shoe factory worker in various capacities. Vadeboncoeur died at Haverhill on October 16, 1935, at age 77. However Peter Morris suggests that this is a different Eugene Vadeboncoeur, and that the ballplayer died in Denver in 1891. *(Total Baseball; Baseball Necrology; U.S. Federal Census; SABR-Quebec; petermorrisbooks.com; Sporting Life)*

William "Peek-A-Boo" Veach gained his nickname during his pitching days when he checked signals from the bench with runners on base. For the Kansas City Cowboys in 1884, he had twelve complete games and a 3–9, 2.42 ERA record as a pitcher. He later pitched one game—a losing effort—for the Louisville Eclipse in 1887. In Kansas City he played fourteen games as an outfielder; in 1888 he became a full-time first baseman while playing for St. Paul, graduating to the Cleveland Spiders and Pittsburgh Alleghenys in 1890. Despite an anemic .215 career average, he drew enough bases on balls to have a career on-base percentage of .319. During his career he "played in as many leagues as any player in the business." Veach was a lifelong resident of Indianapolis; the census of 1900 shows him as an iron molder, and that of 1920 as a steam fitter. He was a veteran of the Spanish-American War. Veach died in Indianapolis on November 12, 1937, at age 75. *(Total Baseball; Baseball-Reference.com; Sporting News; U.S. Federal Census; Sporting Life)*

Bill Vinton joined the Philadelphia Quakers directly from Phillips Academy in 1884. The *National Police Gazette* noted that he "gives promise of becoming a valuable pitcher." But "his arm soon after gave out." After splitting 1885 between the Quakers and the Philadelphia Athletics, Vinton left the majors with a two-year record of 17–19. He then attended Yale, assisting with the baseball team and becoming "managing editor of the Yale *Courant*." After graduating in 1888, Vinton taught school and went into business, in addition to doing "a great deal of literary work." He died of a heart condition at Pawtucket, RI, on September 3, 1893, at age 28. *(Total Baseball; Baseball-Reference.com; National Police Gazette; New York Times)*

Alex Voss made 20 starts for the Washington Unions in 1884, compiling a 5–14, 3.57 ERA record. Switching to the Kansas City Unions, he had six complete games, resulting in a 0–6 record. During the season Voss also filled in at every position except catcher and fielded above the league average. However at the plate he managed only a .176 average. A rare Southern major leaguer, Voss was born in Roswell, GA. He appears in the 1880 and 1900 censuses as a resident of Cincinnati with an occupation of house painter. At the time of the 1900 census, he was a prisoner in the Cincinnati Work House. In both cases his birth date is listed as a May 1855 rather than 1858 as is shown in all baseball sources. Voss died in Cincinnati on August 31, 1906, at age 48 or, more likely, 51. *(Total Baseball; Baseball-Reference.com; Retrosheet; U.S. Federal Census)*

Moses Fleetwood Walker, a product of Oberlin College and the University of Michigan, where he studied law, was the first black to play in the major leagues, and the last before Jackie Robinson. A slender catcher (159 pounds), he entered the majors in 1884 with the Toledo Blue Stockings, when they moved from the Northwestern League to the American Association. He hit .263 in 42 games, but was often injured. Pitcher Tony Mullane disliked blacks and refused to pay attention to Walker's signals, often crossing him up. Released at the end of the season, Walker worked in the post office and then played minor league ball in Cleveland, Waterbury, Newark and Syracuse. Because of the objection of Cap Anson, all major leagues, and later all organized baseball, banned black players. After leaving baseball in 1889, Walker worked as "businessman, inventor, newspaper editor and author." In 1908 he published a book entitled *Our Home Colony*, advocating that blacks immigrate to Africa. Embittered, he became an alcoholic and died in

Bill Vinton (T. Scott Brandon)

Fleet Walker (Wikimedia Commons)

Cleveland on May 11, 1924, at age 67. *(Baseball-Reference.com; Negro Leagues Baseball Museum e-museum; Sporting Life)*

Oscar Walker, a left-handed outfielder and first baseman, played in one game for his hometown Brooklyn Atlantics in 1875. In 1877 he signed with St. Paul but jumped to Manchester and was banned for contract jumping. In 1879 to returned to the majors with Buffalo, hitting .275 as the regular first baseman, but became the first player to strike out five times in a nine inning game. In 1882 Walker joined the St. Louis Browns of the American Association and became a regular outfielder, leading the AA with seven homers. In 1884, back with Brooklyn, he hit .270 as an outfield regular with the Trolley Dodgers, before finishing with Baltimore in 1885. For his career he hit .254 in 281 games. Born to German parents, Walker is listed as a painter in the 1880 census. He died in Brooklyn on May 20, 1889, at age 35. His widow was left destitute after his long illness and a benefit game was played for her relief. *(Total Baseball; Baseball-Reference.com; U.S. Federal Census; Major League Baseball's "Permanently Ineligible List"; Sporting Life)*

Walt Walker was signed as a "change catcher" by Detroit in March 1884. According to the *Chicago Daily Tribune*, he had "never played in a professional team, but is said to be a good catcher." He played in one game on May 8, going one for four at the plate and scoring a run. He also had two errors. Walker was born in Berlin, MI, to a Scots father and an Irish mother. The 1880 census shows him still in school. Both 1900 and 1910 censuses list him as a patient-inmate of the Eastern Michigan Asylum at Pontiac. Walker died at Pontiac on February 28, 1922, at age 61. *(Chicago Daily Tribune; Total Baseball; Baseball-Reference.com; Boston Daily Globe; U.S. Federal Census)*

Welday Walker, the younger brother of Fleet Walker, followed his brother to the majors via Oberlin College and the University of Michigan. Not the athlete his brother was, he was pressed into service in 1884 because of injuries. In five games the outfielder hit .222. When blacks were banned from the majors at the end of 1884, he played at Waterbury, CT, and in 1887 for the Pittsburgh Keystones of the Negro League. After leaving baseball, he joined his brother in Steubenville, OH, where they managed a hotel and a group of movie theaters. Like his brother, he was angry over the role of blacks and helped in the publishing of a black newspaper which advocated a return of blacks to Africa. Welday Walker died at Steubenville on November 23, 1937, at age 78. *(Baseball-Reference.com; Baseball Encyclopedia; Retrosheet)*

John Ward played center field for the Washington Unions on May 23, 1884. He had a single in four at bats, but in the field he committed an error on his only fielding chance. *Total Baseball* and *Retrosheet* give Ward a Washington, DC, birthplace. However, Peter Morris, who places Ward in his "On the Brink" cases, says he was from East St. Louis. *(Total Baseball; Baseball-Reference.com; Retrosheet; petermorrisbooks.com)*

John Montgomery Ward was approaching a Hall of Fame career as a pitcher with 164 career wins by age 24. He won 22 games for Providence in 1878 and the following season — still only 19 years old — turned in a 47–19 record. After his arm went dead in 1884, he played outfield, throwing with his left hand; in 1885 he shifted to shortstop. In seventeen seasons in the National League with Providence, New York and Brooklyn and the Players Leagues with Brooklyn, Ward hit .275 but reached an inflated .338 in 1887, .335 in 1890 and .328 in 1893. In 17 World Series games he hit .400. He twice led the NL in stolen bases, stealing 111 in 1887. In 1886 he led NL shortstops in fielding.

Monte Ward (Library of Congress)

Ward attended Penn State as a 13-year-old and later graduated from law school. He was captain of the NL champion New York clubs of 1888–1889 and founder of the Brotherhood of Players. After leaving baseball in 1894, he practiced law in New York and served as an agent for players. Discovering golf, he became one of the nation's best amateur golfers. Ward died on vacation at Augusta, GA, on March 4, 1925, at age 65. He was named to the Baseball Hall of Fame in 1964. *(Baseball-Reference.com; Total Baseball; BaseballLibrary. com; New York Times; U.S. Federal Census)*

Fred Warner began his major league career with his hometown Philadelphia Centennials of the National Association in 1875 and played in one game with the A's in the inaugural National League season. Warner was the regular shortstop for Indianapolis in 1878 and the regular third baseman for Cleveland in 1879. Returning to Philadelphia, he played for the Quakers in 1883 before finishing as the regular third baseman for Brooklyn in 1884. He hit as high as .248 in 1878, settling for a .234 average. A good-fielding shortstop — thirty points above the league average — Warner was well below the league average for third basemen in both percentage and range. He worked as a railway conductor after leaving baseball. Only 31 years old, Warner died in Philadelphia on February 13, 1886, following a four-month illness. *(Total Baseball; Baseball-Reference.com; U.S. Federal Census; Sporting Life)*

Bill Watkins spent forty years in organized baseball. The 26-year-old Canadian appeared in 34 games with Indianapolis in 1884, primarily as a third baseman, hitting .205 and fielding .878 — just above the league average. Struck on the head by a pitched ball, he was close to death, and it was said his hair turned white over night as a result. While that was the extent of his playing career, he also served as manager, part of a long career in that capacity. Moving to Detroit, he finished as league runner-up in 1886 and won the league championship and World Series in 1887. His other major league managerial stints were with Kansas City and Pittsburgh in the National League and Kansas City in the American Association. His longest association was with minor league Indianapolis franchises, winning pennants there in 1895, 1897 and 1900. He also served as club president until 1912. After leaving baseball, he became a civic-minded resident of Port Huron, MI, serving as a justice of the peace in Marysville, MI. Suffering from diabetes, Watkins died at Port Huron on June 9, 1937, at age 79. *(Baseball-Reference.com; Baseball Necrology; Minorleaguebaseball.com; Sporting News)*

Bill Watkins (T. Scott Brandon)

Sam Weaver is one of the four-league players. After making one successful start for the 1875 Philadelphia White Stockings in the National Association, he returned to the majors in 1878 as a 31-game loser (despite a 1.95 ERA) for the

National League Milwaukee Cream Citys. When the American Association was formed in 1882, Weaver won 26 games for the Athletics, completing all 41 of his starts. After going 24–22 for the Louisville Eclipse in 1883, he seized the chance to return to Philadelphia to pitch for the Union Association Keystones. His ERA ballooned to 5.76 and his record dropped to 5–10. Two years later he made two starts for the Athletics again, leaving the majors with a 67–80, 3.22 ERA record. Weaver also played in 25 games as an outfielder and first baseman, hitting .207. Bill Lee asserts that from 1887 until 1908 Weaver was a patrolman for the Philadelphia police force, retiring after a serious injury. The 1900 census lists him as a "special police officer." That census also gives him a birth date of July 1850 rather than the listed one of July 1855. Weaver died in Philadelphia on February 1, 1914, at age 63 — or 58. *(Total Baseball; Baseball-Reference.com; Baseball Necrology; U.S. Federal Census)*

Harry Weber caught three games for Indianapolis in 1884, going 0 for 8 as a hitter in his major league career. Little is known of Weber beyond his baseball statistics. *Total Baseball* gives him an Indianapolis birthplace. Harry A. Weber appears in the 1910, 1920 and 1930 censuses for Indianapolis. Born to German parents around 1860, this Harry Weber was listed as a dry goods merchant in the 1910 census and as a stock keeper for a saw factory in that of 1920. *(Total Baseball; Baseball-Reference.com; Retrosheet; U.S. Federal Census)*

Joe Weber, a 22-year-old Canadian from Hamilton, Ontario, played in two games for Detroit on May 30 and July 31, 1884. The outfielder went hitless in eight at bats and committed one error in the field. He was the first Hamilton native to play in the majors. The 1911 Hamilton census shows the 46-year-old Weber living in Hamilton with his wife, two sons and daughter-in-law. Weber died at Hamilton on December 15, 1921, at age 59. *(Baseball-Reference.com; Total Baseball; Canadian Census)*

John Garibaldi "Podge" Weihe debuted as a 20-year-old outfielder with his hometown Cincinnati team in August of 1883. The following season he was a regular outfielder with Indianapolis, hitting .254 in 63 games. His work in the outfield (.864 percentage) was eighteen points above the league average. Born to German parents, Weihe appears in the 1900 census as a police officer, one of Cincinnati's "finest," according to *Sporting Life*. By 1910 he has become a "saloonist," confirming Bill Lee's research. A 1913 report described him as being "as big as a barrel." Weihe died in Cincinnati on April 15, 1914, at age 51. The cause of death was "acute cellulitis of the neck." *(Baseball-Reference.com; Retrosheet; DeadballEra.com; Baseball Necrology; U.S. Federal Census; Sporting Life)*

Curt Welch joined Toledo in 1883 and moved with the club from the Northwestern League into the American Association in 1884. In ten major league seasons with the Blue Stockings, St. Louis, the Athletics, and Baltimore of the AA and Baltimore, Cincinnati and Louisville of the National League, he held regular status as an outfielder each year, leading the AA in fielding in both 1885 and 1886. A career .263 hitter, he hit .271, .282, .278, .282, and .271 in the 1885–89 period and led the AA in doubles in 1889. Welch was "undoubtedly one of the greatest ... outfielders in the history of the game." A career .933 fielder with good range, he fielded more than thirty points above

Curt Welch (Library of Congress)

the league average. However, according to his *Sporting Life* obituary, he became "a wreck from drink." As his health began to deteriorate, he dropped out of the majors in 1893 — at age 31 — and out of baseball in 1894. He then supported his family by his "trade as a potter." The East Liverpool, OH native died at his home of consumption on August 29, 1896. He was 34 years old. *(East Liverpool Review; Total Baseball; Baseball-Reference.com; U.S. Federal Census; Sporting Life)*

Michael "Smiling Mickey" Welch (Welsh) completed all 64 starts as a 20-year-old rookie with Troy in 1880. In 13 seasons — 11 before his arm began to go bad — he worked more than 4800 innings, pitching 500 innings three times, more than 400 three times and more than 300 three times. In the same span he had one 40-win season (44–11 in 1885), three more 30-win seasons and five more 20-win seasons. His 307 career wins were achieved by his 31st birthday. Welch came to Troy from Holyoke, MA, and moved with the club to New York in 1883. There he helped the Giants win world championships in both 1888 and 1889. Like many pitchers of the time, Welch played outfield as well, hitting .224. When he left baseball in 1892, Welch served as a steward for the Elks Club in Nashua, NH, and later as a stadium gatekeeper for the Giants. Born in Brooklyn to Irish parents, the 82-year-old Welch died July 30, 1941, while visiting at Nashua. He was named to the Hall of Fame in 1973. *(Baseball-Reference.com; Total Baseball; Hall of Fame; New York Times; U.S. Federal Census; Sporting News)*

Perry Werden was one of the greatest minor league players of all time. In a career of 25 years (1884–1908) the 220-pounder hit .341 with 169 home runs. As an 18-year-old, he debuted with his hometown St. Louis Maroons, completing 12 of 16 starts for a 12–1, 1.97 ERA record before an arm injury forced him to first base. Werden played with the Maroons, with Toledo and Baltimore of the American Association and with Washington, St. Louis and Louisville of the National League. In five seasons as a regular, he hit .282 with 26 homers, twice leading a league in triples. His fielding percentage was only average for first baseman of the time; however, his range far exceeded the league average. After leading the Western League with 11 homers in 1886, he led the International Association in hitting in 1889. In homer-friendly Nicolet Park in Minneapolis, he had back-to-back seasons of 43 and 45 home runs in 1894–95. After retiring as a player, he managed an independent team and umpired in the Northern League and Dakota League. Werden died of a heart attack in Minneapolis on January 9, 1934, at age 68. *(Baseball-Reference.com; Total Baseball; Baseball Necrology; Encyclopedia of Minor League Baseball; Sporting News; U.S. Federal Census)*

Joe Werrick was the regular shortstop for the St. Paul Saints in their nine-game major league experience in 1884. In 1886 he became the regular third baseman for the American Association Louisville Eclipse, holding that position through 1888. A .250 hitter over four seasons, Werrick reached .285 in inflated 1887 figures. In the field, neither his range nor his percentage reached the average for his contemporaries. Werrick signed with St. Joseph in 1889 and was playing with Portsmouth as late as 1896. Born in St. Paul to Norwegian immigrant parents, Werrick appears in the 1880 census as a "collar maker," confirming

Mickey Welsh (Library of Congress)

Joe Werrick (Library of Congress)

Bill Lee's finding that he was a harness maker by trade. The 1910 census shows him living in Kansas City working in a saddle factory. On May 10, 1943, Werrick died at the state hospital in St. Peter, MN. He was 81 years old. *(Baseball-Reference.com; Total Baseball; Baseball Necrology; U.S. Federal Census; Sporting Life)*

Milton "Buck" West, a left-handed-hitting outfielder, had two major league trials six years apart. In 1884 the *National Police Gazette* noted that the Cincinnati Red Stockings "have caught a good man." West hit .244 in 33 games. After leading the Tri-State League in hits in 1888, he returned to the majors with the Cleveland Spiders in 1890, posting almost identical numbers—a .245 average in 37 games. On neither team did he field well, his .828 percentage being more than fifty points below the league average. The 1880 census shows West still living at home in Mansfield, OH, working as a cigar maker. Bill Lee found that West opened a liquor store and later a restaurant. He died at Mansfield on January 13, 1929, at age 68. *(Total Baseball; National Police Gazette; Baseball Necrology; U.S. Federal Census; Baseball-Reference.com)*

Harry Wheeler joined Providence as a pitcher in 1878, compiling a 6–1 record. After brief trials as an outfielder with Cincinnati and Cleveland in 1879–80, he emerged as a regular with the Cincinnati Red Stockings in 1882 and with Columbus in 1883. He closed his major league experience in 1884, splitting time among the St. Louis Browns and Union League clubs in Kansas City, Chicago, Pittsburgh, and Baltimore. During this odyssey he managed four games for Kansas City, his team losing all four. He final marks were a 7–6, 4.70 ERA pitching record, a .228 batting average and a fielding percentage more than 50 points below the league average. Born in Versailles, IN, Wheeler resided in Cincinnati. In the 1880 census, he is listed as a bartender. Before his death, he became an invalid and also a pauper, saying "I'm broke; I haven't a cent." His wife is credited with developing sliding pads, which he wore inside his uniform. Wheeler died in Cincinnati October 9, 1900, at age 42. *(Baseball-Reference.com; Washington Post; National Police Gazette; U.S. Federal Census)*

Bill White led American Association shortstops in assists three times in a four-year career. Joining the Pittsburgh Alleghenys as a 24-year-old in 1884, he went on to play for Louisville (1886–88), finishing with the AA champion St. Louis Browns in 1888. In all, he hit .241 with a high of .257 in 1886. In the 10-game World Series against the Giants in 1888, he hit .143. After leaving baseball, he served as a "security guard at Riverside Tube Mill," according to Bill Lee. The census of 1910 shows White and his brother Joseph working as bartenders in Bellaire, OH. Born in Bridgeport, OH, to English parents, White died at Bellaire on December 29, 1924, at age 64. *(Baseball Encyclopedia; Baseball-Reference.com; Baseball Necrology; U.S. Federal Census)*

James "Deacon" White began his career as a catcher with the Cleveland Forest Citys of the National Association in 1871. In five NA seasons with Cleveland and Boston, he hit .347 and won a batting title in 1875, hitting .367. When the National League was formed, he helped the White Stockings win the 1876 championship. A year later he hit a league-leading .387 for the NL champion Boston Red Caps before moving on to Cincinnati, Buffalo, Detroit and Pittsburgh. White finished

"Deacon" White (Wikimedia Commons)

his career as a 42-year-old regular with the Buffalo Players League club in 1890. In fifteen seasons in the National/Players League, he hit .303. Dan Brouthers, Hardy Richardson, Jack Rowe, and White comprised the "Big Four" that helped the Detroit Wolverines win the 1887 championship. White played every position but spent most of his NL career as a third baseman. However, in 1879 he caught 75 games that his brother Will pitched in Cincinnati. After leaving baseball, White worked for his brother as an optician and later operated a livery stable and garage in Buffalo. He died at Aurora, IL, on July 7, 1939, at age 91. (Total Baseball; Sporting News; Baseball-Reference.com; SABR Baseball Encyclopedia; Dictionary of Biography — Baseball)

Will White won 229 games in 10 seasons, 226 in seven full seasons (1878–80 and 1882–85). A graduate of the College of Ophthalmics, he was the first major league player to wear glasses on the field. The 23-year-old White joined his brother Deacon in Boston late in 1877, going 2–1. In following seasons, he won 40 or more games three times, and at least 30 twice. In 1879 he completed 75 of 76 games, working 680 innings and winning 43 for the National League Cincinnati Red Stockings. The complete games and innings are major league records. After a stop in Detroit, White returned to Cincinnati in 1882. With his Red Stockings now in the American Association, White led the AA with 40 wins, 52 complete games, eight shutouts and a .769 winning percentage. A year later he led the AA with 43 wins, a 2.09 ERA and six shutouts. Only 31 years old when his arm went bad, White left the majors in 1886 and "became a successful businessman in Buffalo." Following a heart seizure in the water, White drowned in Port Carling, Ontario, on August 31, 1911. He was 56 years old. (Total Baseball; Dictionary of Biography — Baseball; Baseball Library; Baseball-Reference.com)

Warren White (William Warren), born in 1844, was a Civil War veteran who had served with the 14th Heavy Artillery regiment of New York. The Milton, NY, native played with and managed National Association teams in Washington — Olympics (1871), Nationals (1872) and Blue Legs (1873). He was playing manager for the Lord Baltimores in 1874 and played for the Chicago White Stockings in 1875. In all, he hit .260 and fielded much above the league average for third basemen. In 1884 the 40-year-old White, who was serving as secretary for the Union Association, donned a uniform again for four games as an infielder with the Washington club. He had one hit and two RBIs, but also had seven errors in 23 fielding chances. White was a resident of Washington, DC, where, according to the 1880 census, he worked as a Treasury Department clerk. He died at Little Rock, AR, on June 12, 1890, at age 46. (Total Baseball; Baseball-Reference.com; U.S. Federal Census; U.S. Civil War Soldiers)

Milt Whitehead, a 22-year-old Canadian, was the regular shortstop for the St. Louis Maroons in 1884. The switch-hitter did little to help the runaway champions, batting only .207 and fielding twelve points below the league average. Tried as a pitcher, he gave up 14 hits and nine runs in a losing effort. Late in the season he shifted to the Kansas City Cowboys, for whom he played five games as an infielder and catcher, and left the majors with a .207 average. He continued to play in the minors until 1897. In 1891 Denver released him to San Francisco so that he could play on the West Coast. In 1893 he was playing for Stockton, in the most "excellent condition in six years." In April 1897 *Sporting Life* contains a note that Whitehead has been "taken to an insane asylum." Whitehead is still listed as a ball player in the 1900 census when he is a patient at the Southern California State Hospital at Highland. He died at the State Hospital on August 15, 1901, at age 39. *(Total Baseball; Baseball-Reference.com; Baseball Encyclopedia; Sporting Life; U.S. Federal Census)*

Guerdon Whiteley joined the Cleveland Blues in August 1884, purchased from the Chicago reserves. In eight games he hit .147. In 1885 he played in 33 games for the Boston Beaneaters, raising his average to .185. In the outfield he committed 20 errors in 41 games for a .785 percentage — more than a hundred points below the league average. In 1886 he led the New England League with 11 homers while playing with Newburyport. Born in Rhode Island, with an Irish mother, Whiteley — spelled Whitely — appears in the 1880 census, working in a woolen mill. In the 1920 census a Gurdon Whitley, born in 1860, appears in the census for East Greenwich, working as a weaver in a woolen mill. Whiteley died at Cranston, RI, on November 24, 1924, at age 65. *(Total Baseball; Baseball-Reference.com; U.S. Federal Census; Encyclopedia of Minor League Baseball; Sporting Life)*

Ed Whiting became the regular catcher for the Baltimore Orioles in 1882. The Philadelphia native shifted to Louisville in 1883, when he hit .292 as the regular catcher. By 1884 he served as backup to Dan Sullivan with the Eclipse. Whiting finished his major league career in 1886 by going hitless in six games for the Washington Nationals. Sometimes playing under the name Harry Zieber, he hit .255 in 180 major league games. In the 1900 census for Philadelphia, an Ed Whiting — born like the ball player in 1860 in Pennsylvania — is listed as a bartender. He does not appear in the 1910 census. *(Total Baseball; Retrosheet; Washington Post; U.S. Federal Census)*

Art Whitney is identified by *Sporting Life* as the "father of the fielders' glove." Late in his career he began using a glove in the field — previously used only by catchers and first basemen — and other players followed. Despite his light bat, Whitney lasted eleven seasons — nine as a regular — in the majors. The son of a dentist from Brockton, MA, Whitney entered the majors with Worcester in 1880, also playing for Detroit, Providence, Pittsburgh and New York in the National League. He played with Pittsburgh, the Cincinnati Kellys and St. Louis in the American Association, and the New York Players League club. He helped

Art Whitney (Library of Congress)

the Giants win two NL championships. A career .223 hitter, he hit as high as .260 in 1887 figures. As a third baseman or shortstop, he led his league in fielding four times. In later years, according to Bill Lee, Whitney operated a business in Fitchberg, MA, and was associated with a firm that manufactured and distributed sporting goods. *Sporting News* says that Whitney was a representative for A.G. Spalding & Bros. Whitney's brother Frank played for Boston in 1876. Art Whitney died in Lowell, MA, on August 15, 1943, at age 85. *(Sporting Life; Baseball Encyclopedia; Baseball Necrology; Baseball-Reference.com; Sporting News)*

James "Grasshopper Jim" Whitney joined the Boston Beaneaters in 1881, coming from the Knickerbockers. The *New York Times* called him "loose-jointed, tall, raw-boned, and clumsy." However, others judged him to be one of the three "speediest pitchers that ever twirled a ball." The

Jim Whitney (Mark Fimoff)

"Stump" Wiedman (Library of Congress)

hard-throwing right hander worked more than 300 innings for eight consecutive seasons, more than 400 five times and more than 500 twice, including a National League–leading 552 as a rookie. Included in his 191 career wins were two 30-win seasons. He had 37 wins and a league leading 345 strikeouts for the NL champions in 1883. But he also lost more games than he won — including back-to-back thirty-two loss seasons in 1885–86. In addition to Boston, Whitney played for Kansas City, Washington and Indianapolis of the NL and the American Association Athletics. Like his pitching mate Charlie Buffinton, Whitney played outfield when he wasn't pitching, hitting .323 in 1882. Because of failing health, he left baseball in 1890 and entered the "hay and grain" business." He died of consumption at Binghamton, NY, on May 21, 1891, at age 35. (Baseball-Reference.com; Total Baseball; BaseballLibrary.com; Sporting Life; New York Times)

George "Stump" Wiedman practiced "starting the ball low and sailing it up toward the batter's nose." Born in Rochester, NY, to German parents, Wiedman is described as a "Dutchman." His name was spelled "Weidman" in contemporary accounts and also in the census. He entered the majors with Buffalo in late 1880 and a year later posted the lowest ERA in the National League. In nine seasons he won 101 games, including 25 and 20-win seasons with Detroit in 1882–83. But he also lost 156 games, included an 18-inning 1–0 loss to Providence in 1883. He was a 36-game loser for Kansas City in 1886. Wiedman finished his major league career with the New York Metropolitans in 1887 and the New York Giants in 1888. In 1891 he was reported to have "dropped out of sight," but in 1896 he was signed as an NL umpire. Although Cap Anson asked that he be "dismissed for incompetency," Wiedman lasted a full season. He then appears in the 1900 census for Rochester as a saloon keeper. This is confirmed by his obituary in Sporting Life. Following an operation for throat cancer, he died in New York City on March 2, 1905, at age 44. (Total Baseball; Baseball-Reference.com; New York

Times; Chicago Daily Tribune; National Police Gazette; U.S. Federal Census; Sporting Life)

John Wiley played third base for the Washington Unions on June 23, 1884, in a game at Philadelphia. Likely a pick-up player from the Philadelphia area, Wiley went hitless in four at bats and had errors on two of three fielding chances in a 6–5 victory. There were at least two John Wileys, born around 1860, living in Philadelphia in 1880, which makes identification difficult. In addition, *Baseball-Reference.com* and *Baseball Page* do not accept the first name of John. *(Baseball-Almanac.com; Total Baseball; U.S. Federal Census; Baseball-Reference.com; Baseball Page)*

Wash Williams appeared in two games as an outfielder for the Richmond Virginians in 1884. In 1885 he played in one game for the Chicago White Stockings. In all, he collected three hits in 12 at bats for a .250 average, but he misplayed two of four balls hit to him. Sources agree that he was a Philadelphia native. *Baseball-Reference.com* gives a death date of 1890. *Total Baseball* and *Retrosheet* say August 9, 1892. *(Total Baseball; Baseball-Reference.com; Retrosheet)*

Edward "Ned" Williamson hit 27 home runs in 1884, a record that stood until 1919 when Babe Ruth hit 29. Playing in Chicago's Lakefront Park with fences less than 200 feet at the lines and only 300 feet to center, Williamson hit 49 doubles in 1883, when most balls hit over the fence were ground rule doubles; in 1884 all balls hit over the fence were ruled as homers. When the White Stockings moved to West Side Park in 1885, Williamson's home run production dropped to three, though he led the National League in RBIs. The 210-pound Williamson, a product of Philadelphia, had entered the NL with Indianapolis in 1878 and joined the White Stockings a year later. In a 13-year career he hit .255 and led third basemen in fielding five times, with a fielding percentage seventeen points over the league average. Considered the "hardest thrower the game has ever produced," Williamson shifted to shortstop in 1886. After injuring his knee in an exhibition game in Paris in 1889, he finished his career with Chicago in the Players League in 1890. Williamson died at Mountain Valley Springs, AR, on March 3, 1894, at age 36. He was undergoing treatment for dropsy and a liver ailment. *(Chicago Daily Tribune; Washington Post; In Memory of Ned Williamson; A Short History of the Single Season Home Run Record; Baseball-Reference.com)*

Ned Williamson (Library of Congress)

Wills began the 1884 season with the Washington club of the American Association, playing four games in which he hit .133. In July he joined the Kansas City Unions for five games, in which he hit .143. But in nine games—eight as a centerfielder—he handled fourteen of fifteen chances for a .933 average. *(Total Baseball; Baseball-Reference.com)*

George "Tug" Wilson, a 24-year-old outfielder, catcher and infielder, played in 24 games for his hometown Brooklyn Trolley Dodgers in 1884. In these games he managed a .232 batting average and a .889 fielding percentage. George A. Wilson of the right age appears in the 1910 census for Brooklyn, working as a dealer in warehouse teas. The player died in Brooklyn on November 18, 1914, at age 54. *(Total Baseball; Baseball-Reference.com; U.S. Federal Census)*

Bill Wise posted a 23–18, 3.04 ERA record for the seventh place Washington Unions in 1884. His win total constituted almost half of the team's 47 wins. He had pitched well in three starts for Baltimore in 1882 (1–2, 2.77 ERA). When the Union Association folded, Wise was out of the majors. In 1886 he returned to make one start for the Washington Nationals, lasting just three innings, and leaving the majors with a 24–21 record. Wise played 57 games as a position player, hitting .224 for his career. Born in the District of Columbia to parents from Maryland and Virginia, Wise appears in the censuses of 1910, 1920 and 1930. In each he is shown as being a clerk in the U.S. Government Printing Office. He died on May 5, 1940, at the age of 79. *(Baseball-Reference.com; Total Baseball; U.S. Federal Census; SABR Baseball Encyclopedia)*

Sam Wise won the *Boston Globe*'s solid silver bat in 1887 when he hit .334 for Boston. In 1881 he came to Detroit from the Akron club in his hometown. After signing a contract with Cincinnati for 1882, he was offered a "big salary" and jumped to Boston, for whom he played through 1888, helping them win the 1883 NL championship. Boston sold him to Washington in 1889; he then played for the Players League Buffalo Bisons in 1890 and for the American Association Baltimore Orioles in 1891 before returning to Washington in 1892. As a shortstop, he was "not among the first in his position," but "makes up with the stick." A career .272 hitter, Wise hit .311 as a 36-year-old in 1893. Released by Washington in 1894, he played in the Eastern League for Buffalo before retiring in 1897. Wise appears in the 1880 Akron census as a machinist. After leaving the majors he was described as "stringing wires for an electric company." Later he became a fireman. Wise died of appendicitis at Akron on January 22, 1910, at age 62. *(Total Baseball; Boston Globe; National Police Gazette; Washington Post; U.S. Federal Census)*

William "Jimmy" or "Chicken" Wolf, a Louisville native, played almost his entire career with the local Eclipse team. In 1882 the club moved from semi-professional status into the American Association, and Wolf immediately became the regular right fielder. In ten seasons with the club, he hit .290, and helped them win a league championship in 1890. In that season he was the AA batting champion with a .363 average, also leading the league with 197 hits. As an outfielder, he had a .918 fielding percentage — more than thirty points above the league average. Louisville fell to last place in 1891, and Wolf was released. He played three games for the St. Louis Browns in 1892 before finishing with Buffalo of the Eastern League in 1893. Born to German parents, Wolf went to work as an engine driver and assistant captain for the Louisville Fire Department. After receiving a serious head injury in 1900, he was declared "mentally unbalanced" and institutionalized for a time in the Kentucky State Hospital. Released in 1902, he died from the results of the head injury on May 16, 1903 at age 41. *(Total Baseball; Baseball-Reference.com; SABR Biography Project; U.S. Federal Census; Sporting Life)*

Fred Wood, an 18-year-old Canadian, joined the Detroit Wolverines as a reserve in 1884. He caught seven games, also appearing as an outfielder and shortstop. He hit only .048 and allowed seven passed balls in one game. In 1885 he played in one game for Buffalo, leaving the majors with a .065 batting average in 13 games. After suffering a broken finger in 1886, he was released

Sam Wise (Library of Congress)

by Buffalo. In 1887 *Sporting Life* notes that Wood is "done forever with professional baseball." Bill Lee found that Wood served as "general manager for the Shredded Wheat Co. in Niagara Falls, NY, before becoming the Eastern representative for *The Billiards Magazine*." Wood died at New York City from injuries suffered after being hit by a car on August 28, 1933. Fred Wood was the brother of Pete Wood, a pitcher with Buffalo and Pittsburgh. *(Total Baseball; Baseball Reference.com; Chicago Daily Tribune; Baseball Necrology; Sporting Life)*

George Wood, a left-handed hitting outfielder, played thirteen seasons in the majors, twelve as a regular. The Boston native, son of Canadian parents from Prince Edward Island, joined Worcester in 1880, also playing with Detroit, Philadelphia, Baltimore and Cincinnati of the National League, Philadelphia of the Players League and Baltimore and Philadelphia of the American Association. He was playing manager of the A's. A career .273 hitter, he hit .302 for Detroit in 1882 and .309 for the A's in 1891, leading the NL with 7 home runs in 1882. His .895 fielding percentage was 12 points higher than the league average. After leaving the majors in 1892, Wood umpired in the NL, the Eastern League and Southern League. He worked as a ticket taker in the Philadelphia ball park, and then received a state office as a messenger and later clerk for the secretary of the commonwealth of Pennsylvania. Still later he became a marshal of the Public Service Commission, appointed by former teammate John Tener. Wood died at Harrisburg on April 4, 1924, at age 65. *(Baseball Reference.com; Sporting Life; Total Baseball; Chicago Daily Tribune; Washington Post; U.S. Federal Census)*

Jimmy Woulfe had a major league career of 23 games—split between the Red Stockings and the Alleghenys in 1884. The New Orleans–born outfielder hit only .136 and fielded .795—fifty points below the league average. Three years later the *National Police Gazette* carried his picture as treasurer of the Young Men's Gymnastics Club of New Orleans, an organization made up of men from "the first families of New Orleans." Born to Irish parents, Woulfe appears as a resident of New Orleans in the censuses of 1900, 1910 and 1920. He is shown first as a notary public and thereafter as a lawyer. Woulfe died in New Orleans on December 20, 1924, at age 65. *(Total Baseball; Washington Post; National Police Gazette; U.S. Federal Census)*

Frank Wyman played thirty games for the Kansas City Cowboys when that club replaced Altoona in the Union Association in June 1884. Used primarily as an outfielder, Wyman hit only .215, and his work in the field was below the league average. He also pitched in three games—including a complete game loss. In August he shifted to the Chicago Browns, for whom he played two games at first base, before leaving the majors. Born in Haverhill, MA, Wyman worked in the shoe factory there before entering professional baseball and returned to that occupation afterwards. Both the 1900 and 1910 censuses show him as a resident of Haverhill, working as a shoe cutter. Wyman died in Everett, MA, on February 4, 1916, at age 53. *(U.S. Federal Census; Baseball-Reference.com; Total Baseball)*

Ed Yewell played in 27 games as a utility infielder and outfielder for the Washington Nationals in 1884. The 21-year-old Washington, DC, native hit .247. Eleven of his games were at second base, where he fielded .885. When the American Association club disbanded in the first week of August, Yewell played in one game for the Washington Unions, going hitless in four at bats. He

George Wood (T. Scott Brandon)

played for Alexandria in 1885. Both the 1900 census and the 1890 *Washington City Directory* list Yewell as a grocer. Bill Lee's research shows that Yewell worked as a patent attorney; this is confirmed by the census of 1910. Yewell died on September 15, 1940, at age 78. *(Baseball-Reference.com; Total Baseball; Sporting Life; Baseball Necrology; U.S. Federal Census; Washington City Directory)*

Tom York made his major league debut with the Troy Haymakers of the National Association as a 20-year-old in 1871. He also played with the Lord Baltimores, the Philadelphia White Stockings and Hartford Dark Blues in the NA, moving with Hartford into the National League in 1876. In fifteen seasons—five in the NA—he was a regular outfielder thirteen times, leading the NA in fielding in 1873. His career .877 fielding percentage was more than forty points over the league average. A career .271 hitter, York hit over .300 four times with a high of .310 in 1879, a year after he had led the NL with ten triples. As playing manager at Providence, he led the team to a third-place finish in 1878 and a second-place finish in 1881. He played with Cleveland (1883) before finishing his major league career in the American Association with Baltimore in 1884–85. York umpired in both the NL and AA. In later years the Brooklyn native was placed "in charge of the press box gate" at the Polo Grounds. He died in New York City on February 17, 1936, at age 84. *(Total Baseball; Baseball-Reference.com; Boston Daily Globe; U.S. Federal Census; Sporting Life)*

Charles "Chief" Zimmer joined Detroit at the end of 1884, coming from Ironton of the Ohio State League. After an 1886 trial with the Metropolitans, he became a regular with Cleveland of the American Association in 1888, catching 125 games in 1889. A strong hitter, Zimmer hit .340 in 1895 and was over .300 four times on his way to a career .269 average. He led National League catchers in fielding and double plays three times

"Chief" Zimmer (T. Scott Brandon)

each. Cy Young's catcher in Cleveland, Zimmer caught the first of Young's no-hitters. He later played for Louisville and Pittsburgh, closing his major league career as player-manager of the Philadelphia Phillies in 1903. Before leaving baseball in 1907, he managed at Little Rock. Zimmer was born in Marietta, OH, to German parents. The 1920 census simply lists him as a retired baseball player. However, Bill Lee found that Zimmer had been a building inspector "before he opened a cigar store and became a cigar maker." He was also the inventor of "Zimmer's Baseball Game," a table game. Zimmer died in Cleveland on August 22, 1949, at age 88. *(Total Baseball; Baseball-Reference.com; Baseball Encyclopedia; New York Times; Sporting News; U.S. Federal Census)*

Appendix I
Performance of Players by League and Team

In 1861 Joe Start of the Enterprise club of Brooklyn played in seven National Association games, leading all batters with a 4.1 and 1.5 average—four runs per game with one over and one "hands lost" per game with five over. On May 18, 1912, forty-eight-year-old Detroit coach Deacon McGuire, filling in for striking Tiger players, singled in a game in Philadelphia. These two records—fifty-three years apart—represent the alpha and omega of the men of 1884 as active players.

When Start scored more than four runs per game, organized baseball clubs had been in existence fewer than twenty years (since September 23, 1845, when the New York Knickerbocker Base Ball Club was founded) and the practice of organized clubs playing against one another was a year younger—the Knickerbockers had lost to the New York Base Ball Club on June 19, 1846, at the Elysian Fields. By the time of McGuire's single, the structure of major league baseball that would last until 1953—an eight-team American League with clubs in Boston, Chicago, Cleveland, Detroit, New York, Philadelphia, St. Louis and Washington and an eight-team National League with clubs in Boston, Brooklyn, Chicago, Cincinnati, New York, Philadelphia, Pittsburgh and St. Louis—was in its ninth season.

Between Start and McGuire organized baseball went through a number of manifestations. Before there was an organized major league, there were organized baseball clubs. According to Ward and Burns (*Baseball: An Illustrated History*), by 1856 "there were nearly fifty clubs around Manhattan alone." In 1857 the clubs formed a loose federation called National Association of Base Ball Players. Start, like all the players of 1863, was an amateur. When Harry Wright began openly paying players in 1869, baseball entered its second phase.

The better players began to gravitate toward teams with the ability to pay for their services. Wright's Red Stockings employed only one local Cincinnati player, and Wright had no problem with shifting the club to Boston to take advantage of the market there. When the National Association of Professional Baseball Players was formed in 1871, the top clubs were in existence, ready to be organized into a national league stretching from Boston to Rockford, IL. Baseball had entered a third phase.

The formation of the National League in 1876 opened a fourth phase. The control of major league baseball passed from the players to the owners, providing a stability still in evidence today. For six years the National League monopolized professional baseball. The fifth manifestation—the creation of the American Association in 1882—brought for the first time two major leagues competing for top players and also for fan support. This phase of major league baseball was repeated in the creation of the American League in 1901. In 1884 the Union Association extended that competition to a third league as a further test of the strength of the marketplace to support a greater number of teams and of organized baseball to develop enough players of major league caliber to supply the teams. The answer to this fifth phase was a resounding no. Through the creation of the Brotherhood of Professional Baseball Players and its outgrowth, the Players League, in 1890, the players unsuccessfully sought to regain control of the game. So like the fifth phase, the sixth ended in failure.

The players of 1884 were a part of each of these manifestations. While there are no national records, at least five of the 637 players were active in organized baseball prior to the creation of the

National Association. In addition to Cuthbert, the players included Joe Start (Brooklyn Atlantics), Davy Force (New York Mutuals and Washington Olympics), Bob Ferguson (Brooklyn Enterprise), and Dave Eggler (New York Mutuals).

The following sections are intended to serve two purposes. First, the brief history of the clubs of organized major league baseball from 1871 through the opening years of the twentieth century places a frame around the 1884 players. Second, the sections index the 1884 players, showing their performance on those clubs from 1871 through 1912.

A note on club names is perhaps in order here. Today we live in an age when club names and logos are selected to involve the greatest amount of fan identification and support. They are under trademark for merchandizing and advertising purposes, bringing tidy sums to the clubs. As fans, we will likely say, "The Twins are playing the Royals today." Only if the question is "Where are they playing?" do we mention the name of a city. Major league baseball has not always been this way. When baseball clubs were local in the 1850s and '60s, clubs were formal entities and identified as such. But with the first franchise shift — the Cincinnati Red Stockings to Boston — and the formation of national leagues, city identification became more important than club identification. Newspaper accounts of games in 1884 will show that the Chicagos played at the Detroits, not the White Stockings played the Wolverines. Sometimes the league is designated to avoid confusion; i.e., the Philadelphia Unions defeated the Baltimore Unions. The Metropolitans and the Athletics are referred to by club names to distinguish them from their National League counterparts. All this is to say that by the 1880s, club names were generally secondary, often not "official," and subject to change by whim or circumstance. Attempts at retro designations are not always in agreement: St. Paul Saints? St. Paul White Caps? St. Paul Apostles?

While I have tried to minimize confusion, I probably have not always succeeded. Washington clubs in five different leagues were generally known as Nationals. Kansas City clubs in four different leagues were known as Cowboys. The Players League Boston franchise adopted the "Reds" name from the defunct Union Association club and then carried it with them into the American Association. Other franchises such as Cincinnati and Pittsburgh simply picked up and moved from one league to another without changing names. In 1890 some players from the New York Giants moved to the Players League, taking with them the name Giants, while a team also called the Giants remained in the National League.

THE NATIONAL ASSOCIATION (1871–1875)

In the five-year history of the National Association of Professional Baseball Players, twenty-five clubs participated. Some say that the $10 league entry fee helped swell this number. Fifty-eight men who played in 1884 were veterans of the NA.

Baltimore Marylands (1873)

The Marylands, a second entry from Baltimore, had a short history in the National Association, lasting just six games. Without a single win, the club disbanded in July. Like the Lord Baltimores, the Marylands played at Newington Park. Lou Say, a local player, had two hits in three games.

1884 PLAYERS (1)

Name	Years	Games	Record
Lou Say	1873	3	.167

Boston Red Stockings (1871–75)

The Boston Red Stockings were charter members of the National Association. In 1869 the Red Stockings, then based in Cincinnati, had become the first professional baseball club. In 1870 Manager Harry Wright took his best players and the team name and moved to Boston. Playing at South End Grounds, the Red Stockings were the powers of the NA, winning four straight titles after an initial second-place finish. Hall of Fame outfielder and first baseman Jim O'Rourke hit .350, .316 and .291 from 1873 through 1875; catcher Deacon White hit .390, .303 and .366 over the same period. Jack Manning was a regular outfielder in 1875. When the league disbanded, Wright again moved the franchise, this time into the new National League as the Red Caps.

1884 PLAYERS (4)

Name	Years	Games	Record
Juice Latham	1875	16	.269
Jack Manning	1873, 75	109	.270
Jim O'Rourke	1873–75	202	.318
Deacon White	1873–75	210	.351

Brooklyn Atlantics (1872–75)

Founded in 1857, the Atlantic Baseball Club of Brooklyn became the dominant club of the 1860s, winning amateur National Association championships in 1859–61, 1864–66 and 1869. The Atlantics entered the professional version of the National Association in its second season. The team played at Capitoline Grounds in 1872 and at Union Grounds, shared with the Eckfords, thereafter. However, they did not enjoy a winning season in the NA, finishing no higher than sixth. Tommy Bond pitched 55 of the club's 56 games in 1874, winning 22. Bob Ferguson was a three-year regular, also managing the club 1872–74; Jack Burdock and Jack Remsen were regulars twice.

In 1875 the club set a futility record by losing 42 of 44 games. The Atlantics disbanded after that season.

1884 Players (9)

Name	Years	Games	Record
Harry Arundel	1875	1	.000
Tommy Bond	1874	55	22–32
Jack Burdock	1872–73	92	.258
Doc Bushong	1875	1	.600
John Cassidy	1875	41	1–20/.176
Jim Clinton	1874–75	24	1–14/.130
Bob Ferguson	1872–74	144	.265
Barney Gilligan	1875	2	.250
Jack Remsen	1872–73	87	.272

Brooklyn Eckfords (1872)

Eckford Base Ball Club, another of the great clubs of the 1860s, were amateur champions in 1862–63. Formed in 1855 and named for their sponsor, Scottish shipbuilder Henry Eckford, the Eckfords played at Union Grounds in Brooklyn. They were members of the National Association only in 1872, and that season was not a success, as they won only three of 29 games to finish ninth. Candy Nelson became the regular second baseman after joining the club from Troy. Twenty-one-year-old Jim Clinton played six different positions and also managed the club to an 0–11 record. The club disbanded at the end of the season.

1884 Players (3)

Name	Years	Games	Record
Jim Clinton	1872	25	.234
Jim Holdsworth	1872	2	.286
Candy Nelson	1872	18	.250

Chicago White Stockings (1871 and 1874–75)

The White Stockings were formed in 1870, Chicago's attempt to emulate the success of the Cincinnati Red Stockings. In the inaugural National Association season, the White Stockings finished with a 19–9 record and third place. However, in the Great Chicago Fire of October 8–11, 1871, their home field — White Stocking Ground — was destroyed. They did not participate in the league in 1872 and 1873, but with a new ball park — 23rd Street Grounds — they returned to the league in 1874. That season second baseman Levi Meyerle hit .394. Outfielder Paul Hines and shortstop John Peters were two-year regulars. Hines hit .328 in 1875. Fergy Malone managed the White Stockings for 36 games in 1874. The club finished in fifth and seventh place in the last two years of the NA. When the league disbanded, the White Stockings moved into the National League.

1884 Players (8)

Name	Years	Games	Record
Ned Cuthbert	1874	58	.268
Will Foley	1875	3	.250
Davy Force	1874	59	.313
Paul Hines	1874–75	128	.313
Fergy Malone	1874	57	.251
Levi Meyerle	1874	53	.394
John Peters	1874–75	124	.287
Warren White	1875	69	.247

Cleveland Forest Citys (1871–72)

The Forest City Baseball Club was formed in 1870, taking its name from one of the nicknames adopted by the city of Cleveland. By 1871, as an all-professional club, they became a charter member of the National Association, finishing that season with a 10–19 record, for seventh place. In 1872 with a record of 6–16, the club withdrew from the NA in August. Catcher Deacon White hit .322 and .343, but was winless in two games as manager; third baseman Ezra Sutton hit .352 in 1871. Home games were played at National Association Grounds.

1884 Players (5)

Name	Years	Games	Record
Joe Battin	1871	1	.000
Jim Holdsworth	1872	22	.300
Joe Quest	1871	3	.231
Ezra Sutton	1871–72	51	.319
Deacon White	1871–72	51	.329

Elizabeth (NJ) Resolutes (1873)

The Resolute Base-Ball Club of Elizabeth, a city located just west of New York City, was founded in 1866. The club added professional players and entered the National Association in 1873. Soon, however, they found the competition too strong, winning just two of 23 games. Playing at Waverly Fairgrounds, the Resolutes called it a season in late July. Jack Farrow filled in at four positions, Jim Clinton at third base.

1884 PLAYERS (2)

Name	Years	Games	Record
Jim Clinton	1873	9	.237
Jack Farrow	1873	12	.167

Ft. Wayne Kekiongas (1871)

Named for the Miami Indian settlement at the site of what is now Ft. Wayne, the Kekionga Base-Ball Club played the first major league baseball game in history, defeating the Cleveland Forest Citys 2–0. Bobby Mathews' opening-day four-hit shutout allowed him to lead the league in that category. The game was played before 200 fans at the Kekionga Base-Ball Grounds, called Grand Duchess. Formed in 1868, the club was not a success in the National Association, dropping out in August with a 7–12 record.

1884 PLAYERS (1)

Name	Years	Games	Record
Bobby Mathews	1871	19	6–11

Hartford Dark Blues (1874–75)

The Hartford Base Ball Club, called the Dark Blues, were the only new club to enter the National Association in 1874, a year that saw the Marylands, the Washingtons and the Resolutes withdraw. In fact, the club was formed in 1874. Playing at Hartford Ball Club Grounds, the Dark Blues went 16–27 in their initial season. However, by 1875 they had added second baseman Jack Burdock and outfielder Jack Remsen from the Mutuals, third baseman Bob Ferguson and pitcher Tommy Bond from the Atlantics and outfielder Tom York from the Philadelphias. Managed by Ferguson, this new set of Dark Blues finished second. When the NA disbanded, Hartford passed into the new National League.

1884 PLAYERS (10)

Name	Years	Games	Record
Tommy Bond	1875	40	19–16
Steve Brady	1874–75	28	.303
Jack Burdock	1875	74	.294
Bob Ferguson	1875	85	.240
Bill Harbidge	1875	53	.240
Charley Jones	1875	1	.000
Jack Manning	1874	1	.200
Jack Remsen	1875	86	.268
Orator Shaffer	1874	9	.229
Tom York	1875	86	.296

Keokuk (IA) Westerns (1875)

Keokuk, claiming a population of 15,000 in 1875, was the westernmost city in the National Association. Western Baseball Club of Keokuk was formed in 1875 and entered the National Association in the league's final season. But after winning only one of 13 games, the club disbanded on June 16. The Westerns played home games at Walte's Pasture, also called Perry Park, a field with two lakes in the outfield. Rookie Charley Jones was the regular left fielder for the Westerns.

1884 PLAYERS (1)

Name	Years	Games	Record
Charley Jones	1875	12	.275

Lord Baltimores (1872–74)

The Lord Baltimores were named for the founder of Maryland. They were sometimes called the Canaries or Yellow Stockings, names taken from their uniforms. The Lord Baltimores entered the National Association in its second year, finishing second to the Boston Red Stockings. Shortstop Davy Force hit .432 that season, and Bobby Mathews won 25 games. In 1873 the team dropped to third; by 1874 they won only nine of 47 games to finish in last place, disbanding after that season. Force and outfielder Tom York were two-year regulars. Warren White was playing manager in 1874. The Lord Baltimores played home games at Newington Park in Baltimore.

1884 PLAYERS (8)

Name	Years	Games	Record
Davy Force	1872–73	68	.386
Joe Gerhardt	1874	14	.328
Jack Manning	1874	42	.351/4–16
Bobby Mathews	1872	50	25–18
Lou Say	1874	18	.209
Pop Snyder	1874	39	.217
Warren White	1874	45	.264
Tom York	1872–73	108	.286

Middletown (CT) Mansfields (1872)

The Mansfield Baseball Club was named for Civil War general and Middletown native Joseph Mansfield. Founded in 1866, the club remained largely amateur, even as a member of the National Association in 1872. With a supporting population of only 11,000, the Mansfields played at Mansfield Club Grounds. First baseman Tim Murnane (.359) and rookie shortstop Jim O'Rourke (.307) helped the Mansfields to a .301 club batting average. But after winning only five of 24 games, the Mansfields withdrew from the league on August 14.

1884 Players (2)

Name	Years	Games	Record
Tim Murnane	1872	24	.359
Jim O'Rourke	1872	23	.307

New Haven (CT) Elm Citys (1875)

The Elm City club was named from one of the New Haven nicknames. New Haven had been the site of the first public planting of trees—many of them large elms. The Elm Citys entered the National Association in its last year and wound up as one of the "have nots." Winning only seven of 47 games, they finished a distant eighth place and withdrew at the end of the season. Juice Latham went 4–14 as manager of the club. None of the 1884 players held regular status, but Billy Geer, a seven-position player, appeared in 37 games. Except for one game at Brewster Race Track, they played home games at Howard Avenue Grounds.

1884 Players (5)

Name	Years	Games	Record
John Cassidy	1875	6	.136
Billy Geer	1875	37	.244
Fred Goldsmith	1875	1	.500
Jim Keenan	1875	5	.077
Juice Latham	1875	20	.197

New York Mutuals (1871–75)

The Mutuals, dating from 1857, were named for the Mutual Hook and Ladder Company. By 1868 the club had moved from the Elysian Fields to the Union Grounds in Brooklyn, their home throughout their National Association and National League history. In amateur National Association baseball, the Mutuals claimed a championship in 1868. One of the charter members of the National Association in 1871, they had a second-place finish in 1874 but fell to sixth place with a losing record in 1875. When the NA disbanded, the Mutuals became a charter member of the National League. Outfielder Dave Eggler hit .320, .338 and .336 in 1871–73; Bobby Mathews started 182 of 188 games in the 1873–75 period, winning 100. First baseman Joe Start was a five-year regular and 18–7 as manager in 1873; Eggler and second baseman Candy Nelson were regulars for three seasons. Bob Ferguson managed the team to a 16–17 record in 1871.

1884 Players (12)

Name	Years	Games	Record
Jack Burdock	1874	61	.275
Dave Eggler	1871–73	142	.333
Bob Ferguson	1871	33	.241
Chick Fulmer	1872	36	.307
Billy Geer	1874	2	.250
Joe Gerhardt	1875	58	.214
Jim Holdsworth	1873, 75	124	.300
Bobby Mathews	1873–75	187	100–83
Candy Nelson	1873–75	171	.247
Jack Remsen	1874	64	.229
Orator Shaffer	1874	1	.200
Joe Start	1871–75	273	.295

Philadelphia Athletics (1871–75)

The Athletics were founded as the Athletic Base Ball Club in 1860. Charter members of the National Association, they were one of three teams to be members throughout its history. After winning the inaugural league championship, they were never again so successful in the NA, dropping to third in the final season. Among Athletics standouts were Levi Meyerle, who hit .492 in 1871 and Cap Anson, who hit .414, .398, .331 and .324 in the 1872–75 period. Anson also managed the club to a 4–2 record. Ezra Sutton was a three-year regular at third base, hitting .335 in 1873. When the league disbanded, the Athletics became charter members of the National League. They played home games at Jefferson Street Grounds.

1884 Players (11)

Name	Years	Games	Record
Cap Anson	1872–75	222	.364
Joe Battin	1873–74	52	.238
Ned Cuthbert	1871–72	75	.305
Dave Eggler	1875	66	.302
Davy Force	1875	77	.311
Lon Knight	1875	13	.128
Fergy Malone	1871–72	68	.305

Name	Years	Games	Record
Levi Meyerle	1871–72	53	.406
Tim Murnane	1873–74	62	.217
John Richmond	1875	29	.200
Ezra Sutton	1873–75	181	.318

Philadelphia Centennials (1875)

The Centennial Club of Philadelphia — the city's third entry in the National Association — lasted only fourteen games in 1875. Playing in Columbia Park — renamed Centennial Park — the Centennials compiled a 2–12 record, playing their last game on May 26 before withdrawing from the league. According to Daniel Ginsburg, before folding, the club sold shortstop Bill Craver and pitcher George Bechtel to the Athletics, the first player sales in major league history. Twenty-year-old Fred Warner was the club's regular center fielder.

1884 PLAYERS (1)

Name	Years	Games	Record
Fred Warner	1875	14	.246

Philadelphia White Stockings (1873–75)

The Philadelphia Baseball Club is sometimes referred to as the Philadelphias or simply as the Whites. They entered the National Association in its third year, occupying the same Jefferson Street Grounds as the Athletics. In three years of existence, the White Stockings finished second, fourth and fifth in the league. Chick Fulmer was the regular shortstop all three seasons. Levi Meyerle hit .349 in 1873 and .320 in 1875; Jim Holdsworth hit .359 and Dave Eggler .324 for the 1874 club. Fergy Malone was 8–2 as manager in 1873. The White Stockings disbanded with the league.

1884 PLAYERS (13)

Name	Years	Games	Record
Bill Crowley	1875	9	.081
Ned Cuthbert	1873	51	.277
Dave Eggler	1874	58	.318
Chick Fulmer	1873–75	175	.257
Jim Holdsworth	1874	57	.340
Fergy Malone	1873, 75	82	.270
Levi Meyerle	1873, 75	116	.330
Ed McKenna	1874	1	.000
Tim Murnane	1875	69	.272
Orator Shaffer	1875	19	.243
Pop Snyder	1875	66	.243
Sam Weaver	1875	1	1–0
Tom York	1874	50	.250

Rockford Forest Citys (1871)

The Forest City club of Rockford, IL, was a charter member of the National Association. Playing in the Agricultural Society Fair Grounds, a field with trees along the infield foul lines, the Forest Citys finished last in the league with a 4–21 record. Adding to their problems, they were the westernmost club in the league at the time; consequently they had the highest travel costs. Not surprisingly, Forest City disbanded at the end of the season. Playing the first of his 27 seasons, third baseman Cap Anson hit .325. Twenty-year-old Chick Fulmer was the regular shortstop.

1884 PLAYERS (2)

Name	Year	Games	Record
Cap Anson	1871	25	.325
Chick Fulmer	1871	16	.270

St. Louis Brown Stockings (1875)

Already a professional club, the Brown Stockings entered the National Association for the 1875 season. Playing in Grand Avenue Grounds — also called Sportsman's Park I — they finished fourth in the league that season with a 39–29 record. Eighteen-year-old "Pud" Galvin debuted with the Brown Stockings as a change pitcher for George Bradley. Galvin made seven starts for a 4–2, 1.16 ERA record. Joe Battin was the regular second baseman; Ned Cuthbert the regular left fielder. When the NA disbanded, the Brown Stockings became a charter member of the new National League.

1884 PLAYERS (4)

Name	Year	Games	Record
Joe Battin	1875	67	.250
George Bradley	1875	60	33–26
Ned Cuthbert	1875	68	.242
Pud Galvin	1875	8	4–2

St. Louis Red Stockings (1875)

The Red Stockings were an amateur baseball club that decided to go professional in 1875; they then entered the National Association. Their home park was Compton Avenue Baseball Park. In professional competition the Red Stockings lasted only 19 games, of which they won four. First baseman Charlie Hautz was the team's leading hitter with a .301 average. Nineteen-year-old Silver Flint, the regular catcher, managed only five hits in 17 games. In July the team withdrew from the league.

1884 Players (4)

Name	Years	Games	Record
Joe Ellick	1875	7	.222
Silver Flint	1875	17	.082
Charlie Hautz	1875	19	.301
Trick McSorley	1875	15	.212

Troy Haymakers (1871–72)

The Haymakers were formed in 1860 as the amateur Union Club of Lansingburgh. Going professional in 1871, they became charter members of the National Association. Playing home games at Haymakers' Grounds in Lansingburgh, NY, the Haymakers finished sixth in 1871 with a 13–15 record. In fifth place with a 15–10 record, the Haymakers disbanded in July 1872. Twenty-year-old Tom York was the regular center fielder in 1871; Davy Force the regular shortstop in 1872.

1884 Players (3)

Name	Years	Games	Record
Davy Force	1872	25	.408
Candy Nelson	1871	4	.350
Tom York	1871	29	.255

Washington Blue Legs (1873)

This club seems to have been a combination of the previous Washington teams. Four former Nationals and three former Olympics were on the roster. The manager, Nick Young, had managed the Olympics. The team played in Olympic Grounds. They finished the season with an 8–31 record, good for seventh place. Two 18 year olds—shortstop Joe Gerhardt and catcher Pop Snyder—were regulars. Twenty-one year-old outfielder Paul Hines led the team with a .331 batting average.

1884 Players (4)

Name	Years	Games	Record
Joe Gerhardt	1873	13	.214
Paul Hines	1873	39	.331
Pop Snyder	1873	28	.194
Warren White	1873	39	.269

Washington Nationals (1872)

The National Baseball Club—the first of many Washington clubs of that name—was one of the ten present at the formation of the National Association. However, the Nationals did not pay the $10 entry fee, so were not included in the 1871 standings. They began the following season in the NA, but after 11 games, none of which they won, the Nationals withdrew from the league, lasting one day longer than the Olympic Club. Paul Hines played first base, and Warren White played third. White hit .289 for a club that hit .239. They played at National Grounds.

1884 Players (2)

Name	Years	Games	Record
Paul Hines	1872	11	.245
Warren White	1872	10	.289

Washington Olympics (1871–72)

The Olympic Baseball Club of Washington played professionally prior to the opening of the National Association. Charter members of the NA, the Olympics played home games at Olympic Grounds, a park with a capacity of 500. The first season the team posted a 15–15 record, good for fifth place. Shortstop Davy Force hit .278, the team average. In 1872 the club lasted only nine games, disbanding in late May with a 2–7 record.

1884 Players (2)

Name	Years	Games	Record
Davy Force	1871	32	.278
Warren White	1871	1	.000

Washington Washingtons (1875)

Washington had no representation in the National Association in 1874. *Green Cathedrals* calls the 1875 team the Olympics—the team played in Olympic Grounds. *Baseball-Reference.com* calls them the Nationals; Marshall Wright calls them the Washingtons. By whatever name, the team contained only two players from the 1873 team. Not successful in the field, the team lost 23 of 28 games and dropped from the league in July. Lou Say was a backup shortstop.

1884 Players (1)

Name	Years	Games	Record
Louis Say	1875	11	.263

The National League (1876–)

From its inception in 1876 to the beginning of the 20th century, 31 franchises representing 22 cities participated in the National League. Of the 637 major league players in 1884, 390 spent some part of their careers in the NL.

Baltimore Orioles (1892–99)

When the American Association was absorbed into the National League in 1892, Baltimore was one of four AA franchises to make the transition. After a sorry twelfth-place finish in 1892, the Orioles moved up to eighth in 1893 and then into first in 1894. Three consecutive championships followed by two runner-up finishes marked the Orioles as the team of the '90s. Hall of Fame manager Ned Hanlon was the architect of the Orioles' success, developing a scrappy style that featured John McGraw. The Orioles closed the century with a fourth-place finish, but were dropped from the NL when it contracted to eight teams in 1900. The Orioles played their entire NL history in Oriole Park III. Few of the 1884 players were part of the club's glory years. First baseman Dan Brouthers hit .347 for the 1894 champions; third baseman Jim Donnelly hit .328 for the '96 winners; Al Maul's twenty wins helped the '98 runners-up; Joe Quinn was a utility player.

1884 PLAYERS (17)

Name	Years	Games	Record
Dan Brouthers	1894–95	128	.343
Charlie Buffinton	1892	13	4–8
James B. Donnelly	1896	106	.328
Frank Foreman	1892	4	0–3
Joe Gunson	1892	89	.213
Ned Hanlon	1892	11	.163
Bill Johnson	1892	4	.133
Al Maul	1897–98	30	20–7
Jocko Milligan	1893	24	.245
Tony Mullane	1893–94	55	18–25
Joe Quinn	1896–98	111	.273
Harry Stovey	1892–93	82	.262
Cub Stricker	1892	75	.264
Sy Sutcliffe	1892	66	.279
Adonis Terry	1892	1	0–1
Curt Welch	1892	63	.236
George Wood	1892	21	.224

Boston Red Caps/Beaneaters (1876–)

The Red Caps are one of two franchises which have held continuous membership in the National League since 1876. Called the Red Stockings while in the National Association, the Red Caps became known as the Beaneaters in 1882. The current name Braves (from the Boston Tea Party) was adopted in 1912. The club has also used Doves (1907–10), Rustlers (1911) and Bees (1936–40). Their move to Milwaukee in 1953 was major league baseball's first franchise move in fifty years; the team then moved to Atlanta in 1966. The Red Caps/Beaneaters played at South End Grounds through 1887. These grounds were torn down and replaced by a new South End Grounds in 1888. When South End Grounds burned on May 16, 1894, the club played in Congress Street Grounds before moving into a rebuilt South End Grounds on June 20. Braves Field, long time home of the Braves, opened in 1915. Tommy Bond's 80 victories helped the Red Caps win National League championships in 1877 and 1878. "Grasshopper Jim" Whitney's 37 wins and Ezra Sutton's .324 average led the Beaneaters to a pennant in 1883. During the decade of the 1890s, pitcher John Clarkson, outfielder Tommy McCarthy, and catcher King Kelly — Hall of Famers all — led Boston to five pennants in 1891–93 and 1897–98. John Morrill — who managed the team in 1882–88 — was a regular for 13 seasons, primarily as a first baseman. Second baseman Jack Burdock (10 seasons), shortstop Ezra Sutton (10), and third baseman Billy Nash (9), contributed to team stability as did infielder Sam Wise (7) and outfielder Joe Hornung (7). Burdock managed the club in 1883.

1884 PLAYERS (69)

Name	Years	Games	Record
Bill Annis	1884	27	.177
Marty Barrett	1884	3	.000
Charlie Bennett	1889–93	337	.216
Tommy Bond	1877–81	247	149–81
Dan Brouthers	1889	126	.373
Lew Brown	1876–77, 83	117	.234
Tom Brown	1888–89	197	.240
Charlie Buffinton	1882–86	184	104–70
Jack Burdock	1878–88	760	.277
Cliff Carroll	1893	120	.224
John Clarkson	1888–92	242	149–82
Jack Clements	1900	16	.310
John Connor	1884	7	1–4
Bill Crowley	1881, 84	180	.254
Con Daily	1886–87	86	.207
Daisy Davis	1884–85	15	6–9
Pat Dealy	1885–86	50	.250
Pat Deasley	1881–82	110	.255
John Fox	1881	17	6–8
Charlie Ganzel	1890–97	535	.267
Charles Getzein	1890–91	51	27–22
Ed Glenn	1888	20	.154
Tom Gunning	1884–86	87	.186
Mert Hackett	1883–85	152	.210
Walter Hackett	1885	35	.184
Lou Hardie	1890	47	.227

All members of the 1883 National League champion Boston Beaneaters were active in 1884. *Top row:* Joe Hornung, Ezra Sutton, Sam Wise, Jack Burdock; *bottom row:* Charlie Buffinton, Paul Radford, Jim Whitney, John Morrill, Mike Hines, Mertie Hackett and Edgar Smith.

Bill Hawes	1879	38	.184		Blondie Purcell	1885	21	.218
Mike Hines	1883–85, 88	116	.207		Joe Quinn	1888–89, 91–92	417	.245
Paul Hines	1890	69	.264		Charley Radbourn	1886–89	165	78–81
Joe Hornung	1881–88	705	.263		Paul Radford	1883	72	.205
Pete Hotaling	1882	84	.259		Hardy Richardson	1889	132	.304
Sadie Houck	1879–80	92	.253		John Richmond	1880–81	59	.260
Dick Johnston	1885–89	529	.256		Ed Rowen	1882	83	.248
Charley Jones	1879–80	149	.309		Pop Smith	1889–90	193	.238
King Kelly	1887–88, 91–92	442	.289		Pop Snyder	1878–81	203	.227
John Kiley	1891	1	.000		Harry Stovey	1891–92	172	.255
Jack Leary	1880	1	.000		Ezra Sutton	1877–88	977	.287
Fred Lewis	1881	27	.219		Sam Trott	1880	39	.208
Jack Manning	1876 78	130	.259		Deacon White	1877	59	.387
Jim Manning	1884–85	173	.224		Will White	1877	3	2–1
Bobby Mathews	1881–82	39	20–15		Guerdon Whitely	1885	33	.85
Tommy McCarthy	1885, 92–95	552	.296		Jim Whitney	1881–85	266	133–121
Chippy McGarr	1890	121	.236		Sam Wise	1882–88	709	.267
Gene Moriarity	1884	4	.063					
John Morrill	1876–88	1219	.262					
Tim Murnane	1876–77	104	.281					
Billy Nash	1885–89, 91–95	1186	.281					
Dan O'Leary	1880	3	.250					
Jim O'Rourke	1876–7880	277	.309					
Tom Poorman	1885–86	144	.253					
Phil Powers	1880	37	.143					

Brooklyn Bridegrooms (1890–)

The Brooklyn Bridegrooms, 1889 champions of the American Association, jumped to the National League for 1890 and under various names and locations have been members ever since. Known as the Superbas (1899–1910) and later as the Robins—for manager Wilbert Robinson (1914–1931)—the club officially settled on Dodgers, short for Trolley Dodgers, a name they had used when first entering the American Association. In 1958, the franchise relocated to Los Angeles. The Bridegrooms won their initial venture into the NL in 1890, when Adonis Terry and Bob Caruthers combined for 49 wins and Dave Foutz hit .303. King Kelly managed the club for two seasons and Foutz for four, as it sank into the second division. Ned Hanlon joined the club as manager in 1899, bringing with him key players from Baltimore, to form the bases for championships in 1899 and 1900. Deacon McGuire was a backup catcher both years. Outfielder Oyster Burns and Foutz, as pitcher, first baseman and outfielder, were five-year regulars. Dan Brouthers, Bob Caruthers, George Pinkney, Germany Smith, Terry and Ward were regulars twice. In their first NL season the Bridegrooms played in Washington Park I, moving to Eastern Park a year later. In 1898 they moved to a new Washington Park. Ebbets Field was built in 1913.

teams to enter the NL that year. Sam Crane managed the Bisons in 1880. In 1881 they added Dan Brouthers, Deacon White, Jim O'Rourke and Dave Rowe to a lineup that already included Davy Force and Hardy Richardson, supporting the pitching of Pud Galvin. In 1883 Brouthers hit .374, and Galvin won 46 games. Force (shortstop), Richardson (second base) and Galvin were seven-year regulars. Rowe, a catcher and third baseman, was a regular for six seasons. Brouthers at first base and White at third were five- year regulars. O'Rourke was an outfield regular for four seasons. Outfielders Bill Crowley and Jim Lillie held regular status for three seasons. In seven seasons in the NL, Buffalo finished in third place four times, but by 1885, the Bisons fell to seventh place. At the end of the season, they sold off their stars to Detroit and dropped out of the NL, returning to the International League in 1886. For their first five NL seasons they played home games at Riverside Park before shifting to Olympic Park in 1884.

1884 Players (23)

Name	Years	Games	Record
Lady Baldwin	1890	2	1–0
Dan Brouthers	1892–93	229	.336
Pete Browning	1894	1	1.000
Jack Burdock	1891	3	.083
Oyster Burns	1890–95	637	.300
Doc Bushong	1890	16	.236
Bob Caruthers	1890–91	127	41–25/.271
Pop Corkhill	1890	51	.225
Cannon-Ball Crane	1893	3	0–2
Con Daily	1891–95	308	.259
Bones Ely	1891	31	.153
Dude Esterbrook	1891	3	.375
Dave Foutz	1890–96	555	.266/18–11
Al Maul	1899	4	2–0
Tommy McCarthy	1896	104	.249
Deacon McGuire	1899–1901	202	.298
Joe Mulvey	1895	13	.306
George Pinkney	1890–91	261	.291
Danny Richardson	1893	54	.223
Germany Smith	1890, 97	241	.196
Harry Stovey	1893	48	.251
Adonis Terry	1890–91	129	32–32/.264
Monte Ward	1891–92	253	.270

Buffalo Bisons (1879–85)

Buffalo entered the National League from the International Association in 1879, one of four

1884 Players (53)

Name	Years	Games	Record
Dan Brouthers	1881–85	439	.351
Scrappy Carroll	1885	13	.075
James Burke	1882–83	2	0–1
Chub Collins	1884	45	.178
John Connor	1885	1	0–1
Ed Coughlin	1884	1	.250
Cannon-Ball Crane	1885	13	.275
Sam Crane	1880	10	.129
Bill Crowley	1879–80, 85	237	.264
Ed Cushman	1883	7	3–3
One-Arm Daily	1882	29	15–14
Buttercup Dickerson	1885	5	.048
Tom Dolan	1882	22	.157
Denny Driscoll	1880, 85	25	.154
Dave Eggler	1879, 83–84	185	.208
Bones Ely	1884	1	.000
Dude Esterbrook	1880	64	.241
J. Fisher	1885	1	0–1
Davy Force	1879–85	581	.207
Chick Fulmer	1879–80	87	.254
Pud Galvin	1879–85	413	218–179
Art Hagan	1883–84	5	1–4
Moxie Hengle	1885	7	.154
Joe Hornung	1879–80	163	.266
Tommy Kearns	1880	2	.000
Jim Keenan	1880	2	.143
Arlie Latham	1880	22	.127
Jim Lillie	1883–85	276	.235
Jack Lynch	1881	20	10–9

Jack Manning	1881	1	.000
Jim McCauley	1885	24	.179
Jim McDonald	1885	5	.000
Mike Moynahan	1880	27	.330
George Myers	1884–85	167	.194
Jim O'Rourke	1881–84	369	.353
John Peters	1881	54	.214
Dick Phelan	1885	4	.125
Tom Poorman	1880	19	.157
Blondie Purcell	1881–82	114	.280
Charley Radbourn	1880	6	.143
Hardy Richardson	1879–85	618	.292
Jack Rowe	1879–85	504	.289
Billy Serad	1884–85	67	23–41
Orator Shaffer	1883	95	.292
Pop Smith	1881	3	.000
Ecky Stearns	1880, 85	58	.191
Tony Suck	1883	2	.000
Sleeper Sullivan	1881	35	.190
Ed Swartwood	1881	1	.333
Oscar Walker	1879–80	106	.262
Deacon White	1881–85	463	.301
Stump Wiedman	1880	17	0–9
Fred Wood	1885	1	.250

Chicago White Stockings (1876–)

One of the charter members of the National League, Chicago has held continuous membership since. Originally named for a uniform color, the team was known as the Colts through the 1890s, as the Orphans briefly at the turn of the century, and as the Cubs since 1902. The White Stockings played at 23rd Street Grounds, Lake Front Park (1878–84), where Ned Williamson hit 27 homers in 1884, West Side Park I (1885–92), South Side Park (1890–91) and West Side Park II (1893–1915). Wrigley Field opened in 1915. One of the great clubs of the 19th century, Chicago had NL championships in 1876, 1880–82 and 1885–86. Second baseman Paul Hines and shortstop John Peters had been regulars on the 1875 National Association club; they along with first baseman Cap Anson, catcher Deacon White and utility player Fred Andrus were members of the 1876 club. Anson finished his career with the 1897 Orphans along with second baseman Fred Pfeffer and pitcher Adonis Terry. Anson held regular status for 22 seasons—usually as a first baseman—managing twenty of those. Infielders Tom Burns and Ned Williamson were 11-year regulars—Burns later succeeding Anson as manager; Pfeffer held down second base for 10 seasons. Outfielders George Gore and Abner Dalrymple and catcher Silver Flint were at their posts for 10 years. King Kelly played wherever needed for seven years. Pitchers Bill Hutchison, Larry Corcoran and Fred Goldsmith were in the starting rotation for seven, five and five seasons. Anson hit .399 in 1881; John Clarkson won 53 games in 1885. Bob Ferguson managed in 1878, preceding Anson.

1884 Players (60)

Name	Years	Games	Record
Fred Andrus	1876, 84	9	.293/1–0
Cap Anson	1876–97	2276	.329
Charlie Bastian	1889	46	.135
George Bradley	1877	55	18–23
Joe Brown	1884	15	.213/4–2
Lou Brown	1879	6	.286
Tom Burns	1880–91	1239	.286
Cliff Carroll	1890–91	266	.272
Bob Caruthers	1893	1	.000
John Cassidy	1878	60	.266
John Clarkson	1884–87	199	137–57
Larry Corcoran	1880–85	270	175–85
Mike Corcoran	1884	1	0–1
George Crosby	1884	3	1–2
Con Daily	1896	9	.074
Abner Dalrymple	1879–86	709	.295
Tom Dolan	1879	1	.000
Charlie Eden	1877	15	.218
Dave Eggler	1877	33	.265
Bob Ferguson	1878	61	.351
Silver Flint	1879–89	680	.241
Ed Gastfield	1885	1	.000
Fred Goldsmith	1880–84	177	107–63
George Gore	1879–86	719	.315
Frank Hankinson	1878–79	102	.231
Bill Harbidge	1878–79	58	.283
Lou Hardie	1886	16	.176
John Hibbard	1884	2	1–1
Paul Hines	1876–77	128	.313
Bill Hutchison	1889–95	367	181–158
Charley Jones	1877	2	.375
King Kelly	1880–86	681	.316
Walt Kinzie	1884	19	.159
Bill Krieg	1885	1	.000
Terry Larkin	1878–79	114	60–49
Chuck Lauer	1890	2	.250
Tom Lee	1884	5	1–4
Tom Lynch	1884	1	0–0
Jim McCauley	1885	3	.167
Bill McClellan	1878	48	.224
Jim McCormick	1885–86	66	51–15
Hugh Nicol	1881–82	73	.201
John Peters	1876–77, 79	73	.201

Name	Years	Games	Record
Fred Pfeffer	1883–89, 91, 96–97	1093	.252
Tom Poorman	1880	7	.200
Phil Powers	1878	8	.161
Shadow Pyle	1887	4	1–3
Joe Quest	1879–82	285	.225
Jack Remsen	1878–79	98	.226
Dave Rowe	1877	2	.286
Milt Scott	1882	1	.400
Orator Shaffer	1879	73	.304
Joe Start	1878	61	.351
Billy Sunday	1883–87	181	.254
Sy Sutcliffe	1884–85	15	.190
Adonis Terry	1894–97	101	.266/41–40
Bill Traffley	1878	2	.111
Deacon White	1876	66	.343
Wash Williams	1885	1	.250
Ned Williamson	1879–89	1065	.260

Cincinnati Red Stockings (1876–1880)

The Red Stockings were a charter member of the National League. However, in five seasons they finished last three times, with a second-place finish in 1878 being their peak. The NL was unhappy that the franchise played Sunday ball games and sold beer in the stands, so expelled them after the 1880 season. The Red Stockings played in Avenue Grounds through 1879 and in Bank Street Grounds in 1880. Third baseman Will Foley and outfielders Charley Jones and Redleg Snyder were regulars on the 1876 team. Foley, Jones and pitcher Will White were three-year regulars. Hall of Fame members King Kelly and Deacon White were regulars twice. In 1879 Kelly hit .348, and Will White won 43 games.

1884 Players (25)

Name	Years	Games	Record
Hick Carpenter	1880	77	.240
Ned Cuthbert	1877	12	.179
Buttercup Dickerson	1878–79	110	.296
Will Foley	1876–77, 79	170	.209
Billy Geer	1878	61	.219
Joe Gerhardt	1878–79	139	.243
Pete Hotaling	1879	81	.279
Charley Jones	1876–77	180	.302
King Kelly	1878–79	137	.321
Jack Manning	1877, 80	105	.274
Mike Mansell	1880	53	.193
Bobby Mathews	1877	15	3–12
Levi Meyerle	1877	27	.327
George Miller	1877	11	.162
Jack Neagle	1879	3	.167
Blondie Purcell	1879–80	89	.283
Charlie Reilley	1880	30	.204
John Reilly	1880	73	.206
Lou Say	1880	48	.199
Pop Smith	1880	83	.207
Redleg Snyder	1876	55	.151
Joe Sommer	1880	24	.182
Harry Wheeler	1879–80	18	.088
Deacon White	1878–80	174	.318
Will White	1878–80	190	91–94

Cincinnati Reds (1890–)

After being an American Association site (1882–89), Cincinnati returned a franchise to the National League in 1890, and has been an NL city since. The original name "Red Stockings" was shortened to Reds and renamed Redlegs for stretches in the 1954–60 period when the name *Reds* had communist implications. The team played in League Park I until 1894 when it moved into League Park II. Crosley Field, their longtime home, was built in 1912. The Reds won no National League honors until 1919, when they won the pennant and the "Black Sox" World Series. Hall of Fame second baseman Bid McPhee played ten of his 18 seasons with the Reds in the National League. Infield mates Arlie Latham and Germany Smith played beside him for six seasons. Manager and first baseman Charlie Comiskey and pitchers Tony Mullane and Frank Foreman were three-year regulars. Buck Ewing, who managed the club in 1895–97, hit .318 in 1896; Mullane won 23 games in 1891.

1884 Players (24)

Name	Years	Games	Record
Kid Baldwin	1890	22	.153
Pete Browning	1891–92	138	.319
Bob Caruthers	1893	13	.292
Charlie Comiskey	1892–94	266	.233
Pop Corkhill	1891	1	.000
Cannon-Ball Crane	1891	15	4–8
Buck Ewing	1895–97	175	.302
Frank Foreman	1890, 95–96	84	38–31
Buster Hoover	1892	14	.176
Jim Keenan	1890–91	129	.174
Joe Knight	1890	127	.312
Bill Kuehne	1892	6	.208
Arlie Latham	1890–95	696	.279
Bid McPhee	1890–99	1224	.278
Tony Mullane	1890–93	128	62–55
Hugh Nicol	1890	50	.210

Name	Years	Games	Record
Tip O'Neill	1892	109	.251
Joe Quinn	1900	74	.274
Charley Radbourn	1891	26	11–13
John Reilly	1890–91	1099	.271
Mike Slattery	1891	41	.209
Germany Smith	1891–96	781	.254
Curt Welch	1892	25	.202
George Wood	1892	30	.196

Cleveland Blues (1879–84)

The Blues were one of four franchises to enter the National League in its fourth year. They used League Park I throughout their six seasons in the league, but finished in the first division only twice, with a high of third in 1880. After a seventh place finish in 1884, the Blues withdrew from the NL, yielding their place to the Union Association champion St. Louis Maroons. First baseman Bill Phillips, shortstop Jack Glasscock and pitcher Jim McCormick were regulars throughout the Blues' history. Heavy-hitting second baseman Fred Dunlap started four seasons, managing in 1882; third baseman Mike Muldoon and outfielders Orator Shaffer and Pete Hotaling each started three. The Scots-born McCormick won 45 games in 1880; Dunlap hit .326 (1883) and .325 (1881).

1884 PLAYERS (50)

Name	Years	Games	Record
Joe Ardner	1884	26	.174
George Bradley	1881–83	94	.231/8–13
Fatty Briody	1882–84	136	.224
Cal Broughton	1883	4	.200
Ernie Burch	1884	32	.210
Doc Bushong	1883–84	125	.203
Charlie Cady	1883	3	.000
Bill Crowley	1883	11	.293
One-Arm Daily	1883	45	23–19
Fred Dunlap	1880–83	342	.302
Charlie Eden	1879	81	.272
Dude Esterbrook	1882	45	.246
Jake Evans	1883–84	170	.248
George Fisher	1884	6	.125
Gid Gardner	1880	10	.188
Barney Gilligan	1879–80	82	.171
Pit Gilman	1884	2	.000
Jack Glasscock	1879–80	494	.258
Frank Hankinson	1880	69	.209
Ned Hanlon	1880	73	.246
Pa Harkins	1884	46	12–32
John Henry	1884	9	.154
Pete Hotaling	1880, 83–84	280	.248
Rudy Kemmler	1881	1	.000
Jim McCormick	1879–84	348	174–162
Sam Moffett	1884	67	.184
Jerrie Moore	1884	9	.200
Mike Moynahan	1881, 84	45	.244
Mike Muldoon	1882–84	292	.230
Willie Murphy	1884	42	.226
The Only Nolan	1881	22	8–14
Bill Phillips	1879–84	537	.264
George Pinkney	1884	36	.313
Phil Powers	1881	5	.067
Blondie Purcell	1881	20	.175
Jack Remsen	1881	48	.174
John Richmond	1882	41	.171
Dave Rowe	1882	24	.258
Orator Shaffer	1880–82	252	.246
Bill Smith	1884	1	.000
Germany Smith	1884	72	.254
Pop Smith	1881	10	.118
Len Stockwell	1879	2	.000
George Strief	1879, 84	79	.181
Billy Taylor	1881	24	.243
John Tilley	1882	15	.089
Fred Warner	1879	76	.244
Harry Wheeler	1880	1	.250
Guerdon Whitely	1884	8	.147
Tom York	1883	100	.260

Cleveland Spiders (1889–1899)

The American Association Cleveland Blues jumped intact to the National League for the 1889 season and promptly finished in sixth place. By 1890 the team had adopted the team name Spiders. The Blues/Spiders played in League Park II until 1891 when they moved to a new League Park III. Led by Hall of Fame outfielder Jesse Burkett and pitcher Cy Young, the club had two second-place finishes in the expanded NL and so qualified for the Temple Cup in both 1895 (when they were champions) and 1896. With the exception of catcher Chief Zimmer — a nine-year regular — and outfielder Chippy McGarr, who started for four seasons, the 1884 players had little to do with the championship teams. Buck Ewing hit .344 in 1893 and McGarr hit .340 in 1895. In 1892 John Clarkson won 25 games—17 with Cleveland. After the 1899 season, the NL contracted to a more manageable eight teams, so the Spiders were dropped from the league.

1884 PLAYERS (22)

Name	Years	Games	Record
Joe Ardner	1890	84	.223
Jersey Bakley	1889	36	12–22

John Clarkson	1892–94	87	41–37	Harry Buker	1884	30	.135
Jack Clements	1899	4	.250	Dick Burns	1883	17	2–12
Jerry Denny	1891	36	.225	Dan Casey	1885	12	4–8
Buck Ewing	1893–94	149	.316	Chub Collins	1885	14	.196
Jay Faatz	1889	117	.231	Frank Cox	1884	27	.135
Charlie Getzein	1891	1	0–1	Sam Crane	1885–86	115	.170
Joe Gunson	1893	21	.260	Harry Decker	1886	14	.222
Chippy McGarr	1893–96	416	.276	James B. Donnelly	1885	56	.232
Tony Mullane	1894	4	1–2	Jerry Dorgan	1885	39	.286
Joe Quinn	1899	147	.286	Mike Dorgan	1881	8	.235
Paul Radford	1889	136	.238	Fred Dunlap	1886–87	116	.274
Edgar Smith	1890	8	1–4	Joe Farrell	1882–84	280	.237
Pop Snyder	1889	22	.188	Will Foley	1881	5	.133
Joe Sommer	1890	9	.229	Tom Forster	1882	21	.092
Len Stockwell	1890	2	.286	Charlie Ganzel	1886–88	209	.258
Cub Stricker	1889	136	.251	Ed Gastfield	1884–85	24	.071
Sy Sutcliffe	1889	46	.248	Bill Geis	1884	75	.177
Peek-A-Boo Veach	1890	64	.235	Joe Gerhardt	1881	80	.242
Buck West	1890	37	.245	Charlie Getzein	1884–88	186	95–86
Chief Zimmer	1889–99	882	.275	Tom Gillen	1886	2	.400

Detroit Wolverines (1881–88)

The Detroit Wolverines entered the National League when the league expelled the Cincinnati Red Stockings after the 1880 season. In eight seasons the Wolverines, playing all home games at Recreation Park, finished in every position except third. After acquiring Dan Brouthers, Jack Rowe, Hardy Richardson and Deacon White from Buffalo, the Wolverines finished as runners up in 1886 and league champions in 1887, defeating the St. Louis Browns in the World Series. The following season the club dropped to fifth place and left the NL. Brouthers hit .338 and Pretzels Getzein won 29 games for the champions, but a year earlier Brouthers had hit .370 and Lady Baldwin had won 42 games. Outfielder Ned Hanlon was a regular throughout the club's history, and catcher Charlie Bennett held regular status seven times. Outfielder George Wood and pitcher Stump Wiedman were five-time regulars; Getzein for four seasons.

1884 Players (82)

Name	Years	Games	Record
Lady Baldwin	1885–88	107	69–35
Dave Beatle	1884	1	.000
Charlie Bennett	1881–88	625	.278
George Bradley	1881	1	.000
Frank Brill	1884	12	2–10
Fatty Briody	1887	33	.227
Cal Broughton	1888	1	.000
Dan Brouthers	1886–88	373	.338
Lew Brown	1881	27	.241
Barney Gilligan	1888	1	.200
Ben Guiney	1883–84	3	.083
Jim Halpin	1885	15	.130
Ned Hanlon	1881–88	830	.261
Sadie Houck	1881, 83	176	.264
Frank Jones	1884	2	.125
Henry Jones	1884	34	.220
Tom Kearns	1882, 84	25	.217
Walt Kinzie	1882	13	.094
Lon Knight	1881–82	169	.239
Jack Leary	1881	3	0–2/.273
Dick Lowe	1884	1	.333
Henry Luff	1882	3	.273
Jim Manning	1885–87	59	.216
Tom Mansell	1883	34	.221
Deacon McGuire	1885, 88	37	.172
Mox McQuery	1885	70	.273
Frank Meinke	1884–85	93	.163/8–24
Jerrie Moore	1885	6	.174
Gene Moriarity	1885	11	.026
Charlie Morton	1885	22	.177
Frank Mountain	1881	7	3–4
Mike Moynahan	1881	1	.250
Tony Mullane	1881	5	1–4
Dan O'Leary	1881	2	.000
Frank Olin	1885	1	.500
Marr Phillips	1885	33	.209
Martin Powell	1881–83	236	.276
Walter Prince	1884	7	.143
Joe Quest	1885	55	.195
Charlie Reilley	1881	19	.171
Hardy Richardson	1886–88	303	.330
Frank Ringo	1885	17	.246
Yank Robinson	1882	11	.179

Name	Years	Games	Record
Jack Rowe	1886–88	340	.301
Edward Santry	1884	6	.182
Milt Scott	1884–85	148	.251
Dupee Shaw	1883–84	54	19–33
Phenonemal Smith	1886	3	1–1
Ecky Stearns	1881	3	.091
Sy Sutcliffe	1888	49	.257
Sam Trott	1881–83	113	.241
Dasher Troy	1881–82	51	.265
Walt Walker	1884	1	.250
Joe Weber	1884	2	.000
Deacon White	1886–88	360	.297
Will White	1881	2	0–2
Art Whitney	1881–82	89	.182
Stump Wiedman	1881–85, 87	196	84–101
Sam Wise	1881	1	.500
Fred Wood	1884	12	.048
George Wood	1881–85	459	.281
Chief Zimmer	1884	8	.069

Hartford Dark Blues (1876–77)

The Dark Blues were charter members of the National League, moving from the National Association. They played in the Hartford Ball Club Grounds. With six regulars from the NA club—Tommy Bond, Jack Burdock, Manager Bob Ferguson, Bill Harbidge, Jack Remsen and Tom York—the Dark Blues finished tied for second in the inaugural NL season. Bond won 31 games that season. By 1877 the Dark Blues had moved to Brooklyn, playing only one game in Hartford, the rest in Union Grounds in Brooklyn. Despite the fact that John Cassidy hit .386 and Joe Start .332, the Dark Blues dropped to third place (in a six-team league) and determined not to field a team in 1878.

1884 Players (11)

Name	Years	Games	Record
Tommy Bond	1876	45	31–13
Jack Burdock	1876–77	127	.259
John Cassidy	1876–77	72	.362
Bob Ferguson	1876–77	127	.261
Bill Harbidge	1876–77	71	.220
Jim Holdsworth	1877	55	.254
Terry Larkin	1877	56	29–25
Jack Remsen	1876	69	.275
Joe Start	1877	60	.332
Live Oak Taylor	1877	2	.375
Tom York	1876–77	123	.270

Indianapolis Hoosiers (1878)

Indianapolis was part of the first expansion of the National League in 1878. The Hoosiers had played in the League Alliance in 1877, winning 23 of 34. But when they moved into the National League, they finished in fifth place out of six teams, winning only 24 of 60 games. At the end of the season, they dropped from the league. Orator Shaffer hit .338 on a team that hit .236. Jim McCormick had a 1.69 ERA for 117 innings, second only to Monte Ward of Providence. Home field for the 1878 season was South Street Park.

1884 Players (8)

Name	Years	Games	Record
Silver Flint	1878	63	.224
Jim McCormick	1878	14	5–8
Candy Nelson	1878	19	.131
The Only Nolan	1878	38	13–22
Joe Quest	1878	62	.205
Orator Shaffer	1878	63	.338
Fred Warner	1878	43	.248
Ned Williamson	1878	63	.232

Indianapolis Hoosiers (1887–89)

After the 1886 season, the St. Louis Maroons relocated to Indianapolis. In three seasons there, the club managed seventh-place finishes in 1888 and 1889 after a last-place finish in 1887. Second baseman Charley Bassett, shortstop Jack Glasscock, third baseman Jerry Denny, outfielder Emmett Seery and pitcher Henry Boyle were three-year regulars. In 1889 Glasscock hit .352, and Boyle won 21 games. In their first season, the Hoosiers played in Seventh Street Park. In 1888 the field was renovated, shifting home plate. After the 1889 season, the club disbanded.

1884 Players (22)

Name	Years	Games	Record
Ed Andrews	1889	40	.306
Tug Arundel	1887	43	.197
Charley Bassett	1887–89	374	.239
Henry Boyle	1887–89	121	49–69
Tom Brown	1887	36	.179
John Cahill	1887	68	.205
Larry Corcoran	1887	3	0–2
Con Daily	1888–89	119	.235
Jerry Denny	1887–89	381	.280
Dude Esterbrook	1888	64	.220
Gid Gardner	1887	18	.175
Charlie Getzein	1889	45	18–22
Jack Glasscock	1887–89	369	.309
Mert Hackett	1887	42	.238
Paul Hines	1888–89	254	.292
Bill Johnson	1887	11	.190
John Kirby	1887	8	1–6

Name	Years	Games	Record
Sam Moffett	1887–88	13	3–10
George Myers	1887–89	178	.220
Jumbo Schoeneck	1888–89	64	.238
Emmett Seery	1887–89	382	.254
Jim Whitney	1889	9	2–7

Kansas City Cowboys (1886)

When Detroit purchased the Buffalo team to acquire key players such as Dan Brouthers and Hardy Richardson, the National League accepted Kansas City as a replacement franchise. Playing at Association Park, called "The Hole," the Cowboys suffered through a 31–90 season, besting only Washington. Grasshopper Jim Whitney and Stump Wiedman together lost 68 games; Al Myers and Charley Bassett were the only regulars to hit over .250. Outfielder Dave Rowe managed the team. At season end, the Cowboys were themselves replaced by the Pittsburgh Alleghenys. Kansas City never again held an NL franchise.

1884 Players (14)

Name	Years	Games	Record
George Baker	1886	1	.250
Charley Bassett	1886	90	.260
Fatty Briody	1886	56	.237
James B. Donnelly	1886	113	.201
Mert Hackett	1886	62	.217
Jim Lillie	1886	114	.175
Larry McKeon	1886	3	0–2
Mox McQuery	1886	122	.247
Al Myers	1886	118	.277
Paul Radford	1886	122	.229
Frank Ringo	1886	16	.232
Dave Rowe	1886	105	.240
Jim Whitney	1886	46	12–32
Stump Wiedman	1886	51	12–36

Louisville Colonels (1892–99)

In 1892 when the American Association merged with the National League, Louisville was one of four AA clubs invited to play in the expanded league. This was not a happy decision, as the Colonels finished no higher than ninth in the twelve-team league and in three of the eight seasons finished in last place. In four of the eight seasons their attendance was also at the bottom of the league. After the 1899 season, when the NL cut to eight teams, Louisville was dropped. The Colonels played home games in three renditions of Eclipse Park. Most of the 1884 players played bit roles for the Colonels, as only outfielder Tom Brown and second baseman Fred Pfeffer were three-year regulars. Pete Browning hit .355 in 57 games in 1893.

1884 Players (15)

Name	Years	Games	Record
Charley Bassett	1892	79	.214
Dan Brouthers	1895	24	.309
Tom Brown	1892–94	404	.239
Pete Browning	1892–93	98	.350
Jerry Denny	1893–94	104	.263
Jack Glasscock	1895	18	.338
Bill Kuehne	1892	76	.167
Doggie Miller	1896	98	.275
Fred Pfeffer	1892–95	364	.272
George Pinkney	1893	118	.235
Danny Richardson	1894	116	.253
Emmett Seery	1892	42	.201
Curt Welch	1893	14	.170
Perry Werden	1897	131	.302
Chief Zimmer	1899	75	.298

Louisville Grays (1876–77)

Louisville was a charter member of the National League, finishing fifth that season. In 1877 the club finished second. However, four Louisville players—pitcher Jim Devlin, outfielder George Hall, shortstop Bill Craver and utility player Al Nichols—were implicated in a fixing scandal, and the club withdrew from the NL at the end of that season. They had played home games at St. James Court. Second baseman Joe Gerhardt hit .304 in 1877; he and catcher Pop Snyder were regulars both seasons the club was in existence.

1884 Players (8)

Name	Years	Games	Record
Jim Clinton	1876	16	.338
Bill Crowley	1877	61	.282
Chick Fulmer	1876	66	.273
Joe Gerhardt	1876–77	124	.280
Bill Holbert	1876	12	.256
Juice Latham	1877	59	.285
Orator Shaffer	1877	61	.285
Pop Snyder	1876–77	117	.229

Milwaukee Cream Citys (1878)

Milwaukee came to the National League in 1878 from the League Alliance, one of the minor league organizations. Playing at the Milwaukee Base-Ball Grounds, the Cream Citys won only fifteen of sixty league contests, finishing in last place, 26 games behind champion Boston. Twenty-year-old outfielder Abner Dalrymple hit .354, second best in the league. At the end of the season the club withdrew from the NL.

1884 PLAYERS (9)

Name	Years	Games	Record
Charlie Bennett	1878	49	.245
George Creamer	1878	50	.212
Abner Dalrymple	1878	61	.354
Joe Ellick	1878	3	.154
Will Foley	1878	56	.271
Bill Holbert	1878	45	.185
John Peters	1878	55	.309
Sam Weaver	1878	45	12–31

New York Gothams/Giants (1883–)

In 1883 the National League returned to New York City in the form of Troy. The Trojans, in need of financial help, moved into the larger metropolitan market. Initially the club was known as the Gothams—to distinguish them from the American Association Metropolitans. By 1885, because of a number of larger-than-average players, the team became known as Giants. The Gothams originally played at the Southeast Diamond of the Polo Grounds. In 1889 a new Polo Grounds was built and the Giants played briefly at St. George Cricket Grounds before moving into the new park. Another edition of the Polo Grounds opened in 1891, and the Giants played in it until 1911. Then in 1912 they moved into the final version of the Polo Grounds, their home until they moved to San Francisco in 1958. The Giants teams that won the NL and the World Series in 1888–89 had six Hall of Fame performers: Monte Ward, Buck Ewing, Jim O'Rourke and Roger Connor in the field and Mickey Welch and Tim Keefe on the mound. Connor (first base) Ward (shortstop) and Welch were regulars nine times; Ewing (catcher) seven times, O'Rourke (outfield) six times; Pete Gillespie (outfield) and Keefe five times; Danny Richardson (second base) and Mike Dorgan (outfield) four times. In 1885 Connor hit .371 and Welch won 44 games; a year later Keefe won 42 games. Ewing came back to manage the Giants in 1900.

1884 PLAYERS (55)

Name	Years	Games	Record
Bob Barr	1891	5	0–4
Charley Bassett	1890–92	265	.245
Buck Becannon	1887	1	.000
Ed Begley	1884	31	12–18
Dan Brouthers	1904	2	.000
Jim Brown	1884	1	0–1
Oyster Burns	1895	33	.307
Ed Caskin	1883–4, 86	196	.236
Elmer Cleveland	1888	9	.235
Roger Connor	1883–89, 91, 93–94	1120	.319
Larry Corcoran	1885–86	4	2–1/.278
Cannon-Ball Crane	1888–89, 92–93	98	37–44
Sam Crane	1890	4	.000
Pat Deasley	1885–87	125	.274
Jerry Denny	1890–91	118	.214
James B. Donnelly	1897	23	.188
Mike Dorgan	1883–87	425	.281
Dude Esterbrook	1885–86, 90	256	.266
Buck Ewing	1883–89, 91–92	734	.306
John Ewing	1891	33	.204
Frank Foreman	1893	2	0–1
Joe Gerhardt	1885–87	236	.172
Pete Gillespie	1883–87	474	.283
Jack Glasscock	1890–91	221	.296
George Gore	1887–89, 91–92	478	.279
Sandy Griffin	1884	16	.177
Frank Hankinson	1883–84	199	.226
John Henry	1890	37	.243
Joe Hornung	1890	120	.238
John Humphreys	1883–84	49	.105
Tim Keefe	1885–89, 91	172	174–82
King Kelly	1893	20	.269
Jimmy Knowles	1892	16	.153
Arlie Latham	1989	4	.000
Tommy Loughran	1884	9	.103
Charlie Manlove	1884	3	.000
Al Maul	1901	3	0–3
Alex McKinnon	1884	116	.272
Jocko Milligan	1893	42	.231
Candy Nelson	1887	1	.000
Hank O'Day	1889	10	9–1
Tip O'Neill	1883	23	.197
Jim O'Rourke	1885–89, 91–92, 1904	807	.299
Dave Orr	1883	1	.000
Henry Oxley	1884	2	.000
Fred Pfeffer	1896	4	.143
Gracie Pierce	1883	18	.081
Danny Richardson	1884–89, 91	696	.258
Hardy Richardson	1892	64	.214
Mike Slattery	1888–89	115	.251
Dasher Troy	1883	85	.215

Name	Years	Games	Record
Monte Ward	1883–89, 93–94	1070	.279
Mickey Welch	1883–92	427	238–146
Art Whitney	1885–89	219	.218
Stump Wiedman	1887–88	3	1–2

New York Mutuals (1876)

The Mutuals were charter members of the National League. Playing in Union Grounds in Brooklyn, they finished sixth in that inaugural season. First baseman Joe Start hit .277, fifty points over the team average; Bobby Mathews started 55 of the team's 56 games. Citing financial hardships, the club refused to make the final road trip into the West. The result was that the NL expelled the Mutuals at the end of the season.

1884 PLAYERS (6)

Name	Years	Games	Record
Davy Force	1876	1	.000
Jim Holdsworth	1876	52	.266
Terry Larkin	1876	1	0–1
Bobby Mathews	1876	56	21–34
Jim McGuinness	1876	1	.000
Joe Start	1876	56	.277

Philadelphia Athletics (1876)

The Athletics were charter members of the National League and finished seventh in the inaugural season. Levi Meyerle finished fifth in the league in run production and slugging. But when they were unable to finish their schedule because of financial problems, they—along with the New York Mutuals—were dropped from the league. The Athletics played home games at Jefferson Street Grounds.

1884 PLAYERS (8)

Name	Years	Games	Record
Doc Bushong	1876	5	.048
Dave Eggler	1876	39	.299
Davy Force	1876	60	.232
Lon Knight	1876	55	10–22/.250
Fergy Malone	1876	22	.229
Levi Meyerle	1876	55	.340
Ezra Sutton	1876	54	.297
Fred Warner	1876	1	.000

Philadelphia Quakers/Phillies (1883–)

In 1883 the National League determined to place a franchise in Philadelphia to compete with the American Association Athletics. They did this by relocating the Worcester club. Known first as the Quakers, the club adopted the more familiar Phillies team name in 1890. The club played initially in Recreation Park, moving to Huntington Grounds in 1887. When this park burned in 1894, the club played briefly at the University of Pennsylvania, at a temporary Huntington Grounds, before moving into the Baker Bowl in 1895. The club finished runners-up in 1887 and had twelve first-division finishes in the 19th century. Catcher Jack Clements, with the club for 14 seasons, was a regular ten times. Sid Farrar was a fixture at first base for seven seasons; third baseman Joe Mulvey and outfielder Jim Fogarty for six; and second baseman Ed Andrews for five. But the greatest Quaker of them all was Charlie Ferguson. Dead at age 25, Ferguson had 99 wins and a .288 batting average in just four seasons.

1884 PLAYERS (64)

Name	Years	Games	Record
Hezekiah Allen	1884	1	.667
Ed Andrews	1884–89	557	.261
Charlie Bastian	1885–88	349	.196
Dan Brouthers	1896	57	.344
Charlie Buffinton	1887–89	159	77–50
Dan Casey	1886–89	142	72–59
Jack Clements	1884–97	997	.289
John Coleman	1883–84	133	.238/17–63
Roger Connor	1892	155	.294
Bill Conway	1884	1	.000
Paul Cook	1884	3	.083
John Crowley	1884	48	.244
Tony Cusick	1884–87	84	.198
Harry Decker	1889–90	16	.204
Jerry Denny	1891	19	.288
Mike DePangher	1884	4	.200
Conny Doyle	1883	16	.221
Sid Farrar	1883–89	816	.253
Jack Farrell	1886	17	.183
Bob Ferguson	1883	86	.258
Charlie Ferguson	1884–87	183	99–64
Jim Fogarty	1884–89	660	.247
Bill Gallagher	1883	2	.000
Charlie Ganzel	1885–86	35	.164
Gid Gardner	1888	1	.667
Buck Gladman	1883	1	.000
Emil Gross	1883	57	.307
Tom Gunning	1887	28	.260
Art Hagan	1883	17	1–14
Bill Harbidge	1883	73	.221
Lou Hardie	1884	3	.375
Hardie Henderson	1883	1	0–1

Name	Years	Games	Record
Charlie Hilsey	1883	3	.100
Buster Hoover	1884	10	.190
Arthur Irwin	1886–89	345	.233
Joe Kappel	1884	4	.067
Tim Keefe	1891–93	72	32–29
Joe Knight	1884	6	.250
Fred Lewis	1883	38	.250
Tom Lynch	1884–85	26	.248
Jack Manning	1883–85	309	.265
Al Maul	1887, 1900	12	6–5
Tommy McCarthy	1886–87	26	.186
Al McCauley	1890	112	.244
Bill McClellan	1883–84	309	.246
Jim McElroy	1884	13	1–12
Deacon McGuire	1886–88	103	.261
Barney McLaughlin	1887	50	.220
Cyclone Miller	1884	1	0–1
Sparrow Morton	1884	2	0–2
Joe Mulvey	1883–89, 92	682	.259
Con Murphy	1884	3	0–3
Al Myers	1885, 89–91	420	.245
Billy Nash	1896–98	189	.252
Jack Neagle	1883	18	.164
The Only Nolan	1885	7	1–5
Blondie Purcell	1883–84	200	.260
Shadow Pyle	1884	1	0–1
Jack Remsen	1884	12	.209
Frank Ringo	1883–84	86	.173
Ed Sixsmith	1884	1	.000
Edgar Smith	1883	1	0–1
Phenomenal Smith	1890–91	27	9–13
Billy Sunday	1890	31	.261
Gene Vadeboncoeur	1884	4	.214
Bill Vinton	1884–85	30	13–16
Fred Warner	1883	39	.227
George Wood	1886–89	422	.262
Chief Zimmer	1903	37	.220

Pittsburgh Alleghenys (1887–)

The Pittsburgh Alleghenys moved intact from the American Association to the National League in 1887, replacing Kansas City. The name Pirates, given to the franchise in 1891, came from their "pirating" of Players League players that had been granted to other teams. In the 19th century the Pirates had a runner-up finish in 1893, but had losing records seven times in 13 seasons. "Old Bones" Ely was a Pirate regular for six seasons, as was catcher and infielder Doggie Miller. Pitcher Pud Galvin was a Pirate starting pitcher for four seasons. Infielder Bill Kuehne, pitcher Cannon-Ball Morris, and outfielder Billy Sunday all held regular status for three seasons. Fred Dunlap managed in 1889; Jack Clements in 1890; Tom Burns in 1892. After Fred Clarke and Honus Wagner joined the Pirates in 1900, they began the twentieth century with a second place finish and then won three consecutive championships. The Pirates began in the NL playing in Recreation Park, moving to Exposition Park in 1891. Forbes Field was built in 1909.

1884 Players (37)

Name	Years	Games	Record
Sam Barkley	1887	89	.224
Tom Brown	1887	47	.245
Pete Browning	1891	50	.291
Tom Burns	1892	12	.205
Cliff Carroll	1888	5	.000
Fred Carroll	1887–89, 91	574	.281
John Coleman	1887–88, 90	234	.262/0–2
Pop Corkhill	1891–92	109	.200
Sam Crane	1890	22	.195
Abner Dalrymple	1887–88	149	.215
Harry Decker	1890	92	.274
James B. Donnelly	1897	44	.193
Fred Dunlap	1888–90	220	.240
Bones Ely	1896–1901	742	.256
Pud Galvin	1887–89, 91–92	246	125–110
Jack Glasscock	1893–94	152	.309
Ned Hanlon	1889–91	235	.252
Guy Hecker	1890	86	.226/2–9
Hardie Henderson	1888	5	1–3
Paul Hines	1890	31	.182
Bill Kuehne	1887–89	558	.240
Chuck Lauer	1889	4	.188
Al Maul	1888–89, 91	17	2–8
Jim McCormick	1887	36	12–23
Alex McKinnon	1887	48	.340
Doggie Miller	1887–93	757	.263
Cannon-Ball Morris	1887–89	114	49–50
Jack Rowe	1889	75	.259
Phenomenal Smith	1890	5	1–3
Pop Smith	1887–89	325	.208
Billy Sunday	1888–90	287	.243
Ed Swartwood	1892	13	.238
Adonis Terry	1892–94	57	30–16
Peek-A-Boo Veach	1890	8	.300
Deacon White	1889	55	.253
Art Whitney	1887	119	.260
Chief Zimmer	1900–02	193	.262

Providence Grays (1878–85)

Providence entered the National League in 1878 as one of three new clubs. Bolstered by key players from Boston and the defunct Hartford Dark Blues, Providence finished second that season. They won league championships in 1879 and 1884 and had runner-up finishes in 1880–82. Paul Hines was the leading hitter for both championship clubs—.357 in 1879 and .312 in 1884. Monte Ward won 47 games in 1879; Charley Radbourn won 59 in 1884. Key Grays included Hines, an eight-year outfield regular, first baseman Joe Start (seven), second baseman Jack Farrell (six), third baseman Jerry Denny (5), Radbourn (5), Ward (5) and catcher Barney Gilligan (4). Mike Dorgan managed in 1880; Farrell in 1881. After dropping to fourth place with a losing record in 1885, the Grays dropped out of the league. Throughout their NL history, Providence played at Messer Street Grounds.

1884 PLAYERS (48)

Name	Years	Games	Record
Harry Arundel	1884	1	1–0
Charley Bassett	1884–85	109	.143
George Bradley	1880	82	.227/13–8
Lew Brown	1878–79, 81	129	.276
Cliff Carroll	1882–85	285	.246
John Cassidy	1883	89	.238
John Cattanach	1884	1	0–0
Ed Conley	1884	8	4–4
Fred Corey	1878	4	.143
Cannon-Ball Crane	1885	1	.000
Con Daily	1885	60	.260
Jerry Denny	1881–85	460	.248
Mike Dorgan	1880	79	.246
Jack Farrell	1879–85	534	.251
Barney Gilligan	1881–85	329	.220
Emil Gross	1879–81	168	.281
Mike Hines	1885	1	.000
Paul Hines	1878–85	705	.309
Sadie Houck	1880	49	.201
Arthur Irwin	1883–85	259	.245
Rudy Kemmler	1879	2	.143
Sam Kimber	1885	1	0–1
Lon Knight	1885	25	.160
Tim Manning	1882, 85	31	.090
Bobby Mathews	1879, 81	41	16–14
Bill McClellan	1881	68	.166
Jim McCormick	1885	4	1–3
Cyclone Miller	1884	6	3–2
Joe Mulvey	1883	4	.125
Tim Murnane	1878	49	.239
Miah Murray	1884	8	.185
Henry Myers	1881	1	.000
Sandy Nava	1882–84	91	.176
Dan O'Leary	1879	2	.429
Jim O'Rourke	1879	81	.348
John Peters	1880	86	.228
Charley Radbourn	1881–85	296	193–89
Paul Radford	1884–85	202	.220
Charlie Reilley	1882	3	.182
Dupee Shaw	1885	49	23–26
Edgar Smith	1883, 85	3	1–0/.231
Joe Start	1879–85	590	.297
Charlie Sweeney	1882–84	64	.266/24–15
Dasher Troy	1882	4	.235
Monte Ward	1878–82	374	.246/145–86
Harry Wheeler	1878	7	.148
Art Whitney	1882	11	.075
Tom York	1878–82	362	.285

St. Louis Brown Stockings (1876–77)

Coming from the National Association, the Brown Stockings were charter members of the National League, finishing second in the inaugural season. George Bradley started every game, winning 45. The 1877 team finished fourth in the six-team league and the club withdrew before the 1878 season. The Brown Stockings played home games in Sportsman's Park I. Of the 1884 players, only third baseman Joe Battin was with the club both years, and his .300 average in 1876 dropped to .199 in 1877.

1884 PLAYERS (8)

Name	Years	Games	Record
Joe Battin	1876–77	121	.255
George Bradley	1876	64	45–19
Ned Cuthbert	1876	63	.247
Mike Dorgan	1877	60	.308
Davy Force	1877	58	.262
Jack Gleason	1877	1	.250
Ed McKenna	1877	1	.200
Jack Remsen	1877	33	.260

St. Louis Browns/Perfectos/Cardinals (1892–)

When the American Association merged with the National League in 1892, St. Louis was one of four AA clubs to survive the merger. The Browns fared poorly in their first seven years in the NL, finishing no higher than ninth in the 12-team league. The club moved from Sportsman's Park II to Robison Field in 1893, continuing there until 1920, when they joined the American League Browns in Sportsman's Park IV. The Browns adopted the name Perfectos in 1899 and in 1900 the now-used name Cardinals. Only 11 of the 26 men from 1884 held regular positions with the club. Roger Connor and Joe Quinn were three-year regulars; Perry Werden and Doggie Miller were regulars twice. Many of the others such as Pete Browning, Pud Galvin, Charlie Getzein, Bill Kuehne, George Gore and Germany Smith made brief end-of-career appearances in St. Louis. Doggie Miller hit .339 in 1894. Bob Caruthers was one of five managers used in 1892; Connor managed in 1896.

1884 PLAYERS (26)

Name	Years	Games	Record
Tom Brown	1895	83	.217
Pete Browning	1894	2	.143
Hick Carpenter	1892	1	.333
Cliff Carroll	1892	101	.273
Bob Caruthers	1892	143	.277/2–10
Jack Clements	1898	99	.257
Roger Connor	1894–97	350	.304
James B. Donnelly	1898	1	1.000
Bones Ely	1893–95	288	.279
Pud Galvin	1892	12	5–6
Charlie Getzein	1892	13	5–8
Jack Glasscock	1892–93	187	.272
George Gore	1892	20	.205
Sandy Griffin	1893	23	.196
Joe Gunson	1893	40	.272
Bill Hutchison	1897	6	1–4
Bill Kuehne	1892	6	.167
Arlie Latham	1896	8	.200
Doggie Miller	1894–95	248	.315
Gene Moriarity	1892	47	.175
George Pinkney	1892	78	.172
Joe Quinn	1893–96, 98, 1900	548	.264
Germany Smith	1898	51	.159
Cub Stricker	1892	28	.204
Perry Werden	1892–93	274	.266
Jimmy Wolf	1892	3	.143

St. Louis Maroons (1885–86)

After a runaway domination of the Union Association in 1884, the Maroons moved into the National League in 1885, replacing Cleveland. After finishing in last place in their initial NL trial, they advanced two places to sixth in 1886. At the end of that season, the franchise shifted to Indianapolis for 1887. First baseman Alex McKinnon (.294 and .301) and shortstop Jack Glasscock (.280 and .325) were among the few bright spots. Second baseman Fred Dunlap, outfielder Joe Quinn and pitcher Henry Boyle were also two-year regulars, Dunlap managing in 1885. In St. Louis the Maroons played in Palace Park of America, as they had in the UA.

1884 PLAYERS (29)

Name	Years	Games	Record
George Baker	1885	38	.122
Al Bauers	1886	4	0–4
Henry Boyle	1885–86	102	25–39/.217
Jim Brennan	1885	3	.100
Fatty Briody	1885	62	.195
Dick Burns	1885	1	0–0
John Cahill	1886	125	.199
Ed Caskin	1885	71	.179
Sam Crane	1886	39	.172
One-Arm Daily	1885	11	3–8
Jerry Denny	1886	119	.257
Tom Dolan	1885–86	18	.192
Fred Dunlap	1885–86	177	.245
Jack Glasscock	1885–86	232	.304
Jack Gleason	1885	2	.143
John Kirby	1885–86	55	16–34
Charlie Krehmeyer	1885	1	.000
Fred Lewis	1885	45	.293
Alex McKinnon	1885–86	222	.298
Trick McSorley	1885	2	.500
George Myers	1886	79	.190
Dick Phelan	1885	2	.250
Joe Quinn	1885–86	172	.221
Dave Rowe	1885	16	.161
Emmett Seery	1885–86	185	.214
Orator Shaffer	1885	69	.195
Sy Sutcliffe	1885	16	.122
Charlie Sweeney	1885–86	88	16–27/.240
Rooney Sweeney	1885	3	.091

Syracuse Stars (1879)

Syracuse entered the National League in 1879 as one of the replacements for the Milwaukee and Indianapolis clubs. But the Stars could manage no higher than seventh place and withdrew at the end of the season. They played home games at Star Park I. Hick Carpenter, Jack Farrell, Jimmy Macullar, Blondie Purcell (who was also the change pitcher), John Richmond, Mike Mansell and Bill Holbert were the regulars; Mike Dorgan managed the club. Farrell hit .303.

1884 PLAYERS (11)

Name	Years	Games	Record
Hick Carpenter	1879	65	.203
George Creamer	1879	15	.217
Mike Dorgan	1879	59	.267
Jack Farrell	1879	54	.303
Bill Holbert	1879	59	.201

Name	Years	Games	Record
Jimmy Macullar	1879	64	.211
Mike Mansell	1879	67	.215
Tom Mansell	1879	1	.250
John McGuinness	1879	12	.294
Blondie Purcell	1879	63	.260
John Richmond	1879	62	.213

Troy (NY) Trojans (1879–82)

Troy entered the National League in 1879 after Indianapolis and Milwaukee had dropped out. In four seasons, the Trojans did not have a winning record, finishing no higher than fourth. They played at Putnam Grounds in 1879, at Haymakers' Grounds in Lansingburgh in 1880–81, and at Troy Ball Club Grounds in Watervliet in 1882. The franchise was moved to New York for the 1883 season. John Cassidy and Bob Ferguson were with the club throughout. Ferguson was a three-year regular, as was Roger Connor, Ed Caskin, Jake Evans and Bill Holbert. Mickey Welch won 34 games in 1880; Connor hit .332, .292 and .330.

1884 Players (29)

Name	Years	Games	Record
George Bradley	1879	63	13–40/.247
Fatty Briody	1879	1	.000
Dan Brouthers	1879–80	42	.267
Ed Caskin	1879–81	215	.237
John Cassidy	1879–82	206	.226
Roger Connor	1880–82	249	.317
Buttercup Dickerson	1880	30	.193
Jake Evans	1879–81	202	.241
Buck Ewing	1880–82	154	.256
Bob Ferguson	1879–82	279	.266
Gid Gardner	1879	2	.167
Pete Gillespie	1880–82	240	.264
Fred Goldsmith	1879	8	2–4
Frank Hankinson	1881	85	.193
Bill Harbidge	1880–82	41	.220
Thorny Hawkes	1879	64	.208
Bill Holbert	1879–82	181	.211
Jim Holdsworth	1882	1	.000
Tim Keefe	1880–82	100	41–59
Terry Larkin	1880	6	0–5
Mike Lawlor	1880	4	.111
Tom Mansell	1879	40	.243
Frank Mountain	1880	2	1–1
Candy Nelson	1879	28	.264
Fred Pfeffer	1882	85	.218
Charlie Reilley	1879	62	.229
Chief Roseman	1882	82	.236
John Shoupe	1879	11	.091
Mickey Welch	1880–82	138	69–64

Washington Senators (1892–99)

The Washington Senators moved from the American Association when that league merged with the National League in 1892. They played their eight NL seasons at Boundary Field. The Senators had no first-division finishes and were consistently among the bottom three clubs in the 12-team league. When the NL reduced to eight teams in 1900, the Senators were dropped. Deacon McGuire, one of two 1884 players to make the transition into the NL, was with the club each year, until traded to Brooklyn on July 14, 1899. In the 1894–97 stretch he hit .306, .336, .321 and .343. Tom Brown, Henry Larkin, and Paul Radford each held regular status for two seasons. Brown managed in 1897–98. Al Maul was a front line pitcher for three seasons, leading the NL in ERA in 1895.

1884 Players (17)

Name	Years	Games	Record
Tom Brown	1895–98	202	.280
Jim Field	1898	5	.095
Frank Foreman	1892	11	2–4
Jack Glasscock	1895	25	.230
Henry Larkin	1892–93	200	.295
Arlie Latham	1899	6	.167
Al Maul	1893–97	91	38–44
Deacon McGuire	1892–99	787	.297
Jocko Milligan	1892	88	.276
Joe Mulvey	1893	55	.235
Jim O'Rourke	1893	129	.287
Paul Radford	1892–94	356	.242
Danny Richardson	1892	142	.240
Hardy Richardson	1892	10	.108
Yank Robinson	1892	67	.179
Cub Stricker	1893	59	.179
Sam Wise	1893	122	.311

Washington Statesmen (1886–1889)

The Washington Statesmen entered the National League from the Eastern League in 1886 as a replacement franchise for Buffalo. The club played at Swampoodle Grounds but were not a success in the league, with three cellar finishes and a seventh place in their four seasons. After the 1889 season they were dropped from the league to make a place for the Cincinnati Red Stockings, who were leaving the American Association. Outfielder Paul Hines, a two-year regular, hit .312 and .308. Cliff Carroll, Jim Donnelly, Al Myers and Billy O'Brien were also two-year starters. Dupee Shaw had 13 of the team's 29 wins in 1886. Jim Whitney had 24- and 18-win seasons.

1884 Players (39)

Name	Years	Games	Record
Tug Arundel	1888	17	.196
Phil Baker	1886	81	.222
Bob Barr	1886	23	3–18
Cliff Carroll	1886–87	214	.238
Larry Corcoran	1886	21	.185/0–1
Cannon-Ball Crane	1886	80	.171/1–7
Sam Crane	1887	7	.300
One-Arm Daily	1887	6	0–6
Pat Dealy	1887	58	.259
Pat Deasley	1888	34	.157
Harry Decker	1886	7	.217
James B. Donnelly	1887–89	243	.200
Jack Farrell	1886–87	134	.227
Davy Force	1886	68	.182
John Fox	1886	1	0–1
Gid Gardner	1888	1	.333
Barney Gilligan	1886–87	109	.193
Buck Gladman	1886	44	.138
Walt Goldsby	1886	6	.222
Jackie Hayes	1886	26	.191
John Henry	1886	4	.357
Paul Hines	1886–87	244	.310
Sadie Houck	1886	52	.215
Arthur Irwin	1889	85	.233
John Irwin	1887–89	103	.273
Jimmy Knowles	1886	115	.215
Bill Krieg	1886–87	52	.254
John Morrill	1889	44	.185
Miah Murray	1888	12	.095
Al Myers	1887–89	283	.225
Billy O'Brien	1887–89	248	.248
Hank O'Day	1886–89	95	28–61
Dupee Shaw	1886–88	69	20–47
Joe Start	1886	31	.221
Perry Werden	1888	3	.300
Ed Whiting	1886	6	.000
Jim Whitney	1887–88	86	42–42
Bill Wise	1886	1	0–1
Sam Wise	1889	121	.250

Worcester Ruby Legs (1880–82)

The Worcester Ruby Legs entered the National League in 1880, replacing Syracuse. In three seasons the club finished fifth, eighth and eighth. Playing in Agricultural County Fair Grounds Race Track, the Ruby Legs had few fans—once as few as six. Before the 1883 season, the franchise was shifted to Philadelphia. Harry Stovey, Art Irwin, and George Creamer were regulars all three seasons. Doc Bushong and Fred Corey were regulars twice. Stovey led the NL in both homers and triples in 1880. Buttercup Dickerson hit .316 and Pete Hotaling .309 in 1881. Mike Dorgan managed the club in 1881; Tommy Bond in 1882.

1884 Players (33)

Name	Years	Games	Record
Charlie Bennett	1880	51	.228
Tommy Bond	1882	8	.133/0–1
Doc Bushong	1880–82	186	.191
Hick Carpenter	1881	83	.216
John Clarkson	1882	3	1–2
Jim Clinton	1882	26	.163
Fred Corey	1880–82	156	.221/15–37
George Creamer	1880–82	246	.211
Buttercup Dickerson	1880–81	111	.310
Jerry Dorgan	1880	10	.200
Mike Dorgan	1881	51	.277
Joe Ellick	1880	5	.056
Jake Evans	1882	80	.213
Billy Geer	1880	2	.000
Jim Halpin	1882	2	.000
Jackie Hayes	1882	78	.270
Pete Hotaling	1881	77	.309
Art Irwin	1880–82	219	.246
John Irwin	1882	1	.000
Lon Knight	1880	49	.239
Fred Mann	1882	19	.234
Frank McLaughlin	1882	15	.218
Ed Merrill	1882	2	.125
Frank Mountain	1882	5	0–5
Candy Nelson	1881	24	.282
Tom O'Brien	1882	22	.202
Dan O'Leary	1882	6	.182
Charlie Reilley	1881	2	.375
Pop Smith	1881	11	.073
Harry Stovey	1880–82	242	.275
Billy Taylor	1881	6	.107
Art Whitney	1880	76	.222
George Wood	1880	81	.245

American Association (1882–1891)

In the ten-year existence of the American Association, 26 clubs representing 19 cities participated. Of the 637 players of 1884, 408 spent some part of their careers in the AA.

Baltimore Orioles (1882–89)

The Baltimore Orioles were charter members of the American Association when it formed in

1882. In their first eight years in the league, the Orioles finished in the first division only one time — in 1887, when they finished third. After the 1889 season — a fifth-place finish — the club folded. Originally tenants of Newington Park, the old grounds used by the National Association clubs, the Orioles moved to Oriole Park in 1883. Like most professional baseball clubs from Baltimore, this one was named for the indigenous bird.

Of 79 players from 1884, 55 were with the club for only one season — 25 for ten or fewer games. Third baseman Joe Sommer spent six seasons in Baltimore—five as a regular. Thirty-six of the players held regular status for one or more seasons. Oyster Burns, Jim Clinton, Jumbo Davis, Bob Emslie, Jack Farrell, Chris Fulmer, Mike Muldoon, Bill Greenwood, Blondie Purcell, Ecky Stearns, and Sam Trott were two-year regulars. The three-year regulars were pitcher Hardie Henderson and middle infielders Jimmy Macullar and Tim Manning.

Emslie posted 32 wins in 1884; Henderson had 27 and 25 wins in 1884–85; Phenomenal Smith had 25 in 1887. Burns hit .341 in 1887; in 1883 Clinton and Davis hit .313 and .309. Shortstop Henry Myers was manager in the first season.

1884 Players (79)

Name	Years	Games	Record
John Ake	1884	13	.192
George Baker	1883	7	.227
Phil Baker	1883	28	.273
George Bradley	1888	1	.000
Cal Broughton	1883	9	.188
Joe Brown	1885	5	0–4
Tom Brown	1882	45	.304
Oyster Burns	1884–85, 1887–88	332	.300
Pat Burns	1884	6	.200
Dennis Casey	1884–85	100	.274
Monk Cline	1882	44	.221
Jim Clinton	1883–4, 1886	221	.281
Bill Conway	1886	7	.143
Jumbo Davis	1886–87	190	.274
Buttercup Dickerson	1884	13	.214
Tom Dolan	1886	38	.152
Dave Eggler	1883	53	.188
Bob Emslie	1883–85	87	44–40
Jake Evans	1885	20	.221
Tom Evers	1882	1	.000
Jack Farrell	1888–89	145	.205
Joe Farrell	1886	73	.209
Jim Field	1885	38	.208
Frank Foreman	1885 89	54	25–22
John Fox	1883	20	6–13
Chris Fulmer	1886–89	204	.339
Bill Gallagher	1883	16	.164
Gid Gardner	1883–84, 85	127	.234
Walt Goldsby	1888	45	.236
Fred Goldsmith	1884	4	3–1
Bill Greenwood	1887–88	233	.233
Pa Harkins	1888	1	0–1
Jackie Hayes	1887	8	.143
Hardie Henderson	1883–86	177	65–105
John Henry	1885	10	.265
Buster Hoover	1886	40	.217
Joe Hornung	1889	135	.229
Sadie Houck	1886	61	.192
Charles F. Householder	1882	74	.254
Bill Jones	1882	4	.067
John Kerins	1889	16	.283
Jack Leary	1882–83	7	.207
Charlie Levis	1885	1	.250
Jimmy Macullar	1884–86	292	.199
Jack Manning	1886	137	.223
Tim Manning	1883–85	169	.207
Jerry McCormick	1883	93	.262
Chippy McGarr	1889	3	.143
Jumbo McGinnis	1886	26	11–13
Jim McLaughlin	1884	3	1–2
Bill Mountjoy	1885	6	2–4
Mike Muldoon	1885–86	203	.226
Henry Myers	1882	69	.180
Sandy Nava	1885–86	10	.188
Jack Neagle	1883	6	1–4
Jack O'Brien	1888	57	.224
Tom O'Brien	1883, 85	41	.257
John Peltz	1888	1	.250
Gracie Pierce	1882	41	.199
Abner Powell	1886	11	.179
Phil Powers	1885	9	.118
Blondie Purcell	1886–88	267	.143
Billy Reid	1883	24	.278
Dave Rowe	1883	59	.313
Jim Roxburgh	1884	2	.500
Lou Say	1883	74	.256
Milt Scott	1886	137	.190
Phenomenal Smith	1887–88	93	39–49
Joe Sommer	1884–89	672	.240
Ecky Stearns	1883–85	260	.228
Rooney Sweeney	1885	25	.208
Billy Taylor	1886	10	1–6
Bill Traffley	1884–86	147	.171
Sam Trott	1884–85, 1887–88	208	.262
Oscar Walker	1885	4	.000
Ed Whiting	1882	74	.260

Name	Years	Games	Record
Bill Wise	1882	3	1–2
George Wood	1889	3	.200
Tom York	1884–85	105	.232

Baltimore Orioles (1890–91)

A new club with the same name was entered into the American Association on August 26, 1890, to replace the Brooklyn Gladiators. Playing in Oriole Park II, this version of the Orioles won fifteen of 34 games in 1890 and finished fourth in the league in 1891. When the American Association merged into the National League after the 1891 season, these Orioles were one of four clubs to make the transition. The 1884 players made a modest contribution to Oriole success. Five held regular status. Bill Johnson, a two-year regular, hit .295 in 24 games in 1890. Only Joe Sommer had played with the first Orioles.

1884 Players (7)

Name	Years	Games	Record
Jersey Bakely	1891	8	4–2
Lou Hardie	1891	15	.232
Bill Johnson	1890–91	153	.275
Joe Sommer	1890	38	.256
Curt Welch	1890–91	151	.253
Perry Werden	1891	139	.290
Sam Wise	1891	103	.247

Boston Reds (1891)

After the Players League folded at the end of the 1890 season, the champion Reds were one of two clubs invited to join the American Association for 1891. Eight players from the 1890 team made the move with the club into the AA. Playing in Congress Street Grounds, the Reds captured the final American Association pennant. The club disbanded with the league at the end of the season.

Six of the 1884 players held regular status with the Reds: Dan Brouthers, Cub Stricker, and Paul Radford on the infield; Tom Brown and Hardy Richardson in the outfield, and Charlie Buffinton on the mound. Brouthers led the league in hitting; Brown led in runs and hits; Buffinton led in winning percentage. Art Irwin managed the club.

1884 Players (9)

Name	Year	Games	Record
Dan Brouthers	1891	130	.350
Tom Brown	1891	137	.321
Charlie Buffinton	1891	58	29–9
Art Irwin	1891	6	.118
John Irwin	1891	19	.222
King Kelly	1891	4	.267
Paul Radford	1891	133	.259
Hardy Richardson	1891	74	.255
Cub Stricker	1891	139	.216

Brooklyn Gladiators (1890)

In the shuffling of teams following the creation of the Players League, the Brooklyn Bridegrooms and Cincinnati Red Stockings left the American Association to join the National League. The Baltimore Orioles and Kansas City Cowboys folded. One of the franchises added to the American Association was a new Brooklyn club called the Gladiators. Playing home games in Ridgewood Park, the club did not fare well. Anchored in eighth place with a 26–73 record, the Gladiators folded on August 25.

Five of the eight Gladiators who had played in 1884 held regular status, including the entire infield. Jumbo Davis was the leading hitter after joining the club from St. Louis.

1884 Players (8)

Name	Year	Games	Record
Jumbo Davis	1890	38	.303
Frank Fennelly	1890	45	.247
Joe Gerhardt	1890	99	.203
Jack Lynch	1890	1	0–1
Con Murphy	1890	12	3–9
Candy Nelson	1890	60	.251
Billy O'Brien	1890	96	.278
John Peltz	1890	98	.227

Brooklyn Trolley Dodgers (1884–1889)

Under various names—Grays, Chelseas, Atlantics, Quicksteps—this Brooklyn club played in the Eastern League (1881–82) and Interstate Association (1883) before entering the American Association in 1884 when that league expanded. After finishing ninth in the twelve-team league in 1884, Brooklyn had winning seasons in 1886 (third) and 1888 (second) before winning the 1889 pennant. That year the club played a nine-game World Series against the New York Giants, losing six games to three. Because of the number of young players becoming married, the club became generally known as the Bridegrooms in 1888. Following the championship season, the Bridegrooms shifted to the National League for the 1890 season. The home grounds were Washington Parks I and in 1889 Washington Park II.

Of the 48 Dodgers who had played in 1884, 29 played only one season with the club. Adonis Terry played all six seasons and held regular status every year. Twenty-eight other players held regular status for at least one season. John Cassidy, Dave Foutz, Bob Caruthers, Jimmy Peoples, and Bill Phillips were regulars for two seasons; Pitchers Pa Harkins and Henry Porter, infielder Bill McClellan and outfielder Ed Swartwood were three-year men; infielder George Pinkney and outfielder Germany Smith were five-year regulars.

After coming over from the St. Louis Browns, Bob Caruthers turned in 29 and 40-win seasons. Earlier Henry Porter had 33 and 27 wins. In 1888 Dave Orr hit .305; in 1885 Bill Phillips hit .302.

1884 Players (48)

Name	Years	Games	Record
Ike Benners	1884	49	.201
Ernie Burch	1886–87	162	.270
Jack Burdock	1888	70	.122
Oyster Burns	1888–89	103	.298
Doc Bushong	1888–89	94	.196
Bob Caruthers	1888–89	153	.237/69–26
John Cassidy	1884–85	160	.239
Jim Conway	1884	13	3–9
Jack Corcoran	1884	52	.211
Pop Corkhill	1888–89	157	.265
Jerry Dorgan	1884	4	.308
John Farrow	1884	16	.190
Dave Foutz	1888–89	278	.276/15–7
Billy Geer	1884	107	.210
Bill Greenwood	1884	92	.216
Pa Harkins	1885–87	92	39–50
Jackie Hayes	1884–85	58	.160
Hardie Henderson	1886–87	27	15–12
Mike Hines	1885	3	.077
Bill Holbert	1888	15	.120
Pete Hotaling	1885	94	.257
Charles F. Householder	1884	76	.242
Charlie Jones	1884	25	.178
Ed Kennedy	1886	6	.182
Sam Kimber	1884	41	18–20
Jimmy Knowles	1884	41	.235
Bill Krieg	1885	17	.150
Jim McCauley	1886	11	.233
Bill McClellan	1885–88	463	.253
Jack O'Brien	1887	30	.228
Dave Orr	1888	99	.305
Jimmy Peoples	1886–88	239	.223
Bill Phillips	1885–87	372	.278
George Pinkney	1885–89	670	.264
Henry Porter	1885–87	142	75–64
Paul Radford	1888	90	.218
Jack Remsen	1884	81	.223
Charlie Robinson	1885	11	.150
Chief Roseman	1887	1	.333
Bill Schenck	1885	1	.000
Phenomenal Smith	1885	1	0–1
Germany Smith	1885–89	540	.249
Joe Strauss	1886	9	.250
Ed Swartwood	1885–87	312	.268
Adonis Terry	1884–89	378	94–107/.249
Oscar Walker	1884–85	95	.270
Fred Warner	1884	84	.222
Tug Wilson	1884	24	.232

Cincinnati Kellys (1891)

After the 1890 season, the American Association lost four clubs. Among the replacements was a new franchise in Cincinnati, put together quickly. Some sources refer to the club as the Porkers in reference to the pork-producing area; most sources give it the name of the manager: Hall of Fame member Mike "King" Kelly. The Kellys or Kelly's Killers did not fare well. Turning down an offer to play across the river in Covington, KY, the club opted to play in the East End Grounds. Few fans found the grounds. After winning only 43 of 100 games, the club disbanded on August 17 and was replaced the next day by Milwaukee.

Six of the seven Kellys who had played in 1884 held regular status. Kelly led the club in hitting; Cannon-Ball Crane led AA pitchers with a 2.45 ERA.

1884 Players (7)

Name	Years	Games	Record
Ed Andrews	1891	83	.211
Charlie Bastian	1891	1	.000
Cannon-Ball Crane	1891	32	14–14
King Kelly	1891	82	.297
Yank Robinson	1891	97	.178
Emmett Seery	1891	97	.285
Art Whitney	1891	93	.199

Cincinnati Red Stockings (1882–1889)

When the National League expelled the Red Stockings in 1880 for playing Sunday games and selling beer at the ball park, Cincinnati was left without a major league team. In 1882 when the American Association was formed, the Red Stockings were among its charter members. Winners of the inaugural AA pennant, the Red Stockings finished in the first division in six of eight seasons in that league, with runner-up finishes in 1884 and 1887. They played home games in Bank Street Grounds in 1882–83 and League Park I in 1884–89. The franchise was invited to rejoin the National League in 1890 in the reorganization caused by the creation of the Players League.

A number of the 1884 players enjoyed extended careers in Cincinnati. Twenty-two of the 42 Red Stockings were with the club more than one year. Both Bid McPhee and Hick Carpenter were eight-year players; Long John Reilly and Pop Snyder each lasted seven seasons. Multi-year regulars included second baseman McPhee and third baseman Carpenter (eight seasons each) first baseman Reilly (seven), outfielder Pop Corkhill (six), shortstop Frank Fennally (four), catcher Pop Snyder (four), pitchers Will White and Tony Mullane (four each), outfielders Charley Jones and Hugh Nicol (three each), catchers Jim Keenan and Kid Baldwin (two each), and outfielder Joe Sommer and shortstop Chris Fulmer (two each).

Both White and Mullane posted strong seasons in Cincinnati uniforms. White had 40-, 43-, and 34-win seasons in the 1882–84 period; Mullane had 33, 31 and 26 wins in 1886–88. Carpenter hit .342 in 1882; Reilly hit .339 in 1884, one of four seasons over .300; Jones hit .314 and .322 in 1884–85; Corkhill hit .311 in the inflated 1887 season.

Snyder managed the club from 1882 through the first 38 games of 1884; White managed the remainder of the 1884 season.

1884 Players (42)

Name	Years	Games	Record
Kid Baldwin	1885–89	344	.228
Frank Berkelbach	1884	6	.240
Hick Carpenter	1882–89	892	.269
Jim Clinton	1885	105	.238
Pop Corkhill	1883–88	685	.268
Ren Deagle	1883–84	22	13–9
Frank Fennelly	1885–88	526	.253
Chick Fulmer	1882–84	202	.254
Charley Jones	1883–87	482	.301
Jim Keenan	1885–89	299	.261
Rudy Kemmler	1882	3	.091
Fred Lewis	1886	77	.318
Henry Luff	1882	28	.233
Jimmy Macullar	1882–83	93	.225
Tom Mansell	1884	65	.248
Leech Maskrey	1887	27	.194
Jumbo McGinnis	1887	8	3–5
Larry McKeon	1885–86	52	28–21
Bid McPhee	1882–89	911	.263
George Miller	1884	6	.250
Bill Mountjoy	1883–85	51	29–20
Tony Mullane	1886–89	188	101–69
Hugh Nicol	1887–89	382	.236
Jimmy Peoples	1884–85	76	.170
Abner Powell	1886	19	.230
Phil Powers	1882–85	96	.204
Icicle Reeder	1884	3	.143
John Reilly	1883–89	801	.301
Billy Serad	1887–88	28	12–14
Gus Shallix	1884–85	36	17–14
Pop Snyder	1882–88	296	.250
Joe Sommer	1882–83	177	.283
Ecky Stearns	1882	49	.257
Lou Sylvester	1886	17	.182
Tug Thompson	1882	1	.200
Bill Tierney	1882	1	.000
Bill Traffley	1883	30	.200
Podge Weihe	1883	1	.250
Buck West	1884	33	.244
Harry Wheeler	1882	76	.250
Will White	1882–86	208	136–69
Jimmy Woulfe	1884	8	.147

Cleveland Blues (1887–1888)

Without a major league team after the 1884 National League Blues folded, Cleveland received an American Association franchise for 1887, replacing the Pittsburgh Alleghenys, who had shifted to the National League. The new club, also called the Blues — apparently short for Bluebirds — played home games in League Park II. Finishing in last place in 1887, they improved to sixth place in 1888. After that season, they also made the shift into the National League.

Among the 1884 players, only outfielder Pete Hotaling — who hit .299 in 1887 — and tiny second baseman Cub Stricker were regulars both seasons.

1884 Players (17)

Name	Years	Games	Record
Gus Alberts	1888	102	.206
Jersey Bakely	1888	61	25–33
Scrappy Carroll	1887	57	.199
One-Arm Daily	1887	16	4–12
Jay Faatz	1888	120	.264
Ed Hogan	1888	78	.227
Pete Hotaling	1887–88	224	.278
John Kirby	1887	5	0–5
Fred Mann	1887	64	.309

Name	Years	Games	Record
Bill McClellan	1888	22	.222
Deacon McGuire	1888	26	.255
Phil Reccius	1887	62	.205
Jimmy Say	1887	16	.375
Pop Snyder	1887–88	138	.237
Cub Stricker	1887–88	258	.249
Charlie Sweeney	1887	36	.226
Chief Zimmer	1887–88	79	.239

Columbus Buckeyes (1883–84)

When the American Association expanded from six teams to eight in 1883, one of the added clubs was the Columbus Buckeyes. In their first season, the club finished sixth, winning only 32 games. However, in 1884 they went 69–39, finishing second to the New York Metropolitans. Despite success on the field, Columbus was one of the clubs dropped to reduce the AA to a more manageable eight teams for 1885. Named for the Ohio state tree, the team played home games in Recreation Park.

In a remarkable show of stability, eight men— first baseman Jim Field, second baseman Pop Smith, shortstop John Richmond, third baseman Bill Kuehne, outfielders Tom Brown and Fred Mann, catcher Rudy Kemmler and pitcher Frank Mountain—were regulars in both 1883 and 1884. The club did not hit very well, with Richmond's .283 average in 1883 the high mark. On the other hand, Ed Morris won 34 games in 1884, and Mountain had 26 and 23 win seasons.

1884 PLAYERS (19)

Name	Years	Games	Record
Al Bauers	1884	3	1–2
Tom Brown	1883–84	204	.273
John Cahill	1884	59	.219
Fred Carroll	1884	69	.278
Ed Dundon	1883–84	52	9–20
Jim Field	1883–84	181	.243
Pete Fries	1883	3	.300
Rudy Kemmler	1883–84	145	.204
Bill Kuehne	1883–84	205	.232
Fred Mann	1883–84	195	.262
Tom Mansell	1884	28	.185
Cannon-Ball Morris	1884	52	34–13
Frank Mountain	1883–84	101	49–50
Gracie Pierce	1883	11	.171
John Richmond	1883–84	197	.267
Bill Schwartz	1883	2	.250
Pop Smith	1883–84	205	.249
Tom Sullivan	1884	4	2–2
Harry Wheeler	1883	82	.226

Columbus Solons (1889–91)

A new Columbus team entered the American Association for the 1889 season, replacing the Cleveland Blues, who had shifted to the National League. Playing in the new Recreation Park, the Solons or Senators—named from the fact that Columbus is the Ohio state capital—finished sixth in 1889, improved to second in 1890, and returned to sixth in 1891. When the AA disbanded at the end of the 1891 season, the franchise folded.

Neither shortstop Henry Easterday nor outfielder John Sneed played two full seasons for the Solons, but they were the only two-year regulars among the 1884 players. Bill Kuehne and Rudy Kemmler played for both the Columbus Buckeyes and Columbus Solons. Kuehne was a regular for both. Dave Orr was the only .300 hitter.

1884 PLAYERS (9)

Name	Years	Games	Record
Elmer Cleveland	1891	12	.171
James B. Donnelly	1891	17	.241
Henry Easterday	1889–90	153	.167
Bill Greenwood	1889	118	.225
Rudy Kemmler	1889	8	.115
Bill Kuehne	1891	68	.215
Dave Orr	1891	134	.327
Jimmy Peoples	1889	29	.230
John Sneed	1890–91	227	.276

Indianapolis Hoosiers (1884)

When the American Association expanded for the 1884 season, one of the added franchises was Indianapolis. Though *Green Cathedrals* calls the team the Blues, most sources refer to them as the Hoosiers, taken from the state's traditional nickname. Playing in Seventh Street Park, the Hoosiers fared poorly against AA competition, finishing in 12th place with a 29–78 record. When the AA returned to an eight-team format for 1885, Indianapolis was dropped from the league.

Catcher Jim Keenan hit .293 for a club that collectively hit .233. Only three men—first baseman John Kerins, shortstop Marr Phillips and outfielder John Peltz—played in as many as 70 games. Pitcher Larry McKeon started 60 of the 107 games, winning 18. He was the only pitcher with an ERA under 4.00. Infielder Bill Watkins managed the club to a 4–18 record for the final 22 games.

1884 Players (35)

Name	Years	Games	Record
Jake Aydelott	1884	12	5–7
Bob Barr	1884	16	3–11
Marty Barrett	1884	5	.077
Bob Blakiston	1884	6	.222
Tommy Bond	1884	5	0–5
Bill Butler	1884	9	.226
Pat Callahan	1884	61	.260
Chub Collins	1884	38	.225
Harry Decker	1884	4	.267
James B. Donnelly	1884	40	.254
Jerry Dorgan	1884	34	.298
Pete Fries	1884	1	.333
Jim Holdsworth	1884	5	.111
Jim Keenan	1884	68	.293
John Kerins	1884	94	.214
Charlie Levis	1884	3	.200
Marshall Locke	1884	7	.241
Mac MacArthur	1884	6	1–5
Al McCauley	1884	17	.189
Larry McKeon	1884	61	18–41
Ed Merrill	1884	55	.179
Frank Monroe	1884	2	.000
Gene Moriarity	1884	10	.216
Jon Morrison	1884	44	.264
George Mundinger	1884	3	.250
John Peltz	1884	106	.219
Marr Phillips	1884	97	.269
Charlie Reising	1884	2	.000
Charlie Robinson	1884	20	.287
John Sneed	1884	27	.216
Tug Thompson	1884	24	.206
Jim Tray	1884	6	.286
Bill Watkins	1884	34	.204
Harry Weber	1884	3	.000
Podge Weihe	1884	63	.254

Kansas City Cowboys (1888–1889)

When the New York Metropolitans ceased to exist after the 1887 season, a franchise in Kansas City filled the vacancy. Thus, major league baseball returned to Kansas City after a two-year hiatus from the closing of the National League club in 1885. Being the farthest west of any major league city until 1958 and being one of the hubs of the cattle industry, Kansas City's major league clubs invariably bore the name Cowboys. The 1888 club played in Association Park and finished in last place with a 43–89 record. The 1889 club changed to Exposition Park and moved up one notch to seventh with a 55–82 record. At the end of the season the club disbanded.

Second baseman Sam Barkley and third baseman Jumbo Davis were regulars in both seasons. Davis hit .267 for a club that hit only .218 in 1888. Ecky Stearns and Barkley hit .286 and .284 the following season. Jim Conway won 19 games in 1889; Henry Porter made 54 starts, winning 18 in 1888. Dave Rowe, Barkley, and Bill Watkins managed the 1888 club; Watkins managed in 1889.

Fatty Briody and Rowe had both played with the NL Cowboys; John Kirby had played with the UA Cowboys.

1884 Players (19)

Name	Years	Games	Record
Sam Barkley	1888–89	161	.234
Jim Brennan	1888	34	.169
Fatty Briody	1888	13	.208
Monk Cline	1888	73	.235
Jim Conway	1889	41	19–19
Jumbo Davis	1888–89	183	.266
Henry Easterday	1888	115	.190
Ed Glenn	1888	3	.000
Joe Gunson	1889	34	.213
Frank Hankinson	1888	37	.174
Charley Jones	1888	6	.160
John Kirby	1888	5	1–4
Jim Manning	1889	132	.204
Chippy McGarr	1889	25	.287
Bill Phillips	1888	129	.236
Henry Porter	1888–89	59	18–40
Dave Rowe	1888	32	.172
Ecky Stearns	1889	139	.286
Tom Sullivan	1888–89	34	10–24

Louisville Eclipse (1882–91)

The Eclipse, Louisville's second major league team, was formed in 1882, becoming a charter member of the American Association. It was one of three clubs to hold continuous membership throughout the ten-year history of the AA. Winners of the pennant in 1890, they also finished last twice—in both 1889 and 1891. The team played in Eclipse Park, named for the club. However, in 1885, the club took the now more familiar name of Colonels. When the American Association merged with the National League after the 1891 season, Louisville was one of the former AA clubs invited to join the expanded National League for 1892.

On one hand Louisville was a very stable club. Outfielder Jimmy Wolf was a ten-year regular, winning a batting title for the 1890 champions. Outfielder Pete Browning and pitcher and first baseman Guy Hecker were eight-year regulars. Browning hit over .300 seven times with three batting titles. Hecker was a 52-game winner in 1884. First baseman Paul Cook and outfielder Leech Maskrey each started for four seasons; outfielder, catcher and first baseman John Kerins, third baseman Joe Werrick, and shortstop Bill White started for three. Second baseman Joe Gerhardt, first baseman Juice Latham, infielder Tom McLaughlin, third baseman Phil Reccius, and catcher Dan Sullivan all started two seasons.

On the other hand, 22 of the 54 players from 1884 had "pass-through" careers in Louisville, playing fewer than 20 games each.

Browning, Monk Cline, McLaughlin, Ed Merrill, Reccius and Wolf were all local players.

Gerhardt managed in 1883; Kerins had a seven-game managerial stint in 1888; Dude Esterbrook (2–8) and Wolf (14–51) tried their hand at management in 1889.

1884 Players (54)

Name	Years	Games	Record
Wally Andrews	1884, 89	40	.197
Lew Brown	1883	14	.183
Pete Browning	1882–89	874	.343
Monk Cline	1884–85, 91	117	.291
John Connor	1885	4	1–3
Paul Cook	1886–89, 91	310	.219
Joe Crotty	1882 85	44	.148
Ren Deagle	1884	12	4–6
Buttercup Dickerson	1884	8	.143
Denny Driscoll	1884	13	.188
Henry Easterday	1890	7	.083
Bones Ely	1886	10	.156
Dude Esterbrook	1888–89	34	.255
John Ewing	1888–89	61	14–43
Eddie Fusselback	1888	1	.250
Billy Geer	1885	14	.118
Joe Gerhardt	1883–84, 91	186	.237
Bill Gleason	1889	16	.241
Jack Gleason	1883	84	.299
Guy Hecker	1882–89	619	171–137/.290
Bill Hunter	1884	2	.143
John Irwin	1891	14	.273
Jack Jones	1883	2	.000
John Kerins	1885–89	429	.263
Charles Krehmeyer	1885	7	.226
Bill Kuehne	1891	41	.277
Juice Latham	1883–84	165	.213
Jack Leary	1883	40	.188
Henry Luff	1883	6	.174
Leech Maskrey	1882–86	391	.227
Tom McLaughlin	1883–85	252	.204
Ed Merrill	1882	1	—
Joe Miller	1885	98	.183
Tony Mullane	1882	55	30–24
Miah Murray	1885	12	.186
Gracie Pierce	1882	9	.303
Walter Prince	1883	4	.182
Phil Reccius	1882–88	198	.240
Chief Roseman	1890	2	.250
Jimmy Say	1882	1	.250
Bill Schenck	1882	60	.260
Pop Smith	1882	3	.182
Len Stockwell	1884	2	.111
Joe Strauss	1885–86	76	.215
Dan Sullivan	1882–85	180	.243
Sleeper Sullivan	1883	1	.000
Tom Sullivan	1886	9	2–7
Lou Sylvester	1886	45	.227
Peek-A-Boo Veach	1887	1	.000
Sam Weaver	1883	46	24–22
Joe Werrick	1886–88	393	.253
Bill White	1886–88	316	.258
Ed Whiting	1883–84	100	.264
Jimmy Wolf	1882–91	1195	.290

Milwaukee Brewers (1891)

When the Cincinnati Kellys folded in August 1891, they were replaced by the Milwaukee Brewers on August 18. The Brewers had left the Western Association on August 16. Playing the final 36 games of the Cincinnati schedule, the Brewers went 21–15. Like Milwaukee clubs since, the team took the name Brewers from Milwaukee's strong brewing industry. They played home games at Borchert Field. At the end of the season the American Association disbanded, and the Brewers returned to the Western Association for 1892.

Abner Dalrymple was a regular outfielder, one of four regulars who hit over .300; Gus Albert was the most active of four third basemen.

1884 Players (2)

Name	Years	Games	Record
Gus Alberts	1891	12	.098
Abner Dalrymple	1891	32	.311

New York Metropolitans (1883–1887)

Founded in 1880 as an independent professional team, the Metropolitans became a member

METROPOLITAN BASEBALL NINE 1882.
SARONY.
Copyright 1882, by N. Sarony.
37 UNION SQUARE, N.Y.

The 1882 New York Metropolitans were an independent team. *Top row:* Jack Lynch, Charlie Reipschlager, Tip O'Neill, Edward Kennedy, John Clapp, John Doyle, Frank Hankinson, Steve Brady. *Bottom row:* Tom Mansell, Terry Larkin, Candy Nelson and Long John Reilly. All except Clapp and Doyle played in the majors in 1884.

of the American Association in its first expansion in 1883. Playing in the Polo Grounds, the team finished fourth in 1883, and followed that by winning the 1884 pennant. What followed was a series of seventh-place finishes. In 1886 the club moved to St. George Cricket Field, but this move did not improve the gate or the team's performance. After the 1887 season, the Brooklyn Trolley Dodgers purchased the franchise to acquire key players and protect their territory.

Outfielder Chief Roseman was a regular outfielder for the Metropolitans throughout their five-year history. First baseman Dave Orr, shortstop Candy Nelson, outfielder Steve Brady and pitcher Jack Lynch were four-year regulars. Orr hit .354, .342, .338 and .368. Nelson hit .305 in 1883. Lynch had 37 wins in 1883. The three-year regulars included third baseman Frank Hankinson, catcher Bill Holbert, outfielder Ed Kennedy and pitcher Ed Cushman. Third baseman Dude Esterbrook, catcher Charlie Reipschlager, second baseman Tom Forster and pitcher Tim Keefe were regulars for two years. Keefe had 41 wins in 1883 and 37 wins for the 1884 league champions.

While Orr, Roseman, Hobert and Nelson were members of the club in all five seasons, twenty players played in only one season. Catchers Henry Oxley and Tony Murphy each played in one game.

Bob Ferguson managed the club for 1886 and part of 1887; Orr had an eight-game stint in 1887.

1884 PLAYERS (36)

Name	Years	Games	Record
Buck Becannon	1884–85	11	3–8
Ed Begley	1885	20	4–9
Steve Behel	1886	59	.205
Steve Brady	1883–86	441	.264
Cal Broughton	1885	11	.146
Sam Crane	1883	96	.235
Clarence Cross	1887	16	.200
Doug Crothers	1885	18	7–11
Joe Crotty	1886	14	.170
Ed Cushman	1885–87	86	35–49

Name	Years	Games	Record
Dude Esterbrook	1883–84, 87	235	.274
Tom Forster	1885–86	124	.207
Joe Gerhardt	1887	85	.221
Frank Hankinson	1885–87	357	.247
Ed Hogan	1887	32	.200
Bill Holbert	1883–87	311	.213
Sadie Houck	1887	10	.152
Charley Jones	1887	62	.255
Tim Keefe	1883–84	126	78–44
Edward Kennedy	1883–85	293	.204
Jimmy Knowles	1887	16	.250
Jack Lynch	1883–87	200	100–95
Tom McLaughlin	1886	74	.136
Jon Morrison	1887	9	.118
Tony Murphy	1884	1	.333
Candy Nelson	1883–87	492	.258
Tom O'Brien	1887	31	.194
Dave Orr	1883–87	450	.348
Henry Oxley	1884	1	.000
Gracie Pierce	1884	5	.250
Paul Radford	1887	128	.265
Charlie Reipschlager	1883–86	233	.224
Chief Roseman	1883–87	495	.257
Dasher Troy	1884–85	152	.251
Stump Wiedman	1887	12	4–8
Chief Zimmer	1886	6	.158

Philadelphia Athletics (1882–1890)

This edition of the Philadelphia Athletics was a charter member of the American Association at its founding in 1882. Playing in Oakdale Park, the Athletics finished third in the inaugural season. Shifting to Jefferson Street Grounds—their home through 1890—the club won the 1883 pennant. After third-place finishes in 1888 and 1889, they plunged into the cellar in 1890. The club disbanded after that season.

Juice Latham managed the 1882 A's; Lon Knight, the pennant-winning manager, piloted the club in 1883–84; Harry Stovey managed the 1885 club.

1884 Players (68)

Name	Years	Games	Record
Tug Arundel	1882	1	.000
Al Atkinson	1884, 86–87	82	42–36
Jake Aydelott	1886	2	0–2
Jersey Bakely	1883	8	5–3
Kid Baldwin	1890	24	.233
Jud Birchall	1882–84	225	.252
Bob Blakiston	1882–84	148	.240
George Bradley	1883, 86–88	90	.212/16–7
Jim Brennan	1889	31	.221
Jim Brown	1886	1	0–1
John Coleman	1884–86, 89	251	.259/6–7
Jim Conway	1885	2	0–1
Fred Corey	1883–85	269	.260
Bill Crowley	1883	23	.250
Ed Cushman	1885	10	3–7
Henry Easterday	1890	19	.147
Bob Emslie	1885	4	0–4
Frank Fennelly	1888–89	153	.255
Elmer Foster	1884	4	.182
Eddie Fusselback	1885	5	.316
Bill Gleason	1888	123	.224
Jack Gleason	1886	77	.187
Bill Greenwood	1882	7	.300
Tom Gunning	1888–89	31	.207
Charlie Hilsey	1884	6	.208
Sadie Houck	1884–85	201	.278
Bill Hughes	1885	4	.188
John Irwin	1886	3	.231
Joe Kappel	1890	56	.240
Bill Kienzle	1882	9	.333
Lon Knight	1883–85	234	.256
Ted Larkin	1884–89	726	.305
Juice Latham	1882	74	.285
Fred Mann	188287	84	.260
Mike Mansell	1884	20	.200
Bobby Mathews	1883–87	172	106–61
Chippy McGarr	1886–87	208	.285
Cyclone Miller	1886	19	10–8
Jocko Milligan	1884–87	303	.279
Frank Mountain	1882	9	2–6
Mike Moynahan	1883–84	96	.307
Jack O'Brien	1882–86, 90	468	.273
Tom Poorman	1887–88	232	.250
Martin Powell	1885	19	.160
Blondie Purcell	1885, 88–90	323	.290
Joe Quest	1886	42	.207
Marshall Quinton	1885	7	.207
John Richmond	1882	18	.185
Frank Ringo	1885	2	.000
Chief Roseman	1887	21	.219
Ed Rowen	1883–84	53	.232
Jim Roxburgh	1887	2	.125
Jimmy Say	1882	22	.207
Lou Say	1882	49	.226
Taylor Shafer	1890	69	.172
Orator Shaffer	1885–86, 90	123	.279
Frank Siffell	1884–85	10	.148
Phenomenal Smith	1884, 85, 88–89	10	4–6
Pop Smith	1882	20	.92
Harry Stovey	1883–89	824	.302
Cub Stricker	1882–85	374	.239
George Strief	1885	44	.274

Bobby Mathews, who won the first major league game ever played in 1871 was still active in 1887. He is shown in the lower right corner of this Kalamazoo Bats team card of the Philadelphia A's. Others in the photograph are *(top row)* Fred Mann, Harry Stovey, Wilbert Robinson, and Tom Poorman; *(middle row)* Chippy McGarr, Denny Lyons, Manager Charles Mason, Henry Larkin, and Lou Bierbauer; *(bottom row)* Gus Weyhing, Jocko Milligan, and George Townsend beside Mathews. Mann, Stovey, Poorman, McGarr, Larkin, Milligan and Mathews were all 1884 veterans.

Bill Sweeney	1882	20	9–10
Billy Taylor	1884–85, 87	37	20–17
Bill Vinton	1885	7	4–3
Sam Weaver	1882, 86	44	26–17
Curt Welch	1988–90	364	.274
Jim Whitney	1890	7	2–2

1884 Players (5)			
Name	Years	Games	Record
Pop Corkhill	1891	83	.209
Ted Larkin	1891	133	.279
Jocko Milligan	1891	118	.303
Joe Mulvey	1891	113	.254
George Wood	1891	132	.309

Philadelphia Athletics (1891)

After the Philadelphia Athletics folded in 1890, the American Association replaced them with the Players League Philadelphia entry — also called the Athletics. These Athletics played at Forepaugh Park, as they had when they played in the PL. The club finished fourth in 1891 behind Boston, St. Louis and Baltimore. At the end of the season, both the league and the club disbanded.

The five players from 1884 were all regulars for these Athletics. Jocko Milligan and Ted Larkin had been regulars for the original Athletics. While managing the team to a 67–55 record, George Wood led the club in hitting.

Pittsburgh Alleghenys (1882–1886)

The Pittsburgh Alleghenys were a charter member of the American Association. The team played home games in Exposition Park. Following Ohio River flooding which submerged the Lower Field, they moved to the park's Upper Field. In 1884 they settled in Recreation Park. After a second-place finish in the American Association in 1886, the franchise jumped to the National League to replace Kansas City.

In the five-year history of the franchise, it turned over 63 players, none of whom were with the club more than three seasons. Only infielder Joe Battin and outfielder Ed Swartwood were considered regulars for three seasons; Battin managed in 1883–84. Catcher Fred Carroll, pitchers Cannon-Ball Morris and Denny Driscoll, infielders George Creamer (who also managed in 1884) and Art Whitney and outfielders Tom Brown, Fred Mann, Mike Mansell and Billy Taylor held regular status for two seasons. Bob Ferguson also managed in the 1884 season.

Franchise best in hitting were Swartwood, who hit .329 and .356 in 1882–83, and Brown, who hit .307 in 1886. Among pitchers Morris won 39 and 41 games in 1885–86 and Hall of Famer Pud Galvin added 29 wins in 1886.

1884 Players (63)

Name	Years	Games	Record
Gus Alberts	1884	2	.200
Harry Arundel	1882	14	4–10
Sam Barkley	1886	122	.266
Bob Barr	1883	26	6–18
Joe Battin	1882–84	175	.204
Frank Beck	1884	3	.333
Tom Brown	1885–86	223	.295
Fred Carroll	1885–86	193	.281
Ed Colgan	1884	48	.155
George Creamer	1883–84	189	.220
Buttercup Dickerson	1883	85	.249
Connie Doyle	1884	15	.293
Denny Driscoll	1883–84	64	31–30
Charlie Eden	1884–85	130	.258
Jay Faatz	1884	29	.241
Jim Field	1885	56	.239
Tom Forster	1884	35	.222
John Fox	1884	7	1–6
Pud Galvin	1885–86	61	32–28
Ed Glenn	1886	71	.191
Jack Gorman	1884	8	.148
Charlie Hautz	1884	7	.208
Jackie Hayes	1883–84	118	.253
Jim Keenan	1882	25	.219
Rudy Kemmler	1882, 85	42	.233
Jimmy Knowles	1884	46	.231
Bill Kuehne	1885–86	221	.214
Chappy Lane	1882	57	.178
Chuck Lauer	1884	13	.114
Jack Leary	1882	60	.292
Fred Mann	1885–86	215	.251
Mike Mansell	1882–84	202	.251
Jim McDonald	1884	38	.159
Frank McLaughlin	1883	29	.219
Pete Meegan	1885	18	7–8
Doggie Miller	1884–86	214	.222
Bill Morgan	1882	17	.258
Bill Morgan	1883	32	.158
Ed Morris	1885–86	127	80–44
Charlie Morton	1882	25	.282
Frank Mountain	1885–86	23	.133/1–6
Jack Neagle	1883–84	70	14/38
Bill Nelson	1884	3	1–2
The Only Nolan	1883	7	0–7
Henry Oberbeck	1883	2	.222
John Peters	1882–84	87	.271
Marr Phillips	1885	4	.267
Joe Quest	1884	12	.209
Billy Reid	1884	19	.243
John Richmond	1885	34	.206
Frank Ringo	1885–86	18	.209
Milt Scott	1885	55	.248
Frank Smith	1884	10	.250
Phenomenal Smith	1884	1	0–1
Pop Smith	1885–86	232	.232
George Strief	1882	79	.195
Dan Sullivan	1886	1	.000
Fleury Sullivan	1884	51	16–35
Ed Swartwood	1882–84	272	.325
Billy Taylor	1882–83	153	.269
Live Oak Taylor	1884	41	.211
Bill White	1884	74	.227
Art Whitney	1884–86	249	.242

Richmond Virginians (1884)

The Virginians or Virginias began 1884 as members of the Eastern League. On August 4 the club "disbanded" and on August 5 replaced Washington in the American Association. Playing home games at Allen's Pasture, a field without fences, the club went 12–30 for the rest of the 1884 season. When the AA returned to eight clubs in 1885, Richmond was dropped from the majors.

Among the regulars, catcher John Hanna and second baseman Terry Larkin came from the disbanded Washington club. The leading hitter, outfielder Mike Mansell, came from the Athletics. Three other regulars — including pitchers Pete Meegan and Ed Dugan — all "graduated" with the club from the Eastern League.

1884 Players (19)

Name	Years	Games	Record
Wes Curry	1884	2	0–2
Bill Dugan	1884	9	.107
Ed Dugan	1884	20	5–14
Ted Firth	1884	1	0–1
Ed Ford	1884	2	.000
Ed Glenn	1884	43	.246
Walt Goldsby	1884	11	.225
John Hanna	1884	22	.194

Dick Johnston	1884	39	.281
Terry Larkin	1884	40	.201
Mike Mansell	1884	29	.301
Pete Meegan	1884	22	7–12
Bill Morgan	1884	6	.100
Billy Nash	1884	45	.199
Jim Powell	1884	41	.245
Marshall Quinton	1884	26	.234
Bill Schenck	1884	42	.205
Andy Swan	1884	3	.500
Wash Williams	1884	2	.250

Rochester Hop-Bitters (1890)

The Hop-Bitters were an expansion franchise for the American Association in 1890, as they along with Toledo, Syracuse and a new Brooklyn team replaced Brooklyn, Cincinnati, Baltimore and Kansas City. Playing at Culver Park in Rochester, the Hop-Bitters finished with a 63–63 record, good for fifth place. At the end of the season, the club dropped from the AA, playing in the Eastern Association for the 1891 season.

Seven of the 1884 players held regular status. Bob Barr was fourth in the AA in wins; outfielder Sandy Griffin led the Hop-Bitters in hitting.

1884 Players (9)

Name	Years	Games	Record
Bob Barr	1890	57	28–24
Jim Field	1890	52	.202
Bill Greenwood	1890	124	.222
Sandy Griffin	1890	107	.307
Jimmy Knowles	1890	123	.281
Deacon McGuire	1890	87	.299
Tom O'Brien	1890	73	.190
Marr Phillips	1890	64	.206
Phil Reccius	1890	1	.000

St. Louis Browns (1882–1891)

The St. Louis Browns were a charter member of the American Association and were one of the two teams—the other being Louisville—to survive the ten seasons the AA was in operation. After finishing fifth in a six-team league in 1882, they had nine consecutive first division finishes. In 1885 they began a run of four consecutive pennants, and finished runners-up three times. During their entire AA tenure the Browns played in Sportsman's Park. Originally called the Brown Stockings like their National League predecessors, the club shortened the name to Browns by 1883. When the AA folded after the 1891 season, the Browns became the third St. Louis team to enter the National League.

A core of solid players formed the basis of the Browns championship franchise. Charles Comiskey was a nine-year fixture at first base. Arlie Latham anchored the other corner of the infield for seven seasons; Yank Robinson and St. Louis native Bill Gleason were the middle infielders for five and six seasons respectively.

Tip O'Neill held one outfield position for seven seasons; Hugh Nicol held one for four and Curt Welch for three. Future Hall of Famer Tommy McCarthy was a four-year regular after the championship run. O'Neill had seasons of .350, .328, .435, .335, .335, and 321. McCarthy hit .350 and .310 in 1890–91; Fred Lewis hit .301 and .323 in 1883–84.

Two remarkable athletes—Bob Caruthers and Dave Foutz—were keys to the pennant winners. Among the best pitchers in the American Association—both were 40-game winners—they were also among the better hitters in the league and rotated among the outfielders. Foutz had 33, 41 and 25-win seasons in 1885–87; at the same time Caruthers had 40, 33 and 29 wins. Jumbo McGinnis won 25, 28 and 24 in the 1882–84 period; Tony Mullane had 35 wins in 1883.

After short stints of managing in 1883 and 1884, Comiskey ran the club for five of the next six seasons. Ned Cuthbert, Ted Sullivan, McCarthy, John Kerins, Chief Roseman and Joe Gerhardt also had turns at the helm.

1884 Players (57)

Name	Years	Games	Record
Nin Alexander	1884	1	.000.
Sam Barkley	1885	106	.268
Cal Broughton	1885	4	.059
Ed Brown	1882	17	.183
Doc Bushong	1885–87	245	.245
Bob Caruthers	1884–87	268	.313/106–38
Charlie Comiskey	1882–89, 91	1036	.273
Joe Crotty	1882	8	.143
Ned Cuthbert	1882–83	81	.211
Daisey Davis	1884	25	10–12
Jumbo Davis	1889–90	23	.240
Pat Deasley	1883–84	133	.228
Tom Dolan	1883–84	116	.229
James B. Donnelly	1890	11	.333
John Ewing	1883	1	.000
Dave Foutz	1884–87	302	.296/114–48
Chick Fulmer	1884	1	.000
Eddie Fusselback	1882	35	.228
Joe Gerhardt	1890	37	.256

Name	Years	Games	Record
Bill Gleason	1882–87	659	.275
Jack Gleason	1882–83	87	.252
Walt Goldsby	1884	5	.200
Jack Gorman	1883	1	.000
Charlie Hodnett	1883	4	2–2
Rudy Kemmler	1886	35	.138
John Kerins	1890	18	.127
Walt Kinzie	1884	2	.111
Charlie Krehmeyer	1884	21	.229
Arlie Latham	1883–89	839	.267
Johnny Lavin	1884	16	.212
Fred Lewis	1883–84	122	.314
Tom Mansell	1883	28	.402
Tommy McCarthy	1888–91	540	.306
Jim McCauley	1884	1	.000
Chippy McGarr	1888	34	.235
Jumbo McGinnis	1882–86	153	88–61
Trick McSorley	1886	5	.150
Jocko Milligan	1888–89	135	.315
Charlie Morton	1882	9	.063
Tony Mullane	1883	83	35–15/.225
Hugh Nicol	1883–86	383	.243
Henry Oberbeck	1883	4	.000
Tip O'Neill	1884–89, 91	785	.343
Joe Quest	1883–84	100	.216
Yank Robinson	1885–89	602	.255
Chief Roseman	1890	80	.341
John Shoupe	1882	2	.000
George Strief	1883–84	130	.216
Al Struve	1884	2	.286
Dan Sullivan	1885	17	.117
Sleeper Sullivan	1882–83	59	.186
Lou Sylvester	1887	29	.223
Oscar Walker	1882	76	.239
Curt Welch	1885–87	381	.277
Harry Wheeler	1884	5	.263
Bill White	1888	76	.175
Art Whitney	1891	3	.000

Syracuse Stars (1890)

The Stars moved from the International Association to the American Association in 1890 as one of four replacement teams. Playing in Stars Park II, Syracuse finished in seventh place. At the end of the season the franchise withdrew from the AA and played in the Eastern League in 1891.

Four of the nine players from 1884 made significant contributions to Syracuse in 1890. First baseman Mox McQuery had a career year, hitting .308. Barney McLaughlin (shortstop) and Bones Ely (outfield) were also regulars. Dan Casey led the pitching staff with 40 complete games and 19 wins.

1884 Players (8)

Name	Years	Games	Record
Joe Battin	1890	29	.210
Dan Casey	1890	45	19–22
Pat Dealy	1890	18	.182
Mike Dorgan	1890	33	.216
Bones Ely	1890	119	.262
Barney McLaughlin	1890	86	.264
Mox McQuery	1890	122	.308
John Peltz	1890	5	.176

Toledo Blue Stockings (1884)

The Toledo Blue Stockings were champions of the Northwestern League in 1883. When the American Association expanded to 12 teams in 1884, Toledo joined Indianapolis, Brooklyn and Washington as new entries. Toledo fared best of the newcomers, ending in eighth place. However, at the end of the season, the club was dropped from the AA fold. Home games were played in League Park—except for a September 13 game, played in Tri-County Fair Grounds.

Rookie second baseman Sam Barkley and pitcher Tony Mullane were the most successful of the Blue Stockings. Barkley hit .306, while Mullane completed 64 games in a 36-win season. He was also third on the club in hits. In addition to Barkley, catcher Deacon McGuire, outfielder Curt Welch, and pitcher-outfielder Hank O'Day all began extended major league careers with the Blue Stockings in 1884. Fleet Walker and his brother Welday Walker were the first and last blacks to play in the majors before 1948. Charlie Morton managed the club.

1884 Players (20)

Name	Years	Games	Record
Tug Arundel	1884	15	.085
Sam Barkley	1884	104	.306
Ed Brown	1884	42	.176
Sim Bullas	1884	13	.089
Ed Kent	1884	1	0–1
Chappy Lane	1884	57	.228
Deacon McGuire	1884	45	.185
Trick McSorley	1884	21	.250
George Meister	1884	34	.193
Joe Miller	1884	105	.239
Joe Moffett	1884	56	.201
Charlie Morton	1884	32	.162
Tony Mullane	1884	95	.276/36–26
Hank O'Day	1884	41	9–28/.211
Frank Olin	1884	26	.256
Tom Poorman	1884	94	.233

John Tilley	1884	17	.179
Fleet Walker	1884	42	.263
Welday Walker	1884	5	.222
Curt Welch	1884	109	.224

Toledo Maumees (1890)

The Toledo Maumees — named for the river and historical region that forms part of the city of Toledo — entered the American Association, one of four new teams replacing clubs lost to the National League or to closure. They played home games at Speranza Park. Like the earlier Blue Stockings, the Maumees finished ahead of the other expansion clubs; with a 68–64 record, they finished fourth. However, like the Blue Stockings, the Maumees were dropped from the league at the end of the season, making Manager Charlie Morton a double Toledo loser.

Outfielder Ed Swartwood, in his last season as a regular, hit .327 and was second in the AA in on-base percentage. First baseman Perry Werden, in his first year as a regular, hit .295, leading the AA with 20 triples. Thirty-eight-year-old Ed Cushman was second on the club in innings and complete games.

1884 Players (5)

Players	Years	Games	Record
Ed Cushman	1890	40	17–21
John Peltz	1890	20	.200
John Sneed	1890	9	.200
Ed Swartwood	1890	126	.327
Perry Werden	1890	128	.295

Washington Nationals (1884)

The Washington Nationals entered the American Association in 1884 when the league expanded to twelve teams. These AA Nationals, playing at Athletic Park, were in direct competition with the Union Association Nationals, playing at Capitol Grounds. The Unions outlasted the Americans, who disbanded on August 4, after having won only twelve of 63 games.

With a .200 team batting average and a team ERA over 4.0, the Nationals struggled. Only eight players appeared in as many as half of the games. Bob Barr's nine wins represented three fourths of the Nationals' victories. Shortstop Frank Fennelly and second baseman Thorny Hawkes joined Barr as above average performers.

Almost a third of the players — Jack Beach, Lyman Drake, Frank Farley, Alex Gardner, John Hamill, Jones, Sam King, and Ed Trumbull — had no major league life beyond Washington.

1884 Players (25)

Name	Years	Games	Record
Bob Barr	1884	32	9–23
Jack Beach	1884	8	.097
Lyman Drake	1884	2	.286
Tom Farley	1884	14	.212
Frank Fennelly	1884	62	.292
Alex Gardner	1884	1	.000
Buck Gladman	1884	56	.156
Walt Goldsby	1884	6	.375
John Hamill	1884	19	2–17
John Hanna	1884	23	.066
Thorney Hawkes	1884	38	.278
John Humphreys	1884	49	.176
Jones	1884	4	.294
John Kiley	1884	14	.214
Sam King	1884	12	.178
Bill Morgan	1884	45	.173
Henry Mullin	1884	34	.142
Willie Murphy	1884	5	.476
Frank Olin	1884	21	.386
Walter Prince	1884	43	.217
Edgar Smith	1884	14	.088
Andy Swan	1884	5	.143
Ed Trumbull	1884	25	.116/1–9
Wills	1884	4	.133
Ed Yewell	1884	27	.247

Washington Statesmen (1891)

The Statesmen entered the American Association as part of the reorganization following the breakup of the Players League. Home field was the new Boundary Field with trees overhanging the outfield fence. The Statesmen finished in last place in the AA. However, at the end of the season they were invited to join the expanded National League.

Among the 1884 players, only first baseman Mox McQuery, outfielder Paul Hines, catcher Deacon McGuire and pitcher Frank Foreman held regular status with the Statesmen. McGuire was in a class by himself, hitting .313. Foreman won 18 games for a club that won only 44. Outfielder Sy Sutcliffe hit .353 and first baseman Allen McCauley .282 in backup roles.

Sam Trott, Pop Snyder and Sandy Griffin all had stints as managers of the Statesmen.

1884 Players (16)

Name	Year	Games	Performance
Jersey Bakely	1891	13	2–10
Jumbo Davis	1891	12	.318

Name	Years	Games	Record
Fred Dunlap	1891	8	.200
Frank Foreman	1891	43	18–20
Sandy Griffin	1891	20	.275
Paul Hines	1891	54	.282
Al McCauley	1891	59	.282
Deacon McGuire	1891	114	.303
Tom McLaughlin	1891	14	.268
Mox McQuery	1891	68	.241
Miah Murray	1891	2	.000
Mike Slattery	1891	15	.283
Pop Smith	1891	27	.178
Pop Snyder	1891	8	.185
Sy Sutcliffe	1891	53	.353
Sam Trott	1891	12	Manager

UNION ASSOCIATION (1884)

In the course of its single season of existence, the Union Association saw thirteen clubs participate. Only Baltimore, Boston, Cincinnati, St. Louis and Washington lasted the entire season; the other three positions were filled by Altoona, Chicago, Kansas City, Milwaukee, Philadelphia, Pittsburgh, St. Paul and Wilmington. Of the year's players, 272 played in the Union Association. Of these, 102 played only in the UA.

Altoona Mountain Citys (1884)

Altoona, PA (pop. 25,000), was a charter member of the Union Association located between the league's East Coast cities and the Midwest. Playing home games in Columbia Park, the club averaged just over a thousand fans for 17 home games. However, the team won only six of 25 games before disbanding on May 31. According to Donald Dewey and Nicolas Acocella, fans referred to the team as the Pride or the Ottawas. A bare majority of sources today call the team Mountain Citys; many refer to team as the Unions.

John Murphy won five of the team's six victories. Germany Smith was the club's leading hitter.

1884 Players (17)

Name	Years	Games	Record
Charlie Berry	1884	7	.240
James Brown	1884	21	.250/1–9
Pat Carroll	1884	11	.265
Joe Connors	1884	3	.091
Clarence Cross	1884	2	.571
George Daisey	1884	1	.000
Charlie Dougherty	1884	23	.259
John Grady	1884	9	.306
Frank Harris	1884	24	.263
Harry Koons	1884	21	.231
Jack Leary	1884	8	.091
Charlie Manlove	1884	2	.429
Jerrie Moore	1884	20	.313
John Murphy	1884	25	5–6/.149
George Nofsker	1884	7	.040
Taylor Shafer	1884	19	.284
Germany Smith	1884	25	.315

Baltimore Monumentals (1884)

Baltimore had one of the eight charter franchises in the Union Association. The franchise name comes from the fact that Baltimore was referred to as the Monument City in the 19th Century. The Monumentals were one of only five franchises to complete the season, finishing in fourth place with a 58–47 record—third place among teams that played a complete season. Home games were played at Bellair Lot, except for one game played at Monumental Park. The club disbanded with the league after the 1884 season.

Bill Sweeney led the UA in starts, innings and wins. Outfielder Emmett Seery played in every game while leading the team in hitting. But 19 of the 36 Monumentals played in fewer than ten games.

1884 Players (36)

Name	Years	Games	Record
Al Atkinson	1884	8	3–5
Frank Bahret	1884	2	.000
Joe Battin	1884	17	.102
Frank Beck	1884	5	.100
Pat Burns	1884	1	.500
John Cuff	1884	3	.091
Ned Cuthbert	1884	44	.202
Jerry Dorsey	1884	2	.000
Joe Ellick	1884	7	.148
Eddie Fusselback	1884	68	.284
Gid Gardner	1884	1	.250
Bernie Graham	1884	42	.269
Tom Lee	1884	21	5–8/.280
Charlie Levis	1884	87	.228
Chris McFarland	1884	3	.214
Bill Morgan	1884	2	.222
James Morris	1884	1	.000
John O'Brien	1884	18	.247
Henry Oberbeck	1884	33	.184
Dick Phelan	1884	101	.246
Yank Robinson	1884	102	.267

Name	Years	Games	Record
John A. Ryan	1884	6	3–2
Lou Say	1884	78	.239
Jumbo Schoeneck	1884	16	.250
Scott	1884	13	.226
Emmitt Seery	1884	105	.311
Taylor Shafer	1884	3	.077
Alexander Skinner	1884	1	.333
Smith	1884	1	0–1
Phenomenal Smith	1884	9	3–3
Joe Stanley	1884	6	.238
Tony Suck	1884	3	.300
Bill Sweeney	1884	62	40–21
Rooney Sweeney	1884	48	.226
Bill Tierney	1884	1	.333
Harry Wheeler	1884	17	.261

Boston Reds (1884)

The Boston Reds were one of the eight charter member of the Union Association and were one of the five who actually completed the season. Their 58–51 record, allowed them to finish fifth in the league. The team played home games at Dartmouth Grounds. When the UA disbanded after the 1884 season, so did the club. Red has been a favorite part of team names in Boston, beginning with the Red Stockings and Red Caps and continuing to the present Red Sox.

Rookie Ed Crane, who would later lead AA pitchers in ERA, led the Reds in hitting as an outfielder and catcher. After starting 28 games for Detroit, Dupee Shaw arrived in Boston in time to win 21 games. Tim Murnane came out of a six-year retirement to manage the club and play first base.

1884 Players (25)

Name	Years	Games	Record
Tommy Bond	1884	23	13–9
Lew Brown	1884	85	.231
James Burke	1884	45	19–15
Kid Butler	1884	71	.169
Ed Callahan	1884	4	.385
Cannon-Ball Crane	1884	101	.285
Charlie Daniels	1884	3	.273
Clarence Dow	1884	1	.333
Joe Flynn	1884	9	.226
Walter Hackett	1884	103	.243
John Irwin	1884	105	.234
Tommy McCarthy	1884	53	.215
Jim McKeever	1884	16	.136
Henry Mullin	1884	2	.000
Tim Murnane	1884	76	.235
Murphy	1884	1	.000
Tom O'Brien	1884	103	.263
Elias Peak	1884	1	.667
Charlie Reilley	1884	3	.000
John Rudderham	1884	1	.250
Patrick Scanlan	1884	6	.292
Dupee Shaw	1884	44	21–15
Art Sladen	1884	2	.000
Mike Slattery	1884	106	.208
Fred Tenney	1884	4	3–1

Chicago Browns (1884)

The Chicago Browns were charter members of the Union Association. The team played some home games in White Stocking Field but most at South Side Park. After remaining in Chicago until August 20, the Browns relocated to Pittsburgh. The Chicago record was 34–39.

The Browns had only one .300-hitting regular and a team average of .234. However, One-Arm Daily had 44 complete games, 403 strikeouts and a 2.43 ERA. A quarter of the players appeared in two or fewer games. Eleven players moved with the franchise to Pittsburgh. Second baseman Moxie Hengle managed the club in Chicago; he did not make the move to Pittsburgh.

1884 Players (32)

Name	Years	Games	Record
Al Atkinson	1884	8	4–4
Charlie Baker	1884	12	.155
Charlie Berry	1884	5	.117
Frank Bishop	1884	4	.188
Charlie Briggs	1884	49	.170
Charlie Cady	1884	6	3–1
Phil Corriden	1884	2	.143
Dan Cronin	1884	1	.250
One-Arm Daily	1884	46	22–23
Joe Ellick	1884	74	.254
Charles Fisher	1884	1	.667
Will Foley	1884	19	.282
Frank Foreman	1884	3	1–2
Gid Gardner	1884	22	.247
Bernie Graham	1884	1	.200
Emil Gross	1884	23	.358
Moxie Hengle	1884	19	.203
John Horan	1884	20	3–6/.088
Charles W. Householder	1884	66	.233
Harry Koons	1884	1	.000
Bill Krieg	1884	61	.229
Jack Leary	1884	10	.175
Steve Matthias	1884	37	.275
Chippy McGarr	1884	19	.157
Frank McLaughlin	1884	15	.239
Cyclone Miller	1884	1	1–0

Name	Years	Games	Record
Art Richardson	1884	1	.000
Jumbo Schoeneck	1884	72	.325
Alexander Skinner	1884	1	.333
Tony Suck	1884	43	.144
Harry Wheeler	1884	20	.223
Frank Wyman	1884	2	.375

Cincinnati Outlaw Reds (1884)

The Outlaw Reds were a charter franchise of the Union Association and one of its stronger members. With a 69–36 record, they finished second to the St. Louis Maroons among clubs that completed the season. The Outlaw Reds played home games at the 2,000 seat Bank Street Grounds. At the end of the 1884 season, the Union Association folded and the club disbanded.

The Outlaw Reds featured three 20-game winners—all with ERAs below 3.00; Jim McCormick had a 1.54 ERA. Led by Martin Powell, the Outlaw Reds hit .271. McCormick, shortstop Jack Glasscock and catcher Fatty Briody were added in mid season. Sam Crane managed the club.

1884 Players (23)

Name	Years	Games	Record
Charlie Barber	1884	55	.201
George Bradley	1884	58	25–15
Fatty Briody	1884	22	.337
Dick Burns	1884	79	.306/23–15
Elmer Cleveland	1884	29	.322
Sam Crane	1884	80	.233
Joe Crotty	1884	21	.262
John Ewing	1884	1	.000
Jack Glasscock	1884	38	.419
Bill Harbidge	1884	82	.279
Bill Hawes	1884	79	.278
Jack Jones	1884	69	.261
John Kelly	1884	38	.282
Ed Kennedy	1884	13	.208
Jim McCormick	1884	27	21–3
Frank McLaughlin	1884	16	.239
Mox McQuery	1884	35	.280
Lou Meyers	1884	2	.000
Dan O'Leary	1884	32	.258
Martin Powell	1884	43	.319
Fred Robinson	1884	3	.231
Pop Schwartz	1884	29	.236
Lou Sylvester	1884	82	.267

Kansas City Cowboys (1884)

When the Altoona franchise ceased operation on May 31, 1884, Kansas City was awarded a Union Association franchise and began operation on June 7. As a frontier town, Kansas City quickly developed a practice of naming major league teams "Cowboys." This practice was followed by the National League entry of 1885, the American Association team (1886–87) and the Federal League team of 1915. The UA Cowboys won only 16 of 79 games for a .203 percentage, making them even less successful than the team they replaced. Like many unsuccessful teams, the Cowboys tried a high number of players to try to find a winning combination. As a result only three players—rookies Kid Baldwin, Barney McLaughlin and Taylor Shafer—played in as many as half of the games. And they often played out of position. Baldwin, primarily a catcher, played five positions; the seventeen-year-old Shafer played in five; McLaughlin played in six, including pitcher. The Cowboys also went through three managers, going 0–4 under Harry Wheeler, 3–13 under Matt Porter and 13–46 under Ted Sullivan. Having played home games at Athletic Park, Kansas City disbanded with the league at the end of the season.

1884 Players (51)

Name	Years	Games	Record
Nin Alexander	1884	19	.138
Jersey Bakely	1884	6	2–3
Kid Baldwin	1884	50	.194
Charlie Bastian	1884	11	.196
Charlie Berry	1884	29	.246
Bob Black	1884	38	.247/4–9
Howard Blaisdell	1884	4	0–3/.313
Charlie Cady	1884	2	.000
Ed Callahan	1884	3	.364
Jim Chatterton	1884	4	.133
Joe Connors	1884	3	0–1/.091
Clarence Cross	1884	25	.215
Doug Crothers	1884	3	1–2
Jim Cudworth	1884	32	.147
Jumbo Davis	1884	7	.207
John Deasley	1884	13	.175
Harry Decker	1884	23	.133
James H. Donnelly	1884	6	.130
Bill Dugan	1884	3	.000
Al Dwight	1884	12	.233
Joe Ellick	1884	2	.000
Charles Fisher	1884	10	.200
Frank Foreman	1884	1	0–1
Jack Gorman	1884	8	.129
Tom Gorman	1884	25	.321
Ernie Hickman	1884	17	4–13
Bill Hutchison	1884	2	1–1

Name	Years	Games	Record
John Kirby	1884	2	0–1
Frank Kreeger	1884	1	0–1
Henry Luff	1884	5	.053
Barney McLaughlin	1884	42	.228
Frank McLaughlin	1884	32	.228
Henry Oberbeck	1884	27	.189
Billy O'Brien	1884	4	.235
Matthew Porter	1884	3	.083
Jimmy Say	1884	2	.250
Lou Say	1884	17	.200
Emmett Seery	1884	1	.500
Taylor Shafer	1884	44	.171
Joe Strauss	1884	16	.200
George Strief	1884	15	.107
Pat Sullivan	1884	31	.193
Ted Sullivan	1884	3	.333
Jerry Sweeney	1884	31	.264
Jerry Turbidy	1884	13	.224
Peek-A-Boo Veach	1884	27	.134/3–9
Alex Voss	1884	8	0–6
Harry Wheeler	1884	14	.258
Milt Whitehead	1884	5	.136
Wills	1884	5	.143
Frank Wyman	1884	30	.218

Milwaukee Cream Citys (1884)

Milwaukee participated in the Northwestern League in 1884. When Pittsburgh disbanded on September 19, Milwaukee was invited to join the Union Association, playing their first game on September 27. The team won eight of twelve games played, giving them second place in the league in terms of percentage. The team disbanded with the league at the end of 1884. They played home games in Wright Street Grounds. There is considerable disagreement about the team name. Of six sources, two used Cream Citys, a name taken from the cream colored brick used in much of Milwaukee construction; two use Brewers, taken from the city's long brewing tradition; two refer to them by uniform color — Grays.

None of the twelve players used by the Cream Citys were pick-up players, added for the UA schedule. Nine of the 12 had no previous major league experience; five played no major league games after 1884; Lady Baldwin, Cal Broughton, Al Myers and Henry Porter used the Milwaukee experience as a springboard for extended careers.

1884 PLAYERS (12)

Name	Years	Games	Record
Lady Baldwin	1884	7	.222/1–1
Steve Behel	1884	9	.242
George Bignall	1884	4	.222
Cal Broughton	1884	11	.308
Ed Cushman	1884	4	4–0
Anton Falch	1884	5	.111
Thomas Griffin	1884	11	.220
Ed Hogan	1884	11	.081
Tom Morrissey	1884	12	.170
Al Myers	1884	12	.326
Henry Porter	1884	10	3–3/.275
Tom Sexton	1884	12	.234

Philadelphia Keystones (1884)

The Philadelphia Keystones were charter members of the Union Association. Taking their name from Pennsylvania's state nickname — and also an earlier amateur club in the city — the team played home games in Keystone Park. However, the Keystones were one of the less successful members of the UA. Philadelphia was then a three-team city, so the Keystones competed with the National League Quakers and the American Association Athletics for fan support. On September 19, 1884, with a record of 21–46, the club disbanded.

Jersey Bakely had two thirds of the Keystones' wins. Buster Hoover hit .364 on a team that hit .245 in a league that also hit .245. Seventeen of the 29 Keystones played 10 or fewer games. Ten played in the majors only in 1884. Fergy Malone finished his managerial career with the Keystones.

1884 PLAYERS (29)

Name	Years	Games	Record
Jersey Bakely	1884	43	14–25
Pat Carroll	1884	5	.158
Jack Clements	1884	41	.282
Clarence Cross	1884	2	.222
Con Daily	1884	2	.000
Dave Drew	1884	2	.444
Henry Easterday	1884	28	.243
J. Fisher	1884	10	1–7
Joe Flynn	1884	52	.249
Robert Foster	1884	1	.333
Bill Gallagher	1884	3	1–2
Billy Geer	1884	9	.250
Tom Gillen	1884	29	.155
Buster Hoover	1884	63	.364
Bill Johnson	1884	1	.000
Bill Jones	1884	4	.143
Bill Kienzle	1884	67	.254
Henry Luff	1884	26	.270
Fergy Malone	1884	1	.250
Al Maul	1884	1	0–1
Jerry McCormick	1884	67	.285

Name	Years	Games	Record
John McGuinness	1884	53	.236
Levi Meyerle	1884	3	.091
John O'Donnell	1884	1	.250
George Pattison	1884	2	.000
Elias Peak	1884	54	.195
Chris Rickley	1884	6	.200
John Siegel	1884	8	.226
Sam Weaver	1884	17	5–10

Pittsburgh Stogies (1884)

The Chicago Browns relocated in Pittsburgh on August 20, 1884. There the club posted a 7–11 record before disbanding on September 19. The franchise record was 41–50. Home field in Pittsburgh was Exposition Park. Eleven of the 14 Stogies came with the franchise; second baseman George Strief, third baseman Joe Battin and catcher Kid Baldwin were added. Battin served as manager for six games; shortstop Joe Ellick for 12.

1884 Players (14)

Name	Years	Games	Record
Al Atkinson	1884	9	2–6
Charlie Baker	1884	3	.083
Kid Baldwin	1884	1	1.000
Joe Battin	1884	17	.188
Charlie Berry	1884	2	.100
One-Arm Daily	1884	10	5–4
Joe Ellick	1884	18	.163
Gid Gardner	1884	16	.266
Charles W. Householder	1884	17	.258
Bill Krieg	1884	10	.359
Jumbo Schoeneck	1884	18	.286
George Strief	1884	15	.208
Tony Suck	1884	10	.171
Harry Wheeler	1884	17	.233

St. Louis Maroons (1884)

The St. Louis Maroons were by far the most successful team in the Union Association. Bankrolled by Henry Lucas, who served as club president as well as league president, the Maroons compiled a 94–19 record, finishing 21 games ahead of runner-up Cincinnati. They played home games at Palace Park of America, which had a 10,000 seating capacity. Before the start of the 1885 season, the National League admitted the Maroons to replace Cleveland. This move ended the history of the Union Association.

In Fred Dunlap, Bill Taylor, Buttercup Dickerson and Orator Shaffer, the Maroons had four of the top five hitters in the UA. Dunlap led in batting, runs, hits, homers, and slugging. Shaffer led in doubles.

1884 Players (23)

Name	Years	Games	Record
George Baker	1884	80	.164
Henry Boyle	1884	65	.260
Jim Brennan	1884	56	.216
Ed Callahan	1884	1	.000
John Cattanach	1884	2	1–1
Dan Cronin	1884	1	.000
Buttercup Dickerson	1884	46	.365
Tom Dolan	1884	19	.188
Fred Dunlap	1884	101	.412
Bill Gleason	1884	92	.324
Charles Hodnett	1884	14	12–2
Fred Lewis	1884	8	.300
C.V. Matterson	1884	1	1–0
Joe Quinn	1884	103	.270
Dave Rowe	1884	109	.293
Tom Ryder	1884	8	.250
Orator Shaffer	1884	106	.360
Sleeper Sullivan	1884	2	1–0/.111
Ted Sullivan	1884	31	Mgr.
Charlie Sweeney	1884	33	24–7
Bill Taylor	1884	43	25–4/.366
Perry Werden	1884	18	12–1/.237
Milt Whitehead	1884	99	.211

St. Paul Saints (1884)

St. Paul began the 1884 season as a charter member of the Northwestern League. However, Bay City, MI, withdrew from the league on July 22, beginning a process that led to the demise of the league on September 3. When the Wilmington franchise withdrew from the Union Association, St. Paul was invited to fill their place on the schedule and began league play on September 27. While the club had played Northwestern League games at Fort Street Grounds, it had no home games in the Union Association, compiling a 2–6 record with one tie game. The franchise disbanded with the league at the end of the season. Most sources accept the team name "Saints." However, *Baseball-Reference.com* calls the team "Apostles," and *Nineteenth Century Baseball* and the *Baseball-Almanac.com* refer to it as "White Caps."

Pitcher and outfielder James Brown, second baseman Moxie Hengle and outfielder John Tilley were additions to the team. For first baseman Steve Dunn, outfielder Bill Barnes and pitcher Lou Galvin, this was their major league experience. Catcher Charles Ganzel went on to play thirteen seasons in the National League.

1884 Players (11)

Name	Years	Games	Record
Bill Barnes	1884	8	.200
Jim Brown	1884	6	1–4
Scrappy Carroll	1884	9	.097
Pat Dealy	1884	5	.133
Steve Dunn	1884	9	.250
Lou Galvin	1884	3	0–2
Charlie Ganzel	1884	7	.217
Moxie Hengle	1884	9	.152
Billy O'Brien	1884	8	.233
John Tilley	1884	9	.154
Joe Werrick	1884	9	.074

Washington Nationals (1884)

Washington was one of the charter franchises of the Union Association, and one of five to complete the 1884 season. Playing in Capitol Grounds, the club finished with a 47–65 record, good for fifth place. Known as the Nationals, the UA club had the same team name as the contemporary American Association club. When the Union Association folded, the Washington franchise moved into the Eastern League for the 1885 season and disbanded at the end of that season.

The Nationals tried 51 players over the course of the season. More than half (27) played ten or fewer games; Almost the same number (26) played only in 1884. Phil Baker, Tom Evers, Harry Moore, Alex Voss and Bill Wise were the only players to appear in half the Nationals' games.

1884 Players (51)

Name	Years	Games	Record
Gus Alberts	1884	4	.250
Phil Baker	1884	86	.288
Al Bradley	1884	1	.000
Chick Carroll	1884	4	.250
Marty Creegan	1884	9	.152
One-Arm Daily	1884	2	1–1
Jim Deasley	1884	31	.216
David Drew	1884	13	.302
Tom Evers	1884	109	.232
John Ewing	1884	1	.200
Franklin	1884	1	.000
Chris Fulmer	1884	48	.276
Charlie Gagus	1884	42	10–9/.247
Jim Green	1884	10	.139
Joe Gunson	1884	45	.139
Jim Halpin	1884	46	.185
Bill Hughes	1884	14	.122
Pop Joy	1884	36	.215
Charlie Kalbfus	1884	1	.200
John Kelly	1884	4	.357
Terry Larkin	1884	17	.243
Mike Lawlor	1884	2	.000
Mike Lehane	1884	3	.333
Charlie Levis	1884	1	.000
Milo Lockwood	1884	20	.209
Jerry McCormick	1884	42	.217
Jim McDonald	1884	2	.167
Frank McKee	1884	3	.231
Ed McKenna	1884	32	.188
William McLaughlin	1884	10	.189
McRemer	1884	1	.000
Harry Moore	1884	111	.336
Peter Morris	1884	1	.000
John Mulligan	1884	1	.250
William Nusz	1884	1	.000
Frank Olin	1884	1	.000
Maury Pierce	1884	2	.143
Abner Powell	1884	48	.283/6–12
Walter Prince	1884	1	.250
Icicle Reeder	1884	3	.167
Bill Rollinson	1884	1	.000
John M. Ryan	1884	7	.143
John Shoupe	1884	1	.750
Fred Tenney	1884	32	.235
Art Thompson	1884	1	0–1
Alex Voss	1884	63	5–14/.192
John Ward	1884	1	.250
Warren White	1884	4	.056
John Wiley	1884	1	.000
Bill Wise	1884	85	23–18/.233
Ed Yewell	1884	1	.000

Wilmington Quicksteps (1884)

Wilmington Quicksteps were runaway leaders of the Eastern League in 1884. On August 12, with a 50–12 record, they withdrew in order to join the Union Association, replacing the Philadelphia Keystones. The Quicksteps were overmatched in most games and saw their record drop to 2–15. On September 15, scheduled to play Kansas City, the Quicksteps faced a game with empty stands. At that point Wilmington forfeited the game and withdrew from the league. The Quicksteps have been Delaware's only major league club.

Only nine of the 20 Quicksteps played in as many as half the team's games. Hitting only .175 as a team, the Quicksteps saw only four players produce 10 or more hits.

1884 Players (20)

Name	Years	Games	Record
Jersey Bakely	1884	2	0–2
Charlie Bastian	1884	17	.200
Ike Benners	1884	6	.045
Oyster Burns	1884	2	.143
Dan Casey	1884	2	1–1
Dennis Casey	1884	2	.250
John Cullen	1884	9	.194
Tony Cusick	1884	11	.147
George Fisher	1884	8	.069
Tom Lynch	1884	16	.276
Bill McCloskey	1884	9	.100
Jim McElroy	1884	1	0–1
John Munce	1884	7	.190
John Murphy	1884	10	0–6/.065
Henry Myers	1884	6	.125
The Only Nolan	1884	9	1–4/.273
John M. Ryan	1884	2	.167
Jimmy Say	1884	16	.220
Redleg Snyder	1884	17	.192
Fred Tenney	1884	1	0–1

Players League (1890)

The Players League was created by the Brotherhood of Professional Baseball Players as an attempt to wrest control of baseball from the owners and return it to the players. This attempt lasted only one season. The eight PL teams all finished the season; 63 players from 1884 participated.

Boston Reds (1890)

Managed by King Kelly, the Boston Reds won the first and only Players League championship in 1890. They were the first occupants of Congress Street Grounds. When the League disbanded, the Reds as a team were invited to become a member of the American Association for 1891. Nine of the 1884 players were regulars. Hardy Richardson led the PL in hits and RBIs and was second in homers; Dan Brouthers led in on-base percentage; Harry Stovey stole 97 bases while finishing third in runs and homers; Tom Brown was second in runs and stolen bases. Old Hoss Radbourn led pitchers in winning percentage.

1884 Players (11)

Name	Years	Games	Record
Dan Brouthers	1890	123	.330
Tom Brown	1890	128	.276
Art Irwin	1890	96	.260
Dick Johnston	1890	2	.111
King Kelly	1890	89	.326
John Morrill	1890	2	.143
Billy Nash	1890	129	.266
Joe Quinn	1890	130	.301
Charley Radbourn	1890	45	27–12
Hardy Richardson	1890	130	.326
Harry Stovey	1890	118	.297

Brooklyn Wonders (1890)

Playing home games at Eastern Park, the Monte Ward–managed Wonders finished second in the Players League with a 76–56 record. The Wonders disbanded with the league at the end of the season. Veterans of 1884 held down four of the regular positions for the Wonders. First baseman Dave Orr was second in the PL in batting and RBIs. Ward, who played shortstop, was third in hits and fourth in runs scored.

1884 Players (8)

Name	Years	Games	Record
Ed Andrews	1890	94	.253
Paul Cook	1890	58	.252
Con Daily	1890	46	.250
Jack Hayes	1890	12	.190
Con Murphy	1890	23	4–10
Dave Orr	1890	107	.373
Emmett Seery	1890	104	.223
Monte Ward	1890	128	.337

Buffalo Bisons (1890)

Jack Rowe, one of the "Big Four" that had made Buffalo a National League power in the early 1880s, helped organize the Players League Buffalo club in 1890. Fellow "Four" member Deacon White — now 42 years old — was also on the Buffalo roster. However, the Bisons plunged into last place with a 36–96 record. The pitching staff had a team ERA over six runs per game. Rowe managed the team to a 27–72 record before being succeeded by Jay Faatz. The club played home games at Olympic Park II. It disbanded with the PL at the end of the season. Lady Baldwin, Faatz, Rowe and White ended their careers here.

1884 Players (6)

Name	Years	Games	Record
Lady Baldwin	1890	7	2–5
Jay Faatz	1890	32	.189
John Irwin	1890	77	.234
Jack Rowe	1890	125	.250

Name	Years	Games	Record
Deacon White	1890	122	.260
Sam Wise	1890	119	.293

Chicago Pirates (1890)

Charlie Comiskey left the St. Louis Browns to manage the Chicago Players League club. Playing at South Side Park II, also known as Brotherhood Park, the Pirates played .547 ball but finished fourth, as only Buffalo hit worse. Headed by outfielder Tip O'Neill, five of the veteran 1884 players held regular status. At the end of the season, the Pirates disbanded, and Comiskey returned to the Browns.

1884 Players (6)

Name	Years	Games	Record
Charlie Bastian	1890	80	.191
Charlie Comiskey	1890	88	.244
Arlie Latham	1890	52	.229
Tip O'Neill	1890	137	.302
Fred Pfeffer	1890	124	.257
Ned Williamson	1890	73	.195

Cleveland Infants (1890)

The Cleveland Infants, managed initially by Henry Larkin, finished seventh in the 1890 season and disbanded with the league at the end of the season. The club played at Brotherhood Park. Headed by Pete Browning, four Cleveland regulars hit over .300, giving the Infants the highest team batting average in the league. But the pitching staff had the second highest ERA in the league.

1884 Players (8)

Name	Years	Games	Record
Jersey Bakely	1890	43	12–25
Jim Brennan	1890	59	.253
Pete Browning	1890	118	.373
Henry Larkin	1890	125	.332
Paul Radford	1890	122	.292
Pop Snyder	1890	13	.188
Cub Stricker	1890	127	.244
Sy Sutcliffe	1890	99	.329

New York Giants (1890)

The New York Players League club not only captured key players from the 1889 National League New York club, but also usurped their nickname. Even with four future Hall of Fame players and a gaudy .284 team batting average, these Giants finished third in the Players League with a 74–57 record. Roger Conner led the PL in homers and slugging and was fourth in hitting and fifth in runs scored. Jim O'Rourke finished third in hitting and fourth in RBIs. John Ewing led PL pitchers in strikeouts per game. Buck Ewing managed the club. The Giants played home games in the fourth version of the Polo Grounds, also known as Brotherhood Park. Key regulars such as Connor, the Ewings, O'Rourke, George Gore, Danny Richardson and Tim Keefe returned to the NL Giants for 1891.

1884 Players (13)

Name	Years	Games	Record
Roger Connor	1890	123	.349
Cannon-Ball Crane	1890	43	16–19
Fred Dunlap	1890	1	.500
Buck Ewing	1890	83	.338
John Ewing	1890	35	18–12
George Gore	1890	93	.318
Dick Johnston	1890	77	.242
Tim Keefe	1890	30	17–11
Hank O'Day	1890	43	22–13
Jim O'Rourke	1890	111	.360
Danny Richardson	1890	123	.256
Mike Slattery	1890	97	.307
Art Whitney	1890	119	.219

Philadelphia Quakers (1890)

The Quakers shared Forepaugh Park with the American Association Philadelphia Athletics in 1890. With a 68–63 record, the Quakers finished fifth in the League. As in New York, the Philadelphia Players League club absorbed key players from the National League Quakers—Charlie Buffinton, Sid Farrar, Jim Fogarty, Joe Mulvey and George Wood came from the NL Quakers—and adopted their name. The NL team then adopted the name Phillies. Fogarty (7–9) and Buffinton (61–54) managed the team.

1884 Players (6)

Name	Years	Games	Record
Charlie Buffinton	1890	42	19–15
Sid Farrar	1890	127	.254
Jim Fogarty	1890	91	.239
Jocko Milligan	1890	62	.295
Joe Mulvey	1890	120	.287
George Wood	1890	132	.289

Pittsburgh Burghers (1890)

Using a core group of eight National League Pittsburgh Alleghenys, the Pittsburgh Burghers participated in the Players League in 1890. The Burghers were the first tenants of Exposition Park III, but could manage no higher than a 60–68, sixth-place finish. Yank Robinson finished second in the league in walks; Pud Galvin and Ed Morris finished third and fourth in fewest walks allowed. Ned Hanlon finished fourth in stolen bases. Hanlon managed the club. The club disbanded with the league at the end of the season. Fred Carroll, Galvin, Hanlon, and Al Maul returned to the NL Pittsburgh club.

1884 PLAYERS (7)

Name	Years	Games	Record
Fred Carroll	1890	111	.298
Pud Galvin	1890	26	12–13
Ned Hanlon	1890	118	.298
Bill Kuehne	1890	126	.239
Al Maul	1890	45	15–12/.259
Cannon-Ball Morris	1890	18	8–7
Yank Robinson	1890	98	.229

AMERICAN LEAGUE (1901–)

The American League existed in 1900 as a minor league. By 1901 it was challenging the National League as a second major league, picking up franchises rejected by the National League or locating in cities wanting a major league club. Few of the 1884 players were still active in 1901, but four — pitcher Frank Foreman, catcher Deacon McGuire, shortstop Bones Ely and second baseman Joe Quinn — played on one or more of the new AL clubs.

Baltimore Orioles (1901–02)

Admitted to the American League in January 1901, the Baltimore Orioles contested the first two AL pennants. In 1901 they finished fifth; a year later they were dead last with a 50–88 record. Like their predecessors in the AA and NL, they took the name Orioles; they played home games in Oriole Park IV. At the end of 1902, the franchise was purchased by New York and became the Highlanders and later the Yankees. Frank Foreman came to the Orioles in 1901 from Boston, logging 12 wins that season.

1884 PLAYER (1)

Name	Years	Games	Record
Frank Foreman	1901–02	26	12–8

Boston Somersets (1901–)

The Somersets were also admitted to the American League in January 1901. The club played at Huntington Avenue Baseball Grounds until the 1912 season, when Fenway Park was built. In the first decade of the 20th Century the team had league championships in 1903–04, a world championship in 1903 and eight first-division finishes. The club became known as the Pilgrims in 1903, and in 1907 adopted the more familiar Red Sox name. Deacon McGuire was a playing manager in both 1907 and 1908.

1884 PLAYERS (2)

Name	Years	Games	Record
Frank Foreman	1901	1	0–1
Deacon McGuire	1907–08	7	.600

Cleveland Bluebirds (1901–)

Cleveland had been a member of the American League in 1900, when it did not have major league classification. Initially the club took the original nickname of the old National League franchise of the 1880s. However, in 1902 it took the name Bronchos and in 1903 the Naps for manager Napoleon Lajoie. The now familiar Indians nickname was adopted in 1915 to honor Native American star Louis Sockalexis. In the first decade of the century, the club had five first division finishes, topped by a second place finish in 1908. They played in League Park III. Deacon McGuire managed Cleveland (1909–11), playing his last game as manager.

1884 PLAYERS (1)

Name	Years	Games	Record
Deacon McGuire	1908, 1910	2	.286

Detroit Tigers (1901–)

Detroit was a charter member of the American League, moving with the league into major status in 1901. In the first decade of the century the club had six first division finishes and three AL championships. Until Navin Field was built in 1912, the Tigers played at Bennett Park, named for Charlie Bennett, long time Detroit Wolverines catcher. This was the site of World Series games in 1907–1909. Deacon McGuire was the club's regular catcher in 1902 and 1903. He played his last game in 1912 while serving as a coach.

1884 Players (1)

Name	Years	Games	Record
Deacon McGuire	1902–03, 1912	146	.240

New York Highlanders (1904–)

Over the objections of the National League, the American League placed a team in New York City in 1904. New York baseball men purchased the Baltimore franchise and built a new ballpark on the highest point in New York City. Hilltop Park was the home of the Highlanders until 1912. In 1913 the club took the now familiar name Yankees and moved to the Polo Grounds. Yankee Stadium was completed in 1923. The club had second place finishes in 1904, 1906 and 1910. Deacon McGuire was the regular catcher for the 1904 Highlanders.

1884 Players (1)

Name	Years	Games	Record
Deacon McGuire	1904–07	225	.230

Philadelphia Athletics (1901–)

The Philadelphia Athletics joined the American League in January 1901 prior to the AL's elevation to major status. Connie Mack became manager of the club that season. Playing originally in Columbia Park, the A's moved to Shibe Park — their home for the remainder of their stay in Philadelphia — in 1909. In the first decade of the century the A's boasted of one world championship in 1910, two other AL championships and two second place finishes. The club moved to Kansas City in 1954 and then to Oakland in 1968. Bones Ely was a reserve shortstop for the 1901 club.

1884 Players (1)

Name	Years	Games	Record
Bones Ely	1901	45	.216

Washington Senators (1901–)

The Senators played in the American League in 1900 and moved into major status with the league. Initially they played in American League Park I, moving to American League Park II in 1904. Griffith Stadium was built in 1911. In the first decade of the century they suffered four seventh-place finishes and four last-place finishes. Thirty-nine-year-old Bones Ely was the regular shortstop in 1902. At age 37, Joe Quinn was a reserve second-baseman for the 1901 club.

1884 Players (3)

Name	Years	Games	Record
Bones Ely	1902	105	.262
Jim Manning	1901	Manager	61–72
Joe Quinn	1901	66	.252

Appendix II
Birth and Mortality Summary

So far as we know, there were 637 men who played major league baseball in 1884. But one says that number with some care. Baseball research is an ongoing process; records are constantly being emended. In some recent cases, researchers have given the records once thought to be those of two men to just one, resulting in the loss of a player. For example, Taylor Shafer has now been awarded the records of both Frank Shaffer and Taylor Shaffer. In other cases, a new major leaguer is created when researchers separate records. As an example, Robert Foster has now been given a portion of the records long held by Elmer Foster. In still other cases, players have simply been traded. Emory Nusz has disappeared from the major league ranks, his place taken by his brother William. So while 637 is the present number, it may not be the final number.

Through the work of SABR's Biographical Research Committee, we know more about those who played than ever before. Players who were once just last names are being fleshed out with first names, birth dates and places, and death dates and places. At the same time, research tools are improving—even for amateur researchers. For example, *Ancestry.com* has made census data available, allowing us to locate key information about players' place of birth, parentage, occupation and family relationships. More and more historical newspapers are also now available, allowing us to find obituaries for missing players.

What conclusions can we draw about the group of men who played in 1884?

Place of Birth

Of the 637 players, we have reasonably reliable birth data at this time on 622. Not surprisingly, the lion's share of players came from the more heavily populated Atlantic seaboard. A group of nine states running from Massachusetts through the District of Columbia accounted for 364 players—almost 59 percent of the total. The three states of Pennsylvania (113), New York (104) and Massachusetts (74) accounted for 291 players—almost 47 percent of the group. Ken Burns' contention in *Baseball: An Illustrated History* that baseball was a game with urban roots is borne out by these birth data. The city of Philadelphia alone produced 73 players; greater New York City produced 54; greater Boston had 23; Washington, DC, had 14. Eight were born in Providence, seven each in Buffalo and Baltimore, and six each in Pittsburgh and New Haven.

The Middle West with heavy representation from Illinois (44 players), Ohio (39) and Missouri (20) furnished 136 players—less than a quarter of the total. But the urban trend continued. Twenty of the Illinois players hailed from Chicago; seventeen of Missouri's total were from St. Louis—in addition to three East St. Louis, IL, players. Fourteen of Ohio's total were from Cincinnati with more from its Kentucky suburbs.

The South, with few metropolitan areas, furnished only 31 players, and this figure may be exaggerated. Mississippi's Doug Crothers grew up in St. Louis, and Georgia's Alex Voss spent most of his life in Cincinnati. A player once thought to be a son of Arkansas, Edward "Chick" Carroll, has since lost both his first name and place of birth. Even in the South the urban trend continued. Four of Kentucky's fourteen players came from the Cincinnati suburbs of Newport and Covington. Louisville was home for six players; New Orleans produced five of Louisiana's six, and Richmond produced four of Virginia's six, with another coming from the DC suburb of Alexandria.

Only sixteen players were born in the area west of the Sabine River–Missouri River–Red River of the North corridor. This is not surprising since only Texas (1845), California (1850), Oregon (1859), Kansas (1861) and Nevada (1864) held statehood before 1884. When Detroit shortstop Walt Kinzie was born in Kansas in 1859, it was still a territory. Kinzie, whose parents were natives of Illinois, soon became a Chicago resident. The other fifteen Westerners were Californians — most from the Bay Area. In fact, seven players attended St. Mary's College. There New York City shortstop Jerry Denny, Brooklyn-born lefty "Cannon-Ball" Morris, and Chicago-born right-hander Hank O'Day joined locals Fred Carroll, Jim Fogarty, Charlie Gagus, and Jim McElroy.

Fifty-three players — almost 9 percent — were foreign born. Twenty-nine came from Canada; a dozen from Ireland. Germany contributed five (George Meister, Frank Siffell, Bill Kuehne, Gus Shallix and "Pretzels" Getzein); three each came from Scotland (Jim McCormick, Hugh Nicol and Mal MacArthur) and England (Jim Halpin, Tim Manning and Tom Brown); contributing one each were Wales (Peter Morris) and Australia (Joe Quinn).

Nationality

Since the U.S. Federal Census reports birth data on parents as well as children, we have nationality information on 564 of the 637 players.

Of those 564 players, 263 — almost 47 percent — had one or both parents born in the United States. This figure includes the black parents of Fleet and Welday Walker and the Native American mother of Billy Barnes. If 47 percent seems to be a low figure, it serves as a reminder that the United States was still a young country when the 1884 players were born, and that waves of immigrants were starting to arrive. Abraham Lincoln's "four score and seven years ago," spoken at Gettysburg in 1863, came at a time when most of the players were infants or small children; a few were not yet born.

A more startling fact is that 209 players, 37 percent of the known group, had at least one parent born in Ireland. One result of the potato famine in Ireland and the evictions of families from the land in the 1840s was that thousands of Irish families immigrated to Canada or the United States. According to the website *Spartacus*, between 1844 and 1854 "nearly two million people — about a quarter of the population — had emigrated to the United States." Poverty forced most to settle along the Eastern seaboard, accepting jobs in the cities there. According to the website *Answers.com*, "By the 1850s–1860s, 28 percent of all people living in New York, 26 percent in Boston, and 16 percent in Philadelphia had been born in Ireland." It is not surprising then that 44 Irish players were born in New York; 40 in Massachusetts and 23 in Pennsylvania. The surge of Irish immigration continued through the 1850s and '60s as families attempted to reunify. Some Irish emigrated for a second time, those who had settled in Canada migrating on to more industrial cities in the United States. Many Irish also were able to find employment in the mill and factory towns such as Lowell and Fall River in Massachusetts. Even Australian-born Joe Quinn had Irish parents. The Irish impact on major league baseball probably exceeds the known 37 percent. The list of 72 players whose family background is unknown contains names such as Murphy, O'Brien, O'Leary, Ryan, Larkin, Hogan and O'Donnell,

Germans formed one of the largest groups of immigrants to the United States, especially following the failed German Revolution of 1848. Unlike the Irish, the Germans — who tended to be more affluent — moved to the interior of the United States. The online government document "German Immigration Patterns" (*Urban Germans ... Immigration*) specifically mentions Cincinnati, Milwaukee, St. Louis and St. Paul as having large concentrations of Germans. Player totals would suggest that Chicago, Pittsburgh and Louisville were also destination cities for those immigrants. Sixty-six players with German parents were part of the 1884 player pool. Ten were from Pennsylvania, eight each were from Illinois and New York, six were from Missouri and five each were from Kentucky and Ohio.

Thirty-six players had at least one English parent, and 14 had at least one Scots parent. The 28 players listed as Canadian are only those not specifically designated as Irish, English or Scots. Doubtless some Canadians players would fall into one of those groups. Completing the known nationalities were three Norwegian players: Tony Suck, Joe Werrick and Bill Nelson (father); two Welch players: Peter Morris and Abner Powell; two French players: Mike DePangher and Emil Gross (mother); and one Portuguese: Lou Sylvester.

Age

Birthdates — at least a year of birth — are available for 585 of the players. Almost a third of the players (182) for whom we have birth data were born between 1858 and 1860, making the median age around 25.

The only regular older than 40 was 42-year-old first baseman Joe Start of Providence, who hit .276 in 93 games for the National League champion Grays and played in the first World Series ever. He would go on to lead NL first basemen in fielding at age 43 before retiring at age 44. Philadelphia Keystones manager Fergy Malone, another 42-year-old, caught one game for his team, and 40-year-old Warren White, a Civil War veteran, left his position in the league office to play four games as an infielder for the Washington Unions.

Of the other eight players born prior to 1850, three National Association stars were born in 1845. Ned Cuthbert was an outfield regular for the Baltimore Monumentals, Bob Ferguson managed the Pittsburgh Alleghenys, appearing in ten games, and Levi Meyerle made three appearances for his hometown Keystones. Two 37-year-olds were forces in 1884: Deacon White hit .325 as an infield regular for Buffalo and would enjoy six more seasons as a regular; "One Arm" Daily struck out 483 in 500 innings in the Union Association. Three chipper 36-year-old shortstops round out the list. Billy Geer enjoyed his most productive season as a Brooklyn regular; Davy Force led NL shortstops in fielding and Candy Nelson helped the Metropolitans win an AA championship.

Six players born in 1866 played in the majors as 17- or 18-year-olds. Pat Callahan, the youngest of the group, hit .260 in 61 games as the regular third baseman for the Indianapolis Hoosiers, his only major league experience. On the same club Larry McKeon made 60 starts, winning 18 games; Milt Scott, who had played with the White Stockings as a 16-year-old in 1882, hit .247 as the regular first baseman for Detroit. Taylor Shafer was an outfield regular at Altoona and Kansas City, as was Mike Slattery for the Boston Reds. Outfielder and first baseman Bill Hughes played in 14 games for the Washington Unions;

Edward "Chick" Carroll, the Washington shortstop on opening day, has long been listed as a 16-year-old, born in 1868. However, all birth data on Carroll are now disputed. *Baseball-Almanac.com* asserts that Kansas City third baseman and catcher James H. Donnelly, whose records have just been separated from those of James B. Donnelly, was born in January 1867, making him younger than Pat Callahan, who was born in October 1866.

Birth Year	Number of Players
Before 1850	11
1850–51	22
1852–53	29
1854–55	54
1856–57	99
1958–59	123
1860–61	111
1862–63	92
1864–65	45
After 1865	8

Mortality Statistics

Dan Cronin, who played two games in the Union Association, died in Boston on November 30, 1885, the first of 24 players who did not survive the decade of the 1880s. The youngest, Kansas City Unions pitcher Howard Blaisdell, was only 24 when he died on May 30, 1886. Ninety of the 579 players for whom we have a death date did not live into the 20th century. In addition to the usual rash of accidents (eight), suicides (seven) and murders (2), diseases now generally under control took their toll on the ranks of the players. In addition to at least four syphilis-related deaths, four players fell to Bright's disease, four to typhoid, two to malaria and one to dysentery.

In an Internet study, Ed Stephan notes, "It's numbing to read about the many players in the 1870–90s who died in their twenties and thirties, often from alcohol and fighting." Certainly alcoholism was a contributing factor in a number of those deaths. However, more than one-fourth of the young players were carried away by diseases of the lungs, variously described as consumption, tuberculosis, or pulmonary congestion.

Born for the most part before or during the Civil War, more than seventy of the players saw the outbreak of World War II. The oldest, former Detroit outfielder Henry Jones died on May 31, 1955, at age 98. The last to die was Al Maul, a journeyman pitcher who had begun his career with the Philadelphia Keystones in 1884. The 92-year-old Maul died on May 3, 1958.

Age of Players at Death	Number of Deaths
20–29	18
30–39	67
40–49	71
50–59	85
60–69	123
70–79	134
80–89	66
90–99	14

Between Blaisdell and Jones, the median death age for the 579 players was 63. We have no national life expectancy statistics by which to measure this figure. But 19th century statistics are available for Massachusetts, where the life expectancy for a 20-year-old white male in 1878–82 — roughly our group — was 39.8. If this figure held for the nation, then the players would have marginally exceeded expectations for their group.

Bibliography

Databases

Ancestry.com. http://www.ancestry.com. This subscriber Internet service is the source for all the U.S. Federal Censuses, city directories, voter registration lists, military service lists, death indexes and death certificates cited in the book.

LA84 Foundation, "Sports Library." http://www.la84foundation.org/4sl/over_frmst.htm. This is the source for *Sporting Life* and *Baseball Magazine* and *Outing*.

Paper of Record. http://www.paperofrecord.com. This digital newspaper service is the source for *Sporting News*.

ProQuest Historical Newspapers. http://www.umi.com/en-US/catalogs/databases/detail/pq-hist-news.shtml. Formerly provided for members of the Society for American Baseball Research, this University of Michigan service provides digital copies of nineteenth and early twentieth century *New York Times, Chicago Daily Tribune, Chicago, Washington Post, Los Angeles Times, Boston Globe, Boston, Atlanta Constitution, National Police Gazette*.

Russo, Mark. *The Deadball Era: Where Every Player Is Safe at Home*. http://www.thedeadballera.com/. This omnibus site is a storehouse for information on deceased players. It contains obituaries and photographs, in addition to the lists of post baseball occupations, causes of death for players who died young, as well as lists of suicides, accidents, and murders.

Player Records

Baseball Almanac: Where What Happened Yesterday Is Preserved Today. http://www.baseball-almanac.com.

The Baseball Encyclopedia: The Complete and Official Record of Major League Baseball. 8th ed. New York: Macmillan, 1990.

The Baseball Page. http://http.thebaseballpage.com.

Forman, Sean I. *Baseball-Reference.com*. http://www.baseball-reference.com.

Retrosheet. http://www.retrosheet.org/.

Society for American Baseball Research. *SABR Baseball Encyclopedia*. http://members.sabr.org/members.cfm?a=rtl&rtl=enc&enc=crd&pid=238.

Thorn, John, Pete Palmer, Michael Gershman, and David Pietrusza, with Matthew Silverman and Sean Lahman, eds. *Total Baseball: The Official Encyclopedia of Major League Baseball*. 6th ed. New York: Total Sports, 1999.

General Sources

Baseball: An Illustrated History. Narrative by Geoffrey Ward. Based on a documentary filmscript by Geoffrey C. Ward and Ken Burns. New York: Knopf, 1994.

Baseball and Philosophy: Thinking Outside the Batter's Box. Edited by Eric Bronson. Foreword by Bill Littlefield. Peru, IL: Open Court, 2004.

Baseball Fever. http://www.baseball-fever.com/content.php.

Baseball Historian: Where Faded Memories Return. http://www.baseballhistorian.com/index.cfm.

Benswanger, William E. "Professional Baseball in Pittsburgh." http://www.upress.pitt.edu/htmlSourceFiles/pdfs/9780822959700exr.pdf.

Biographies—The D's: Elmwood Cemetery's List of Honor. http://historicelmwood.org/modules/tinycontent/print.php?id=7

Bullpen. A collaborative encyclopedia sponsored by Baseball-Reference.com.

Burgess, Bill III. "Umpires Register." *Baseball Guru.com*. http://baseballguru.com/bburgess/analysisbburgess17.html.

Charlton, James, and others. *Charlton's Baseball Chronology*. http://www.baseballlibrary.com/chronology/.

"Cincinnati Police Officers Killed in the Line of Duty 1776–1900." *Greater Cincinnati Police Historical Society Museum*. http://www.gcphs.com/cincinnatiofficers_killed_1876-1900.

The Complete New York Clipper Baseball Biographies: More than 800 Sketches of Players, Managers, Owners, Umpires, Reporters and Others, 1859–1903. Compiled by Jean-Pierre Caillault. Foreword by John Thorn. 2 vols. Jefferson, NC: McFarland, 2009.

Curry, Richard. "Saginaw Old Golds History." http://www.saginawoldgolds.com/History.htm.

Deadball Stars of the National League. Written by the Deadball Era Committee of the Society for American Baseball Research. Edited by Tom Simon. Foreword by Keith Obermann. Dulles, VA: Brassey's, 2004.

Dewey, Donald, and Nicholas Acocella. "The Ballclubs: Altoona Mountain Citys." *That's Baseball*. http://thatsbaseball1.tripod.com/id92.htm.

1883 Brooklyn Atlantics Scorecard (Possibly the Earliest

Known "Dodgers" Scorecard). AmericanMemorabilia.com.

Eldred, Rich. "Timothy Hayes Murnane." *Baseball's First Stars*. Edited by Frederick Ivor-Campbell, et al. Cleveland: SABR, 1996.

Filichia, Peter. *Professional Baseball Franchises: From the Abbeville Athletics to the Zanesville Indians*. New York: Facts on File, 1993.

Find a Grave. http://www.findagrave.com/cgi-bin/fg.cgi?page=gr&GRid=11818440.

Ginsburg, Daniel E. *The Fix Is In: A History of Baseball Gambling and Game Fixing Scandals*. Jefferson, NC: McFarland, 1995.

Hardball Times. http://www.hardballtimes.com/main/article/this-annotated-week-in-baseball-history-march-11-17-1953/.

In Memory of Ned Williamson, October 24, 1857–March 3, 1894. http://www.nedwilliamson.us/.

"Irish Americans." *Answers.com*. http://www.answers.com/topic/irish-american.

"Irish Immigration." *Spartacus*. http://www.spartacus.schoolnet.co.uk/USAEireland.htm.

James, Bill. *The New Bill James Historical Baseball Abstract*. New York: Free Press, 2001.

Jeffre, Jay. "The Jay Ballers of the World." Futility Infielders.com. http://www.futilityinfielder.com/leadoff03.html.

Johnson, Lloyd, and Miles Wolfe, eds. *The Encyclopedia of Minor League Baseball: The Official Record of Minor League Baseball*. 2nd ed. Durham, NC: Baseball America, 1997.

Kaese, Harold. *The Boston Braves 1871–1953*. New York: Putnam, 1948.

Lee, Bill. *The Baseball Necrology: The Post-Baseball Lives and Deaths of Over 7,600 Major League Players and Others*. Jefferson, NC: McFarland, 2003.

Lowry, Philip J. *Green Cathedrals: The Ultimate Celebration of Major League and Negro League Ballparks*. New York: Walker, 2006.

Marlin, Brooks. "Major League Baseball's 'Permanently Ineligible' List." Everything2. http://everything2.com/title/Major+League+Baseball%2527s+%2522permanently+ineligible%2522+list.

Morris, Peter. *Peter Morris, Baseball Historian*. http://www.petermorrisbooks.com. 2007–2009.

National Baseball Hall of Fame. *A Short History of the Single Season Home Run Record*. http://www.exhibits.baseballhalloffame.org/ss_home_run/williamson.htm.

National Baseball Hall of Fame and Museum. "Welch, Mickey." http://www.baseballhall.org/hof/welch-mickey.

Negro Leagues Baseball Museum emuseum: Electronic Resources for Teachers. http://www.coe.ksu.edu/nlb emuseum/history/szplayers.html.

The New York Mets Hall of Records. www.hagenspan.com/NYMHall/mets.html.

19cbaseball. Compiled by E. Miklich. http://www.19cbaseball.com/.

Pajot, Dennis. "Anton Falch — Ballplayer, but Much More in Life." Seamheads.com.

"The Personification of Coolness," *New York Times*. http://www.adonisterry.tripod.com/.

Seymour, Harold. *Baseball: The Golden Age*. New York: Oxford University Press, 1989.

Society for American Baseball Research. *The Baseball Biography Project*. http://bioproj.sabr.org/. Among its 1,271 biographies, this project now has biographies for 39 of the 1884 players.

Society for American Baseball Research. *SABR Biographical Committee Newsletter*. http://www.sabr.org/cmsFiles/Files/ACF7FA.pdf

Society for American Baseball Research. *SABR Collegiate Database*. http://www.ncaa-baseball.com/sabr/database.

Society for Baseball Research: Schott-Pelican Chapter. *History of New Orleans Baseball*. http://www.sabrneworleans.com/history.html.

Soos, Troy. *Before the Curse: The Glory Days of New England Baseball, 1858–1918*. Jefferson, NC: McFarland, 1997.

Sports Illustrated/cnn. http://www.sportsillustrated.cnn.com/.

Stephan, Ed. *For Love, for Money, for Real Money: Life Expectancy Among 19th Century Baseball Players*. http://www.edstephan.org/webstuff/es.19thBB.html.

Thorn, John. "When Baseball Was Big in Kingston." *Thorn Pricks*. http://thornpricks.blogspot.com/2006/05/when-baseball-was-big-in-kingston.html.

Thornley, Stew. "Minneapolis Millers." http://stewthornley.net/millers.html.

"The Top 100 Cubs of All Time — #48 George Gore." *Bleed Cubbie Blue*. http://www.bleedcubbieblue.com/2007/1/2/164852/5362.

"Umpire Rulings in a Triple Play (Trickery, Confusion, Decision)." Assembled by Frank Hamilton. http://tripleplays.sabr.org/tp_tcd.htm.

"Urban Germans." *Immigration....* http://memory.loc.gov/learn///features/immig/alt/german6.html.

Vaccaro, Frank. "One-Arm Daily: 20Ks?" *The National Pastime*, 1999. Society for American Baseball Research.

Voigt, David Quentin. *America Through Baseball*. Chicago: Nelson-Hall, 1976.

"The Watsons." http://www.flls.org/weedsport/watson.html.

Wolfe, H. Scott. "The Babe Ruth of His Day." http://www.galenahistorymuseum.org/abnerdalrymple.htm.

Wright, Marshall D. *Nineteenth Century Baseball: Year-by-Year Statistics for the Major League Teams, 1871 through 1900*. Jefferson, NC: McFarland, 1996.

Zingg, Paul J. and Mark D. Medeiros. *Runs, Hits, and an Era: The Pacific Coast League 1903–1958*. Champagne: University of Illinois Press, 1994.

Zingler, David. "Bobby Mathews." *Simply Baseball Notebook: Forgotten in Time*. http://z.lee28.tripod.com/sbnsforgottenintime/id26.html.

Index

A.G. Spalding & Bros. *see* Spalding, Albert
age 226
Agricultural County Fair Grounds Race Track (Worcester) 199
Agricultural Society Fair Grounds (Rockford) 182
Ake, John 10, 200
Akron, OH 11, 18, 106, 121, 122, 160, 163, 174
Albany, NY 30, 64, 66, 81, 93, 104, 106, 129, 138
Alberts, Gus 10, 203, 206, 210, 219
Albion College 112
Alexander, William "Nin" 10, 211, 216
Alexandria, VA 19, 112, 176, 224
Alice, ID 10
All-America team 34, 44
Allegheny, PA 87, 120
Allen, Hezekiah "Ki" 10, 194
Allen's Pasture (Richmond) 210
Allentown, PA 100, 115
Alton, IL 63, 130
Altoona, PA 10, 13, 23, 105, 152
Altoona Mountain Citys (UA) 4, 6, 21, 26, 34, 41, 46, 50, 56–57, 78, 83, 98, 102, 105, 118, 124, 128, 149, 152, 214
American Association (AA) 101; cities 3; clubs and players 199–214; pennant race 6–7; umpires 55, 60, 61, 76, 96, 97, 104, 107, 111, 133, 154, 176
American Civil War 18, 170, 226
American League: alignment (1903–1953) 177; clubs and players 222–223
American League Park (Washington) 223
Ames, IA 158
Ancestry.com 224
Andrews, Ed 11, 191, 194, 202, 220
Andrews, Wally 11, 206
Andrus, Fred 12, 187
Annis, Bill 12, 184
Anson, Adrian "Cap" 1, 5, 12–13, 62, 121, 158, 164, 172, 181, 182, 187
Ardner, Joe 13, 189
Arundel, Harry 13, 179, 196, 210
Arundel, John "Tug" 13, 191, 199, 208, 212

Ashland, OH 103
Association Park (Kansas City) 192, 205
Astoria, NY 24
Athletic Park (Kansas City) 216
Athletic Park (Washington) 213
Atkinson (Atkisson), Al 14, 208, 214, 215, 218
Atlanta 13, 38, 58, 77, 96, 98, 106, 136, 137, 152, 156, 158
Atlantic Association 154
Atlantic City, NJ 66, 96, 141
Atlantic League 76, 88, 115
Attleboro, MA 30, 72
Auburn, NY 14, 56, 106
Augusta, GA 58, 102, 107, 150, 157, 161, 166
Aurora, IL 106, 170
Austin, NV 33
Avenue Grounds (Cincinnati) 188
Aydelott, Jake 14, 205, 208

Bahret, Frank 14, 214
Bakely (Bakley), Edward "Jersey" 14, 189, 200, 203, 208, 213, 216, 217, 220, 221
Baker, Charlie 15, 215, 218
Baker, George 6, 15, 192, 197, 200, 218
Baker, Phil 15, 199, 200, 219
Baker Bowl (Philadelphia) 194
Baldwin, Charles "Lady" 15, 186, 190, 217, 220
Baldwin, Clarence "Kid" 16, 188, 203, 208, 216, 218
Baltimore, MD 50, 54, 61, 68, 87, 104, 106, 108, 117, 127, 128 147, 148, 150, 162
Baltimore Lord Baltimores (NA) 68, 73, 105, 107, 147, 153, 170, 176, 180
Baltimore Marylands (NA) 147, 178
Baltimore Monumentals (UA) 4, 6, 14, 18, 20, 30, 47, 49, 56 60, 70, 72, 78, 102, 110, 119, 120, 128, 129, 133, 144, 146, 147, 148, 149, 150, 151, 152, 154, 157, 160, 161, 162, 169, 214–215
Baltimore Orioles (AA) 4, 6, 10, 14, 15, 24, 25, 26, 27, 28, 30, 36, 38, 39, 41, 51, 54, 55, 59, 60–61, 63, 64, 66, 68, 69, 70, 72, 77, 79,

82, 84, 84, 85, 87, 88, 90, 91, 94, 96, 102, 104, 105, 106, 109, 111, 114, 121, 122, 126, 127, 129, 132, 134, 135, 136, 137, 140, 145, 146, 147, 148, 152, 154, 155, 161, 163, 165, 167, 168, 171, 174, 175, 176, 199–201
Baltimore Orioles (AL) 68, 81, 222
Baltimore Orioles (NL) 5, 26, 55, 68, 80, 81, 108, 117, 122, 138, 155, 156, 158, 162, 167, 168, 175, 184
Bangor, ME 21
Bank Street Grounds (Cincinnati) 188, 203, 216
Barber, Charlie 16, 216
Barkley, Sam 17, 195, 205, 210, 211, 212
Barnes, Bill 17, 218–219, 226
Barr, Bob 17, 193, 199, 205, 210, 211, 213
Barrett, Marty 17, 184, 205
Bartlesville, OK 10
Bartletts (Lowell, MA) 83
Bassett, Charley 17–18, 191, 192, 193, 196
Bastian, Charlie 18, 187, 194, 202, 216, 220, 221
Batavia, IL 24
Battin, Joe 18, 179, 181, 182, 196, 209–210, 212, 214, 218
Bauer (Bauers), Al 18–19, 197, 204
Bay Area (CA), 22, 54, 82, 115
Bay City, MI 21, 37, 69, 97, 218
Beach, Jack 19, 213
Beatle, Dave 19, 190
Beaver, KS 95
Becannon, James "Buck" 19, 193, 207
Beck (Hengstebeck), Frank 20, 210, 214
Begley (Bagley), Ed 20, 193, 207
Behel, Steve 20, 207, 217
Belfast, ME 161
Bellair Lot (Baltimore) 214
Bellaire, OH 169
Belleview, KY 95
Belmont, MA 37
Beloit, WI 25, 78
Belvidere, IL 22
Benners, Ike 20–21, 202, 220
Bennett, Charlie 21, 184, 190, 193, 199, 223
Bennett Park (Detroit) 21, 222

231

Bennington, VT 104
Berea, OH 57
Berkelbach, Frank 21, 203
Berkeley, CA 60
Berkeley, MI 77
Berlin, Germany 63
Berlin, MI 165
Berry, Charlie 21, 214, 215, 216, 218
Berry, Charlie, Jr. 21
Beverly, MA 123
Bierbauer, Lou 209
Big Beaver, MI 133
"Big Four" 142, 170, 220
Bignell, George 21, 217
Binghamton, NY 36, 59, 102, 109, 110, 111, 163, 172
Birchall, Judson 22, 208
Birmingham, AL 87, 106, 121, 155, 158
Birmingham, MI 146
birthplaces 224, 225
Bishop, Frank 22, 215
Black, Bob 22, 216
"Black Sox" scandal 40
Blackstone, MA 50
Blackwood, NJ 14
Blaisdell, Howard "Dick" 22, 216, 226
Blakiston (Blackstone), Bob 22, 205, 208
Blandinsville, IL 89
Blong, Joe 18
Bloomington, IL 139
Boecke, George *see* Baker, George
Bond, Tommy 22–23, 179, 180, 184, 191, 199, 205, 215
Boonville, MO 57
Borchert Field (Milwaukee) 206
Boston, MA 23, 26, 32, 45, 51, 56, 57, 81, 89, 90, 95, 104, 105, 108, 112, 113, 115, 119, 123, 125, 139, 141, 142, 150, 151, 152, 160, 162, 175
Boston Beacons 142
Boston Beaneaters (NL) 4, 5, 12, 17, 21, 22, 26, 27, 28, 33, 37, 40, 47, 49, 51, 52, 69, 71, 72, 76, 79, 80, 82, 83, 86, 87, 88, 91, 92, 94, 96, 102, 103, 105, 107, 108, 111, 119, 126, 130, 135, 136, 137, 138, 139, 142, 143, 145, 152, 153, 156, 159, 163, 169, 171, 174, 184–185
Boston Blues 105
Boston Journal 119
Boston Red Caps *see* Boston Beaneaters
Boston Red Sox *see* Boston Somersets
Boston Red Stockings (NA) 101, 105, 123, 131, 169, 178
Boston Reds (AA) 26, 27, 89, 90, 95, 96, 139, 142, 156, 201
Boston Reds (PL) 26, 27, 28, 91, 95, 119, 126, 138, 142, 156, 220
Boston Reds (UA) 4, 6, 22, 26, 30, 32, 44, 46, 51, 57, 67, 80, 89, 90, 108, 112, 122, 123, 129, 132, 140, 146, 147, 149, 150, 151, 162, 215

Boston Somersets (AL) 68, 112, 129, 222
Boston Unions 112, 122
Boundary Field (Washington) 198, 213
Bowden College 90
Boxford, MA 66
Boyle, Henry 6, 23, 191, 197, 218
Boyle, Jimmy 1
Bradford, MA 22
Bradford, PA 53, 102
Bradley, Al 23–24, 219
Bradley, George 6, 24, 75, 182, 187, 189, 190, 196, 198, 200, 208, 216
Brady, Steve 24, 180, 207
Brady's Bend, PA 23
Braintree, MA 105, 159
Brandywine, PA 86
Braves Field (Boston) 184
Brennan, Jim (Jack) (John Gottleib Doering) 24, 197, 205, 208, 218, 221
Brewster Race Track (New Haven) 181
Bridgeport, CT 20, 40, 132, 146, 150
Bridgeport, OH 169
Briggs, Charlie 24, 215
Brill (Briell) Frank 24, 190
Briody, Charles "Fatty" 25, 189, 190, 192, 197, 198, 205, 216
Bristol, NH 137
Bristol, RI 81
Bristow, VA 144
Brockton, MA 21, 83, 135
Bronx, NY 104
Brooklyn, NY 29, 30, 31, 36, 37, 39, 42, 43, 50, 58, 59 64, 65, 84, 96, 100, 117, 119, 120, 124, 127, 141, 145, 147, 61, 165, 168, 173, 176
Brooklyn Atlantics (NA) 13, 22, 29, 31, 36, 39, 57, 64, 65, 74, 141, 154, 165, 179
Brooklyn Bridegrooms (NL) 5, 15, 26, 27, 29, 30, 31, 35, 43, 44, 49, 60, 66, 69, 81, 108, 112, 123, 128, 132, 135, 142, 152, 155, 162, 165, 185–186
Brooklyn Eagle 77
Brooklyn Eckfords (NA) 39, 87, 127, 179
Brooklyn Gladiators (AA) 51, 73, 104, 127, 129, 132, 201
Brooklyn Grays 162
Brooklyn Trolley Dodgers (AA) 6, 20, 28, 29, 30, 31, 35, 36, 41, 42, 43, 46, 56, 64, 65, 69, 72, 79, 82, 84, 86, 87, 88, 91, 95, 96, 97, 98, 109, 119, 133, 134, 135, 139, 141, 143, 145, 147, 152, 156, 160, 162, 165, 166, 173, 201–202
Brooklyn Wonders (PL) 11, 42, 49, 84, 124, 132, 148, 165, 220
Brookville, NY 87
Brotherhood of Professional Baseball Players 87, 119, 133, 142, 166
Brotherhood Park (Chicago) *see* South Side Park

Brotherhood Park (Cleveland) 221
Brotherhood Park (New York) *see* Polo Grounds
Broughton, Cal 25, 189, 190, 200, 207, 211, 217
Brouthers, Dan 1, 4, 142, 170, 184, 186, 190, 192, 193, 194, 198, 201, 220
Brown, Ed 26, 211, 212
Brown, Jim 26, 193, 208, 214, 218–219
Brown, Joe 26, 187, 200
Brown, Lew 26–27, 184, 187, 190, 196, 206, 215
Brown, Tom 27, 184, 191, 192, 195, 197, 198, 200, 201, 204, 210, 220, 225
Brown University 18, 161
Browning, Louis "Pete" 1, 5, 27, 47, 186, 188, 192, 195, 197, 205–206, 221
Buckskin (Ross County), Ohio 157
Buffalo, NY 30, 34, 52, 53, 59, 65, 88, 93, 101, 102, 125, 126, 145, 155, 170, 174
Buffalo Bisons (NL) 4, 26, 30, 34, 39, 40, 44, 45, 47, 49, 50, 54, 55, 57, 59, 60, 61, 66, 68, 69, 70, 81, 85, 87, 93, 94, 101, 103, 104, 105, 109, 110, 121, 125, 131, 133, 134, 135, 137, 138, 142, 145, 148, 149, 152, 155, 157, 160, 165, 169, 172, 174, 186–187
Buffalo Bisons (PL) 15, 145, 170, 174, 220–221
Buffinton, Charlie 5, 28, 172, 184, 185, 194, 201, 221
Buker, Harry 28, 190
Bullas, Sim 28, 212
Burch, Ernie 28–29, 151, 189, 202
Burdock, John "Black Jack" 29, 179, 180, 181, 184, 185, 186, 191, 202
Burke, James 30, 186, 215
Burkett, Jesse 189
Burns, Dick 6, 30, 190, 197, 216
Burns, Pat 30, 200, 214
Burns, Thomas "Oyster" 30, 186, 193, 200, 202, 220
Burns, Tom 30–31, 187, 195
Bushong, Albert "Doc" 31, 179, 186, 189, 194, 199, 202, 211
Butler, Bill 31, 123, 205
Butler, Frank "Kid" 32, 215
Butte, MT 118, 136

Cady, Charles 32, 189, 215, 216
Cahill, John "Patsy" 32, 191, 197, 204
Caledonia, NY 42
California League 22, 54, 82, 110
Callahan, Ed 32, 215, 216, 218
Callahan, Pat 33, 205, 226
Cambridge, MA 37, 72, 74, 80, 94
Cambridge (MA) Reds 56
Camden, NJ 21, 60, 98, 154, 157
Canada 118, 122, 166, 170
Canadian League 134
Canandaigua, NY 109, 152

Canton, OH 150
Capitol Grounds (Washington) 219
Capitoline Grounds (Brooklyn) 179
Carbondale, PA 74, 95
Carlisle, OH 75
Carlton, Steve 135
Carpenter, Warren "Hick" 33, 188, 197, 199, 203
Carroll, Cliff 33–34, 184, 187, 195, 196, 197, 199
Carroll, Edward "Chick" 34, 219, 224, 226
Carroll, Fred 34, 119, 195, 204, 210, 222, 225
Carroll, John "Scrappy" 34, 186, 203, 218–219
Carroll, Pat 34–35, 214, 217
Carthage, NY 88
Caruthers, Bob 5, 35, 186, 187, 188, 197, 202, 211
Casey, Dan 35–36, 190, 194, 212, 220
Casey, Dennis 35, 36, 200, 220
Caskin (Caskins), Ed 36, 193, 197, 198
Cassidy, John 36, 179, 181, 187, 191, 196, 198, 202
Catonsville, MD 163
Cattanach, John 36–37, 196, 218
Centennial Park *see* Columbia Park (Philadelphia)
Center, IN 14
Central League 98, 101, 137
Charleston, SC 14, 75, 105
Charlestown, MA 57, 113, 150
Charlottesville, VA 65
Chatham, Ontario 99
Chattanooga, TN 40, 54, 102, 108, 118, 150
Chatterton, Jim 37, 216
Chester, PA 91, 149
Cheyenne, WY 95
Chicago, IL 13, 22, 24, 25, 26, 28, 32, 34, 40, 49, 67, 68, 69, 72, 73, 74, 79, 85, 87, 88, 95, 97, 98, 106, 109, 115, 121, 122, 130, 133, 134, 147, 148, 150, 157, 158, 224
Chicago Blues 115
Chicago Browns (UA) 4, 6, 14, 15, 21, 22, 24, 32, 44, 46, 50, 60, 66, 68, 78, 79, 85, 87, 89, 98, 102, 107, 111, 113, 117, 120, 141, 147, 150, 157, 169, 175, 215–216
Chicago City League 72, 74, 97, 106, 147
Chicago Colts *see* Chicago White Stockings (NL)
Chicago Orphans *see* Chicago White Stockings (NL)
Chicago Pirates (PL) 18, 40, 101, 131, 133, 173, 221
Chicago Reserves 147, 171
Chicago White Stockings (NA) 68, 86, 105, 116, 133, 170, 179
Chicago White Stockings (NL) 4, 5, 12, 13, 17, 24, 26, 30, 33, 36, 37, 42, 46, 49, 51, 54, 55, 59, 65, 67, 72, 77, 81, 82, 85, 86, 89, 94, 97, 98, 101, 102, 104, 109, 110, 125, 128, 130, 133, 135, 136, 137, 138, 141, 145, 148, 149, 155, 157, 158, 162, 169, 173, 187–188
Chicopee, MA 163
Chillicothe, IL 99
Cincinnati, OH 22, 33, 47, 59, 60, 62, 88, 92, 94, 113, 115, 116, 140–141, 149, 150, 154, 156, 157, 158, 164, 167, 169
Cincinnati Kellys (AA) 11, 18, 44, 95, 148, 171, 202
Cincinnati Outlaw Reds (UA) 4–6, 16, 24, 25, 30, 38, 45, 47, 62, 75, 82, 83, 92, 94, 95, 110, 113, 114, 116, 130, 136, 143, 147, 161, 216
Cincinnati Red Stockings (AA) 4–6, 16, 21, 33, 39, 43, 52, 65, 69, 83, 91, 94, 95, 97, 103, 104, 106, 111, 113, 114, 116, 121, 122, 128, 133, 135, 136, 140, 148, 149, 153, 154, 155, 161, 162, 167, 169, 170, 174, 175, 202–203
Cincinnati Red Stockings (NA) 2, 16, 49, 177
Cincinnati Red Stockings (NL) 33, 43, 54, 69, 72, 73, 92, 94, 107, 116, 127, 137, 140, 147, 151, 154, 169, 170, 188
Cincinnati Reds (NL) 28, 40, 44, 81, 87, 88, 94, 99, 101, 114, 122, 128, 130, 131, 138, 141, 151, 152, 167, 175, 188–189
Cincinnati Work House 164
Claire County, Ireland 158
Clapp, John 207
Clarke, Fred 195
Clarksboro, NY 142
Clarkson, Arthur "Dad" 37
Clarkson, John 5, 37, 184, 187, 189–190, 199
Clarkson, Walter 37
Clay Grove, IA 33
Clemens, Roger 50
Clements, Jack 37–38, 184, 190, 194, 197, 217
Cleveland, Elmer 38, 193, 204, 216
Cleveland, Grover 38
Cleveland, OH 13, 28, 33, 78, 88, 103, 114, 157, 164
Cleveland Bluebirds (AL) 112, 222
Cleveland Blues (AA) 10, 14, 34, 50, 62, 87, 88, 105, 109, 112, 139, 141, 147, 153, 156, 160, 176, 203–204
Cleveland Blues (NL) 5–6, 13, 24, 25, 29, 31, 32, 47, 50, 52, 54, 58, 59, 61, 66, 72, 73, 74, 75, 81, 82, 85, 88, 94, 95, 97, 109, 118, 121, 122, 124, 128, 134, 136, 137, 139, 141, 142, 145, 149, 151, 152, 155, 157, 161, 162, 166, 169, 171, 176, 189
Cleveland Forest Citys (NA) 18, 87, 138, 159, 169, 179
Cleveland Indians *see* Cleveland Bluebirds (AL)
Cleveland Infants (PL) 14, 24, 27, 100, 139, 154, 156, 158–159, 221
Cleveland Naps *see* Cleveland Bluebirds (AL)
Cleveland Spiders (NL) 13, 14, 37, 62, 80, 111, 122, 125, 154, 155, 156, 158, 164, 169, 176, 189–190
Clifton Heights, PA 42
Cline, John "Monk" 38, 200, 205, 206
Clinton, James "Big Jim" 39, 179, 180, 192, 199, 200, 203
Clinton, IL 14
Clinton, NY 72, 74
club names 178
Coatesville, PA 86, 149
Cohoes, NY 104
"Cold Cases of the Diamond" 53
"Colder Cases of the Diamond" 30
Coleman, John 39, 194, 195, 208
Colgan, William "Ed" 39, 157, 210
College of Opthalmics 170
Collins, Charles "Chub" 39–40, 186, 190, 205
Columbia, OH 153
Columbia Park (Altoona) 214
Columbia Park (Philadelphia) 182, 223
Columbus, GA 36
Columbus, OH 14, 19, 58, 75, 93, 105, 121, 129
Columbus Buckeyes (AA) 4–5, 18, 27, 32, 34, 58, 66, 69, 105, 120, 121, 134, 143, 147, 152, 158, 169, 204
Columbus Solons (AA) 38, 55, 59, 79, 95, 99, 132, 133, 153, 204
Comiskey, Charles 5, 40, 188, 211, 221
Comiskey Park (Chicago) 40
Compton Avenue Baseball Park (St. Louis) 182
Congress Street Grounds (Boston) 184, 201, 220
Conley, Ed 40, 196
Connecticut League 65, 85, 104, 132
Connor, John 40, 184, 186, 206
Connor, Roger 5, 41, 193, 194, 197, 198, 221
Connors, Joe (Joseph C. O'Connor) 41, 214, 216
Conway, Bill 41, 194, 200
Conway, Dick 41
Conway, Jim 41–42, 202, 205, 208
Conway, Pete 41
Cook, Paul 42, 194, 206, 220
Corcoran, Jack 42, 202
Corcoran, Larry 5, 42, 187, 191, 193, 199
Corcoran, Mike 42–43, 187
Cordova, IL 155
Corey, Fred 43, 196, 199, 208
Corkhill, John "Pop" 6, 43–44, 186, 188, 195, 202, 209
Cornell University 130
Corridan, Phil 44, 215
Cortland, NY 135
Coughlin, Ed 44, 186

Covington, KY 115, 154, 224
Covington, LA 123
Cox, Frank 44, 190
Crane, Edward "Cannon-Ball" 44–45, 186, 188, 193, 196, 199, 202, 215, 221
Crane, Sam 45, 186, 190, 193, 195, 197, 199, 207, 216
Cranston, RI 171
Craver, Bill 192
Creamer (Triebel), George 45–46, 193, 197, 199, 210
Creegan, Mark (Marcus Kragen) 46, 219
Cronin, Dan 46, 215, 218, 226
Crosby, George 46, 187
Crosley Field (Cincinnati) 188
Cross (Crause), Clarence 46, 207, 214, 216, 217
Crothers, Doug 46–47, 207, 216, 224
Crotty, Joe 47, 206, 207, 211, 216
Crowley, Bill 47, 182, 184, 186, 189, 208
Crowley, John 47, 147
Cuba 126
Cuban Blues 84
Cudworth, Jim 48, 216
Cuff, John 48, 214
Cullen, John 48, 220
Culver Park (Rochester) 211
Cumberland, MD 34, 50
Curry, Wes 48–49, 210
Cushman, Ed 7, 49, 186, 207.208, 213, 217
Cusick, Andrew "Tony" 49, 194, 220
Cuthbert, Edgar "Ned" 49, 177, 178, 179, 181, 182, 188, 196, 211, 214, 226

Daily (Dailey), Cornelius "Con" 49–50, 184, 186, 187, 191, 196, 217, 220
Daily, Hugh "One Arm" (Harry Criss) 6, 50, 186, 189, 197, 199, 203, 215, 218, 219, 226
Daisey, George 50, 214
Dakota League 168
Dallas, TX 47, 77
Dalrymple, Abner 4, 5, 50–51, 187, 193, 195, 206
Danbury, CT 126
Daniels, Charlie 51, 215
Danvers, MA 36, 72, 84
Danville, IL 125
Darlington, WI 57
Dartmouth Grounds (Boston) 215
Davenport, IA 130, 141
Davis, James "Jumbo" 51, 200, 201, 205, 213, 216
Davis, John Henry Albert "Daisy" 51, 184, 211
Dayton, OH 146
Deagle, Ren 51–52, 203, 212
Dealy, Pat 52, 184, 199, 212, 219
Deasley, Gertrude 52
Deasley, John 52, 216, 219
Deasley, Pat 52, 184, 193, 199, 211

Decker, Harry 53, 190, 194, 195, 199, 205, 216
"Decker Safety Catcher's Mit" 53
Dedham, MA 96
Dee, Jim 53
Defiance, OH 121
DeKalb County, IL 29
Delaware 48
Delaware Club (New York) 110
Denny, Jerry 54, 190, 191, 192, 193, 194, 196, 197, 226
Denver, CO 24, 51, 62, 109, 115, 129, 145, 163, 170
DePangher, Mike 54, 194, 225
Deppens (Kentucky) 139
Derby (England) 28
Des Moines, IA 134, 138, 155, 162
Detroit, MI 12, 14, 20, 21, 39, 77, 79, 91, 104, 139, 133
Detroit Athletic Club 79
Detroit Tigers (AL) 112, 117, 177, 222–223
Detroit Wolverines (NL) 5, 15, 19, 21, 24, 25, 26, 28, 30, 35, 39, 44, 45, 53, 55, 56, 5864, 68, 69, 71, 72, 73, 88, 92, 93, 94, 102, 103, 105, 106, 112, 113, 114, 115, 118, 119, 120, 121, 122, 130, 134, 136, 137, 138, 140, 142, 143, 144, 145, 147, 148, 149, 152, 155, 158, 163, 165, 166, 167, 169, 171, 172, 174, 175, 176, 190–191
Devlin, Jim 192
Dickerson, Louis "Buttercup" 6, 54, 186, 188, 198, 199, 200, 206, 210, 218
Digby, Nova Scotia 152
Dolan, Tom 54–55, 186, 187, 197, 200, 211, 218
Donnelly, James B. 55, 184, 190, 192, 193, 195, 197, 199, 204, 205, 211
Donnelly, James H. 56, 216, 226
Dorgan, Jerry 56, 190, 199, 202, 205
Dorgan, Mike 5, 56, 190, 193, 196, 197, 199, 212
Dorsey, Jerry 56, 214
Dougherty, Charlie 56–57, 214
Dover, NH 37
Dow, Clarence 57, 215
Doyle, Cornelius "Conny" 57, 194, 210
Doyle, John 57, 207
Dracot, MA 150
Drake, Lyman 57, 213
Drew, Dave 57, 217, 219
Driscoll, Denny 57
Driscoll, John "Denny" 57, 186, 206, 210
Dubuque, IA 40, 146
Duck Lake, MI 112
Dudley, MA 163
Duffy, Hugh 108
Dugan, Bill 57–58, 210, 216
Dugan, Ed 57–58, 210
Duluth, MN 10, 21
Dundas, Ontario 40
Dundas (Ontario) Standards 39

Dundon, Ed 58, 204
Dunlap, Fred 6, 58–59, 189, 190, 195, 197, 214, 218, 221
Dunn, Steve 59, 218–219
Dwight, Albert Ward 58, 216

Eagle, AK 66
Eagle River, WI 40, 79
Earlville, IL 20
East End Grounds (Cincinnati) 202
East Greenwich, RI 171
East Liverpool, OH 168
East Moline, IL 83
East Orange, NJ 26, 126
East St. Louis, IL 39, 86, 157, 165, 224
East Setauket, NY 43
Easterday, Henry 59, 204, 205, 206, 208, 217
Eastern League 18, 20, 29, 30, 35, 36, 41, 42, 49, 57, 58, 64, 70, 79, 97, 98, 99, 102, 110, 123, 124, 130, 131, 137, 148, 152, 154, 174, 175, 201, 210, 212, 219
Eastern Michigan Asylum (Pontiac), 165
Eastern Park (Brooklyn) 186, 220
Easton, PA 109, 112
Eau Claire, WI 103, 149
Ebbets Field (Brooklyn) 186
Eckford, Henry 179
Eclipse Park (Louisville) 192, 205
Economy, PA 103
Eden, Charlie 59, 187, 189, 210
Edinburg, TX 106
Eggler, Dave 59, 178, 181, 182, 186, 187, 194, 200
Elizabeth, NJ 21
Elizabeth Resolutes (NA) 39, 64, 180
Ellick, Joe 60, 183, 193, 199, 214, 215, 216, 218
Elmira, NY 142
Elmwood Park, IL 116
El Paso, TX 33, 57
Ely, Fred "Bones" 60, 186, 195, 197, 206, 212, 223
Elyria, OH 75
Elysian Fields (New York) 177
Empire State League 62
Emslie, Bob 6, 60–61, 200, 208
England 27, 28, 101, 106
Englewood, NJ 68
English League 28
Enterprise Club (Brooklyn) 65, 177
Erie, PA 49, 66, 99
Esterbrook, Thomas "Dude" 5, 61, 186, 189, 191, 193, 201, 206, 207–208
Evans, Uriah "Bloody Jake" 61, 189, 198, 199, 200
Evanston, IL 29
Evansville, WI 25, 103
Everett, MA 175
Evers, Johnny 61, 133
Evers, Tom 6, 61–62, 200, 219

Ewing, John "Long John" 62, 193, 206, 211, 216, 219, 221
Ewing, William "Buck" 5, 52, 62, 188, 189–190, 193, 198, 221
Exposition Park (Kansas City) 205
Exposition Park (Pittsburgh) 195, 209, 218, 222

Faatz, Jay 62, 190, 203, 210, 221
Fairfield, ME 144
Falch, Anton 63, 217
Fall River, MA 28, 49, 65, 77, 80, 106, 110, 129, 162, 225
Falls, PA 159
Fallston, MD 147
"Fan" 158
Farley, Lawrence "Tom" 63, 213
Farnham, MA 48
Farrar, Sid 63, 194, 221
Farrell, Jack 63–64, 194, 196, 197, 200
Farrell, Joe 64, 190, 200
Farrow, Jack 64, 180, 199, 202
Fayetteville, NY 79
Fennelly, Frank 65, 201, 203, 208, 213
Fenway Park (Boston) 222
Ferguson, Bob 65, 178, 179, 180, 181, 187, 191, 194, 198, 207, 226
Ferguson, Charlie 1, 5, 65, 194
Field, Jim 66, 198, 200, 204, 210, 211
Firth, John "Ted" 66, 210
Fisher (Fish), Charles 66, 215, 216
Fisher, George 66, 189, 220
Fisher, J. 66, 186, 217
Fitchburg, MA 136, 171
Flint, Frank "Silver" 67, 70, 83, 183, 187, 191
Flushing, NY 24
Flynn, Joe 67, 215, 217
Flynn, John 67
Fogarty, Jim 67–68, 70, 194, 221, 225
Foley, Will 68, 179, 188, 190, 193, 215
Fonthill, Ontario 152
Forbes Field (Pittsburgh) 195
Force, David "Wee Davy" 68, 178, 179, 180, 181, 183, 186, 194, 196, 197, 226
Ford, Ed 68, 210
Foreman, Brownie
Foreman, Frank 68, 184, 188, 193, 198, 200, 213–214, 215, 216, 222
Forepaugh Park (Philadelphia) 209, 221
Forest Citys (Cleveland) 151
Forster, Tom 68–69, 190, 207–208, 210
Ft. Edward, NY 121
Fort Smith, AR 10,
Fort Street Grounds 218
Fort Wayne, IN 115, 117, 134
Fort Wayne Kekiongas (NA) 6, 107, 180
Foster, Elmer 69, 208, 224
Foster, Robert 69, 217, 224
Foutz, Dave 5, 69, 186, 202, 212

Fox, John 69, 184, 197, 200, 210
Franklins (Chicago) 72
Frederick, MD 128
Freeport, IL 83
Fresno, CA 93
Fries, Pete 69, 204, 205
Fulmer, Charles "Chick" 69–70, 181, 182, 186, 192, 203, 211, 219
Fulmer, Chris 70, 200
Fulmer, Washington 70
Fusselback (Fusselbach), Eddie 70, 206, 208, 211, 214

Gagus (Geggus), Charlie 70, 219, 225
Gallagher, Bill 70, 194, 200, 217
Galveston, TX 96
Galvin, James "Pud" 4, 70–71, 182, 186, 195, 197, 210, 222
Galvin, Lou 71, 218–219
Ganzel, Charlie 71–72, 184, 190, 194, 219
Ganzel, Foster "Babe" 72
Ganzel, John 72
Garden Cities (Chicago) 106
Garden City, NY 101
Gardner, Alex 72, 213
Gardner, Frank W. "Gid" 72, 189, 191, 194, 198, 199, 200, 214, 215, 218
Gastfield, Ed 72, 187, 190
Geer, George H. 73
Geer, William H. "Billy" 72–73, 181, 188, 199, 202, 206, 217, 226
Geis (Geiss), Bill 73, 190
Geis, Emil 73
Gerard County, KY 114
Gerhardt, Joe 73, 180, 181, 183, 188, 190, 192, 193, 201, 206, 208, 211
"German Battery, " 72
Germany 74, 115, 149, 150
Getzein, Charles "Pretzels" 5, 72, 73–74, 184, 190, 191, 197, 225
Gig Harbor, WA 113
Gillen, Tom 74, 190, 217
Gillespie, Pete 74, 193, 198
Gilligan, Barney 74–75, 179, 189, 190, 196, 199
Gilman, Pit 75, 189
Girard College 97, 117
Gladman (Gladmon), James "Buck" 75, 194, 199, 213
Glasscock, Jack 75–76, 189, 191, 192, 193, 195, 197, 198, 216
Gleason, Bill 76, 206, 208, 211–212, 218
Gleason, Jack 76, 196, 197, 206, 208, 212
Glendale, CA 145, 155
Glenn, Edward "Mouse" 76–77, 184, 205, 210
Gloucester, NJ 4, 50
Goldsby, Walt 77, 199, 200, 210, 212, 213
Goldsmith, Fred 77, 181, 187, 198, 200
Gore, George 5, 77–78, 187, 193, 197, 221
Gorman, Jack 78, 210, 212, 216

Gorman, Tom 78, 216
Grady, John 78, 214
Grafton, MA 33
Graham, Bernie 78, 214, 215
Grand Avenue Grounds see Sportsman's Park
Grand Duchess see Kekionga Base-Ball Grounds
Grand Rapids, MI 35, 44, 92, 93
Gray, Jim 78
Gray, Reddy 78
Great Chicago Fire 179
Great Falls, MT 39
Green, Jim 78, 219
Green Valley, CA
Greenfield, OH 157
Greenhood and Moran (Oakland, CA) 22
Greenwood, Bill 78, 200, 202, 204, 208, 211
Griffin, Thomas 79, 217
Griffin, Tobias "Sandy" 79, 193, 197, 211, 213–214
Griffith, Clark 133
Griffith Stadium (Washington) 223
Gross, Emil 79, 194, 196, 215, 225
Guelph, Ontario 162
Guiney, Ben 79, 190
Gunning, Tom 79–80, 91, 184, 194, 208
Gunson, Joe 80, 184, 190, 197, 205, 219
Guthrie, OK 29

Hackett, Mortimer "Mertie" 80, 184, 191, 192
Hackett, Walter 80–81, 184, 215
Hagan, Art 81, 186, 194
Hall, George 192
Halpin, Jim 81, 190, 199, 219, 225
Hamill, John 81, 213
Hamilton, OH 118
Hamilton, Ontario 93, 104, 106, 160, 167
Hamilton (Ontario) Clippers 40, 119, 134
Hancock County, IN 44
Hankinson, Frank 81, 187, 189, 193, 198, 205, 207–208
Hanlon, Edward "Ned" 5, 81, 184, 186, 189, 190, 195, 222
Hanna, John 82, 210, 213
Harbidge (Harbridge), Bill 82, 180, 187, 191, 194, 198, 216
Hardie, Lou 82, 184, 187, 194, 200
Harkins, John "Pa" 82–83, 189, 200, 202
Harris, Frank 83, 214
Harrisburg, PA 88, 109, 175
Hartford, CT 12, 24, 44, 51, 56, 85, 90, 102, 105, 108, 122, 124, 141, 159
Hartford Ball Club Grounds (Hartford) 180
Hartford Dark Blues (NA) 22, 24, 29, 65, 82, 92, 105, 141, 149, 176) 180
Hartford Dark Blues (NL) 22, 29,

36, 65, 82, 87, 99, 141, 155, 161, 176) 191
Harvard University 23
Hastings, MI 15
Hastings, NE 141
Hautz, Charlie 83, 183, 210
Havana, Cuba 45
Haverhill, MA 22, 32, 84, 163, 175
Haverly Club (San Francisco) 115
Hawes, Bill 83, 185, 216
Hawkes, Thorny 83–84, 198, 213
Hayes, John "Jackie" 84, 199, 200, 202, 210, 220
Haymakers' Grounds (Lansingburgh) 183
Hecker, Guy 5, 84, 195, 206
Henderson, James "Hardie" 6, 84–85, 194, 195, 200, 202
Hengle, Emery "Moxie" 85, 186, 215, 218–219
Henry, John 12, 85, 189, 193, 199, 200
Hibbard, John 85, 187
Hickman, Ernie 85–86, 216
Hilltop Park (New York) 223
Hilsey, Charlie 86, 195, 208
Hines, Mike 80, 86, 185, 196, 202
Hines, Paul 5, 86, 179, 183, 185, 187, 191, 195, 196, 199, 213–214
Hoboken, NJ 48
Hodnett, Charlie 86, 212, 218
Hogan, Eddie 87, 217
Hogan, Mortimer "Ed" 87, 203, 208
Holbert, Bill 87, 141, 192, 193, 197, 198, 202, 207–208
Holdsworth, James "Long Jim" 87, 179, 181, 182, 191, 194, 198, 205
"The Hole" see Association Park
Hollywood, CA 85
Holy Cross, College of 23, 40, 79, 108, 111
Holyoke, MA 17, 30, 68, 74, 119, 124, 163, 168
Honesdale, PA 30
Hoover, William "Buster" 6, 87, 188, 195, 200, 217
Horan, Patrick "John" 87, 215
Hornung, Joe 87–88, 185, 186, 193, 200
"Hot Cold Cases" 119
Hotaling, Pete 88, 185, 188, 189, 199, 200, 203
Houck, Sargent "Sadie" 88, 185, 190, 196, 199, 200, 208
Householder, Charles F. 88, 200, 202
Householder, Charles W. 89, 215, 218
Houston, TX 31, 54
Howard Avenue Grounds (New Haven) 181
Howard's Beach, NY
Hudson, MA 15, 143
Hughes, Bill 89, 208, 219, 226
Humphreys, John 89, 193, 212

Hunter, Bill 89, 206
Hunter, George 89
Huntington Avenue Baseball Grounds (Boston) 222
Huntington Grounds (Philadelphia) 194
Hutchison, Bill 89, 187, 197, 216
Hyattsville, MD 86
Hyde Park, IL 85, 139
Hyde Park, MA 139

Idaho, Springs, CO 10
Illinois State Penitentiary (Joliet), 83
Indianapolis, IN 11, 35, 44, 83, 103, 108, 113, 164, 166, 167
Indianapolis Hoosiers (AA) 4, 6, 7, 14, 17, 22, 31, 33, 39, 53, 55, 56, 69, 87, 94, 95, 102, 103, 104, 108, 112, 115, 118, 119, 120, 123, 132, 134, 141, 143, 153, 162, 163, 166, 167, 204–205
Indianapolis Hoosiers (NL) 11, 13, 18, 23, 27, 32, 42, 49, 54, 61, 67, 72, 73, 76, 80, 86, 91, 97, 109, 118, 125, 127, 128, 138, 147, 148, 149, 166, 172, 173, 191–192
"Infinite ERA Club" 44
International League 44, 59, 61, 80, 81, 83, 88, 99, 104, 120, 124, 134, 143, 159, 168, 212
Interstate Association 60, 65, 82, 96, 201
Interstate League 11, 23, 111
Ireland 50, 104, 111, 113, 122
Ironton, OH 176
Irwin, Art 89–90, 195, 196, 199, 201, 220
Irwin, John 90, 199, 201, 206, 208, 215
Italian-American Sports Hall of Fame 54
Ithaca, NY 109
Ixonia, WI 120

Jackson, Stonewall 19
Jackson, MI 163
Jacksonville, FL 161
Jamestown, NY 52, 146
Janesville, WI 25, 103, 121
Jaxons (Jackson, MI) 163
Jefferson, MT 136
Jefferson Street Grounds (Philadelphia) 181, 182, 194, 208
Jensen, FL 148
Jersey City, NJ 24, 30, 42, 47, 87, 98, 122, 128, 137, 141
Johnson, Bill 90–91, 184, 191, 200, 217
Johnston, Dick 58, 91, 185, 211, 220, 221
Johnstown, PA 38
Jones, Bill 91, 200, 217
Jones, Charles F. 91–92, 202
Jones, Charles W. (Benjamin Wesley Rippy) 92, 135, 180, 185, 187, 188, 203, 205, 208
Jones, Frank 92, 190
Jones, Henry 92, 190, 226

Jones, Uriah "Jack" or "Ryerson" 92–93, 206, 215
Joy, Aloysius "Pop" 93, 219

Kalamazoo, MI 86
Kalbfus, Charlie 93, 219
Kankakee, IL 32
Kansas City, KS 60, 106
Kansas City, MO 52, 58, 60, 63, 78, 89, 97, 103, 106, 129, 135, 143, 148, 169
Kansas City Cowboys (AA) 13, 17, 24, 25, 38, 41, 51, 59, 76, 80, 81, 92, 97, 106, 111, 134, 135, 145, 158, 166, 205
Kansas City Cowboys (NL) 15, 18, 25, 55, 80, 103, 113, 114, 125, 139, 143, 145, 166, 172, 192
Kansas City Cowboys (UA) 4, 7, 10, 14, 16, 18, 21, 22, 32, 37, 41, 46, 48, 51, 52, 52, 56, 57, 59, 60, 66, 68, 78, 85, 89, 97, 98, 103, 113, 128, 135, 147, 148, 149, 156, 157, 158, 160, 163, 164, 169, 170, 173, 175, 216–217
Kappel, Henry "Heinie" 93
Kappel, Joe 93, 195, 208
Kearns, Tom 93, 186, 190
Keefe, Tim 5, 45, 52, 93–94, 141, 193, 195, 198, 207–208, 221
Keenan, Jim 94, 181, 186, 188, 203, 204–205, 210
Kekionga Base-Ball Grounds (Ft. Wayne) 180
Kelly, John F. 94, 215, 219
Kelly, John O. "Kick" 94
Kelly, Michael "King" 1, 5, 94–95, 185, 186, 187, 188, 193, 201, 202, 220
Kemmler, Rudy (Rudolph Kemler) 95, 189, 196, 203, 204, 210, 212
Kennebunkport, ME 12
Kennedy, Ed 95, 202, 215
Kennedy, Edward 95, 207–208
Kent, Ed 95, 212
Kent, OH 106
Kentucky Insane Asylum 140
Keokuk Westerns (NA) 92, 180
Kerins, John 95–96, 200, 204–205, 212
Keystone Park (Philadelphia) 217
Kienzle, Bill 96, 208, 217
Kiley, John 96, 185, 213
Kimber, Sam 96–97, 196, 202
King, Sam 97, 213
Kingston, NY 91
Kingston, OH 121
Kingston, PA 163
Kinzie, Walt 97, 187, 190, 212, 226
Kirby, John 97, 197, 203, 205, 217
Knickerbocker Base Ball Club (New York) 177
Knight, Joe 97, 188, 194
Knight, Lon (Alonzo Letti) 97, 181, 190, 194, 196, 199, 208
Knowles, Jimmy 97–98, 193, 199, 202, 208, 210, 211
Koons, Harry 98, 214, 215
Koufax, Sandy 6

Kreeger, Frank 98, 217
Krehmeyer, Charles 98, 197, 206, 212
Krieg, Bill 98–99, 187, 199, 202, 215, 218
Kuehne (Knelme), Bill 99, 188, 192, 195, 197, 204, 206, 210, 222, 226

Ladies Day 136
Lafayette, IN 128
Lafayette College 21
Lake Front Park (Chicago) *see* White Stocking Park (Chicago)
Lake View Brown Stockings 28
Lakeland, KY 28
Lancaster, PA 52
Lane, George "Chappy" 99, 210, 212
Lanesville, IN 141
Lansingburg, NY 23, 25
Laporte, OH 75
Larkin, Frank "Terry" 99–100, 187, 191, 194, 198, 207, 210–211, 219
Larkin, Henry "Ted" 100, 198, 208, 209, 221
L'Assumption College 79
Latham, Arlie 100–101, 186, 188, 197, 198, 211–212, 221
Latham, George "Juice" 101, 178, 181, 192, 193, 206, 208
Lauer, John "Chuck" 101, 187, 195, 210
Laurel, MD
Lavin, Johnny 101–102, 212
Lavinia, OH 19
Lawlor, Mike 102, 198, 219
Lawrence, MA 47, 160, 163
Leadville, CO 69
Leadville (CO) Blues 69, 133
League Alliance 191, 192
League Park (Cincinnati) 188, 202
League Park (Cleveland) 189, 203, 222
League Park (Toledo) 212
Leary, Jack 102, 185, 190, 200, 206, 210, 214, 215
Lebanon, PA 39, 79
Lebanon Valley College 116
Lee, Tom 102, 187, 214
Lehane, James 102, 214
Lehane, Mike 102
Lehigh University 82
Le Mars, IA 22
Levis, Charlie 102, 200, 205, 214, 219
Lewis, Fred 102–103, 185, 195, 197, 203, 211–212, 218
Lewiston, ME 141
Lexington, KY 59
Library of Congress 2
Lillie, Jim 103, 186, 192
Limerick, Ireland 49
Lincoln, Abraham 225
Lincoln, NE 117, 145
Linn, OR 33
Little Rock, AR 170, 176
Littlestown, PA 130
Live Oaks (Lynn, MA) 97

Liverpool, England 81
Lock Haven, PA 26, 135
Locke, Marshall 103, 205
Lockport, IL 53
Lockwood, Milo 103, 219
London, Ontario 59, 120, 121, 140, 162
Long Island City, NY 24
Longview Insane Asylum (Cincinnati), 16, 140
Los Angeles, CA 20, 32, 85, 138, 149, 155
Loughran, Thomas 103, 193
Louisiana, MO 133
Louisville, KY 28, 33, 38, 60, 114, 133, 140, 141, 171, 225
Louisville Colonels (NL) 18, 26, 27, 28, 54, 76, 99, 117, 133, 135, 142, 148, 167, 168, 176, 192
Louisville Eclipse (AA) 4, 5, 11, 26, 27, 38, 40, 42, 47, 51, 54, 57, 59, 60, 61, 62, 70, 72, 73, 76, 84, 89, 90, 92, 95, 98, 99, 101, 102, 103, 106, 114, 115, 117, 122, 124, 134, 137, 139, 145, 147, 152, 155, 156, 157, 158, 161, 164, 167, 168, 169, 171, 174, 205–206
Louisville Grays (NL) 39, 47, 69, 73, 87, 101, 149, 153, 192
Louisville Slugger bat 27
Lowe, Dick 103, 190
Lowell, MA 42, 48, 57 66, 78, 83, 95, 104, 113, 119, 145, 151, 171, 225
Lucas, Henry 4, 218
Ludlow, MA 147
Luff, Henry 103–104, 190, 203, 206, 217
Lynch, Jack 5, 104, 141, 186, 201, 207–208
Lynch, Thomas J. 104, 195, 220
Lynch, Thomas S. 104, 187
Lynhurst, Ontario 97
Lynn, MA 36, 37, 42, 51, 56, 74, 132, 139, 160
Lyons, Denny 209
Lyons, IA 46
Lyons, NY 62

MacArthur, Malcolm "Mac" 104, 205, 225
Mack, Connie 223
Macon, GA 36, 66, 74, 117, 127
Macullar, Jimmy 104, 197–198, 200, 203
Madison, MT 118
Madison, WI 102
Madison County, IL 28
Malatzky, Richard 124, 128
Malden, MA 22
Malone, Fergy 105, 179, 181, 182, 194, 217, 226
Manchester, NH 15, 37, 163, 165
Manhattan, NY 32, 88, 91, 95, 137, 141, 163
Manhattan College 72, 103
Manistee, MI 92
Manlove, Charlie 105, 193, 214
Mann, Fred 105, 199, 203, 204, 208, 209, 210

Manning, Jack 105, 178, 179, 185, 188, 195, 200
Manning, Jim 105–106, 185, 187, 190, 205, 223
Manning, Tim 106, 196, 200, 225
Mansell, John 106
Mansell, Mike 106, 188, 197–198, 203, 208, 210, 211
Mansell, Tom 106, 190, 198, 204, 207, 212
Mansfield, Joseph 181
Mansfield Club Grounds (Middletown) 181
Mansfield, OH 169
Mantle, Mickey 155
Marietta, OH 92, 176
Marion, LA 77
Marlborough, NH 162
Marshall, IL 125
Marshalltown, IA 13, 158
Marysville, MI 166
Maryville, MO 89
Maskrey, Leech 106, 203, 206
Mason, Charles 209
Massachusetts Insane Asylum 111
Massilion State Hospital 121
Mathews, Bobby 6, 107, 129, 180, 181, 185, 188, 194, 196, 208, 209
Mathewson, Christy 152
Matteson, Clifford Virgil "C.V." 107, 218
Matthias, Steve 107–108, 215
Maul, Al 108, 184, 186, 193, 195, 198, 217, 222, 226
Maysville, KY 115
McCarthy, Tommy 6, 108, 185, 186, 195, 211–212, 215
McCauley, Al 108, 195, 205, 213–214
McCauley, Jim 109, 187, 202, 212
McClellan, Bill 109, 187, 195, 196, 202, 204
McCloskey, Bill 109, 220
McCormick, James "Jerry" 109, 200, 217, 219
McCormick, Jim 5–6, 109–110, 157, 187, 189, 191, 195, 196, 216, 225
McDonald, Jim 110, 187, 210, 219
McElroy, Jim 70, 110, 195, 220, 225
McFarland, Chris 110–111, 214
McGarr, James "Chippy" 111, 185, 189–190, 200, 205, 208, 209, 212, 215
McGinnis, George "Jumbo" 111, 200, 203, 212
McGraw, John 77, 81, 101, 184
McGuinness, John 111, 194, 198, 218
McGuire, James "Deacon" 111–112, 130, 177, 186, 190, 195, 198, 204, 211, 212, 213–214, 222–223
McKee, Frank 112, 219
McKeesport, PA 150
McKeever, Jim 112, 215
McKenna, Ed 112, 182, 196, 219
McKenna, F. 112
McKenna, Patrick 112

McKeon, Larry 6, 112–113, 192, 203, 204–205, 226
McKinnon, Alex 113, 193, 195, 197
McLaughlin, Bernard "Barney" 113, 195, 212, 216–217
McLaughlin, Frank 113, 199, 210, 215, 216, 217
McLaughlin, James (or William) 113, 219
McLaughlin, Jim 114, 200
McLaughlin, Tom 114, 206, 208, 214
McPhee, John "Bid" 6, 114, 188, 203
McQuery, William "Mox" 114–115, 190, 192, 212, 213–214, 216
McRemer 115, 219
McSorley, John "Trick" 115, 183, 196, 212
Medford, MA 56
Meegan, Pete 115, 210, 210–211
Meinke, Bob 115
Meinke, Frank 115, 190
Meister, John B. "George" 115, 212, 225
Melrose, MA 63
Memphis, TN 11, 35, 38, 39, 47, 62, 78, 93, 102, 110, 147, 148, 150, 153, 157, 158, 161
Mencken, H.L. 163
Mercer, NJ 160
Mercer, PA 106
Merchantville, NJ 21
Meridian, MS 10
Merkle, Fred 61, 130
Merrill, Ed 115–116, 134, 199, 205, 206
Messer Street Grounds (Providence) 196
Meyerle, Levi 116, 179, 182, 188, 194, 218, 226
Meyers, Lou 116, 216
Middleboro, MA 48
Middletown, CT 56, 73
Middletown Mansfields (NA) 123, 131, 181
"Mighty Casey" 1, 32, 36
Miller, Ed 116
Miller, George 116, 188, 203
Miller, George "Doggie" 116–117, 192, 195, 197, 210
Miller, Joe 117, 206, 212
Miller, Joseph "Cyclone" 117, 149, 195, 196, 208, 215
Milligan, John "Jocko" 117, 184, 193, 198, 208, 209, 212, 221
Milton, NY 170
Milwaukee, WI 12, 57, 63, 69, 102, 121, 125, 152, 157, 159, 162, 225
Milwaukee Base-Ball Grounds (Milwaukee) 192
Milwaukee Brewers (AA) 10, 51, 206
Milwaukee Cream Citys (NL) 21, 45, 51, 60, 68, 87, 133, 167, 192–193
Milwaukee Cream Citys (UA) 6–7, 15, 20, 21, 25, 47, 63, 79, 87, 101, 102, 103, 121, 125, 135, 149, 217

Milwaukee Reserves 120
Milwaukee Whites 63
Minneapolis, MN 46, 56, 85, 99, 112, 117, 121, 123, 137, 168
Mississippi River 10
Missouri Ozarks 14
Mitchellville, MD 108
Mobile, AL 78
Moffett, James 118
Moffett, Joe 118, 212
Moffett, Sam 118, 189, 192
Mohawk, NY 88
Monmouth, NJ 32
Monroe, Frank 118, 205
Montana 46
Montreal, Quebec 131, 146
Monumental Park (Baltimore) 214
Moore, Henry S. "Harry" 6, 118, 219
Moore, Jerrie 118–119, 189, 190, 214
Morgan, Bill (Henry William Morgan) 119, 193, 210, 211, 213, 214
Moriarity, Gene 119, 185, 190, 197
Morrill, John "Honest John" 119, 185, 199, 220
Morris, Ed "Cannon-Ball" 5, 70, 120, 195, 204, 210, 222
Morris, James 120, 214
Morris, Peter (player) 4, 120, 219
Morris, Peter (researcher) 4, 15, 128
Morrison, Jon 120–121, 208
Morrissey, John 121
Morrissey, Tom 121, 217
mortality statistics 226, 227
Morton, Charlie 121, 190, 210, 212, 213
Morton, William "Sparrow" 121, 195
Mt. Vernon, OH 13
Mountain, Frank 121, 190, 198, 199, 204, 208, 210
Mountain Valley Springs, AR 173
Mountjoy, Bill 121, 200, 203
Moynahan, Mike 121–122, 187, 189, 190, 208
Muldoon, Mike 122, 189, 200
Muldoons (Cincinnati) 156
Mullane, Tony 6, 122, 164, 184, 188, 190, 203, 206, 211–212
Mulligan, John 122, 219
Mullin, Henry 122–123, 213, 215
Mulvey, Joe 123, 186, 194–195, 196, 198, 209, 221
Munce, John 123, 220
Mundinger, George 31, 123
Murnane, Tim 123, 181, 182, 185, 196, 215
Murphy, Cornelius "Con" 123–124, 195, 201, 220
Murphy, Francis "Tony" 124, 207–208
Murphy, John 124, 214, 220
Murphy, William "Gentle Willie" 124, 189, 213
Murray, Jeremiah "Miah" 90, 124–125, 196, 199, 206, 214
Muskegon, MI 57
Mutual (New York) 68

Myers, Al 125, 192, 195, 199, 217
Myers, George 125–126, 187, 192, 197
Myers, Henry 126, 196, 200, 220

Napa, CA 110
Napa State Hospital, CA 60
Nash, Billy 58, 91, 126, 185, 195, 211, 220
Nashua, NH 40, 168
Nashville, TN 39, 58, 76, 108, 121, 149, 158
Natchez, MS 47
National Association Grounds (Cleveland) 179
National Association of Base Ball Players 2, 177
National Association of Professional Base Ball Players (NA) 2, 3, 177–183
National Baseball Hall of Fame 4, 5, 6, 13, 26, 37, 40, 41, 62, 81, 93, 94, 108, 114, 123, 132, 139, 143, 165, 178, 184, 188, 189, 193
National Grounds (Washington) 183
National League (NL): alignment (1903–1953) 177; "Black List" 49, 54, 79, 88, 92, 94, 128; cities in 1884 3; clubs and players 183–199; 1884 pennant race 4–5; umpires 60, 61, 83, 85, 88, 90, 94, 97, 104, 110, 111, 125, 129–130, 134, 136, 154, 157, 160, 172, 176
nationality 225
Nationals (Washington D.C.) 163
Naugatuck, CT 123
Nava, Vincent "Sandy" (Irwin Sandy) 54, 126–127, 196, 200
Navin Field (Detroit) 222
Neagle, Jack 6, 126, 188, 195, 200, 210
Needles, CA 110
Negro League 165
Nelson, Bill 126, 210
Nelson, John "Candy" 127, 179, 181, 183, 191, 193, 198, 199, 201, 207–208
New Bedford, MA 86, 156
New Britain, CT 44
New Brunswick, Canada 134
New Brunswick, NJ 82
New Castle, PA 21, 138
New England League 22, 32, 37, 48, 63, 84, 95, 96, 104, 108, 123–124, 139, 145, 146, 171
New Haven, CT 54, 55, 63, 89, 94, 102, 147, 154
New Haven Elm Citys (NA) 36, 72, 77, 94, 101, 103, 181
New London, CT 117
New Orleans, LA 31, 47, 62, 96, 123, 132, 136, 153, 175
New Rochelle, NY 111
New York Base Ball Club 177
New York City 19, 20, 32, 33, 39, 45, 51, 52, 54, 55, 57, 63, 68, 69, 73, 77, 81, 82, 87, 91, 92, 95, 101, 103, 111, 112, 124, 125, 134, 135,

137, 141, 142, 145, 154, 157, 161, 162, 163, 166, 172, 175, 176
New York Evening Journal 45
New York Giants (NL) *see* New York Gothams
New York Giants (PL) 41, 44, 58, 62, 77, 91, 93, 130, 131, 142, 151, 171, 221
New York Gothams (NL) 4, 5, 17, 18, 19, 20, 23, 26, 30, 36, 38, 40, 41, 42, 44, 45, 52, 54, 55, 56, 61, 62, 68, 73, 74, 76, 77, 79, 81, 85, 88, 89, 90, 93, 95, 98, 101, 103, 105, 108 113, 117, 125, 127, 130, 131, 132, 133, 134, 142, 151, 163, 165, 168, 171, 172, 193–194
New York Highlanders (AL) 112, 223
New York Metropolitans (AA) 3, 4, 19, 20, 24, 25, 29, 45, 46, 47, 49, 52, 57, 61, 63, 68, 73, 81, 86, 87, 88, 92, 93, 95, 98, 104, 114, 120, 124, 127, 129, 132, 134, 139, 141, 144–145, 163, 172, 206–208
New York Mutuals (NA) 29, 59, 65, 69, 72, 73, 87, 107, 127, 141, 149, 154, 181
New York Mutuals (NL) 3, 59, 68, 87, 99, 107, 111, 154, 194
New York-Pennsylvania League 146
New York State League 27, 87
New York World 87
New York Yankees *see* New York Highlanders
Newark, NJ 12, 22, 24, 36, 42, 63, 64, 66, 70, 81, 96, 137, 164
Newburyport, MA 171
Newington Park (Baltimore) 178, 180, 200
Newport, KY 116, 148, 224
Newton, MA 80
Niagara Falls, NY 175
Nichols, Al 192
Nicol, Hugh 127–128, 187, 188, 203, 211–212
Nicolet Park (Minneapolis) 168
Niles, CA 155
Noftsker, George 128, 214
Nogales, AZ 33
Nolan, Edward "The Only" 128, 189, 191, 195, 210, 220
Norfolk, VA 47, 108, 110
Norristown, PA 38
North Carolina League 146
Northern League 168
Northwestern League 15, 17, 21, 25, 40, 44, 47, 59, 63, 72, 92, 95, 97, 99, 103, 105, 117, 121, 123, 125, 134, 135, 140, 162, 164, 212, 217, 218
Northwestern University 158
Norwich, CT 54
Norwood, KY 116
Norwood, MA 96
Notre Dame University 13
Nova Scotia, Canada 147
Nusz, Emory 128, 224
Nusz, William 128, 219, 224

Oak Park, IL 106
Oakdale Park (Philadelphia) 208
Oakland, CA 33, 46, 66, 82, 126
Oberbeck, Henry 128, 210, 212, 214, 217
Oberlin College 164, 165
O'Brien, Billy 128–129, 199, 201, 217, 219
O'Brien, Jack (John K. Bryne) 129, 200, 202, 208
O'Brien, John 129, 214
O'Brien, Tom 129, 199, 200, 208, 211, 215
Ocala, FL 33
O'Day, Hank 70, 129–130, 193, 199, 212, 221
O'Donnell, John 130, 218
Ohio-Michigan League 163
Ohio-Pennsylvania League 121
Ohio School for the Deaf 58
Ohio State League 176
Oil City, PA 84
Old Gold Club (Saginaw, MI) 14, 37, 89
Old Judge baseball cards 2, 10
O'Leary, Dan 130, 185, 190, 196, 199, 216
Olin, Frank 130–131, 190, 212, 213, 219
Olin-Mathison Chemical Company 131
Olympic Club (Washington, DC) 68
Olympic Grounds (Washington) 183
Olympic Park (Buffalo) 186, 220
Omaha, NE 12, 34, 39, 78, 93, 95, 152, 157
O'Neill, James "Tip" 131, 189, 193, 207, 211–212, 221
Orinco, NY 15
Oriole Park (Baltimore) 184, 200, 222
O'Rourke, James "Orator" 4, 131–132, 178, 181, 185, 186–187, 193, 196, 198, 221
Orr, Dave 5, 132, 193, 202, 204, 207–208, 220
Oshkosh, WI 72, 147
Oswego, NY 86, 96, 150
Ottawa, IL 141
Our Home Colony 164
Overbrook, NJ 63
Oxley, Henry 132, 193, 207–208
Oyster Bay, NY 87
Ozone Park, NY 163

Pacific Coast League 27
Painesville, OH 11
Palace Park of America (St. Louis) 197, 218
Palisades Park, NJ 81
Palmyra, NY 159
Pana, IL 10
Parkesburg, PA 44
Parkville, MO 143
Paterson, NJ 41, 94, 110, 128, 137, 160
Pattison, George 132, 218

Paw Paw, IL 29
Pawtucket, RI 18, 164
Peabody, MA 97
Peak, Elias 132, 215, 218
Peck and Snyder baseball cards 2
Peltz, John 31, 123, 132, 200, 201, 204–205, 212, 213
Pennsauken, NJ 18
Pennsylvania State League 100, 102, 105, 130
Pennsylvania State University (Penn State) 166
Peoples, Jim 132–133, 202, 203, 204
Peoria, IL 32, 33, 76, 95, 128, 134, 135, 160
Perry Park (Keokuk) 180
Perth Amboy, NJ 64
Peru, IL 104
Peters, John 133, 179, 187, 193, 196, 210
Petersburg, IL 98
Pfeffer, Fred 4, 88, 133, 187–188, 192, 193, 198, 221
Phelan, Dick 133–134, 187, 197, 214
Philadelphia, PA 11, 13, 14, 15, 16, 20, 21, 22, 23, 24, 30, 34, 37, 44, 45, 46, 47, 49, 52, 58, 59, 66, 67, 68, 69, 70, 74, 78, 80, 82, 84–85, 87, 89, 93, 96, 97, 98, 99, 102, 103–104, 105, 108, 109, 112, 116, 117, 122, 123, 124, 125, 129, 132, 133, 143, 144, 149, 150, 152, 155, 156, 160, 166, 167, 171, 173
Philadelphia Athletics (AA) 4, 13, 14, 16, 22, 24, 26, 39, 41, 43, 44, 47, 49, 56, 57, 59, 60, 61, 65, 69, 70, 76, 79, 80, 86, 88, 89, 90, 93, 96, 97, 100, 101, 105, 106, 107, 111, 117, 121, 123, 129, 135, 136, 137, 138, 143, 145, 146, 147, 149, 150, 152, 156, 160, 161, 164, 167, 172, 175, 208–209
Philadelphia Athletics (AL) 129, 223
Philadelphia Athletics (NA) 12, 18, 49, 59, 68, 97, 105, 116, 123, 143, 159, 181–182
Philadelphia Athletics (NL) 3, 31, 68, 97, 105, 116, 159, 166, 194
Philadelphia Centennials (NA) 166, 182
Philadelphia Keystones (UA) 4, 6, 14, 34, 37, 46, 49, 57, 59, 66, 67, 69, 70, 72, 74, 87, 90, 91, 96, 103, 105, 108, 109, 111, 116, 130, 132, 143, 150, 167, 217–218
Philadelphia Phillies *see* Philadelphia Quakers (NL)
Philadelphia Quakers (NL) 4, 5, 6, 10, 11, 12, 18, 26, 28, 32, 35, 37, 39, 41, 47, 49, 53, 54, 54, 57, 63, 65, 68, 70, 71, 72, 75, 79, 81, 82, 84, 86, 87, 89, 90, 93, 94, 97, 103, 104, 105, 108, 109, 110, 112, 113, 114, 117, 121, 123, 125, 126, 127, 128, 137, 141, 143, 146, 150, 152, 158, 163, 164, 166, 175, 176, 194–195

Philadelphia Quakers (PL) 28, 63, 68, 117, 123, 175, 221
Philadelphia White Stockings (NA) 47, 49, 59, 69, 87, 105, 112, 116, 123, 149, 153, 166, 176, 182
Phillips, Bill 134, 189, 202, 205
Phillips, Marr 134, 190, 204–205, 210, 211
Phillips Academy 164
Phillipsburg, NJ 21
Picketts (Chicago) 147
Pierce, Grayson "Gracie" 134, 193, 200, 204, 206, 208
Pierce, Maurice 134, 219
Pine Bluff, AK 77
Pinkney, George 134–135, 186, 189, 192, 197, 202
Pittsburgh, PA 38, 53, 71, 78, 83, 99, 115, 120, 134, 152, 160, 225
Pittsburgh Alleghenys (AA) 4, 6, 10, 13, 17, 18, 20, 27, 34, 39, 46, 53, 54, 57, 62, 65, 66, 69, 70, 76, 78, 83, 84, 85, 94, 95, 97, 99, 101, 102, 105, 106, 110, 113, 115, 117, 119, 120, 121, 127, 128, 130, 133, 134, 138, 140, 143, 148, 152, 152, 156, 157, 160, 161, 169, 171, 175, 209–210
Pittsburgh Alleghenys (NL) 17, 27, 28, 30, 33, 34, 38, 39, 44, 45, 50, 53, 55, 58, 60, 70, 76, 7, 98, 99, 108, 110, 113, 117, 120, 145, 152, 158, 160, 162, 164, 166, 169, 171, 176, 195
Pittsburgh Burghers (PL) 34, 70, 78, 81, 99, 108, 120, 144, 169, 221–222
Pittsburgh Keystones 165
Pittsburgh Pirates see Pittsburgh Alleghenys (NL)
Pittsburgh Stogies (UA) 4, 6, 14, 15, 16, 18, 21, 50, 60, 72, 89, 98, 156, 157, 169, 218
Plainfield, NJ 126
Plank, Eddie 68
Players League (PL): clubs and players 220–222; umpires 87, 97
Pleasanton, CA 32
Polo Grounds (New York) 176, 193, 207, 221, 223
Poorman, Tom 135, 185, 187, 188, 208, 212
Port Carling, Ontario 170
Port Henry, NY 17
Port Huron, MI 120, 166
Port Stanley, Ontario 97
Porter, Henry 21, 135, 202, 205, 217
Porter, Matt 135, 216–217
Portland, ME 12, 37, 41, 47, 57, 109, 123, 132, 138
Portland, OR 33, 60, 93
Portsmouth, OH 168
Pottsville, PA 12, 117
Poughkeepsie, NY 14, 20, 26
Powell, Abner 135–136, 200, 203, 219
Powell, Jim 136, 211
Powell, Martin 136, 190, 208, 216

Powers, Phil 136–137, 185, 188, 189, 200, 203
Prince, Walter 137, 190, 206, 213, 219
Prince Edward Island 132
Princeton, IL 92
Princeton University 82
ProQuest Historical Newspaper Collection 1
Providence, RI 12, 21, 36, 43, 67, 81, 93, 97, 123, 140, 143, 152, 155, 157
Providence Grays (NL) 3, 4, 5, 13, 18, 24, 44 26, 33, 36, 40, 43, 49, 54, 56, 63, 74, 79, 86, 88, 89, 95, 96, 97, 106, 107, 109, 110, 117, 123, 124, 126, 130, 131, 133, 138, 140, 149, 152, 155, 160, 165, 169, 171, 176, 195–196
Puget Sound, WA 105
Purcell, William "Blondie" 137, 185, 187, 188, 189, 195, 197–198, 200, 208
Purdue University 128
Putnam Grounds (Troy) 198
Pyle, Harry Thomas "Shadow" 137, 188, 195

Quebec (Louisville), 163
Quest, Joe 138, 179, 188, 190, 191, 208, 210, 212
Quincy, IL 162
Quincy, MA 72, 146
Quinn, Joe 138, 184, 185, 189, 190, 197, 218, 220, 223
Quinton, Marshall 138, 208, 211

Racine, WI 81
Radbourn, Charles "Old Hoss" 1, 3, 5, 74, 138–139, 157, 185, 187, 189, 196, 220
Radford, Paul 139, 185, 190, 192, 198, 201, 202, 208, 221
Rain Check 136
Raleigh, NC 146
Randolph, MA 56
Ravalli County, MT 136
Reading, PA 10, 24, 34, 98, 100, 115, 117, 137
Reccius, John 47, 139
Reccius, Phil 139, 203, 206, 211
Recreation Park (Columbus) 204
Recreation Park (Detroit) 190
Recreation Park (Philadelphia) 194
Recreation Park (Pittsburgh) 195, 209
Reeder, Edward "Icicle" 140, 203, 219
Reid, Billy 140, 190, 210
Reilley (O'Reilly), Charles 140, 188, 190, 198, 199, 215
Reilly, John "Long John" 6, 128, 189, 203, 207
Reipschlager, Charlie 141, 207–208
Reising, Charlie 141, 205
Remsen, Jack 141, 179, 180, 181, 188, 189, 191, 195, 196, 202
Richardson [Art], 141–142, 216
Richardson, Danny 142, 186, 192, 193, 198, 221

Richardson, Hardy 4, 142–143, 170, 185, 186–187, 190, 192, 193, 198, 201, 220
Richmond, John 143, 182, 185, 189, 197–198, 204, 208, 210
Richmond, VA 68, 136, 137, 150
Richmond Hills, NY 125
Richmond semi-pro 65
Richmond Virginians (AA) 6, 7, 48, 57, 58, 66, 68, 76, 77, 82, 91, 100, 106, 115, 119, 126, 136, 138, 147, 159, 173, 210–211
Rickley, Chris 143, 218
Ridgeway, NJ 117
Ridgewood Park (Brooklyn) 201
Ringo, Frank 143, 190, 192, 195, 208, 210
River Forest, IL 85
Riverside Park (Buffalo) 186
Robeson Field (St. Louis) 196
Robinson, Charlie 143–144, 202, 205
Robinson, Fred 143, 216
Robinson, Jackie 6, 164
Robinson, Wilbert "Uncle Robby" 143, 186, 209
Robinson, William "Yank" 144, 190, 198, 202, 211–212, 214, 222
Rochester, NY 15, 24, 26, 36, 40, 42, 45, 52, 59, 87, 89, 91, 93, 95, 96, 123, 129, 139, 159, 172
Rochester Excelsior Club 42
Rochester Hop-Bitters (AA) 17, 66, 79, 97, 112, 129, 134, 139, 211
Rock Island, IL 149
Rockford, IL 128
Rockford Forest Citys (NA) 12, 69, 182
Rockingham, NH 37
Rockville, MD 88
Roller rink baseball 152
Rollinson, Bill (William Henry Winslow) 144, 219
Rollstones (Fitchburg, MA) 41
Romulus, MI 14
Roseman, James "Chief" 144–145, 198, 202, 206, 207–208, 212
Roseville, GA 164
Rowe, Dave 6, 145, 188, 189, 192, 197, 200, 205, 218
Rowe, Jack 4, 142, 145, 170, 186–187, 191, 195, 220
Rowen, Ed 145–146, 185, 208
Roxburgh, Jim 146, 200, 208
Roxbury, MA 69
Rudderham, John 146, 215
Rutgers College 82
Ruth, Babe 173
Rutherford, NJ 95
Rutland, VT 51
Ryan, John A. 146, 215
Ryan, John M. (Daniel Sheehan) 146, 219, 220
Ryder, Tom 146, 218

SABR see Society for American Baseball Research
Sacarrappa, ME 77
Sacramento, CA 34, 113

Safe Harbor, PA 53
Saginaw, MI 117, 163
St. George Cricket Grounds (New York) 193, 207
St. James Court (Louisville) 192
St. Joseph, MO 10, 168
St. Louis, MO 15, 16, 46, 47, 49, 51, 54, 55, 67, 71, 76, 77, 78, 83, 86, 97, 98, 102, 128, 130, 133, 138, 144, 145, 157, 225
St. Louis Brown Stockings (NA) 18, 24, 49, 70, 182
St. Louis Brown Stockings (NL) 4, 18, 24, 25, 49, 54, 56, 68, 76, 112, 141, 196
St. Louis Browns (AA) 4, 5, 10, 17, 25, 26, 31, 35, 40, 42, 47, 49, 51, 52, 55, 62, 69, 70, 73, 74, 76, 77, 78, 86, 95, 96, 97, 98, 101, 103, 106, 108, 109, 111, 115, 117, 119, 121, 122, 128, 131, 138, 144, 145, 150, 156, 157, 158, 161, 165, 167, 169, 171, 211–212
St. Louis Browns (NL) 27, 28, 33, 37, 41, 55, 60, 70, 72, 76, 77, 79, 80, 89, 99, 101, 117, 135, 138, 152, 156, 158, 168, 174, 196–197
St. Louis Cardinals *see* St. Louis Browns (NL)
St. Louis Maroons (NL) 15, 19, 23, 24, 30, 32, 36, 45, 50, 55, 58, 75–76, 97, 98, 103, 113, 115, 125, 134, 138, 145, 148, 149, 160, 161, 197
St. Louis Maroons (UA) 4, 5, 6, 7, 15, 23, 24, 32, 36, 46, 54, 55, 58, 76, 86, 95, 98, 103, 107, 138, 145, 146, 149, 157, 158, 160, 168, 170, 218
St. Louis Perfectos *see* St. Louis Browns (NL)
St. Louis Red Stockings (NA) 60, 67, 83, 115, 182–183
St. Mary's College 34, 54, 68, 70, 110, 120
St. Paul, MN 17, 34, 71, 109, 114, 121, 138, 155, 162, 165, 168, 225
St. Paul Saints (UA) 7, 17, 26, 34, 52, 59, 71, 85, 128, 162, 168, 218–219
St. Peter State Hospital (MN) 169
St. Thomas, Ontario 61, 89
St. Thomas Atlantics (Ontario) 89, 99
Salem, MA 37, 160
Salinas, CA 89
San Antonio, TX 32, 150
San Diego, CA 33, 114, 138, 161
Sandwich, MA 40
Sandwich, Ontario 79
San Francisco, CA 22, 32, 33, 46, 48, 54, 59, 67, 70, 82, 110, 126, 146, 155, 160, 161, 170
San Quentin Prison, CA 53, 160
San Rafael, CA 34
Santa Ana, CA 89
Santa Cruz County, CA 146
Santry, Ed 147, 191
Saranac Lake, NY 148
Saratoga Springs, NY 39

Saugatuck, CT 10
Savannah, GA 74, 104, 106, 117, 128, 157
Say, Jimmy 147, 204, 206, 208, 217, 220
Say, Lou 147, 178, 180, 183, 188, 200, 215, 217
Scanlon, Patrick 147, 215
Schenck, Bill 147, 202, 206, 211
Schenectady, NY 121
Schoeneck, Lewis "Jumbo" 6, 93, 147, 192, 215, 216, 218
Schonburg, Otto 113
Schuykill Falls, PA 69
Schwartz, William "Pop" 147–148, 204, 216
Scotland 110, 128
Scott, Milt 148, 188, 191, 200, 210
Scranton, PA 69, 79, 139, 155, 163
Sea Cliff, NJ 58
Seattle, WA 24, 46, 105, 136, 147
Seery, Emmett 6, 148, 191–192, 197, 202, 214–215, 217, 220
Seneca Falls, NY 63
Serad, Billy 148–149, 187, 203
Seventh Street Park (Indianapolis) 191, 204
Seville, OH 107
Sexton, Tom 149, 217
Shafer, Taylor 149, 208, 214, 215, 216–217, 224, 226
Shaffer, Frank 149, 224
Shaffer (Shafer), George "Orator" 149, 180, 181, 182, 187, 188, 189, 191, 192, 197, 208, 218
Shaffer, Taylor 149, 224
Shakopee, MN 17
Shallix, Gus (August Schallick) 149, 203, 225
Shaw, Frederick Lander "Dupee" 6, 149–150, 199, 215
Shaw University 144, 190
Sheehan, Ellen 146
Sheehan, Patrick 146
Shelby County, IL 98
Shelby County, TN 153
Shenandoah, PA 136
Shibe Park (Philadelphia) 223
Shippensburg, PA 128
Shoupe, John 150, 198, 212, 219
Siegel, John 150, 218
Siffell, Frank 150, 208, 225
Silver Slugger award 87
Sioux City, IA 22, 42, 76, 160
Sixsmith, Ed 150, 195
Skinner, Alexander 150, 215, 216
Sladon, Art 150–151, 215
Slattery, Mike 151, 189, 193, 214, 215, 221, 226
"Slide, Kelly, Slide" 94
Smith, Bill 151, 189
Smith, Charles "Pop" 151–152, 185, 187, 188, 189, 195, 199, 204, 206, 208, 210, 214
Smith, Edgar 152, 190, 195, 213
Smith, Frank 152, 210
Smith, George "Germany" 152, 186, 189, 197, 202, 214
Smith, John "Phenomenal" (John Francis Gammon) 152, 191, 195, 200, 202, 208, 210, 215
Sneed, John 153, 204, 205, 213
Snyder, Charles "Pop" 153–154, 180, 182, 183, 185, 190, 192, 203, 204, 213–214, 221
Snyder (Schneider), Emanuel Sebastian "Redleg" 154, 188, 220
Society for American Baseball Research (SABR) 1, 34; Biographical Research Committee 72–73, 113, 128, 224
Sockalexis, Louis 111, 222
Solon, OH 103
Somerville, MA 41, 56, 132
Sommer, Joe 154, 188, 190, 200, 203
South Acton, MA 143
South Africa gold fields 124
South Boston, MA 32, 46, 125
South End Grounds (Boston) 178, 184
South Florida 11
South Jersey Institute 93
South Side Park (Chicago) 187, 215
South Street Park (Indianapolis) 191
Southern California State Hospital (Highland), 171
Southern League 11, 14, 27, 32, 36, 38, 47, 58, 77, 78, 102, 104, 106, 117, 121, 123, 130, 134, 137, 149, 157, 158, 161, 175
Spalding, Albert 12, 28, 171
Spalding Club (Chicago) 97
Spanish-American War 18, 164
Speranza Park (Toledo) 213
Spokane, WA 24, 136, 140
Sportsman's Park (St. Louis) 49, 182, 211
Springfield, IL 79, 105, 161
Springfield, MA 26, 30, 42, 45, 105, 124, 144, 147, 163
Springfield, OH 34
Stanley, Joe 154, 215
Stanley, John "Buck" 154
Stanley, NY 109
Star Park (Syracuse) 197, 212
Start, Joe "Old Reliable" 2, 154–155, 177, 178, 181, 188, 191, 194, 196, 199, 226
Staten Island, NY 61, 92, 162
Stearns, Dan "Ecky" 155, 187, 191, 200, 203, 205
Stella, MO 14
Steubenville, OH 165
Stirling, MA 15
Stockton, CA 54, 155, 170
Stockwell, Len 155, 189, 190, 206
Stoneham, MA 12, 63
"Stonewall Infield" 30
Stovey (Stowe), Harry 6, 127, 155, 184, 185, 186, 199, 208, 209, 220
Strauss (Strasser), Joe 156, 202, 206, 217
Streuve, Al 157, 212
Stricker (Streaker), John "Cub" 156, 184, 190, 197, 198, 201, 203–204, 208, 221

Strief, George 156–157, 189, 208, 210, 212, 217, 218
Suck, Tony (Charles Anthony Zuck) 157, 187, 215, 216, 218, 225
Sulfur Springs, OH 99
Sullivan, Dan 157, 171, 206, 210, 211–212
Sullivan, Florence "Fleury" 157, 210
Sullivan, John L. 69
Sullivan, Pat 157, 217
Sullivan, Thomas "Sleeper" 157–158, 187, 206, 212, 218
Sullivan, Timothy "Ted" 158, 216–217, 218
Sullivan, Tom 158, 204, 205, 206
Sulphur Springs, WV 121
Sunday, Billy 158, 188, 195
Sutcliffe, Elmer "Sy" 158–159, 184, 188, 190, 191, 197, 213–214, 221
Sutton, Ezra 3, 159, 179, 182, 185, 194
Sutton, VT 105
Swampoodle Grounds (Washington) 198
Swan, Andy 159–160, 211, 213
Swartwood, Ed 6, 160, 187, 195, 202, 209–210, 213
Sweeney, Bill 6, 160, 209, 214–215
Sweeney, Charlie 5, 6, 126, 160, 196, 197, 204, 218
Sweeney, Jerry 160–161, 217
Sweeney, John "Rooney" 161, 197, 200, 215
Sydney, Australia 138
Sylvan Club (New York City) 81
Sylvan Lake, NY 26
Sylvester, Lou 161, 203, 206, 212, 216, 225
Syracuse Stars (AA) 18, 36, 52, 56, 60, 113, 114, 132, 212
Syracuse Stars (NL) 33, 46, 56, 63, 87, 104, 106, 111, 137, 143, 197–198
Syracuse, NY 51, 56, 58, 62, 63, 66, 73, 79, 93, 106, 109, 114, 124, 127, 164

Tacoma, WA 106, 113
Tamaqua, PA 70
Tarrytown, NY 73
Taunton, MA 21
Taylor, Billy 6, 161, 189, 199, 200, 209, 210, 218
Taylor, Edward "Live Oak" 161, 191, 210
Taylor, Edward S. 161
Taylor, George E. 161
Tecumsehs (London Ontario) 77, 87, 135, 136, 161
Temple Cup 189
Tener, John 175
Tenney, Fred 161–162, 215, 219, 220
Terre Haute, IN 99, 127
Terry, William "Adonis" 41, 141, 162, 184, 186, 187–188, 195, 202
Tewksbury, MA 37, 66
Texas League 24, 47, 98, 158
Thayer, Ernest 32
Thompson, Art 162, 219

Thompson, John "Tug" 162, 203, 205
Three-I League 24, 35, 99, 128, 130
Tierney, Bill 162, 203, 215
Tilley, John 162, 189, 213, 219
Titusville, PA 78
Toledo, OH 62, 82, 93, 99, 104, 117, 121, 140, 149, 162
Toledo Blue Stockings (AA) 6–7, 13, 17, 26, 28 95, 99, 115, 116, 117, 118, 121, 122, 129, 130, 135, 141, 162, 164, 165, 167, 212–213
Toledo Maumees (AA) 49, 132, 153, 160, 168, 213
Topeka, KS 10, 19, 110, 155, 158
Toronto, Ontario 14, 26, 51, 72, 75, 89, 90, 93, 97, 120, 143, 151
Toronto Parkdales 59
Towanda, PA 133
Townsend, George 209
Traffley, Bill 162, 188, 200, 203
Traffley, John 162
Tray, Jim 163, 205
Trenton, NJ 82, 109, 138
Tri-County Fair Grounds (Toledo) 212
Tri-State League 169
Trott, Sam 163, 185, 191, 200, 214
Troy, John "Dasher" 163, 191, 193, 196, 208
Troy, NY 25, 52, 61, 74, 80, 102, 163
Troy Ball Club Grounds (Watervliet) 198
Troy Haymakers (NA) 68, 127, 176, 183
Troy Trojans (NL) 24, 25, 26, 27, 36, 41, 5461, 62, 65, 72, 74, 77, 81, 82, 83, 87, 93, 100, 102, 106, 121, 127, 133, 140, 144, 150, 168, 198
Trumbull, Ed (Edward J. Trembly) 163, 213
Turbidy, Jerry 163, 217
23rd Street Grounds (Chicago) 179
Tyascin, MD 54

Ukiah, CA 48
Union Association (UA): cities 4; clubs and players 214–220; 1884 pennant race 6–7
Union College 109, 121
Union Grounds (Brooklyn) 179, 181
Union Pacific (Omaha) 162
Union Stockyards Club (St. Louis) 76
University of California 3
University of Illinois 146
University of Michigan 85, 164, 165
University of Pennsylvania 3, 31, 80, 194
Upper Darby, PA 41
Utica, NY 34, 77–78, 81, 101–103, 120, 143, 148

Vadeboncoeur, Gene 163, 195
Valley Falls, RI 40

Veach, William "Peek-A-Boo" 163–164, 190, 195, 206, 217
Verplanck, NY 64
Versailles, IN 169
Vincennes, IN 63
Vinton, Bill 164, 195, 209
Virginias (Richmond) 96
Voss, Alex 164, 217, 219, 224

Wagner, Honus 195
Wakefield, MA 150
Wales 120
Walker, Moses Fleetwood 6, 112, 121, 164–165, 212–213, 225
Walker, Oscar 165, 187, 200, 202, 212
Walker, Walt 165, 191
Walker, Welday 6, 165, 212–213, 225
Walte's Pasture see Perry Park
Waltham, MA 44
Waltham Watch Company 161
Ward, John Montgomery "Monte" 5, 165–166, 186, 193–194, 196, 219, 220
Warner, Fred 166, 182, 189, 191, 194, 195, 202
Warren, IL 51
Warren, OH 106
Warren, PA 26
Washington, DC 15, 17, 27, 36, 38, 61, 64, 70, 73, 75, 76, 86, 88, 93, 109, 119, 134, 146, 154, 158, 161, 165, 170, 174, 175
Washington, MD 150
Washington Blue Legs (NA) 73, 86, 153, 170, 183
Washington Nationals 29, 42, 47
Washington Nationals (AA) 4, 6, 17, 19, 57, 63, 65, 72, 75, 77, 81, 82, 84, 89, 91, 96, 97, 119, 122, 124, 130, 137, 152, 159, 163, 173, 175, 213
Washington Nationals (NA) 86, 170, 183
Washington Nationals/Unions (UA) 57, 61, 62, 69, 70, 78, 80, 81, 89, 93, 94, 99, 102, 103, 109, 110, 112, 113, 115, 120, 122, 128, 130, 134, 135, 137, 140, 144, 146, 150, 161, 162, 164, 165, 170, 173–174, 175, 219
Washington Olympics (NA) 68, 170, 183
Washington Park (Brooklyn) 186, 201
Washington Senators (AL) 106, 138, 223
Washington Senators (NL) 27, 66, 68, 76, 100, 101, 108, 112, 117, 123, 131, 139, 142, 144, 156, 174, 198
Washington Statesmen (AA) 5, 14, 51, 58, 68, 79, 86, 108, 112, 114, 125, 151, 152, 154, 159, 163, 213–214
Washington Statesmen (NL) 13, 15, 17, 33, 42, 44, 45, 50, 52, 53, 55, 63, 66, 69, 72, 74, 75, 77, 84, 85, 86, 88, 89, 90, 98, 119, 125,

129, 130, 149, 155, 168, 171, 172, 174, 198–199
Washington Washingtons (NA) 24, 109, 147, 183
Waterbury, CT 20, 41, 112, 164, 165
Watkins, Bill 166, 204–205
Watsons (Weedsport, NY) 62
Wauwatosa, WI 63
Waverly, MD 69
Waverly Fairgrounds (Elizabeth) 180
Wayne, MI 119
Wayne Township, IN 108
Weaver, Sam 166–167, 182, 193, 206, 209, 218
Weber, Harry 167, 205
Weber, Joe 167, 191
Webster, MA 163
Weedsport, NY 62
Weihe, John Garibaldi "Podge" 167, 203, 205
Welch, Curt 167–168, 184, 189, 192, 200, 209, 211–212, 213
Welch (Welsh), Michael "Smiling Mickey" 5, 20, 52, 93, 168, 193–194, 198
Werden, Perry 86, 168, 192, 197, 199, 200, 213, 218
Werrick, Joe 168–169, 206, 219, 225
West, Milton "Buck" 169, 190, 203
West End (Chicago) 74
West Palm Beach, FL 11
West Philadelphia, PA 86
West Side Park (Chicago) 173, 187
Westerly, RI 143
Western Association 38, 61, 85, 104, 106, 141, 145, 162
Western Inter-State League 140
Western League 15, 19, 38, 60, 63, 76, 78, 86, 97, 98, 99, 104, 106, 110, 113, 117, 138, 141, 148–149, 155, 168, 206
Western Reserve College 11
Westfield, MA 162
Westport, CT 10

Weyhing, Gus 209
Wheaton, IL 159
Wheeler, Harry 169, 188, 189, 196, 203, 204, 212, 215, 216, 217, 218
Wheeling, WV 17, 76, 96, 117, 118
White, Bill 169, 206, 210, 212
White, James "Deacon" 4, 141, 145, 169–170, 178, 179, 185, 186–187, 188, 191, 195, 220–221, 226
White, Warren (William Warren) 170, 179, 180, 183, 219, 226
White, Will 1, 121, 170, 185, 188, 191, 203
White Stocking Grounds (Chicago) 4, 179
White Stocking Park (Chicago) 215
Whitehead, Milt 170–171, 217, 218
Whiteley, Guerdon 171, 185, 189
Whiting, Ed (Harry Zieber) 171, 199, 200, 206
Whitney, Art 171, 191, 194, 195, 196, 199, 202, 210, 212, 221
Whitney, Frank 171
Whitney, James "Grasshopper Jim" 5, 86 171–172, 185, 192, 199, 209
Wichita, TX 134
Wiedman (Weidman), George "Stump" 172–173, 187, 190–191, 192, 194, 208
Wiley, John 173, 219
Wilkes-Barre, PA 19, 97, 163
William and Bridget Dugan 58
Williams, Wash 173, 188, 211
Williamson, Edward "Ned" 3, 4, 173, 187–188, 191, 221
Williamsport, PA 26
Wills 173, 213, 217
Wilmington, DE 20, 66, 87, 96
Wilmington Quicksteps 7, 14, 18, 20, 30, 33, 35, 36, 47, 49, 66, 104, 109, 110, 123, 124, 126, 128, 146, 147, 154, 162, 219–220
Wilson, George "Tug" 173, 202
Windham County, CT 78

Wisconsin 71
Wise, Bill 173–174, 199, 201, 219
Wise, Sam 174, 185, 191, 198, 199, 200, 221
Wolf, William "Jimmy" or "Chicken" 38, 47, 174, 197, 205–206
Wood, Fred 174–175, 187, 191, 201
Wood, George 45, 175, 184, 189, 190–191, 195, 199, 209, 221
Wood, Pete 175
Woonsocket, RI
Worcester, MA 12, 72, 81, 111, 123–124, 129
Worcester Ruby Legs (NL) 21, 22, 31, 37, 39, 43, 46, 54, 56, 60, 61, 72, 81, 84, 88, 89, 90, 97, 105, 113, 115, 121, 127, 129, 130, 140, 152, 156, 161, 171, 175, 199
World Series 3, 21, 24, 31, 35, 67, 68, 73–74, 86, 94, 108, 110, 117, 130, 135, 138, 144, 155, 162, 165, 166, 169, 188, 190, 201, 222
World War II 226
Woulfe, Jimmy 175, 203
Wright, Harry 2, 177
Wright Street Grounds (Milwaukee) 217
Wrigley Field (Chicago) 187
Wyman, Frank 175, 216, 217

Yale Law School 132
Yale University 82, 152, 164
Yankee Stadium (New York) 223
Yewell, Ed 175–176, 213, 219
York, Tom 176, 180, 182, 183, 189, 191, 196, 201
York, PA 150, 163
Young, Cy 71, 176, 189
Youngstown, OH 10, 13

Zimmer, Charles "Chief" 176, 189–190, 191, 192, 195, 204, 208
Zimmerman, PA 38
"Zimmer's Baseball Game" 176

www.ingramcontent.com/pod-product-compliance
Lightning Source LLC
Chambersburg PA
CBHW081550300426
44116CB00015B/2829